Taste of Home

QUICK COOKING

ANNUAL RECIPES

Taste of Home

RDA ENTHUSIAST BRANDS, LLC • MILWAUKEE, WI

QUICK COOKING

ANNUAL RECIPES 2019

CAJUN GRILLED SHRIMP
(p. 228)

1610 N. 2nd St., Suite 102, Milwaukee WI 53212-3906

Visit: tasteofhome.com for other Taste of Home books and products.

International Standard Book Number:
D 978-1-61765-844-0
U 978-1-61765-845-7
Component Number:
D 117800067H
U 117800069H
International Standard Serial Number: 1552-6603

Deputy Editor: Mark Hagen
Senior Art Director: Raeann Thompson
Editor: Hazel Wheaton
Art Director: Maggie Conners
Senior Designer: Courtney Lovetere
Designer: Arielle Jardine, Jazmin Delgado
Copy Editor: Amy Rabideau Silvers
Cover Photography: Taste of Home Photo Studio

Pictured on front cover:
Ho Ho Ho Cake, p. 293; DIY Ramen Soup, p. 312; Bacon-Corn Stuffed Peppers, p. 234; Italian Pasta Sauce, p. 256; Quick Carbanara, p. 96; Bavarian Apple-Sausage Hash, p. 86

Pictured on back cover:
Creamy Layered Blueberry Ice Pops, p. 263; Simple Sweet & Tangy Pork Chops, p. 71; Creamy Strawberry Crepes, p. 178; Bacon, Lettuce & Tomato Pizza, p. 163; Golden Squash Soup, p. 57

Printed in USA
1 3 5 7 9 10 8 6 4 2

GREEN TOMATO BLT (p. 52)

SPICY CORN KABOBS (p. 30)

LOADED RED POTATO CASSEROLE (p. 42)

FIESTA RAVIOLI (p. 71)

NO-BAKE CHOCOLATE CHIP CANNOLI CHEESECAKE (p. 301)

Enjoy Family-Favorite Dishes Every Night of the Week

Liven up the dinner table tonight when you serve the comforting dishes your gang craves. Let *Quick Cooking Annual Recipes* show you how!

TASTY YET SIMPLE DISHES are a snap to prepare when you know the shortcuts that get them on the table fast. Luckily, home cooks from coast to coast shared their all-time greats with the pros at the *Taste of Home* Test Kitchen—and each mouthwatering bite is here in this brand-new collection of cooking sensations!

Take a look inside this fantastic edition of *Quick Cooking Annual Recipes,* and you'll find 582 incredible dishes sure to entice the taste buds of everyone at your table. Even your pickiest eater won't be able to turn down these classic recipes made fast.

Pulled from the complete year of *Simple & Delicious* magazine, these are the entrees, snacks and desserts today's family cooks make in a jiffy. You'll also find soups, salads and sides that come together quickly, plus appetizers, breads and other staples that consistently satisfy without taxing your time. With your new edition of *Quick Cooking Annual Recipes* on hand, it's a breeze to make every meal a memorable occasion.

ICONS IN THIS BOOK

FAST FIX
Recipes that are table-ready in just 30 minutes or less.

5 INGREDIENTS
Dishes that use five or fewer ingredients (they may also call for water, salt, pepper, and canola or olive oil).

EAT SMART
Dietitian-approved recipes that are lower in calories, fat and sodium.

FREEZE IT
Freezer-friendly items that include directions for freezing and reheating.

SLOW COOKER
Recipes that use a slow cooker—one of the most convenient kitchen tools.

THAI SALMON BROWN RICE BOWLS (p. 306)

COCONUT KEY LIME THUMBPRINTS (p. 288)

Beat the clock every night with these **600+ RECIPES & TIPS.**

IN THIS EDITION

5-Item Mainstays
This new chapter offers 23 entrees that come together with just a handful of ingredients. What could be better, easier or quicker? Make sure to try Fiesta Ravioli (p. 71) when time is tight.

Easy Odds & Ends
We've updated this section with all of the time-saving meal-in-one specialties you can imagine. Check out popular bites such as the Thai Salmon Brown Rice Bowls (pictured above), as well as salads layered in mason jars and so many others. Up the yum and the fun in your kitchen today!

30-Minute Dinners
You can't go wrong with main courses that are table-ready in just half an hour. That's why there are dozens of no-fuss staples packed into this handy section. Consider juicy Breaded Turkey Breasts (p. 89), Sausage Rice Skillet (p. 98) or Tasty Taco Chopped Salad (p. 109) for those extra-busy nights.

Slow-Cooked Sensations
This cookbook wouldn't be complete without an entire chapter devoted to everyone's favorite cooking device. Simmer a savory meal, and learn how your slow cooker can do the work for sensational soups, sides and sweets.

Delectable Desserts
Saving time doesn't mean skipping dessert. From cakes and pies to bars and cookies, these treats bake up almost effortlessly. Consider a batch of Coconut Key Lime Thumbprints (pictured above) the next time you need a bake sale contribution in a hurry.

Healthy Delights
In addition to nutrition facts on every recipe, you'll find a complete chapter of lightened-up staples (p. 132) as well as easy ideas from our registered dietician to trim down dishes even further. Simply look for the * HEALTH TIP * icon scattered throughout this book.

Appetizers & Beverages

Here's how to get the party started! For casual or formal get-togethers, a party of friends or a family gathering, these appetizers are just the thing. A collection of cocktails helps you raise a toast to fun and friendship, too!

Crunchy Vegetable Dip (p. 14) **Bacon Cheese Spread** (p. 17) **Pomegranate Cosmo** (p. 10)
Kickin' Cauliflower (p. 10) **Garlic Bean Dip** (p. 9)

CRANBERRY-ORANGE VODKA SLUSH

Years ago, my mother made a rosy and refreshing party drink I've never forgotten. The sparkle comes from fruit juices, vodka and lemon-lime soda.
—Melinda Strable, Ankeny, IA

Prep: 15 min. + freezing
Makes: 24 servings

- **9 cups water**
- **2 cups sugar**
- **1 can (12 oz.) frozen cranberry juice concentrate, partially thawed**
- **1 can (12 oz.) frozen orange juice concentrate, partially thawed**
- **¾ cup thawed lemonade concentrate**
- **2 cups vodka**
- **8 cups lemon-lime soda, chilled**

1. In a 5-qt. bowl, mix water and sugar until the sugar is dissolved. Stir in juice concentrates and vodka until blended. Transfer mixture to freezer containers, allowing headspace for expansion; freeze overnight.
2. For each serving, place ⅔ cup slush in a glass and add ⅓ cup soda.

1 cup: 210 cal., 0 fat (0 sat. fat), 0 chol., 10mg sod., 43g carb. (39g sugars, 0 fiber), 0 pro.

FRESH SHRIMP & AVOCADO NACHOS

FRESH SHRIMP & AVOCADO NACHOS

Since I'm such a fan of shrimp any which way and my family loves nachos, I combined my fresh-from-the-garden ingredients with shrimp and avocado for a cool yet satisfying take on the party snack.
—Teri Rasey, Cadillac, MI

Prep: 30 min. + chilling
Makes: 10 servings

- **4 plum tomatoes, chopped**
- **3 tomatillos, husked and chopped**
- **4 jalapeno peppers, seeded and finely chopped**
- **1 small onion, chopped**
- **2 garlic cloves, minced**
- **¼ cup minced fresh cilantro**
- **3 Tbsp. olive oil**
- **2 Tbsp. seasoned rice vinegar**
- **1 Tbsp. lime juice**
- **1½ tsp. sea salt**
- **½ tsp. dried oregano**
- **1 lb. peeled and deveined cooked shrimp (31-40 per lb.), coarsely chopped**

AVOCADO CREAM

- **2 medium ripe avocados, peeled and pitted, divided**
- **½ cup sour cream**
- **2 Tbsp. lime juice**
- **8 cups tortilla chips**
- **1 cup shredded lettuce**

1. In a large bowl, combine the first 11 ingredients. Cover and refrigerate until chilled, at least 30 minutes. Stir in shrimp.
2. For avocado cream, mash one avocado with sour cream and 1 Tbsp. lime juice until smooth. Cube remaining avocado and toss with remaining lime juice.
3. To serve, arrange chips on a large platter. Top with shrimp mixture, cubed avocado, lettuce and avocado cream; serve immediately.

1 serving: 264 cal., 16g fat (3g sat. fat), 72mg chol., 542mg sod., 20g carb. (3g sugars, 3g fiber), 12g pro.

TEST KITCHEN TIP

Seasoned rice vinegar has added sugar and salt; don't substitute regular rice vinegar in this recipe. The avocado cream makes a tasty topping for tacos, quesadillas and even burgers.

FAST FIX

THYME & FIG GOAT CHEESE SPREAD

When I started my herb garden, it took me a while to find a good way to use thyme, but this easy appetizer spread really lets it shine.
—Laura Cox, Columbia, MO

Takes: 15 min. • **Makes:** 1½ cups

- **1 cup crumbled goat cheese**
- **½ cup sour cream**
- **1 Tbsp. honey**
- **½ tsp. minced fresh thyme**
- **½ cup chopped dried figs**
- **¼ cup slivered almonds**
- **Additional minced fresh thyme, optional**
- **Crackers, French bread baguette slices or fresh vegetables**

In a small bowl, beat cheese, sour cream, honey and thyme until smooth; stir in figs and almonds. Sprinkle with additional thyme if desired. Refrigerate until serving. Serve with assorted crackers, baguette slices or vegetables.

2 Tbsp.: 81 cal., 6g fat (3g sat. fat), 14mg chol., 49mg sod., 7g carb. (5g sugars, 1g fiber), 3g pro.

THYME & FIG GOAT CHEESE SPREAD

EAT SMART | FAST FIX

GARLIC BEAN DIP

There isn't a bean that my family does not like. In fact, I serve one kind of bean or another almost every day. This dip is one of our favorite ways to eat them.
—Nancy Testin, Harrington, DE

Takes: 10 min. • **Makes:** 1½ cups

- **1 can (15 oz.) cannellini beans, rinsed and drained**
- **1 Tbsp. cider vinegar**
- **2 garlic cloves, minced**
- **½ tsp. salt**
- **½ tsp. ground cumin**
- **⅓ cup reduced-fat mayonnaise**
- **2 Tbsp. chopped fresh parsley**
- **Baked pita chips or assorted fresh vegetables**

Place the first five ingredients in a food processor; process until almost smooth. Add the mayonnaise and parsley; pulse just until blended. Serve with pita chips or vegetables.

¼ cup dip: 102 cal., 5g fat (1g sat. fat), 5mg chol., 371mg sod., 11g carb. (1g sugars, 3g fiber), 3g pro. **Diabetic exchanges:** 1 starch, 1 fat.

5 INGREDIENTS | FAST FIX

PEAR-APPLE COCKTAIL

Ah, the memories we made when we went to Hawaii—we concocted this drink for our first toast on the island. That makes this drink special.
—Noelle Appel, Arlington, TX

Takes: 5 min. • **Makes:** 6 servings

- **6 cups unsweetened apple juice, chilled**
- **¾ cup pear-flavored vodka, chilled**
- **Cubed fresh pineapple**

In a pitcher, mix apple juice and vodka. Serve over ice. Garnish with pineapple.

1 cup: 178 cal., 0 fat (0 sat. fat), 0 chol., 10mg sod., 28g carb. (24g sugars, 1g fiber), 0 pro.

FAST FIX

GREEK CROSTINI

Greek ingredients make these crostini a deliciously different spin on traditional bruschetta.
—Mary Shivers, Ada, OK

Takes: 25 min. • **Makes:** 2 dozen

- **1 pkg. (8 oz.) cream cheese, softened**
- **¼ cup Greek vinaigrette**
- **¼ tsp. dried minced garlic**
- **½ cup Greek pitted olives, chopped**
- **½ cup roasted sweet red peppers, drained**
- **3 Tbsp. butter, softened**
- **24 slices French bread baguette (¼ in. thick)**
- **¾ cup crumbled goat or crumbled feta cheese**

1. Preheat oven to 400°. In small bowl, combine cream cheese, vinaigrette and garlic. Stir in olives and red peppers just until blended.
2. Spread butter over baguette slices; place on an ungreased baking sheet. Bake until lightly browned, 3-4 minutes. Spread the cream cheese mixture over toasts; sprinkle with goat cheese. Bake until the cheese is softened, 2-3 minutes longer.

1 piece: 100 cal., 8g fat (4g sat. fat), 19mg chol., 182mg sod., 5g carb. (0 sugars, 1g fiber), 2g pro.

5 INGREDIENTS | FAST FIX

SAUSAGE PINWHEELS

These spirals are simple to make but look special on a buffet. Our guests eagerly help themselves—sometimes the eye-catching pinwheels never make it to their plates!
—Gail Sykora, Menomonee Falls, WI

Takes: 30 min. • **Makes:** 1 dozen

- **1 tube (8 oz.) refrigerated crescent rolls**
- **½ lb. uncooked bulk pork sausage**
- **2 Tbsp. minced chives**

1. Preheat oven to 375°. Unroll crescent dough onto a lightly floured surface; press perforations to seal. Roll dough into a 14x10-in. rectangle.
2. Spread sausage on dough to within ½ in. of edges. Sprinkle with chives. Roll up carefully jelly-roll style, starting with a long side; pinch seam to seal. Cut into 12 slices; place 1 in. apart in an ungreased 15x10x1-in. pan.
3. Bake until golden brown and sausage is cooked through, 12-16 minutes.

1 pinwheel: 132 cal., 9g fat (3g sat. fat), 13mg chol., 293mg sod., 8g carb. (1g sugars, 0 fiber), 4g pro.

FAST FIX

POMEGRANATE COSMO

Every soiree needs a signature drink. Colored sugar dresses up this simple cosmo that lets you enjoy a cozy evening with friends and still shake things up.
—*Taste of Home* Test Kitchen

Takes: 10 min. • **Makes:** 1 serving

- **1 Tbsp. coarse red sugar**
- **1½ oz. lemon-lime soda**
- **1½ oz. pomegranate liqueur or cranberry-pomegranate juice**
- **1 oz. X-Rated fusion liqueur**
- **½ oz. Triple Sec**
- **1 oz. cranberry-pomegranate juice**
- **Lemon peel strip, optional**

1. Sprinkle red sugar on a plate. Moisten the rim of a cocktail glass with water; dip rim in the sugar to coat.
2. Fill a shaker three-fourths full with ice. Add soda, liqueurs and juice; cover and shake until condensation forms on outside of shaker, 10-15 seconds. Strain into the prepared glass. If desired, garnish with lemon peel.

1 serving: 209 cal., 0 fat (0 sat. fat), 0 chol., 6mg sod., 29g carb. (28g sugars, 0 fiber), 0 pro.

SAUSAGE PINWHEELS

SPINACH DIP IN A BREAD BOWL

Whenever we get together with friends, I like to prepare this creamy dip. It's the definition of a crowd-pleaser.
—Janelle Lee, Appleton, WI

Prep: 15 min. + chilling
Makes: 15 servings

- **2 cups sour cream**
- **1 envelope (1 oz.) ranch salad dressing mix**
- **1 pkg. (10 oz.) frozen chopped spinach, thawed and well drained**
- **¼ cup chopped onion**
- **¾ tsp. dried basil**
- **½ tsp. dried oregano**
- **1 round loaf of bread (1 lb.)**
- **Raw vegetables**

1. In a large bowl, combine the first six ingredients. Chill for at least 1 hour. Cut a 1½-in. slice off the top of the loaf; set aside. Hollow out the bottom part, leaving a thick shell. Cut or tear the slice from the top of the loaf and the bread from inside into bite-size pieces.
2. Fill the shell with dip; set on a platter. Arrange the bread pieces and vegetables around it and serve immediately.

1 serving: 161 cal., 6g fat (4g sat. fat), 22mg chol., 571mg sod., 20g carb. (2g sugars, 1g fiber), 4g pro.

5 INGREDIENTS | FAST FIX

KICKIN' CAULIFLOWER

Try these savory bites for a zesty appetizer that's healthy, too!
—Emily Tyra, Traverse City, MI

Takes: 25 min. • **Makes:** 8 servings

- **1 medium head cauliflower (about 2¼ lbs.), cut into florets**
- **1 Tbsp. canola oil**
- **½ cup Buffalo wing sauce**
- **Blue cheese salad dressing**

1. Preheat oven to 400°. Toss cauliflower with oil; spread in a 15x10x1-in. pan. Roast until cauliflower is tender and lightly browned, 20-25 minutes, stirring once.
2. Transfer to a bowl; toss with wing sauce. Serve with dressing.

⅓ cup: 39 cal., 2g fat (0 sat. fat), 0 chol., 474mg sod., 5g carb. (2g sugars, 2g fiber), 2g pro.

EAT SMART | FAST FIX

PEACHY JALAPENO GUACAMOLE

Fresh jalapenos and summer-ripe peaches give this creamy guacamole so much flavor. It's got a little kick, but I love that it's not so spicy it burns off my taste buds!
—Colleen Delawder, Herndon, VA

Takes: 15 min. • **Makes:** 1½ cups

- **2 medium ripe avocados, peeled and cubed**
- **2 Tbsp. lime juice**
- **½ tsp. kosher salt**
- **½ tsp. ground cumin**
- **¼ tsp. pepper**
- **1 medium peach, peeled and finely chopped**
- **1 jalapeno pepper, seeded and minced**
- **2 Tbsp. finely chopped red onion**
- **Tortilla chips**

Mash avocados with lime juice, salt, cumin and pepper. Gently stir in peach, jalapeno and red onion. Serve with tortilla chips.

¼ cup: 90 cal., 7g fat (1g sat. fat), 0 chol., 164mg sod., 7g carb. (2g sugars, 4g fiber), 1g pro. **Diabetic exchanges:** 1 fat, ½ starch.

TEST KITCHEN TIP

Leave the seeds in the jalapeno pepper for a little extra heat. We love this guacamole with chips, but it would complement grilled fish or chicken, too.

NORTHWEST CHERRY SALSA

EAT SMART

NORTHWEST CHERRY SALSA

We have five cherry trees—and I like to use every bit of fruit that doesn't get eaten right off of them. We enjoy this salsa on a variety of dishes, especially turkey.
—Margaret Slocum, Ridgefield, WA

Prep: 15 min. + chilling • **Makes:** ¾ cup

- **1 cup fresh or frozen pitted dark sweet cherries, chopped**
- **2 Tbsp. chopped fresh basil**
- **1 Tbsp. finely chopped green pepper**
- **1 tsp. lemon juice**
- **¼ tsp. Worcestershire sauce**
- **¼ tsp. grated lemon zest**
- **⅛ tsp. salt**
- **Dash hot pepper sauce**

Combine all ingredients; refrigerate at least 1 hour. Serve as a condiment with chicken, turkey or pork.

2 Tbsp.: 18 cal., 0 fat (0 sat. fat), 0 chol., 55mg sod., 5g carb. (3g sugars, 0 fiber), 0 pro. **Diabetic exchanges:** 1 free food.

FAST FIX

TWO-PEPPER BRUSCHETTA

This bruschetta is great for a light luncheon or late-night snack!
—Ramona McClung, Idaho Falls, ID

Takes: 20 min. • **Makes:** 2 servings

- **2 Tbsp. chopped sweet yellow pepper**
- **2 Tbsp. chopped green pepper**
- **2 Tbsp. seeded chopped tomato**
- **1 Tbsp. Italian salad dressing**
- **1¼ tsp. chopped green onion**
- **¾ tsp. minced fresh basil or ¼ tsp. dried basil**
- **2 slices French bread (1 in. thick)**
- **2 tsp. grated Parmesan cheese**

Preheat broiler. In a small bowl, toss the first six ingredients. Place bread slices on an ungreased baking sheet; broil 4-6 in. from heat for 2-3 minutes. Turn over; top with the pepper mixture and sprinkle with Parmesan cheese. Broil until heated through, 2-3 minutes longer.

1 piece: 196 cal., 3g fat (1g sat. fat), 2mg chol., 530mg sod., 36g carb. (2g sugars, 2g fiber), 7g pro.

TOMATO FRITTERS

TOMATO FRITTERS

I got this recipe from a friend, then tweaked it for my family's tastes. It's one of our favorite things in the summer. We love them right after they've been fried, when they're still hot and crispy.
—Pam Halter, Bridgeton, NJ

Prep: 15 min. • **Cook:** 5 min./batch
Makes: about 2½ dozen

1 cup all-purpose flour
1 tsp. baking powder
½ tsp. salt
Dash dried basil
Dash dried oregano
Dash pepper
1 large tomato, finely chopped
½ cup chopped onion
½ cup shredded Parmesan cheese
1 jalapeno pepper, seeded and finely chopped
1 garlic clove, minced
1 to 6 Tbsp. water, optional
Oil for deep-fat frying

1. In a large bowl, whisk flour, baking powder, salt, basil, oregano and pepper. Gently stir in tomato, onion, cheese, jalapeno and garlic just until moistened. If the batter seems thick, add water 1 Tbsp. at a time to thin it slightly until it loosens up and mixes easily.
2. In an electric skillet or deep fryer, heat oil to 375°. Drop batter by rounded tablespoonfuls, a few at a time, into hot oil. Fry until fritters are golden brown, about 1½ minutes per side. Drain on paper towels.

1 fritter: 40 cal., 2g fat (0 sat. fat), 1mg chol., 79mg sod., 4g carb. (0 sugars, 0 fiber), 1g pro.

TEST KITCHEN TIP

The water in this recipe is optional; it will depend on how ripe and juicy your tomatoes are. As a test, fry one fritter. If the middle is still undercooked when the exterior is golden brown, add some water to the batter to loosen it and make a slightly thinner fritter.

CREAMSICLE MIMOSAS

Toast Mom with this grown-up beverage. For the kiddos, substitute two bottles (750 milliliters each) of sparkling apple cider for the champagne.
—Deirdre Cox, Kansas City, MO

Prep: 15 min. + freezing
Makes: 16 servings (4 cups frozen mix)

4 tsp. grated orange zest
2½ cups orange juice
1 cup half-and-half cream
¾ cup superfine sugar
2 bottles (750 ml each) champagne or other sparkling wine
Fresh strawberries

1. Place first four ingredients in a blender; cover and process until sugar is dissolved. Transfer to an 8-in. square dish; freeze, covered, 6 hours or overnight.
2. To serve, place ¼ cup orange mixture in each champagne glass. Add champagne to fill the glass. Garnish with strawberries; serve immediately.

1 serving: 138 cal., 2g fat (1g sat. fat), 8mg chol., 8mg sod., 15g carb. (13g sugars, 0 fiber), 1g pro.

SPICED OLIVES

These are best made a week in advance; the olives really reach perfection at 10 days. Double or triple this zippy recipe—you won't regret it!
—Dean Schrock, Jacksonville, FL

Prep: 5 min. + chilling • **Makes:** 1½ cups

1 jar (7 oz.) pimiento-stuffed olives
½ cup tomato juice
1 Tbsp. olive oil
½ to 1 tsp. crushed red pepper flakes
2 garlic cloves, minced
½ tsp. dried basil
½ tsp. dried oregano

Drain olives, discarding the juice; return the olives to the jar. In a small bowl, combine tomato juice, oil, red pepper flakes, garlic, basil and oregano. Pour over the olives; cover and refrigerate for 3-10 days, turning jar daily. Drain before serving.

1 serving: 38 cal., 4g fat (0 sat. fat), 0 chol., 317mg sod., 2g carb. (0 sugars, 0 fiber), 0 pro.

CREAMSICLE MIMOSAS

MAPLE BLACKBERRY MOJITO

FAST FIX

MAPLE BLACKBERRY MOJITO

This refreshing cocktail is how to take advantage of prime berry season during the summer months. I've also used other fruit, including raspberries, kiwi and strawberries. It's made by the glass, so it's easy to make as many as you need!

—Donna Noel, Gray, ME

Takes: 10 min. • **Makes:** 1 serving

- **4 fresh or frozen blackberries, thawed**
- **5 fresh mint leaves**
- **1 Tbsp. maple syrup**
- **1 lime wedge**
- **¼ cup club soda, chilled**
- **1½ oz. light rum**

In a glass, muddle the blackberries and mint with maple syrup. Squeeze lime wedge into the glass. Stir in club soda and rum. Strain into a chilled glass; serve with ice.

1/2 cup: 160 cal., 0 fat (0 sat. fat), 0 chol., 18mg sod., 16g carb. (13g sugars, 1g fiber), 0 pro.

WHITE WINE SANGRIA

Lime, kumquats and two kinds of oranges infuse this quick and easy cocktail with an unforgettable citrus taste.

—Joyce Moynihan, Lakeville, MN

Prep: 10 min. + chilling

Makes: 18 servings (3½ qt.)

- **3 bottles (750 ml each) white wine**
- **1½ cups brandy**
- **¾ cup orange liqueur**
- **½ cup sugar**
- **1 large navel orange, sliced**
- **1 medium blood orange, sliced**
- **3 kumquats, sliced**
- **1 medium lime, sliced**

In a large pitcher, combine wine, brandy and liqueur. Stir in sugar until dissolved. Add remaining ingredients. Refrigerate 1 hour before serving. Serve over ice.

¾ cup: 214 cal., 0 fat (0 sat. fat), 0 chol., 7mg sod., 15g carb. (12g sugars, 1g fiber), 0 pro.

CRUNCHY VEGETABLE DIP

This new recipe was a big hit with my family. Dig in to it as an appetizer or even as a light lunch.

—Dottie Miller, Jonesborough, TN

Prep: 15 min. + chilling

Makes: 16 servings

- **1 pkg. (8 oz.) cream cheese, softened**
- **1 Tbsp. mayonnaise**
- **1 Tbsp. lemon juice**
- **½ tsp. salt**
- **⅛ tsp. pepper**
- **¾ cup grated carrots**
- **½ cup diced celery**
- **½ cup diced green pepper**
- **⅓ cup chopped green onions**
- **Assorted crackers and fresh vegetables**

In a bowl, beat first five ingredients until smooth. Stir in vegetables. Refrigerate, covered, 2-3 hours. Serve with crackers and vegetables.

2 Tbsp.: 60 cal., 6g fat (3g sat. fat), 14mg chol., 129mg sod., 2g carb. (1g sugars, 0 fiber), 1g pro.

5 INGREDIENTS | FAST FIX

PALOMA

Soon after I learned about this cocktail, I brought the ingredients to a family dinner at my parents' house. The next time we got together, my dad had the fixings all set out and ready to go!
—Ian Cliffe, Milwaukee, WI

Takes: 5 min. • **Makes:** 1 serving

- **Dash salt**
- **1½ oz. tequila**
- **½ oz. lime juice**
- **½ cup grapefruit soda or sparkling peach citrus soda**
- **Lime wedge**

In a glass filled with ice, combine salt, tequila and lime juice. Top with soda. Garnish with lime.

1 serving: 148 cal., 0 fat (0 sat. fat), 0 chol., 163mg sod., 14g carb. (13g sugars, 0 fiber), 0 pro.

TEST KITCHEN TIP

Not sure where to find grapefruit soda? Two of the easiest to find are Fresca (the original flavor is grapefruit) and Jarritos (often found in the ethnic foods aisle). Other brands to try: Izze, San Pellegrino, Ting and Whole Foods' pink grapefruit.

FAST COCONUT SHRIMP

Crispy crumbs and coconut nicely coat tender shrimp in this elegant appetizer. The rum and marmalade sauce on the side is a tasty complement.
—Elaine Bonica, Bethel, ME

Prep: 20 min. • **Cook:** 25 min.
Makes: 2 dozen (1⅓ cups sauce)

- **1 large egg**
- **1 Tbsp. water**
- **1 cup panko (Japanese) bread crumbs**
- **1 cup sweetened shredded coconut**
- **1 lb. uncooked shrimp (26-30 per pound), peeled and deveined**
- **Oil for deep-fat frying**
- **1 jar (12 oz.) orange marmalade**
- **¼ cup rum**

1. In a shallow bowl, whisk egg and water. In another shallow bowl, combine bread crumbs and coconut. Dip shrimp into the egg mixture, then roll in crumb mixture.
2. In an electric skillet or deep fryer, heat ¼ in. of oil to 375°. Fry shrimp, a few at a time, until golden brown, 1-2 minutes on each side. Drain on paper towels.
3. Meanwhile, in a small saucepan, bring orange marmalade and rum to a boil. Reduce heat; simmer, uncovered, for 5 minutes. Serve with shrimp.

1 piece: 103 cal., 4g fat (1g sat. fat), 37mg chol., 60mg sod., 13g carb. (10g sugars, 0 fiber), 4g pro. **Diabetic exchanges:** 1 starch, 1 fat.

5 INGREDIENTS | FAST FIX

SWEDISH ROSE SPRITZ

A spritz is a still or sparkling wine-based cocktail served with a small amount of liqueur and a splash of seltzer or soda.
—*Taste of Home* Test Kitchen

Takes: 5 min. • **Makes:** 1 serving

- **3 oz. dry rosé wine**
- **1 oz. elderflower liqueur**
- **Lemon seltzer water**

Fill a wine glass or tumbler three-fourths full of ice. Add wine and elderflower liqueur. Top with a splash of lemon seltzer; stir gently.

Note: For testing, we used St-Germain Elderflower Liqueur.

1 serving: 189 cal., 0 fat (0 sat. fat), 0 chol., 7mg sod., 19g carb. (14g sugars, 0 fiber), 0 pro.

FAST COCONUT SHRIMP

MARINATED OLIVE & CHEESE RING

We love to make Italian meals into celebrations, and an antipasto always kicks off the party. This one is almost too pretty to eat, especially when sprinkled with pimientos, fresh basil and parsley.
—Patricia Harmon, Baden, PA

Prep: 25 min. + chilling
Makes: 16 servings

- **1 pkg. (8 oz.) cream cheese, cold**
- **1 pkg. (10 oz.) sharp white cheddar cheese, cut into ¼-in. slices**
- **⅓ cup pimiento-stuffed olives**
- **⅓ cup pitted Greek olives**
- **¼ cup balsamic vinegar**
- **¼ cup olive oil**
- **1 Tbsp. minced fresh parsley**
- **1 Tbsp. minced fresh basil or 1 tsp. dried basil**
- **2 garlic cloves, minced**
- **1 jar (2 oz.) pimiento strips, drained and chopped**
- **Toasted French bread baguette slices**

1. Cut cream cheese lengthwise in half; cut each half into ¼-in. slices. On a serving plate, arrange the cheeses upright in a ring, alternating cheddar and cream cheese slices. Place olives in center.
2. In a small bowl, whisk vinegar, oil, parsley, basil and garlic until blended; drizzle over cheeses and olives. Sprinkle with pimientos. Refrigerate, covered, at least 8 hours or overnight. Serve with baguette slices.

1 serving: 168 cal., 16g fat (7g sat. fat), 34mg chol., 260mg sod., 2g carb. (1g sugars, 0 fiber), 6g pro.

TEST KITCHEN TIP

This stylish appetizer is super adaptable. Any cheeses will work in place of the cream cheese and sharp cheddar. Just keep the overall weight the same. For more variety, fold thin slices of deli cuts such as pepperoni and salami in half and tuck them between the cheese slices.

5 INGREDIENTS

CHEESE STRAWS

Just a few on-hand ingredients go into these long, crisp cracker sticks. The hand-held snacks make for easy mingling at parties.
—Elizabeth Robinson, Conroe, TX

Prep: 20 min. • **Bake:** 15 min. + cooling
Makes: 2½ dozen

- **½ cup butter, softened**
- **2 cups shredded sharp cheddar cheese**
- **1¼ cups all-purpose flour**
- **½ tsp. salt**
- **¼ tsp. cayenne pepper**

1. Preheat oven to 350°. In a large bowl, beat butter until light and fluffy. Beat in cheese until blended. Combine flour, salt and cayenne; stir into the cheese mixture until a dough forms. Roll into a 15x6-in. rectangle. Cut into thirty 6-in. strips. Gently place the strips 1 in. apart on ungreased baking sheets.
2. Bake 15-20 minutes or until lightly browned. Cool for 5 minutes before removing from pans to wire racks to cool completely. Store in an airtight container.

1 piece: 72 cal., 5g fat (4g sat. fat), 16mg chol., 106mg sod., 4g carb. (0 sugars, 0 fiber), 2g pro.

MARINATED OLIVE & CHEESE RING

QUESO BAKED NACHOS

To create this recipe, I modified a cheesy nachos recipe I found, loading it up with seasoned beef, beans, tomatoes and creamy queso. My family loves it.
—Denise Wheeler, Newaygo, MI

Prep: 25 min. • **Bake:** 10 min.
Makes: 12 servings

- 1 lb. ground beef
- 1 envelope taco seasoning
- ¾ cup water
- 1 pkg. (13 oz.) tortilla chips
- 1 cup refried beans
- 1 jar (15½ oz.) salsa con queso dip
- 2 plum tomatoes, chopped
- ¼ cup minced fresh chives, optional
- ½ cup sour cream

1. Preheat oven to 350°. In a large skillet, cook and crumble beef over medium heat until no longer pink, 5-7 minutes; drain. Stir in taco seasoning and water; bring to a boil. Reduce heat; simmer, uncovered, until thickened, about 5 minutes, stirring mixture occasionally.
2. In an ungreased 13x9-in. baking pan, layer a third of each of the following: chips, beans, beef mixture and queso dip. Repeat layers twice.
3. Bake, uncovered, until heated through, 10-15 minutes. Top with tomatoes and chives; serve immediately with sour cream on the side.

1 serving: 313 cal., 16g fat (5g sat. fat), 29mg chol., 786mg sod., 32g carb. (2g sugars, 2g fiber), 11g pro.

BLACK-EYED SUSAN

FAST FIX
BLACK-EYED SUSAN

The Kentucky Derby has the mint julep; the Preakness has the Black-Eyed Susan. The drink is a sunny mix of vodka, rum, pineapple and orange juices to toast your special events.
—*Taste of Home* Test Kitchen

Takes: 5 min. • **Makes:** 1 serving

- 1 oz. vodka
- 1 oz. light rum
- ½ oz. Triple Sec
- 2 oz. unsweetened pineapple juice
- 2 oz. orange juice
- Lime slice and pitted sweet dark cherry

Place the desired amount of ice in a rocks glass. Pour vodka, rum, Triple Sec and juices into glass. Stir; serve with a lime slice and cherry.

1 serving: 242 cal., 0 fat (0 sat. fat), 0 chol., 3mg sod., 21g carb. (18g sugars, 0 fiber), 0 pro.

FAST FIX
BACON CHEESE SPREAD

Each year, I share Christmas cheer by setting up a buffet at my family's hardware store. This cheese spread is always a big attraction!
—Sharon Bickett, Chester, SC

Takes: 15 min. • **Makes:** 4 cups

- 1 pkg. (12 oz.) bacon strips, chopped
- ½ cup chopped pecans
- 4 cups shredded sharp cheddar cheese
- 2 cups mayonnaise
- 1 small onion, chopped
- 2 Tbsp. finely chopped sweet red pepper
- ⅛ tsp. cayenne pepper
- Assorted crackers

Cook bacon until crisp; drain. In a large bowl, combine the next six ingredients. Stir in bacon. Serve with crackers.

2 Tbsp.: 184 cal., 18g fat (5g sat. fat), 23mg chol., 216mg sod., 1g carb. (0 sugars, 0 fiber), 4g pro.

ZIPPY CURRY DIP

EAT SMART

HOT CRAB PINWHEELS

I got the recipe for these crabmeat bites from a friend. What amazed me most is that my husband, who hates seafood, couldn't stop eating them.
—Kitti Boesel, Woodbridge, VA

Prep: 15 min. + chilling • **Bake:** 10 min.
Makes: 3 dozen

- **1 pkg. (8 oz.) reduced-fat cream cheese**
- **1 can (6 oz.) crabmeat, drained, flaked and cartilage removed**
- **¾ cup diced sweet red pepper**
- **½ cup shredded reduced-fat cheddar cheese**
- **2 green onions, thinly sliced**
- **3 Tbsp. minced fresh parsley**
- **¼ to ½ tsp. cayenne pepper**
- **6 flour tortillas (6 in.)**

1. Beat cream cheese until smooth; stir in crab, red pepper, cheese, green onions, parsley and cayenne. Spread ⅓ cup filling over each tortilla; roll up tightly. Wrap in plastic, twisting ends to seal; refrigerate at least 2 hours.
2. To serve, preheat the oven to 350°. Unwrap rolls; trim the ends and cut each roll into six slices. Place on baking sheets coated with cooking spray. Bake until bubbly, about 10 minutes. Serve warm.

1 pinwheel: 44 cal., 2g fat (1g sat. fat), 10mg chol., 98mg sod., 3g carb. (0 sugars, 0 fiber), 2g pro.

MANGO BLACK BEAN SALSA

EAT SMART | FAST FIX

MANGO BLACK BEAN SALSA

This colorful salsa takes just minutes to prepare—and that's likely how long it will last once you serve it, too! Chopped mango adds bursts of sweetness to the satisfying chip dip.
—Judy Heiser, Uvalde, TX

Takes: 15 min. • **Makes:** 12 servings

- **1 can (15 oz.) black beans, rinsed and drained**
- **1 can (11 oz.) Mexicorn, drained**
- **1 medium mango, peeled and cubed**
- **¼ cup finely chopped onion**
- **¼ cup minced fresh cilantro**
- **2 Tbsp. lime juice**
- **1 tsp. garlic salt**
- **¼ tsp. ground cumin**
- **Baked tortilla chip scoops**

In a large bowl, mix all ingredients except chips. Refrigerate until serving. Serve with chips.

¼ cup: 70 cal., 0 fat (0 sat. fat), 0 chol., 314mg sod., 14g carb. (6g sugars, 2g fiber), 3g pro.
Diabetic exchanges: 1 starch.

FAST FIX

ZIPPY CURRY DIP

It's easy to encourage everyone to eat their vegetables when this creamy dip is served alongside. The curry flavor gets stronger the longer this dips stands, so I like to make it in advance.
—Priscilla Steffke, Wausau, WI

Takes: 10 min. • **Makes:** about 1 cup

- **½ cup sour cream**
- **½ cup mayonnaise**
- **1 Tbsp. sugar**
- **1 tsp. prepared horseradish**
- **1 tsp. grated onion**
- **1 tsp. cider vinegar**
- **½ to 1 tsp. curry powder**
- **½ tsp. garlic salt**
- **Assorted fresh vegetables or potato chips**

In a small bowl, combine the first eight ingredients. Refrigerate until serving. Serve with vegetables or chips.

2 Tbsp.: 137 cal., 14g fat (3g sat. fat), 15mg chol., 198mg sod., 2g carb. (2g sugars, 0 fiber)

Speedy Sides & Salads

A great meal isn't complete without a top-notch side dish to round it out. These fast and easy dishes make any meal better—and some can even take center stage as a meatless meal on their own.

Cumin Rice with Avocado (p. 23) **Never-Fail Scalloped Potatoes** (p. 31) **Basic Buttermilk Salad Dressing** (p. 41) **Chopped Greek Salad** (p. 33) **Black-Eyed Pea Tomato Salad** (p. 39)

BAKED BUTTERNUT SQUASH

5 INGREDIENTS | EAT SMART

BAKED BUTTERNUT SQUASH

I take advantage of fall produce by baking this scrumptious side dish lightly seasoned with cinnamon, nutmeg and brown sugar.
—Heidi Vawdrey, Riverton, UT

Prep: 5 min. • **Bake:** 1 hour
Makes: 6 servings

- **¼ tsp. salt**
- **⅛ tsp. ground cinnamon**
- **⅛ tsp. ground nutmeg**
- **⅛ tsp. pepper**
- **1 small butternut squash (about 2 lbs.)**
- **2 Tbsp. butter, melted**
- **6 tsp. brown sugar, divided**

1. Preheat oven to 350°. Mix seasoning ingredients. Halve squash lengthwise; remove and discard seeds. Place the squash in an 11x7-in. baking dish coated with cooking spray. Brush with melted butter; sprinkle with seasonings.
2. Place 2 tsp. brown sugar in the cavity of each squash half. Sprinkle the remaining brown sugar over the cut surfaces.
3. Bake, covered, 40 minutes. Uncover; bake until the squash is tender, about 20 minutes longer.

1 serving: 120 cal., 4g fat (2g sat. fat), 10mg chol., 136mg sod., 22g carb. (9g sugars, 5g fiber), 2g pro. **Diabetic exchanges:** 1½ starch, ½ fat.

EAT SMART | FAST FIX

PATTYPAN SAUTE

Summer flavors like tomato and sweet red pepper complement sauteed squash in this lovely side. Shredded Parmesan cheese makes it savory and special.
—*Taste of Home* Test Kitchen

Takes: 25 min. • **Makes:** 4 servings

- **2 cups halved pattypan squash**
- **1 medium onion, halved and sliced**
- **2 tsp. canola oil**
- **2 garlic cloves, minced**
- **1 small sweet red pepper, cut into ½-in. pieces**
- **1 cup sliced fresh mushrooms**
- **1 medium tomato, chopped**
- **½ tsp. salt**
- **½ tsp. Italian seasoning**
- **⅛ tsp. pepper**
- **2 Tbsp. shredded Parmesan cheese**

1. In a large nonstick skillet, saute squash and onion in oil for 2 minutes. Add garlic; cook 1 minute longer. Add red pepper and mushrooms; saute until the vegetables are crisp-tender, 5-7 minutes.
2. Stir in the tomato, salt, Italian seasoning and pepper; heat through. Sprinkle with Parmesan cheese.

¾ cup: 73 cal., 3g fat (1g sat. fat), 2mg chol., 343mg sod., 9g carb. (5g sugars, 2g fiber), 3g pro. **Diabetic exchanges:** 2 vegetable, ½ fat.

FAST FIX

SPINACH SALAD WITH POPPY SEED DRESSING

I love to bring this salad to parties or serve it as a healthy lunch. The easy homemade dressing is the best part.

—Nikki Barton, Providence, UT

Takes: 25 min.
Makes: 6 servings (1 cup dressing)

- 4 cups fresh baby spinach
- 4 cups torn iceberg lettuce
- 1½ cups sliced fresh mushrooms
- ½ lb. bacon strips, cooked and crumbled

DRESSING

- ¼ cup red wine vinegar
- ¼ cup chopped red onion
- 3 Tbsp. sugar
- ¾ tsp. salt
- ¼ tsp. ground mustard
- ½ cup canola oil
- 1½ tsp. poppy seeds

1. In a large bowl, combine spinach, lettuce, mushrooms and bacon. Place vinegar, onion, sugar, salt and mustard in a blender or food processor. While processing, gradually add the oil in a steady stream. Transfer to a bowl; stir in poppy seeds.
2. Divide salad among six plates; drizzle with dressing.

1½ cups with about 2 Tbsp. dressing: 280 cal., 24g fat (3g sat. fat), 14mg chol., 557mg sod., 10g carb. (8g sugars, 1g fiber), 6g pro.

CRANBERRY FLUFF

We like this fluffy fruit salad because it's not as sweet as many other fluffs; the tart cranberries keep the sweetness under control! I'm often asked for the secret to this luscious holiday salad.

—M L Hartel, Williston, ND

Prep: 10 min. + chilling
Makes: 10 servings

- 4 cups fresh or frozen cranberries
- 3 cups miniature marshmallows
- ¾ cup sugar
- 2 cups diced unpeeled tart apples
- ½ cup halved green grapes
- ½ cup chopped nuts
- ¼ tsp. salt
- 1 cup heavy whipping cream, whipped

1. Place the cranberries in a food processor; cover and process until finely chopped. Transfer to a large bowl; add marshmallows and sugar. Cover and refrigerate for 4 hours or overnight.
2. Just before serving, stir in the apples, grapes, chopped nuts and salt. Fold in the whipped cream.

¾ cup: 264 cal., 12g fat (6g sat. fat), 27mg chol., 80mg sod., 38g carb. (30g sugars, 3g fiber), 3g pro.

EAT SMART

CUMIN RICE WITH AVOCADO

PICTURED ON P. 21

Cumin, picante sauce and avocado do a terrific job of perking up rice in this any-day side dish.

—Margaret Allen, Abingdon, VA

Prep: 5 min. • **Cook:** 30 min.
Makes: 6 servings

- 2¼ cups water
- 1 Tbsp. butter
- 2 tsp. reduced-sodium chicken bouillon granules
- ¾ tsp. ground cumin
- 1 cup uncooked long grain rice
- ⅓ cup picante sauce
- 1 medium ripe avocado, peeled and cubed
- 2 green onions, sliced

1. Place the first four ingredients in a large saucepan; bring to a boil. Stir in the rice; return to a boil. Reduce the heat; simmer, covered, until the rice is tender, 20-25 minutes.
2. Stir in picante sauce; heat through. Gently stir in avocado and green onions.

⅔ cup: 188 cal., 6g fat (2g sat. fat), 5mg chol., 194mg sod., 31g carb. (1g sugars, 2g fiber), 3g pro. **Diabetic exchanges:** 2 starch, 1 fat.

CRANBERRY FLUFF

5 INGREDIENTS | FAST FIX

STRAWBERRY FETA TOSSED SALAD

I first had this salad when a neighbor served it at a barbecue. I've experimented with ingredients, but this combination is the best. I took it to a baby shower, and there wasn't a seed left in the bowl.
—Lisa Lesinski-Topp, Menomonee Falls, WI

Takes: 10 min. • **Makes:** 6 servings

- **6 cups torn mixed salad greens**
- **2 cups fresh strawberries, sliced**
- **1 pkg. (4 oz.) crumbled feta cheese**
- **¼ cup sunflower kernels**
- **Balsamic vinaigrette**

Place the first four ingredients in a large bowl. To serve, drizzle with vinaigrette; toss to combine.

1 cup: 103 cal., 6g fat (2g sat. fat), 10mg chol., 259mg sod., 8g carb. (3g sugars, 3g fiber), 6g pro.

EAT SMART | FAST FIX

PEA POD CARROT MEDLEY

We grow pea pods, and I wanted to use them in something other than stir-fries—this fit the bill. Its pretty orange glaze and fresh taste always get compliments.
—Josie Smith, Winamac, IN

Takes: 25 min. • **Makes:** 2 servings

- **2 medium carrots, sliced**
- **2 cups fresh sugar snap peas, trimmed**
- **1 tsp. cornstarch**
- **½ tsp. grated orange zest**
- **⅓ cup orange juice**
- **2 tsp. reduced-sodium soy sauce**
- **¼ tsp. salt**

1. Place carrots and enough water to cover in a small saucepan; bring to a boil. Reduce heat; simmer, covered, 5 minutes. Add peas; simmer, covered, until peas are crisp-tender, 2-3 minutes. Drain and remove vegetables from pan; set aside.
2. In same pan, mix remaining ingredients until the cornstarch is dissolved; bring to a boil. Cook and stir until thickened, 1-2 minutes. Add vegetables; toss to coat.

1 cup: 119 cal., 1g fat (0 sat. fat), 0 chol., 535mg sod., 23g carb. (12g sugars, 6g fiber), 6g pro. **Diabetic exchanges:** 2 vegetable, ½ fruit.

5 INGREDIENTS | EAT SMART

GARLIC-ROSEMARY BRUSSELS SPROUTS

My go-to Thanksgiving side dish is healthy and delicious, and doesn't take much time. I use rosemary for my turkey, too.
—Elisabeth Larsen, Pleasant Grove, UT

Prep: 15 min. • **Bake:** 25 min.
Makes: 8 servings

- **¼ cup olive oil**
- **4 garlic cloves, minced**
- **1 tsp. salt**
- **½ tsp. pepper**
- **2 lbs. Brussels sprouts (about 8 cups), trimmed and halved**
- **1 cup panko (Japanese) bread crumbs**
- **1 to 2 Tbsp. minced fresh rosemary**

1. Preheat oven to 425°. Place first four ingredients in a small microwave-safe bowl; microwave on high 30 seconds.
2. Place Brussels sprouts in a 15x10x1-in. pan; toss with 3 Tbsp. oil mixture. Roast 10 minutes.
3. Toss bread crumbs with rosemary and the remaining oil mixture; sprinkle over sprouts. Bake until crumbs are browned and sprouts are tender, 12-15 minutes. Serve immediately.

¾ cup: 134 cal., 7g fat (1g sat. fat), 0 chol., 342mg sod., 15g carb. (3g sugars, 4g fiber), 5g pro. **Diabetic exchanges:** 1½ fat, 1 vegetable, ½ starch.

GARLIC-ROSEMARY BRUSSELS SPROUTS

Just like Mom Made

Homemade potato pancakes are one of the best-ever comfort foods! You can eat them on their own, or as a side to fried fish or chicken.

HOW-TO

Make Potato Pancakes

1. Shred
Using a food processor or box grater, shred the potatoes.

2. Squeeze
Rinse potatoes in cold water. Place potatoes on a towel. Gather up towel ends; squeeze out and discard excess water.

3. Mix
Stir egg, flour, onion, salt and pepper into the potatoes.

4. Heat
Heat ¼ in. of oil in a large nonstick skillet. Working in batches, drop potato mixture by ⅓ cupfuls into oil; press to flatten slightly. Fry both sides until golden brown.

5. Serve
Drain pancakes on paper towels. Serve immediately. Sprinkle with parsley and top with sour cream or applesauce.

FAST FIX

MOM'S POTATO PANCAKES

Old-fashioned potato pancakes are fluffy inside and crispy outside. Mom got this recipe from Grandma, so we've enjoyed it for years.

—Dianne Esposite, New Middletown, OH

Takes: 30 min. • **Makes:** 6 servings

- **4 cups shredded peeled potatoes (about 4 large potatoes)**
- **1 large egg, lightly beaten**
- **3 Tbsp. all-purpose flour**
- **1 Tbsp. grated onion**
- **1 tsp. salt**
- **¼ tsp. pepper**
- **Oil for frying**
- **Chopped parsley, applesauce and sour cream**

2 pancakes: 171 cal., 7g fat (1g sat. fat), 31mg chol., 411mg sod., 24g carb. (1g sugars, 2g fiber), 3g pro.

★★★★★ **READER REVIEW**

"Delicious, and so simple to make. What a great new way to prepare potatoes. Just lovely."

DUBLINLAB TASTEOFHOME.COM

EDAMAME SALAD WITH SESAME GINGER DRESSING

EAT SMART | FAST FIX

EDAMAME SALAD WITH SESAME GINGER DRESSING

This bright salad has a little bit of everything: hearty greens, a nutty crunch, a zip of citrusy goodness and a big protein punch. It's pure bliss in a bowl.

—Darla Andrews, Schertz, TX

Takes: 15 min. • **Makes:** 6 servings

- 6 cups baby kale salad blend (about 5 oz.)
- 1 can (15 oz.) garbanzo beans or chickpeas, rinsed and drained
- 2 cups frozen shelled edamame (about 10 oz.), thawed
- 3 clementines, peeled and segmented
- 1 cup fresh bean sprouts
- ½ cup salted peanuts
- 2 green onions, diagonally sliced
- ½ cup sesame ginger salad dressing

Divide salad blend among six bowls. Top with all remaining ingredients except salad dressing. Serve with dressing.

1 serving: 317 cal., 17g fat (2g sat. fat), 0 chol., 355mg sod., 32g carb. (14g sugars, 8g fiber), 13g pro.

*** HEALTH TIP *** Vitamin C-rich clementines help your body absorb iron from plant sources like the kale and edamame in this salad.

TEST KITCHEN TIP

Edamame is the Japanese name for immature or green soybeans, which are then steamed or boiled. They're available shelled or still in their pods in the frozen vegetable section.

Green onions (also known as scallions) are the immature form of onions before the bulb has grown. Cut green onions thinly on the diagonal to give them a delicate look, especially appropriate to Asian dishes.

5 INGREDIENTS | EAT SMART | FAST FIX

ROASTED SUGAR SNAP PEAS

This is a super fast and fresh way to dress up crisp sugar snap peas. It's a bright complement to so many spring dishes, and is pretty enough for company.

—*Taste of Home* Test Kitchen

Takes: 15 min. • **Makes:** 2 servings

- 1 pkg. (8 oz.) fresh sugar snap peas, trimmed
- 1 Tbsp. chopped shallot
- 2 tsp. olive oil
- ½ tsp. Italian seasoning
- ⅛ tsp. salt

Preheat oven to 400°. Toss together all ingredients; spread in a 15x10x1-in. pan. Roast until the peas are crisp-tender, 8-10 minutes, stirring once.

⅔ cup: 91 cal., 5g fat (1g sat. fat), 0 chol., 153mg sod., 9g carb. (4g sugars, 3g fiber), 4g pro. **Diabetic exchanges:** 2 vegetable, 1 fat.

5 INGREDIENTS | FAST FIX

RASPBERRY POPPY SEED DRESSING

I love this creamy, fresh-tasting dressing! Quick to assemble, it adds a summery gourmet touch when drizzled over a salad.
—Kendra Stoller, Kouts, IN

Takes: 10 min. • **Makes:** 2 cups

- **6 Tbsp. red wine vinegar**
- **½ cup plus 2 Tbsp. sugar**
- **1 tsp. salt**
- **1 tsp. ground mustard**
- **1 cup canola oil**
- **1 cup fresh or frozen raspberries, thawed**
- **1 tsp. poppy seeds**

In a blender, combine the vinegar, sugar, salt and mustard. While processing, gradually add the oil in a steady stream. Add raspberries; cover and process until blended. Stir in poppy seeds. Serve immediately. Refrigerate leftovers.

2 Tbsp.: 161 cal., 14g fat (2g sat. fat), 0 chol., 148mg sod., 10g carb. (8g sugars, 1g fiber), 0 pro.

EAT SMART | FAST FIX

FRUIT & SPINACH SALAD

The combination of sweet fruit and salty feta cheese makes this salad a winner.
—Virginia Dack, Asheville, NC

Takes: 10 min. • **Makes:** 2 servings

- **2 cups fresh baby spinach**
- **1 snack-size cup (4 oz.) mandarin oranges, drained**
- **⅓ cup seedless red grapes, halved**
- **¼ cup crumbled feta cheese**
- **2 Tbsp. chopped walnuts, toasted**
- **1 green onion, chopped**
- **¼ cup oil and vinegar salad dressing**

In a salad bowl, combine the spinach, oranges, grapes, cheese, walnuts and onion. Drizzle with dressing; toss to coat. Serve immediately.

1 serving: 235 cal., 16g fat (2g sat. fat), 8mg chol., 644mg sod., 19g carb. (16g sugars, 2g fiber), 6g pro. **Diabetic exchanges:** 3 fat, 1 vegetable, ½ fruit.

SLOW COOKER

SPICED ACORN SQUASH

Working full time, I didn't always have time to cook the meals my family loved. So I re-created many of our favorites in the slow cooker. This is one of them.
—Carol Greco, Centereach, NY

Prep: 15 min. • **Cook:** 3½ hours
Makes: 4 squash halves

- **¾ cup packed brown sugar**
- **1 tsp. ground cinnamon**
- **1 tsp. ground nutmeg**
- **2 small acorn squash, halved and seeded**
- **¾ cup raisins**
- **4 Tbsp. butter**
- **½ cup water**

1. In a small bowl, mix the brown sugar, cinnamon and nutmeg; spoon into squash halves. Sprinkle with raisins. Top each with 1 Tbsp. butter. Wrap each half individually in heavy-duty foil, sealing tightly.
2. Pour water into a 5-qt. slow cooker. Place squash in slow cooker, cut side up (packets may be stacked). Cook, covered, on high for 3½-4 hours or until the squash is tender. Open foil carefully to allow steam to escape.

Per squash half: 433 cal., 12g fat (7g sat. fat), 31mg chol., 142mg sod., 86g carb. (63g sugars, 5g fiber), 3g pro.

SPICED ACORN SQUASH

CRANBERRY SWEET POTATO BAKE

Sweet potatoes and tart cranberries are a feast for both the eyes and the palate in this beautiful holiday side dish.
—Patricia Kile, Elizabethtown, PA

Prep: 25 min. • **Bake:** 35 min.
Makes: 8 servings

- **1½ lbs. sweet potatoes (about 3 medium), peeled and cut into 1-in. cubes**
- **1½ cups fresh or frozen cranberries, thawed**
- **⅔ cup sugar**
- **⅓ cup orange juice**
- **1 tsp. salt**
- **1 Tbsp. butter**
- **1½ cups granola without raisins**

1. Preheat oven to 350°. Place sweet potatoes in a large saucepan with enough water to cover; bring to a boil. Reduce heat; cook, uncovered, until tender, 10-15 minutes. Drain.
2. Toss cranberries with sugar, orange juice and salt. Spread half of the cranberry mixture in a greased 11x7-in. baking dish. Top with half of the potatoes. Repeat the layers. Dot with butter.
3. Bake, covered, until the cranberries are tender, about 25 minutes. Uncover; sprinkle with granola. Bake 10 minutes.

½ cup: 261 cal., 5g fat (1g sat. fat), 4mg chol., 323mg sod., 54g carb. (29g sugars, 7g fiber), 5g pro.

EAT SMART | FAST FIX

VEGETABLE BARLEY SAUTE

This wonderful side dish can easily be turned into a hearty entree by adding cooked chicken.
—*Taste of Home* Test Kitchen

Takes: 30 min. • **Makes:** 4 servings

- **½ cup quick-cooking barley**
- **⅓ cup water**
- **3 Tbsp. reduced-sodium soy sauce**
- **2 tsp. cornstarch**
- **1 garlic clove, minced**
- **1 Tbsp. vegetable oil**
- **2 carrots, thinly sliced**
- **1 cup cut fresh green beans (2-in. pieces)**
- **2 green onions, sliced**
- **½ cup unsalted cashews, optional**

1. Prepare barley according to package directions. In a small bowl, combine water, soy sauce and cornstarch until smooth; set aside.
2. In a large skillet or wok, saute garlic in oil for 15 seconds. Add carrots and beans; stir-fry for 1 minute. Add onions; stir-fry for 2-3 minutes. Stir the soy sauce mixture; stir into the skillet. Bring to a boil; cook and stir for 1 minute or until thickened. Add barley; heat through. Stir in cashews if desired.

⅔ cup: 148 cal., 4g fat (1g sat. fat), 0 chol., 458mg sod., 24g carb. (3g sugars, 6g fiber), 5g pro. **Diabetic exchanges:** 1½ starch, 1 fat.

SWEET PEPPER PESTO PASTA

What's a family gathering or potluck without at least one pasta salad? This one is tasty warm or cold.
—Karen Hentges, Bakersfield, CA

Prep: 20 min. • **Bake:** 15 min.
Makes: 8 servings

- **20 miniature sweet peppers, seeded and cut into rings**
- **2 tsp. olive oil**
- **½ tsp. garlic powder**
- **4½ cups uncooked bow tie pasta**
- **1 cup prepared pesto**
- **1 can (2¼ oz.) sliced ripe olives, drained**
- **⅓ cup grated Parmesan cheese**

1. Preheat oven to 350°. Toss peppers with oil and garlic powder; spread evenly in a greased 15x10x1-in. pan. Roast until tender, 10-15 minutes. Cool slightly.
2. Cook pasta according to package directions. Drain; rinse with cold water and drain. Place in a large bowl.
3. Stir in pesto, olives and peppers. Refrigerate, covered, until serving. Sprinkle with cheese.

1 cup: 308 cal., 14g fat (3g sat. fat), 3mg chol., 493mg sod., 37g carb. (3g sugars, 3g fiber), 9g pro.

EAT SMART | FAST FIX

HERBED TUNA & WHITE BEAN SALAD

This quick and delicious salad can be made special for guests—or yourself—by grilling fresh tuna steaks instead of using canned.
—Charlene Chambers, Ormond Beach, FL

Takes: 15 min. • **Makes:** 4 servings

- **4 cups fresh arugula**
- **1 can (15 oz.) no-salt-added cannellini beans, rinsed and drained**
- **1 cup grape tomatoes, halved**
- **½ small red onion, thinly sliced**
- **⅓ cup chopped roasted sweet red peppers**
- **⅓ cup pitted Nicoise or other olives**
- **¼ cup chopped fresh basil**
- **3 Tbsp. extra virgin olive oil**
- **½ tsp. grated lemon zest**
- **2 Tbsp. lemon juice**
- **1 garlic clove, minced**
- **⅛ tsp. salt**
- **2 cans (5 oz. each) albacore white tuna in water, drained**

Place the first seven ingredients in a large bowl. Whisk together oil, lemon zest, lemon juice, garlic and salt; drizzle over the salad. Add the tuna and toss gently to combine.

2 cups: 319 cal., 16g fat (2g sat. fat), 30mg chol., 640mg sod., 20g carb. (3g sugars, 5g fiber), 23g pro. **Diabetic exchanges:** 3 fat, 2 lean meat, 1 starch, 1 vegetable.

TEST KITCHEN TIP

Kalamata olives, though stronger in flavor, would be a good substitute for Nicoise olives. Extra virgin olive oil adds a subtle fruity flavor to the dressing, but plain olive oil could be used instead.

HERBED TUNA &
WHITE BEAN SALAD

EAT SMART

SOUTH-OF-THE-BORDER CITRUS SALAD

Orange, grapefruit and jicama add color and texture to this out-of-the-ordinary fruit salad. Sometimes I'll toss in slices of mango and cucumber for extra fun.
—Mary Fuller, SeaTac, WA

Prep: 20 min. + chilling
Makes: 6 servings

- **3 medium pink grapefruit**
- **3 medium oranges**
- **1 cup julienned peeled jicama**
- **2 Tbsp. minced fresh cilantro**
- **2 Tbsp. lime juice**
- **¼ tsp. ground cinnamon**

1. Cut a thin slice from the top and bottom of each grapefruit and orange; stand fruit upright on a cutting board. With a knife, cut off the peel and outer membrane from each fruit. Cut fruit crosswise into slices; place in a large bowl.
2. Add the remaining ingredients; toss to combine. Transfer to a platter; refrigerate, covered, until serving.

¾ cup: 70 cal., 0 fat (0 sat. fat), 0 chol., 2mg sod., 17g carb. (13g sugars, 3g fiber), 1g pro.
Diabetic exchanges: 1 fruit.

SPICY CORN KABOBS

SPICY CORN KABOBS

Corn on the cob becomes a tangy delight when grilled, dotted with sour cream and cheese, and zinged with a splash of lime.
—Leah Lenz, Los Angeles, CA

Prep: 10 min. • **Grill:** 25 min.
Makes: 6 servings

- **6 medium ears husked sweet corn, halved crosswise**
- **¼ cup sour cream**
- **¼ cup mayonnaise**
- **½ cup grated cotija cheese or Parmesan cheese**
- **2 tsp. chili powder**
- **¼ tsp. cayenne pepper, optional**
- **6 lime wedges**

1. Insert a metal or soaked wooden skewer into the cut end of each piece of corn. Grill, covered, over medium heat until the corn is tender, 25-30 minutes, turning often.
2. In a small bowl, combine sour cream and mayonnaise; spread over the corn. Sprinkle with cheese, chili powder and, if desired, cayenne. Serve with lime wedges.

2 kabobs: 205 cal., 13g fat (4g sat. fat), 20mg chol., 222mg sod., 19g carb. (3g sugars, 3g fiber), 6g pro.

EAT SMART | FAST FIX

COLORFUL COUSCOUS

We love it when side dishes pop with color, like the red and yellow pepper accents you'll see in this light and fluffy couscous. It's a scrumptious and welcome switch from baked potatoes or rice.
—*Taste of Home* Test Kitchen

Takes: 25 min. • **Makes:** 6 servings

- **2 Tbsp. olive oil**
- **5 miniature sweet peppers, julienned**
- **⅓ cup finely chopped onion**
- **2 garlic cloves, minced**
- **1 can (14½ oz.) chicken broth**
- **¼ cup water**
- **½ tsp. salt**
- **¼ tsp. pepper**
- **1 pkg. (10 oz.) couscous**

In a large saucepan, heat oil over medium-high heat; saute peppers, onion and garlic until tender, 2-3 minutes. Stir in broth, water, salt and pepper; bring to a boil. Stir in couscous. Remove from heat; let stand, covered, 5 minutes. Fluff with a fork.

¾ cup: 220 cal., 5g fat (1g sat. fat), 2mg chol., 498mg sod., 37g carb. (2g sugars, 2g fiber), 7g pro.

5 INGREDIENTS | FAST FIX

ROASTED RED PEPPER GREEN BEANS

This recipe showcases a creamy sauce with shallot-and-chive cheese. The toasted pine nuts add crunch. Just a few ingredients—so easy!
—Becky Ellis, Roanoke, VA

Takes: 20 min. • **Makes:** 10 servings

- **2 lbs. fresh green beans, trimmed**
- **1 Tbsp. butter**
- **½ cup pine nuts**
- **Dash salt**
- **1 pkg. (5.2 oz.) shallot-chive spreadable cheese**
- **1 jar (8 oz.) roasted sweet red peppers, drained and chopped**

1. In a pot of boiling water, cook the green beans until tender, 6-8 minutes.
2. Meanwhile, in a large skillet, melt butter over medium heat. Add pine nuts; cook and stir until lightly browned, 3-4 minutes. Remove from heat; sprinkle with salt.
3. Drain beans; return to pot. Place cheese over warm beans to soften; toss to coat. Add red peppers; toss to combine. Sprinkle with pine nuts. Serve immediately.

¾ cup: 152 cal., 12g fat (5g sat. fat), 18mg chol., 341mg sod., 9g carb. (3g sugars, 3g fiber), 4g pro.

EAT SMART

NEVER-FAIL SCALLOPED POTATOES

PICTURED ON P. 21

Take the chill off any blustery day and make something special to accompany meaty entrees. These creamy scalloped potatoes are sure to be a favorite.
—Agnes Ward, Stratford, ON

Prep: 25 min. • **Bake:** 1 hour
Makes: 6 servings

- **2 Tbsp. butter**
- **3 Tbsp. all-purpose flour**
- **1 tsp. salt**
- **¼ tsp. pepper**
- **1½ cups fat-free milk**
- **½ cup shredded reduced-fat cheddar cheese**
- **2 lbs. red potatoes, peeled and thinly sliced (about 4 cups)**
- **1 cup thinly sliced onions, divided**

1. Preheat oven to 350°. In a small saucepan, melt butter; stir in the flour, salt and pepper until smooth. Gradually whisk in milk. Bring to a boil, stirring constantly; cook and stir until thickened, about 2 minutes. Remove from heat; stir in cheese until melted.
2. Coat an 8-in. square baking dish with cooking spray. Place half of the sliced potatoes in the dish; layer with ½ cup of the onion and half of the cheese sauce. Repeat the layers.
3. Bake, covered, 50 minutes. Uncover; bake until bubbly and the potatoes are tender, 10-15 minutes longer.

¾ cup: 215 cal., 6g fat (4g sat. fat), 18mg chol., 523mg sod., 32g carb. (5g sugars, 3g fiber), 8g pro. **Diabetic exchanges:** 2 starch, 1 fat.

ROASTED RED PEPPER GREEN BEANS

EAT SMART | FAST FIX

CITRUS FENNEL SALAD

I guarantee guests will love the taste of this distinctive salad. The bright, pleasant orange flavor pairs well with tender pieces of fennel.

—Marion Karlin, Waterloo, IA

Takes: 20 min. • **Makes:** 8 servings

- **2 large fennel bulbs**
- **2 Tbsp. olive oil**
- **1 Tbsp. butter**
- **6 Tbsp. orange juice**
- **3 Tbsp. lemon juice**
- **1 tsp. salt**
- **½ tsp. coarsely ground pepper**
- **2 large navel oranges, peeled and sliced**
- **Salad greens**

1. Remove fronds from fennel bulbs; set aside for garnish. Cut bulbs into thin slices. In a large skillet, saute fennel slices in oil and butter until crisp-tender.
2. Stir in the juices, salt and pepper. Bring to a boil; reduce the heat to medium. Cook and stir until the fennel is tender, 5-6 minutes.
3. Remove from the heat; stir in orange segments. Serve over salad greens; top with reserved fennel fronds.

½ cup: 89 cal., 5g fat (1g sat. fat), 4mg chol., 336mg sod., 11g carb. (6g sugars, 3g fiber), 1g pro. **Diabetic exchanges:** 1 vegetable, 1 fat, ½ fruit.

CITRUS FENNEL SALAD

EAT SMART | FAST FIX

GRILLED PATTYPANS

Just a few minutes and a handful of ingredients are all you'll need for this scrumptious side dish. Hoisin sauce and rice wine vinegar give grilled pattypans Asian flair.

—*Taste of Home* Test Kitchen

Takes: 15 min. • **Makes:** 6 servings

- **6 cups pattypan squash (about 1½ lbs.)**
- **¼ cup apricot spreadable fruit**
- **2 tsp. hoisin sauce**
- **1 tsp. rice vinegar**
- **½ tsp. sesame oil**
- **¼ tsp. salt**
- **⅛ tsp. ground ginger**

1. Place squash in a grill wok or basket coated with cooking spray. Grill, covered, over medium heat until tender, 4 minutes on each side.
2. Meanwhile, in a small bowl, combine the remaining ingredients. Transfer the squash to a serving bowl; add sauce and toss gently.

Note: If you do not have a grill wok or basket, use a disposable foil pan. Poke holes in the bottom of the pan with a meat fork to allow the liquid to drain.

¾ cup: 54 cal., 0 fat (0 sat. fat), 0 chol., 127mg sod., 12g carb. (8g sugars, 1g fiber), 1g pro. **Diabetic exchanges:** 1 vegetable, ½ starch.

BRUSSELS SPROUTS WITH BACON VINAIGRETTE

I'd never tried Brussels sprouts until I made this salad. It won me over and even charmed my family. Bacon and apples spruce up the flavor.

—Stephanie Gates, Waterloo, IA

Prep: 40 min. • **Cook:** 10 min. + chilling
Makes: 12 servings

- **3 lbs. fresh Brussels sprouts**
- **10 bacon strips, chopped**
- **1 medium red onion, halved and thinly sliced**
- **⅔ cup white wine vinegar**
- **⅓ cup honey**
- **¼ cup Dijon mustard**
- **2 medium apples, thinly sliced**

1. Trim and thinly slice Brussels sprouts. Transfer to a large bowl. In a large skillet, cook bacon over medium heat until crisp, stirring occasionally. Remove with a slotted spoon; drain on paper towels. Discard the drippings, reserving ¼ cup in the pan.
2. Add onion to the drippings; cook and stir over medium-high heat until tender, 3-5 minutes. Stir in vinegar, honey and mustard. Cook and stir for 1 minute. Add the bacon and apples to Brussels sprouts. Drizzle with the onion mixture; toss to coat. Refrigerate for at least 3 hours before serving.

1 cup: 166 cal., 7g fat (3g sat. fat), 11mg chol., 274mg sod., 21g carb. (13g sugars, 5g fiber), 6g pro.

*** HEALTH TIP *** Brussels sprouts are an excellent source off Vitamin K, which is important for healthy bones.

EAT SMART

PARMESAN POTATO WEDGES

I recommend serving these wedges alongside a salad for a light lunch or as a side dish with a chicken or beef entree.
—Beth Ask, Ulster, PA

Prep: 10 min. • **Bake:** 30 min.
Makes: 8 servings

- **¼ cup grated Parmesan cheese**
- **1 tsp. garlic salt**
- **½ tsp. garlic powder**
- **½ tsp. dried oregano**
- **½ tsp. paprika**
- **4 medium baking potatoes (about 8 oz. each)**
- **Cooking spray**

Preheat oven to 400°. Mix the first five ingredients. Cut each potato lengthwise into eight wedges; place in a parchment-lined 15x10x1-in. pan. Spritz with cooking spray; sprinkle with cheese mixture. Bake until tender, about 30 minutes.

4 wedges: 101 cal., 1g fat (0 sat. fat), 2mg chol., 297mg sod., 20g carb. (1g sugars, 2g fiber), 3g pro. **Diabetic exchanges:** 1½ starch.

VANILLA YOGURT AMBROSIA

This simple fruit salad is so yummy. I have served it many times, and it's always one of the first dishes to go. Fat-free vanilla yogurt also works well as the dressing.
—Sherry Hulsman, Louisville, KY

Takes: 15 min. + chilling
Makes: 6 servings

- **1 can (20 oz.) pineapple tidbits, drained**
- **1 can (11 oz.) mandarin oranges, drained**
- **1½ cups green grapes**
- **1 cup miniature marshmallows**
- **½ cup sweetened shredded coconut**
- **¾ cup vanilla yogurt**
- **¼ cup chopped pecans, toasted**

In a serving bowl, combine the pineapple, oranges, grapes, marshmallows and coconut. Fold in the yogurt. Cover and refrigerate for at least 1 hour. Just before serving, stir in pecans.

¾ cup: 234 cal., 7g fat (3g sat. fat), 2mg chol., 56mg sod., 44g carb. (39g sugars, 2g fiber), 3g pro. **Diabetic exchanges:** 2 fruit, 1 fat.

PARMESAN POTATO WEDGES

EAT SMART | FAST FIX

CHOPPED GREEK SALAD

PICTURED ON P. 21

While living in San Diego during college, I had a favorite Greek casual dining spot. Now that I'm back in my hometown, I've recreated some dishes from the diner—it takes me right back!
—Jenn Tidwell, Fair Oaks, CA

Takes: 20 min. • **Makes:** 4 servings

- **4 cups chopped romaine**
- **1 can (15 oz.) garbanzo beans or chickpeas, rinsed and drained**
- **2 celery ribs, sliced**
- **1 medium tomato, chopped**
- **⅓ cup sliced Greek olives**
- **⅓ cup crumbled feta cheese**
- **¼ cup finely chopped pepperoncini**

DRESSING

- **2 Tbsp. minced fresh basil**
- **2 Tbsp. pepperoncini juice**
- **2 Tbsp. extra virgin olive oil**
- **1 Tbsp. lemon juice**
- **¼ tsp. salt**
- **¼ tsp. pepper**

Place the first seven ingredients in a large bowl. In a small bowl, whisk together the dressing ingredients. Drizzle over salad; toss to combine. Serve immediately.

1½ cups: 235 cal., 14g fat (2g sat. fat), 5mg chol., 617mg sod., 22g carb. (4g sugars, 6g fiber), 7g pro. **Diabetic exchanges:** 2 fat, 1½ starch, 1 lean meat, 1 vegetable.

*** HEALTH TIP *** To make this a healthy vegan salad, replace the feta cheese with toasted pine nuts.

TEST KITCHEN TIP

Kalamatas are the most widely known Greek olives. They are almond-shaped and deep purple-black in color.

It's Easy Being Green!

Elegant and exotic-looking, artichokes are surprisingly easy to prepare. And freshly roasted artichoke leaves dipped in aioli (or just melted butter) are divine!

5 INGREDIENTS | EAT SMART

ROASTED ARTICHOKES WITH LEMON AIOLI

Petals of savory artichoke leaves are delicious dipped into a creamy lemon aioli. It may seem intimidating to roast whole artichokes, but the steps couldn't be simpler—and the earthy, comforting flavor is a definite payoff.
—*Taste of Home* Test Kitchen

Prep: 20 min. • **Bake:** 50 min.
Makes: 4 servings

- **4 medium artichokes**
- **2 Tbsp. olive oil**
- **½ medium lemon**
- **½ tsp. salt**
- **¼ tsp. pepper**

AIOLI

- **¼ cup mayonnaise**
- **¼ cup plain Greek yogurt**
- **½ tsp. minced fresh garlic**
- **¼ tsp. grated lemon zest**
- **Dash pepper**

2 halves with 2 Tbsp. aioli: 233 cal., 19g fat (3g sat. fat), 5mg chol., 446mg sod., 16g carb. (2g sugars, 7g fiber), 4g pro.

TEST KITCHEN TIP

To clean an artichoke, rinse it under cold water. Use a soft kitchen brush to gently remove the natural, light film that is produced as the artichoke grows, which can give it a bitter taste. The edible parts of an artichoke are the base of the petals, the center core of the stem and the heart. The fuzzy choke at the center is not edible.

HOW-TO

Prepare and Roast Artichokes

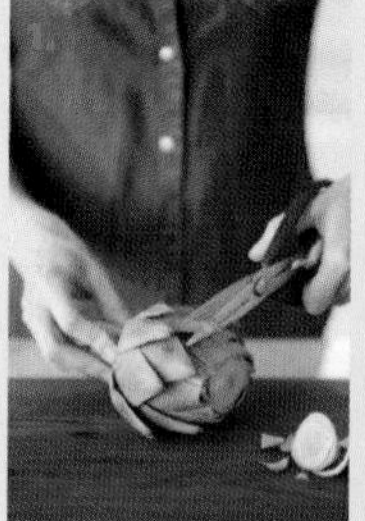

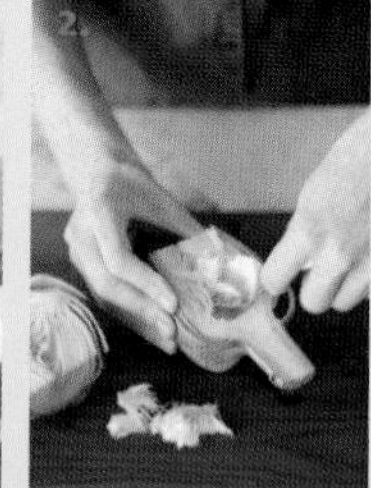

1. Trim
Preheat oven to 400°. Cut 1 in. from the top of each artichoke. Using scissors, cut off tips of outer leaves.

2. Prep
Cut each artichoke in half lengthwise. With a spoon, carefully scrape and remove the fuzzy center. Rub lemon over the cut sides of the artichokes; sprinkle with salt and pepper.

3. Bake
Drizzle oil in a 15x10x1-in. baking pan. Place artichokes in the pan, cut side down; sprinkle with lemon juice. Cover pan with foil; bake on a lower rack until tender and a center leaf pulls out easily, 50-55 minutes.

4. Serve
Mix the aioli ingredients; refrigerate until serving. Serve with artichokes.

NUTTY BARLEY BAKE

When I first brought this dish to holiday dinners, many had only ever seen barley in soup. They have since dubbed me the barley lady, and now I wouldn't dare bring anything but this dish!
—Renate Crump, Los Angeles, CA

Prep: 15 min. • **Bake:** 1¼ hours
Makes: 6 servings

- **1 medium onion, chopped**
- **1 cup medium pearl barley**
- **½ cup slivered almonds or pine nuts**
- **¼ cup butter, cubed**
- **½ cup minced fresh parsley**
- **¼ cup thinly sliced green onions**
- **¼ tsp. salt**
- **⅛ tsp. pepper**
- **2 cans (14½ oz. each) beef broth**
- **Additional parsley and green onions, optional**

1. Preheat oven to 350°. In a large skillet, saute the onion, barley and nuts in butter until barley is lightly browned. Stir in the parsley, green onions, salt and pepper.
2. Transfer to a greased 2-qt. baking dish. Stir in broth. Bake, uncovered, for 1¼ hours or until the barley is tender and the liquid is absorbed. If desired, sprinkle with additional parsley and green onions.

¾ cup: 257 cal., 13g fat (5g sat. fat), 20mg chol., 704mg sod., 30g carb. (2g sugars, 7g fiber), 7g pro.

FAST FIX
AVOCADO ROMAINE SALAD

This salad truly represents my state, since avocados and almonds grow in such abundance here. I love it because I can toss it together in minutes.
—Jeanne Ellermeyer, Walnut Creek, CA

Takes: 20 min. • **Makes:** 6 servings

- **½ cup olive oil**
- **2 Tbsp. white vinegar**
- **2 Tbsp. lemon juice**
- **¼ to ½ tsp. salt**
- **¼ tsp. ground mustard**
- **¼ tsp. paprika**
- **Dash seasoned salt**

SALAD

- **1 bunch romaine, torn (about 5 cups)**
- **1 medium ripe avocado, quartered and sliced**
- **4 green onions, sliced**

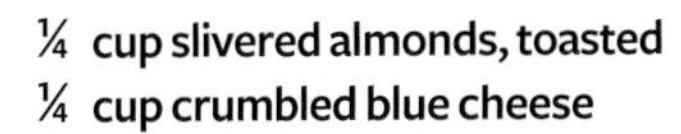

- **¼ cup slivered almonds, toasted**
- **¼ cup crumbled blue cheese**

For the dressing, whisk together the first seven ingredients. Place salad ingredients in a large bowl. Drizzle with dressing just before serving.

1 cup: 257 cal., 26g fat (4g sat. fat), 4mg chol., 329mg sod., 6g carb. (1g sugars, 4g fiber), 4g pro.

EAT SMART
COLCANNON POTATOES

Every Irish family has its own version of this classic dish. My recipe comes from my father's family in Ireland. It's part of my annual St. Pat's menu, along with lamb chops, carrots and soda bread.
—Marilou Robinson, Portland, OR

Prep: 25 min. • **Cook:** 35 min.
Makes: 12 servings

- **1 medium head cabbage (about 2 lbs.), shredded**
- **4 lbs. medium potatoes (about 8), peeled and quartered**
- **2 cups whole milk**
- **1 cup chopped green onions**
- **1½ tsp. salt**
- **½ tsp. pepper**
- **¼ cup butter, melted**
- **Minced fresh parsley**
- **Crumbled cooked bacon**

1. Place cabbage and 2 cups of water in a large saucepan; bring to a boil. Reduce heat; simmer, covered, until cabbage is tender, about 10 minutes. Drain, reserving the cooking liquid; remove cabbage from pan and keep warm.
2. In same pan, combine potatoes and the reserved cooking liquid. Add more water to cover the potatoes; bring to a boil. Reduce heat; cook, uncovered, until the potatoes are tender, 15-20 minutes. Meanwhile, place milk, green onions, salt and pepper in a small saucepan; bring just to a boil and remove from heat.
3. Drain potatoes; place in a large bowl and mash. Add milk mixture; beat just until blended. Stir in cabbage. To serve, drizzle with butter; top with parsley and bacon.

1 cup: 168 cal., 5g fat (3g sat. fat), 14mg chol., 361mg sod., 27g carb. (6g sugars, 4g fiber), 4g pro. **Diabetic exchanges:** 2 starch, 1 fat.

COLCANNON POTATOES

EAT SMART | FAST FIX

SHAVED FENNEL SALAD

This salad tastes even more impressive than it looks. It has an incredible crunch thanks to the cucumbers, radishes and apples. And the finish of fennel fronds adds just the faintest hint of licorice flavor.
—William Milton III, Clemson, SC

Takes: 15 min. • **Makes:** 8 servings

- **1 large fennel bulb, fronds reserved**
- **1 English cucumber**
- **1 medium Honeycrisp apple**
- **2 Tbsp. extra virgin olive oil**
- **½ tsp. kosher salt**
- **¼ tsp. coarsely ground pepper**
- **2 radishes, thinly sliced**

With a mandoline or vegetable peeler, cut the fennel, cucumber and apple into very thin slices. Transfer to a large bowl; toss with olive oil, salt and pepper. Top with radishes and reserved fennel fronds to serve.

¾ cup: 55 cal., 4g fat (1g sat. fat), 0 chol., 138mg sod., 6g carb. (4g sugars, 2g fiber), 1g pro. **Diabetic exchanges:** 1 vegetable, 1 fat.

TEST KITCHEN TIP

Try adding a squeeze of lemon! A little bit of acid would complement the simple dressing nicely. It's easy to modify this recipe based on your taste and what you have on hand: Add more or less fennel, apple and cucumber, as you please.

OVEN-ROASTED POTATOES

5 INGREDIENTS | FAST FIX

OVEN-ROASTED POTATOES

Fragrant rosemary, fresh or dried, gives these potatoes a distinctive and subtle taste. Simple to prepare, yet elegant in color and flavor, this dish is a wonderful addition to any menu.
—Margie Wampler, Butler, PA

Takes: 30 min. • **Makes:** 8 servings

- **2 lbs. small unpeeled red potatoes, cut into wedges**
- **2 to 3 Tbsp. olive oil**
- **2 garlic cloves, minced**
- **1 Tbsp. minced fresh rosemary or 1 tsp. dried rosemary, crushed**
- **½ tsp. salt**
- **¼ tsp. pepper**

1. Preheat oven to 450°. Place potatoes in a 13x9-in. baking dish. Drizzle with oil. Sprinkle with garlic, rosemary, salt and pepper; toss gently to coat.
2. Bake until the potatoes are golden brown and tender, 20-30 minutes.

1 cup: 114 cal., 4g fat (0 sat. fat), 0 chol., 155mg sod., 18g carb. (1g sugars, 2g fiber), 2g pro.

5 INGREDIENTS

THYME-BAKED APPLE SLICES

I often make these apples as an alternative to potatoes when serving meat. My family even asks for seconds!
—Constance Henry, Hibbing, MN

Prep: 15 min. • **Bake:** 25 min.
Makes: 6 servings

- **4 cups apple cider**
- **¼ cup butter, cubed**
- **8 large Braeburn apples (about 4 lbs.)**
- **3½ tsp. minced fresh thyme, divided**

1. Preheat oven to 400°. Place cider in a large saucepan. Bring to a boil; cook until liquid is reduced to ⅔ cup, 18-20 minutes. Remove from heat; stir in butter.
2. Peel and cut each apple into eight wedges. In a large bowl, toss apples with ¼ cup of the reduced cider and 3 tsp. thyme. Transfer to a foil-lined 15x10x1-in. baking pan. Bake 10 minutes.
3. Drizzle with remaining reduced cider. Bake until tender, 12-15 minutes longer. Sprinkle with the remaining thyme.

¾ cup: 264 cal., 8g fat (5g sat. fat), 20mg chol., 78mg sod., 51g carb. (42g sugars, 3g fiber), 1g pro.

HERBED FRENCH FRIES

With fresh herbs and other seasonings, this delicious recipe is a healthy, easy and quick way to make french fries without frying them in deep fat.
—Lora Glenn, Elkader, IA

Prep: 15 min. • **Bake:** 40 min.
Makes: 2 servings

- **1 Tbsp. olive oil**
- **¾ tsp. minced fresh basil**
- **¾ tsp. minced fresh oregano**
- **¾ tsp. minced fresh rosemary**
- **1 small garlic clove, minced**
- **¼ tsp. Italian seasoning**
- **⅛ tsp. salt**
- **⅛ tsp. pepper**
- **Dash chili powder**
- **2 medium potatoes, peeled and cut into thin strips**

1. In a small bowl, combine the first nine ingredients. Add potatoes; toss to coat.

2. Transfer to a 15x10x1-in. baking pan coated with cooking spray. Bake at 400° until tender, 40-45 minutes, turning once.

1½ cups: 188 cal., 7g fat (1g sat. fat), 0 chol., 153mg sod., 30g carb. (2g sugars, 2g fiber), 3g pro. **Diabetic exchanges:** 2 starch, 1 fat.

EAT SMART

PINEAPPLE-PAPAYA SLAW

This tropical slaw is bursting with flavor from fresh fruit, cilantro and red bell pepper. To save time, purchase packaged shredded cabbage. If you can't find papaya, substitute mango.
—*Taste of Home* Test Kitchen

Prep: 20 min. + chilling
Makes: 8 servings

- **½ cup pineapple juice**
- **¼ cup olive oil**
- **2 Tbsp. lime juice**
- **2 Tbsp. minced fresh cilantro**
- **½ tsp. ground cumin**
- **¼ tsp. salt**
- **6 cups shredded cabbage (about 1 small)**
- **1½ cups chopped peeled papaya**
- **1½ cups cubed fresh pineapple**
- **1 small sweet red pepper, chopped**

Whisk together the first six ingredients. Place the remaining ingredients in a large bowl. Drizzle with dressing; toss to coat. Refrigerate, covered, for at least 2 hours. Stir before serving.

1 cup: 112 cal., 7g fat (1g sat. fat), 0 chol., 87mg sod., 13g carb. (7g sugars, 2g fiber), 1g pro. **Diabetic exchanges:** 1½ fat, 1 vegetable, ½ fruit.

*** HEALTH TIP *** Thanks to the pineapple, papaya, bell pepper and cabbage, this side dish covers more than 75 percent of the recommended daily value for vitamin C.

PINEAPPLE-PAPAYA SLAW

ORZO WITH SPINACH & PINE NUTS

I've shared this salad many times with the teachers at my school, who now request it specifically. It's best to add the tomatoes just before serving so they won't soften from the heat and moisture.
—Kate Whitehead, Lindenhurst, IL

Prep: 10 min. • **Cook:** 25 min.
Makes: 12 servings

- **1 pkg. (16 oz.) orzo pasta**
- **1 cup pine nuts**
- **1 garlic clove, minced**
- **½ tsp. dried basil**
- **½ tsp. crushed red pepper flakes**
- **¼ cup olive oil**
- **1 Tbsp. butter**
- **2 pkg. (6 oz. each) fresh baby spinach**
- **1 tsp. salt**
- **¼ tsp. pepper**
- **¼ cup balsamic vinegar**
- **2 cups crumbled feta cheese**
- **1 large tomato, finely chopped**

1. In a large saucepan, cook pasta according to package directions.
2. Meanwhile, in a Dutch oven over medium heat, cook the pine nuts, garlic, basil and pepper flakes in oil and butter just until the nuts are lightly browned.
3. Add the spinach, salt and pepper; cook and stir just until the spinach is wilted, 4-5 minutes longer. Transfer to a large bowl.
4. Drain pasta. Stir into the spinach mixture. Drizzle with vinegar; sprinkle with cheese and tomato.

¾ cup: 313 cal., 15g fat (4g sat. fat), 13mg chol., 411mg sod., 33g carb. (3g sugars, 3g fiber), 12g pro.

EAT SMART | FAST FIX

MODERN WALDORF SALAD

A Waldorf salad inspired my pasta dish. I use smoked turkey, apples, strawberries and orecchiette. Rotisserie chicken and other fruits would also taste delicious.
—Sonya Labbe, West Hollywood, CA

Takes: 30 min. • **Makes:** 4 servings

- **2 cups uncooked orecchiette or small tube pasta (about 6 oz.)**
- **¼ cup reduced-fat plain yogurt**
- **2 Tbsp. mayonnaise**
- **2 Tbsp. 2% milk**
- **4 tsp. Dijon mustard**
- **½ tsp. dried thyme, optional**
- **1 medium apple, chopped**
- **1 Tbsp. lemon juice**
- **½ lb. thick-sliced deli smoked turkey, cut into bite-size pieces**
- **1 cup quartered fresh strawberries**
- **1 celery rib, sliced**
- **¼ cup toasted chopped walnuts, optional**

1. Cook pasta according to the package directions. Drain; rinse with cold water and drain well.
2. Meanwhile, to make the dressing, mix yogurt, mayonnaise, milk, mustard and, if desired, thyme until blended. In another bowl, toss apple with lemon juice.
3. In a large bowl, combine the pasta, apple, turkey, strawberries and celery. Add the dressing; toss gently to coat. If desired, sprinkle with walnuts. Refrigerate until serving.

1½ cups: 313 cal., 8g fat (1g sat. fat), 24mg chol., 606mg sod., 42g carb. (8g sugars, 3g fiber), 19g pro. **Diabetic exchanges:** 2 starch, 2 lean meat, 1 fat, ½ fruit.

5 INGREDIENTS | EAT SMART | FAST FIX

WHITE BEANS & SPINACH

This skillet side dish is a variation of a recipe I received from my Italian mother. I've prepared spinach like this for years—especially since my children like it this way!

—Lucia Johnson, Massena, NY

Takes: 10 min. • **Makes:** 2 servings

- **2 Tbsp. water**
- **2 garlic cloves, minced**
- **8 cups fresh spinach (about 6 oz.)**
- **¾ cup canned cannellini beans, rinsed and drained**
- **⅛ tsp. salt**
- **Dash cayenne pepper**
- **Dash ground nutmeg**

Place water, garlic and spinach in a large skillet. Cook, covered, over medium heat just until tender, 2-3 minutes, stirring occasionally. Stir in the remaining ingredients; heat through.

½ cup: 116 cal., 1g fat (0 sat. fat), 0 chol., 561mg sod., 21g carb. (1g sugars, 7g fiber), 7g pro. **Diabetic exchanges:** 1½ starch.

ITALIAN ARTICHOKE-GREEN BEAN CASSEROLE

My mother and I made changes to a cookbook recipe to create this casserole. We increased the amount of vegetables, and it now receives rave reviews at get-togethers. It's definitely not your average green bean casserole!

—Denise Klibert, Shreveport, LA

Prep: 25 min. • **Bake:** 25 min.
Makes: 10 servings

- **6 cups cut fresh green beans (about 1½ lbs.)**
- **⅓ cup olive oil**
- **1 medium onion, chopped**
- **2 garlic cloves, minced**
- **3 cans (14 oz. each) water-packed artichoke hearts, drained and chopped**
- **½ cup minced fresh parsley**
- **Pinch cayenne pepper**
- **Pinch pepper**
- **1 cup seasoned bread crumbs**
- **1 cup grated Parmesan cheese, divided**

1. Preheat oven to 350°. In a large saucepan, bring 6 cups water to a boil. Add green beans; cook, uncovered, just until crisp-tender, 3-4 minutes. Drain and set aside.
2. In a 6-qt. stockpot, heat the oil over medium heat. Add onion; cook and stir until tender, 3-4 minutes. Add garlic; cook 1 minute longer. Add beans, artichoke hearts, parsley, cayenne and pepper. Stir in bread crumbs and ¾ cup cheese.
3. Transfer to a greased 11x7-in. baking dish. Sprinkle with remaining cheese. Bake until lightly browned, 25-30 minutes.

¾ cup: 207 cal., 10g fat (2g sat. fat), 7mg chol., 616mg sod., 22g carb. (3g sugars, 2g fiber), 8g pro. **Diabetic exchanges:** 2 fat, 1 starch, 1 vegetable.

WHITE BEANS & SPINACH

BLACK-EYED PEA TOMATO SALAD

PICTURED ON P. 21

Spending time in the kitchen with my aunt was such fun—she was an amazing cook and teacher. This flavorful salad was one of her specialties.

—Patricia Ness, La Mesa, CA

Prep: 20 min. + chilling
Makes: 12 servings

- **4 cans (15½ oz. each) black-eyed peas, rinsed and drained**
- **3 large tomatoes, chopped**
- **1 large sweet red pepper, chopped**
- **1 cup diced red onion**
- **4 bacon strips, cooked and crumbled**
- **1 jalapeno pepper, seeded and diced**
- **½ cup canola oil**
- **¼ cup sugar**
- **¼ cup rice vinegar**
- **2 Tbsp. minced fresh parsley**
- **1½ tsp. salt**
- **½ tsp. pepper**
- **⅛ tsp. garlic powder**

Combine the first six ingredients. In another bowl, whisk together remaining ingredients. Add to bean mixture; toss to coat. Refrigerate, covered, at least 6 hours or overnight. Stir just before serving.

Note: Wear disposable gloves when cutting hot peppers; the oils can burn skin. Avoid touching your face.

¾ cup: 242 cal., 11g fat (1g sat. fat), 3mg chol., 602mg sod., 29g carb. (9g sugars, 5g fiber), 9g pro. **Diabetic exchanges:** 2 starch, 2 fat.

CRUMB-TOPPED
MACARONI & CHEESE

CRUMB-TOPPED MACARONI & CHEESE

Everyone loves this grown-up macaroni and cheese. It's tasty when made with sharp cheddar and cream cheese, too. Throw in some crispy bacon for a twist.
—Jennifer Standing, Taos, NM

Prep: 30 min. • **Bake:** 10 min.
Makes: 8 servings

- **2 cups uncooked elbow macaroni**
- **½ cup butter, divided**
- **½ tsp. crushed red pepper flakes**
- **¼ cup all-purpose flour**
- **1½ cups whole milk**
- **2 cups shredded Gruyere cheese or Swiss cheese**
- **1 carton (8 oz.) mascarpone cheese**
- **4½ tsp. Dijon mustard**
- **¼ tsp. salt**
- **⅛ tsp. pepper**
- **¾ cup panko (Japanese) bread crumbs**
- **1 Tbsp. Italian seasoning**

1. Preheat oven to 425°. In a 6-qt. stockpot, cook macaroni according to package directions for al dente; drain and return to pot.
2. Meanwhile, in a medium saucepan, heat ¼ cup butter and pepper flakes over medium heat until butter is melted. Stir in flour until smooth; gradually whisk in milk. Bring to a boil, stirring constantly; cook and stir until thickened, 1-2 minutes.
3. Stir in Gruyere, mascarpone, mustard, salt and pepper until blended. Add sauce to macaroni, tossing to combine. Transfer to a greased 13x9-in. baking dish.
4. Melt remaining butter. Add panko and Italian seasoning; toss to coat. Sprinkle over macaroni. Bake, uncovered, until topping is golden brown, 10-15 minutes.

¾ cup: 473 cal., 36g fat (21g sat. fat), 102mg chol., 487mg sod., 23g carb. (3g sugars, 1g fiber), 16g pro.

COWBOY BAKED BEANS

Baked beans are a perennial favorite at barbecues and potlucks. My meaty recipe uses a variety of beans and has a perfect smoky taste.
—Joe Sherwood, Tryon, NE

Prep: 25 min. • **Bake:** 50 min.
Makes: 12 servings

COWBOY BAKED BEANS

- **1 lb. ground beef**
- **1 lb. bacon, cooked and crumbled**
- **2 cups barbecue sauce**
- **1 can (16 oz.) butter beans, rinsed and drained**
- **1 can (15¾ oz.) pork and beans**
- **1 can (15½ oz.) navy beans, rinsed and drained**
- **1 can (15 oz.) black beans, rinsed and drained**
- **2 medium onions, chopped**
- **¼ cup packed brown sugar**
- **¼ cup molasses**
- **2 Tbsp. balsamic vinegar**
- **2 tsp. ground mustard**
- **2 tsp. Worcestershire sauce**
- **1 tsp. salt**
- **1 tsp. garlic powder**
- **1 tsp. pepper**

Preheat oven to 350°. In a Dutch oven, cook beef over medium heat until no longer pink; drain. Stir in the remaining ingredients. Transfer to a greased 13x9-in. baking dish. Bake, uncovered, until heated through, 50-60 minutes.

¾ cup: 350 cal., 12g fat (4g sat. fat), 34mg chol., 1232mg sod., 43g carb. (18g sugars, 8g fiber), 20g pro.

EAT SMART | FAST FIX

BASIC BUTTERMILK SALAD DRESSING

PICTURED ON P. 21

When serving salad to a crowd, this easy recipe comes in handy. It makes a full quart of creamy, delicious dressing to toss with favorite greens and veggies.
—Patricia Mele, Lower Burrell, PA

Takes: 5 min.
Makes: 32 servings (1 qt.)

- **2 cups mayonnaise**
- **2 cups buttermilk**
- **1 Tbsp. onion powder**
- **1 Tbsp. dried parsley flakes**
- **1½ tsp. garlic powder**
- **½ tsp. salt**
- **½ tsp. celery salt**
- **¼ tsp. pepper**

Whisk together all ingredients. Refrigerate, covered, until serving.

2 Tbsp.: 98 cal., 10g fat (2g sat. fat), 2mg chol., 155mg sod., 1g carb. (1g sugars, 0 fiber), 1g pro. **Diabetic exchanges:** 2 fat.

LOADED RED POTATO CASSEROLE

LOADED RED POTATO CASSEROLE

The flavor of this potato casserole reminds me of the potato skins many restaurants offer as an appetizer.
—Charlane Gathy, Lexington, KY

Prep: 25 min. • **Bake:** 20 min.
Makes: 8 servings

- **16 small red potatoes (about 1¾ lbs.)**
- **½ cup 2% milk**
- **¼ cup butter, cubed**
- **½ tsp. pepper**
- **⅛ tsp. salt**
- **1½ cups shredded cheddar cheese, divided**
- **½ cup crumbled cooked bacon**
- **1 cup sour cream**
- **2 Tbsp. minced fresh chives**

1. Preheat oven to 350°. Place potatoes in a 6-qt. stockpot; add water to cover. Bring to a boil. Reduce heat; cook, uncovered, until tender, 15-20 minutes. Drain; return to pot.
2. Mash potatoes, gradually adding milk, butter, pepper and salt. Spread into a greased 3-qt. baking dish; sprinkle with 1 cup cheese and bacon. Dollop with sour cream; sprinkle with chives and the remaining cheese.
3. Bake, uncovered, until heated through and cheese is melted, 20-25 minutes.

¾ cup: 187 cal., 12g fat (7g sat. fat), 23mg chol., 245mg sod., 15g carb. (2g sugars, 1g fiber), 6g pro.

CHILES RELLENOS

I find that chilies improve almost any recipe that uses cheese! Sometimes I add shredded cooked chicken after the chili layer to make this into a main dish.
—Irene Martin, Portales, NM

Prep: 10 min. • **Bake:** 50 min.
Makes: 8 servings

- **1 can (7 oz.) whole green chilies**
- **2 cups shredded Monterey Jack cheese**
- **2 cups shredded cheddar cheese**
- **3 large eggs**
- **3 cups whole milk**
- **1 cup biscuit/baking mix**
- **Seasoned salt to taste**
- **Salsa**

1. Preheat oven to 325°. Split chilies; rinse and remove seeds. Dry on paper towels. Arrange chilies in an 11x7-in. baking dish. Top with cheeses.
2. In a large bowl, beat the eggs; add milk and biscuit mix. Pour mixture over cheese. Sprinkle with salt. Bake until golden brown, 50-55 minutes. Serve with salsa.

1 cup: 352 cal., 24g fat (14g sat. fat), 144mg chol., 598mg sod., 15g carb. (5g sugars, 0 fiber), 19g pro.

5 INGREDIENTS | EAT SMART | FAST FIX

SHREDDED KALE & BRUSSELS SPROUTS SALAD

This salad is a simple and delicious way to eat your superfoods! It gets even better in the fridge, so I make it ahead. I use a homemade honey mustard dressing, but any type works just fine.
—Alexandra Weisser, New York, NY

Takes: 15 min. • **Makes:** 6 servings

- **1 small bunch kale (about 8 oz.), stemmed and thinly sliced (about 6 cups)**
- **½ lb. fresh Brussels sprouts, thinly sliced (about 3 cups)**
- **½ cup pistachios, coarsely chopped**
- **½ cup honey mustard salad dressing**
- **¼ cup shredded Parmesan cheese**

Toss together all ingredients.

1 cup: 207 cal., 14g fat (2g sat. fat), 8mg chol., 235mg sod., 16g carb. (5g sugars, 4g fiber), 7g pro. **Diabetic exchanges:** 3 fat, 2 vegetable, ½ starch.

CRISPY BAKED ZUCCHINI FRIES

I coat zucchini strips with a mixture of panko bread crumbs, Parmesan cheese and spices, then bake them until they're crispy and golden brown. Delicious!
—Matthew Hass, Ellison Bay, WI

Prep: 25 min. • **Bake:** 20 min.
Makes: 4 servings

- **2 medium zucchini**
- **1 cup panko (Japanese) bread crumbs**
- **¾ cup grated Parmesan cheese**
- **2 tsp. smoked paprika**
- **½ tsp. garlic powder**
- **¼ tsp. ground chipotle pepper**
- **¼ tsp. salt**
- **¼ tsp. pepper**
- **⅓ cup all-purpose flour**
- **2 large eggs, beaten**
- **3 Tbsp. olive oil**

1. Preheat oven to 425°. Cut each zucchini in half lengthwise and then in half crosswise. Cut each piece lengthwise into ¼-in. slices.
2. In a shallow bowl, mix bread crumbs, cheese and seasonings. Place flour and eggs in separate shallow bowls. Dip zucchini slices in flour, then in egg and then in crumb mixture, patting to help coating adhere. Place on a greased rack in a foil-lined rimmed baking pan. Drizzle with oil. Bake until golden brown, 20-25 minutes.

1 serving: 289 cal., 18g fat (5g sat. fat), 106mg chol., 510mg sod., 21g carb. (3g sugars, 2g fiber), 12g pro.

COMPANY RICE

This colorful side dish is a proven favorite with family and friends. One of my son's friends always requested the rice when he came over for dinner. It's delicious served with grilled salmon, beef, turkey, lamb roast or ham.
—Jayne Shiley, Campbellsport, WI

Prep: 10 min. • **Cook:** 55 min.
Makes: 10 servings

- **1 celery rib, thinly sliced**
- **1 large carrot, finely chopped**
- **1 small onion, finely chopped**
- **2 Tbsp. butter**
- **5 cups chicken broth**
- **1 cup uncooked wild rice**
- **1 cup uncooked long grain rice**
- **⅔ cup dried cherries or cranberries**
- **½ cup chopped pecans, toasted**

1. In a large saucepan, saute the celery, carrot and onion in butter until tender. Stir in broth and wild rice. Bring to a boil. Reduce the heat; cover and simmer for 25 minutes.
2. Add long grain rice; cover and simmer 20 minutes longer. Stir in the cherries; cook until the liquid is absorbed, about 5 minutes longer. Just before serving, stir in the pecans.

⅔ cup: 238 cal., 7g fat (2g sat. fat), 9mg chol., 516mg sod., 38g carb. (7g sugars, 2g fiber), 5g pro.

Almond Wild Rice: Omit the long grain rice, dried cherries and chopped pecans. Add 1 cup uncooked brown rice with broth and wild rice. Bring to a boil. Reduce heat; cover and simmer until the rice is tender and liquid is absorbed, 45-50 minutes. Remove from the heat; stir in 1 cup toasted slivered almonds, ½ cup minced fresh parsley and ¼ tsp. each salt and pepper.

CRISPY BAKED ZUCCHINI FRIES

CHEESE & GRITS CASSEROLE

Grits are a staple in southern cooking. Serve this as a brunch item with bacon and eggs or as a side dish for dinner.
—Jennifer Wallis, Goldsboro, NC

Prep: 10 min. • **Bake:** 30 min. + standing
Makes: 8 servings

- **4 cups water**
- **1 cup uncooked old-fashioned grits**
- **½ tsp. salt**
- **½ cup 2% milk**
- **¼ cup butter, melted**
- **2 large eggs, lightly beaten**
- **1 cup shredded cheddar cheese**
- **1 Tbsp. Worcestershire sauce**
- **⅛ tsp. cayenne pepper**
- **⅛ tsp. paprika**

1. Preheat oven to 350°. In a large saucepan, bring water to a boil. Slowly stir in grits and salt. Reduce heat; cover and simmer until thickened, 5-7 minutes. Cool slightly. Gradually whisk in the milk, butter and eggs. Stir in cheddar cheese, Worcestershire sauce and cayenne.
2. Transfer to a greased 2-qt. baking dish. Sprinkle with paprika. Bake, uncovered, until bubbly, 30-35 minutes. Let stand 10 minutes before serving.

¾ cup: 202 cal., 12g fat (7g sat. fat), 86mg chol., 335mg sod., 17g carb. (1g sugars, 0 fiber), 7g pro

Chili Cheese Grits: Omit Worcestershire and cayenne. With the cheese, stir in 2 Tbsp. canned chopped green chilies.

5 INGREDIENTS | EAT SMART

GERMAN RED CABBAGE

Sunday afternoons were a time for family gatherings when I was a kid. While the uncles played cards, the aunts made German treats such as this traditional red cabbage.
—Jeannette Heim, Dunlap, TN

Prep: 10 min. • **Cook:** 65 min.
Makes: 10 servings

- **1 medium onion, halved and sliced**
- **1 medium apple, sliced**
- **1 medium head red cabbage, shredded (about 8 cups)**
- **⅓ cup sugar**
- **⅓ cup white vinegar**
- **¾ tsp. salt, optional**
- **¼ tsp. pepper**

In a large Dutch oven coated with cooking spray, cook and stir onion and apple over medium heat until onion is tender, about 5 minutes. Stir in remaining ingredients; cook, covered, until the cabbage is tender, about 1 hour, stirring occasionally. Serve warm or cold.

1 cup: 64 cal., 0 fat (0 sat. fat), 0 chol., 23mg sod., 16g carb. (12g sugars, 2g fiber), 1g pro. **Diabetic exchanges:** 1 vegetable, ½ starch.

FAST FIX

GREEN SALAD WITH TANGY BASIL VINAIGRETTE

A tart and tangy dressing turns a basic salad into something special. It works for weeknight dining but is good enough for company and pairs so well with just about anything.
—Kristin Rimkus, Snohomish, WA

Takes: 15 min. • **Makes:** 4 servings

- **3 Tbsp. white wine vinegar**
- **4½ tsp. minced fresh basil**
- **4½ tsp. olive oil**
- **1½ tsp. honey**
- **¼ tsp. salt**
- **⅛ tsp. pepper**
- **6 cups torn mixed salad greens**
- **1 cup cherry tomatoes, halved**
- **2 Tbsp. shredded Parmesan cheese**

In a small bowl, whisk the first six ingredients until blended. In a large bowl, combine salad greens and tomatoes. Drizzle with vinaigrette; toss to coat. Sprinkle with cheese.

1 cup: 89 cal., 6g fat (1g sat. fat), 2mg chol., 214mg sod., 7g carb. (4g sugars, 2g fiber), 3g pro. **Diabetic exchanges:** 1 vegetable, 1 fat.

GERMAN RED CABBAGE

GREEK POTATO CASSEROLE

EAT SMART

ROASTED FENNEL & PEPPERS

Fennel makes for a tasty change of pace in this versatile side that goes well with grilled meats. Best of all, it's full of flavor and it doesn't seem light at all!
—*Taste of Home* Test Kitchen

Takes: 30 min. • **Makes:** 6 servings

2 fennel bulbs, halved and sliced
2 medium sweet red peppers, cut into 1-in. pieces
1 medium onion, cut into 1-in. pieces
3 garlic cloves, minced
1 Tbsp. olive oil
½ tsp. salt
½ tsp. pepper
½ tsp. rubbed sage
Fresh sage leaves, thinly sliced, optional

1. Preheat oven to 425°. Place the fennel, peppers, onion and garlic in a 15x10x1-in. baking pan coated with cooking spray. Drizzle with oil; sprinkle with salt, pepper and rubbed sage. Toss to coat.
2. Bake, uncovered, until vegetables are tender, 20-25 minutes, stirring twice. Garnish with fresh sage if desired.

⅔ cup: 67 cal., 3g fat (0 sat. fat), 0 chol., 240mg sod., 10g carb. (5g sugars, 4g fiber), 2g pro. **Diabetic exchanges:** 1 vegetable, ½ fat.

GREEK POTATO CASSEROLE

A crunchy golden brown topping and tangy yogurt and feta make this recipe a winner. You can loosen the mixture with a few tablespoons of milk if necessary.
—Cheryl Woodson, Liberty, MO

Prep: 20 min. • **Bake:** 40 min.
Makes: 8 servings

1 can (14 oz.) water-packed artichoke hearts, rinsed, drained and chopped
1 pkg. (10 oz.) frozen chopped spinach, thawed and squeezed dry
¾ cup plain yogurt
1 pkg. (4 oz.) crumbled tomato and basil feta cheese
3 Tbsp. pitted Greek olives, chopped
2 Tbsp. minced chives
1 tsp. lemon-pepper seasoning
⅛ tsp. pepper
1 pkg. (24 oz.) refrigerated mashed potatoes

TOPPING

½ cup panko (Japanese) bread crumbs
¼ cup grated Parmesan cheese
2 Tbsp. butter, melted
1 tsp. minced fresh rosemary or ½ tsp. dried rosemary, crushed

Preheat oven to 350°. In a large bowl, combine the first eight ingredients. Stir in mashed potatoes. Transfer to a greased 11x7-in. baking dish. Combine the topping ingredients and sprinkle over casserole. Bake, uncovered, until golden brown, 40-45 minutes.

¾ cup: 250 cal., 13 g fat (9 g sat. fat), 29 mg chol., 752 mg sod., 24 g carb., 4 g fiber, 9 g pro.

Quick Soups & Sandwiches

For lunches, dinners and everything in between, soups and sandwiches are classic comfort food. Served individually or paired, these delicious recipes are always surefire hits.

Zippy Egg Salad (p. 51) **Open-Faced Turkey Sandwich** (p. 50) **Grilled Eggplant Panini with Basil Aioli** (p. 57) **Pumpkin Sausage Soup** (p. 49) **Turkey Guacamole Wraps** (p. 53)

FAST FIX

CHEESY EGG QUESADILLAS

Here's my fun spin on breakfast for dinner. These egg quesadillas are so easy to make, full of protein and plain delicious any time of day.

—Barbara Blommer, Woodland Park, CO

Takes: 25 min. • **Makes:** 2 servings

- **3 large eggs**
- **3 Tbsp. 2% milk**
- **⅛ tsp. pepper**
- **1 Tbsp. plus 2 tsp. butter, divided**
- **4 flour tortillas (8 in.)**
- **½ cup refried beans**
- **¼ cup salsa**
- **⅔ cup shredded cheddar cheese**
- **Sour cream and additional salsa, optional**

1. Preheat oven to 425°. Whisk together the first three ingredients. In a large nonstick skillet, heat 1 Tbsp. butter over medium heat. Add the egg mixture; cook and stir until eggs are thickened and no liquid egg remains. Remove from heat.
2. Place two tortillas on a baking sheet. Spread with beans; top with eggs, salsa, cheese and remaining tortillas. Melt remaining butter; brush over tops.
3. Bake until golden brown and cheese is melted, 10-12 minutes. If desired, serve with sour cream and additional salsa.

1 quesadilla: 738 cal., 38g fat (18g sat. fat), 344mg chol., 1248mg sod., 67g carb. (3g sugars, 5g fiber), 30g pro.

ARBORIO RICE & WHITE BEAN SOUP

EAT SMART | FAST FIX

ARBORIO RICE & WHITE BEAN SOUP

Soup is the ultimate winter food, and this satisfying soup is low in fat and comes together in less than 30 minutes.

—Deanna McDonald, Muskegon, MI

Takes: 30 min. • **Makes:** 4 servings

- **1 Tbsp. olive oil**
- **3 garlic cloves, minced**
- **¾ cup uncooked Arborio rice**
- **1 carton (32 oz.) vegetable broth**
- **¾ tsp. dried basil**
- **½ tsp. dried thyme**
- **¼ tsp. dried oregano**
- **1 pkg. (16 oz.) frozen broccoli-cauliflower blend**
- **1 can (15 oz.) cannellini beans, rinsed and drained**
- **2 cups fresh baby spinach**
- **Lemon wedges, optional**

1. In a large saucepan, heat oil over medium heat; saute garlic 1 minute. Add rice; cook and stir 2 minutes. Stir in broth and herbs; bring to a boil. Reduce heat; simmer, covered, until rice is al dente, about 10 minutes.
2. Stir in the frozen vegetables and the beans; cook, covered, over medium heat until heated through and the rice is tender, 8-10 minutes, stirring occasionally. Stir in spinach until wilted. If desired, serve with lemon wedges.

1¾ cups: 303 cal., 4g fat (1g sat. fat), 0 chol., 861mg sod., 52g carb. (2g sugars, 6g fiber), 9g pro.

*** HEALTH TIP *** Neutral flavor and tender skin make white beans a versatile addition to any soup or stew. They add almost 4 grams of fiber per serving in this recipe. If you want to cut sodium, use reduced-sodium broth.

TEST KITCHEN TIP

The Arborio rice cooks up tender with a texture that is smoother than long grain rice. A combination of fresh and frozen veggies make this soup easy to throw together. The pieces of broccoli and cauliflower are large, but cut easily with your spoon.

FAST FIX
QUICK MEXICAN BEAN SOUP

I can whip up this soup in very little time; it's one of my busy-day favorites. Green chilies and chili powder give it oomph.
—Colleen Delawder, Herndon, VA

Takes: 20 min. • **Makes:** 4 servings

- **1 can (16 oz.) butter beans, rinsed and drained**
- **1 can (15½ oz.) small white beans or navy beans, rinsed and drained**
- **1 can (14½ oz.) no-salt-added diced tomatoes, undrained**
- **1 can (4 oz.) chopped green chilies**
- **1 Tbsp. minced fresh cilantro**
- **1½ tsp. chili powder**
- **½ tsp. onion powder**
- **1½ cups vegetable stock**
- **Crumbled queso fresco and additional cilantro, optional**

In a large saucepan, combine first eight ingredients; bring to a boil. Reduce heat; simmer, covered, until flavors are blended, about 10 minutes. If desired, top with cheese and additional cilantro.

1⅓ cups: 214 cal., 1g fat (0 sat. fat), 0 chol., 893mg sod., 45g carb. (4g sugars, 12g fiber), 14g pro.

FAST FIX
PUMPKIN SAUSAGE SOUP

PICTURED ON P. 47

This soup is well suited to my low-carb lifestyle. It's definitely soul food in a bowl and very simple to prepare.
—Paula Diaz, Billings, MT

Takes: 30 min. • **Makes:** 8 servings (3 qt.)

- **1 lb. bulk Italian sausage**
- **2 cups sliced fresh mushrooms**
- **1 medium onion, finely chopped**
- **4 garlic cloves, minced**
- **1 carton (32 oz.) unsalted chicken stock**
- **1 can (15 oz.) pumpkin**
- **1 Tbsp. sugar or sugar substitute equivalent**
- **½ tsp. ground cinnamon**
- **2 tsp. Italian seasoning**
- **1 tsp. ground turmeric**
- **½ tsp. ground ginger**
- **¼ to ½ tsp. ground nutmeg**
- **½ cup heavy whipping cream**
- **⅓ cup cold water**
- **⅓ cup cornstarch**
- **2 cups shredded smoked cheddar cheese**

1. In a Dutch oven, cook the sausage, mushrooms and onion over medium-high heat until sausage is no longer pink and vegetables are tender, 8-10 minutes, breaking up sausage into crumbles; drain. Add garlic; cook 1 minute longer. Add stock, pumpkin, sugar and seasonings. Bring to a boil; reduce heat. Cover and simmer 10 minutes.
2. Stir in cream. In a small bowl, mix the water and cornstarch until smooth. Stir into the pan. Bring to a boil; cook and stir until thickened, 1-2 minutes. Add cheese; cook and stir until melted.

1½ cups: 371 cal., 27g fat (13g sat. fat), 76mg chol., 782mg sod., 16g carb. (5g sugars, 2g fiber), 16g pro.

QUICK MEXICAN BEAN SOUP

5 INGREDIENTS | FAST FIX

ITALIAN SAUSAGE & BEAN SOUP

The combo of sausage, beans and coleslaw mix may sound unusual, but it is delicious. The recipe doubles easily to serve a crowd.

—Stacey Bennett, Locust Grove, VA

Takes: 30 min. • **Makes:** 6 servings (2 qt.)

- **1 lb. bulk hot Italian sausage**
- **2 cans (15½ oz. each) great northern beans, rinsed and drained**
- **1 pkg. (16 oz.) coleslaw mix**
- **1 jar (24 oz.) garlic and herb spaghetti sauce**
- **3 cups water**

In a Dutch oven, cook the sausage over medium heat until no longer pink; drain. Stir in the remaining ingredients. Bring to a boil. Reduce heat; simmer, uncovered, until flavors are blended, 16-20 minutes.

1⅓ cups: 416 cal., 21g fat (8g sat. fat), 53mg chol., 1411mg sod., 35g carb. (9g sugars, 12g fiber), 23g pro.

FAST FIX

RANCH BLT WRAPS

I first sampled these tasty BLT wraps at a bridal luncheon years ago. Now I frequently make them for our weekly neighborhood dinners.

—Darla Wester, Meriden, IA

Takes: 15 min. • **Makes:** 8 servings

- **½ cup mayonnaise**
- **½ cup sour cream**
- **2 Tbsp. ranch salad dressing mix**
- **¼ tsp. crushed red pepper flakes**
- **8 flour tortillas (8 in.), room temperature**
- **16 cooked bacon strips**
- **2 to 3 cups shredded lettuce**
- **2 cups chopped seeded tomato**
- **Green and sweet red pepper strips, optional**

Mix first four ingredients; spread onto tortillas. Top with remaining ingredients and roll up.

1 wrap: 402 cal., 25g fat (7g sat. fat), 27mg chol., 890mg sod., 32g carb. (2g sugars, 2g fiber), 13g pro.

ITALIAN SAUSAGE & BEAN SOUP

FAST FIX

OPEN-FACED TURKEY SANDWICH

PICTURED ON P. 47

It doesn't get much cozier than these delightful suppertime sandwiches. They're an easy way to use up leftover turkey, and I love how the thick toast soaks up that creamy sauce.

—Carol Hull, Hermiston, OR

Takes: 30 min. • **Makes:** 4 servings

- **2 Tbsp. butter**
- **½ cup finely chopped onion**
- **¼ cup finely chopped celery**
- **2 Tbsp. all-purpose flour**
- **1 cup chicken stock**
- **1 cup evaporated milk**
- **4 oz. cream cheese, cubed**
- **1 cup frozen peas**
- **2 cups chopped cooked turkey (about 10 oz.)**
- **½ tsp. salt**
- **¼ tsp. pepper**
- **4 slices Texas toast or other thick-sliced bread, toasted**
- **Chopped tomato and minced fresh parsley, optional**

1. In a large saucepan, heat butter over medium-high heat; saute onion and celery until tender, 4-6 minutes. Stir in flour until blended; cook and stir until golden brown. Gradually stir in stock and milk. Bring to a boil, stirring constantly; cook and stir until thickened, 4-6 minutes.
2. Add cream cheese, peas, turkey, salt and pepper; cook and stir until blended and heated through. Serve over toast. If desired, top with tomato and parsley.

1 open-faced sandwich: 488 cal., 24g fat (13g sat. fat), 135mg chol., 917mg sod., 35g carb. (11g sugars, 3g fiber), 32g pro.

*** HEALTH TIP *** Switching to reduced-fat cream cheese will cut saturated fat by about 25 percent. Be careful to not boil after it's been added; just heat through.

TEST KITCHEN TIP

One 12-ounce can of evaporated milk contains a little over 1½ cups. Leftover milk can be refrigerated for up to five days. Stir leftover evaporated milk into your morning coffee or when making mashed potatoes or macaroni and cheese for a richer flavor.

EAT SMART | FAST FIX

CREAMY CORN CRAB SOUP

Corn really stars in this delectable recipe, and crabmeat makes it a little more special. It will get high marks from both busy cooks and lovers of flavorful homemade food.
—Carol Ropchan, Willingdon, AB

Takes: 30 min. • **Makes:** 6 servings

- **1 medium onion, chopped**
- **2 Tbsp. butter**
- **3 cups chicken broth**
- **3 cups frozen corn**
- **3 medium potatoes, peeled and diced**
- **1 can (6 oz.) crabmeat, drained, flaked and cartilage removed**
- **1 cup whole milk**
- **¼ tsp. pepper, plus more for optional topping**
- **Minced chives and crushed red pepper flakes, optional**

1. In a large saucepan, saute onion in butter until tender. Add the broth, corn and potatoes; bring to a boil. Reduce heat; cover and simmer for 15 minutes. Remove from the heat; cool slightly.
2. In a blender, puree half of the corn mixture. Return to pan. Stir in the crab, milk and pepper; cook over low heat until heated through (do not boil). If desired, top with fresh cracked pepper, chives and crushed red pepper flakes.

1¼ cups: 219 cal., 6g fat (3g sat. fat), 44mg chol., 702mg sod., 33g carb. (6g sugars, 3g fiber), 10g pro. **Diabetic exchanges:** 2 starch, 1 lean meat, 1 fat.

5 INGREDIENTS | FAST FIX

CHICKEN CORDON BLEU STROMBOLI

If chicken cordon bleu and stromboli had a baby, this would be it! You can pair it with jarred or homemade Alfredo sauce or classic Mornay sauce on the side for dipping.
—Cyndy Gerken, Naples, FL

Takes: 30 min. • **Makes:** 6 servings

- **1 tube (13.8 oz.) refrigerated pizza crust**
- **4 pieces thinly sliced deli ham**
- **1½ cups shredded cooked chicken**
- **6 slices Swiss cheese**
- **1 Tbsp. butter, melted**
- **Roasted garlic Alfredo sauce, optional**

1. Preheat oven to 400°. Unroll pizza dough onto a baking sheet. Layer with ham, chicken and cheese to within ½ in. of edges. Roll up jelly-roll style, starting with a long side; pinch seam to seal and tuck ends under. Brush with melted butter.
2. Bake until crust is dark golden brown, 18-22 minutes. Let stand 5 minutes before slicing. If desired, serve with Alfredo sauce for dipping.

1 slice: 298 cal., 10g fat (4g sat. fat), 53mg chol., 580mg sod., 32g carb. (4g sugars, 1g fiber), 21g pro.

TEST KITCHEN TIP

Don't let this stand too long before slicing and eating, or the underside of the crust will get soft. Leftover rotisserie chicken is an excellent alternative in this stromboli.

CHICKEN CORDON BLEU STROMBOLI

FAST FIX

ZIPPY EGG SALAD

PICTURED ON P. 47

A touch of mustard and lemon juice gives this refreshing lunch option extra pep.
—Annemarie Pietila, Farmington Hills, MI

Takes: 10 min. • **Makes:** 2 servings

- **3 Tbsp. mayonnaise**
- **1½ tsp. prepared mustard**
- **⅛ tsp. salt**
- **⅛ tsp. pepper**
- **⅛ tsp. lemon juice**
- **3 hard-boiled large eggs, coarsely chopped**
- **1 Tbsp. minced green onion**
- **2 slices bread**
- **Diced tomato, optional**

Mix the first five ingredients. Stir in the eggs and green onion. Serve on bread. If desired, top with tomato.

1 open-faced sandwich: 332 cal., 24g fat (5g sat. fat), 281mg chol., 530mg sod., 16g carb. (3g sugars, 1g fiber), 12g pro.

GREEN TOMATO BLT

HAM & BEAN SOUP

When I was a cook in a restaurant years ago, this was our best-selling soup. One taste and your family will surely agree it's a winner!
—Mary Detweiler, Middlefield, OH

Prep: 15 min. • **Cook:** 35 min.
Makes: 8 servings (2 qt.)

- **¾ lb. fully cooked ham, cubed**
- **1 medium onion, chopped**
- **2 garlic cloves, minced**
- **2 Tbsp. butter**
- **2 cans (15½ oz. each) great northern beans, rinsed and drained**
- **3 cups chicken broth**
- **2 cups water**
- **1 cup diced peeled potatoes**
- **¾ cup diced carrots**
- **¾ cup diced celery**
- **¼ tsp. pepper**
- **½ cup frozen peas**
- **2 Tbsp. minced fresh parsley**

In a large saucepan, saute ham, onion and garlic in butter until the onion is tender. Add the next seven ingredients; cover and simmer until the vegetables are tender, about 30 minutes. Add peas and cook until heated through, about 5 minutes longer. Stir in parsley.

1 cup: 185 cal., 7g fat (3g sat. fat), 30mg chol., 1079mg sod., 18g carb. (3g sugars, 4g fiber), 13g pro.

FAST FIX

GREEN TOMATO BLT

I absolutely love tomatoes—any kind, any size. And here in the South, that includes fried green tomatoes. I created a special summer sandwich to show them off.
—Hillian Holmgren, Del Rio, TX

Takes: 30 min. • **Makes:** 2 servings

- **2 medium green tomatoes**
- **¼ cup all-purpose flour**
- **¼ cup cornmeal**
- **½ tsp. salt**
- **¼ cup 2% milk**
- **¼ cup canola oil**
- **¼ cup prepared ranch salad dressing**
- **2 green onions, chopped**
- **1 tsp. snipped fresh dill or ¼ tsp. dill weed**
- **2 onion rolls, split**
- **4 cooked bacon strips**
- **2 Bibb or Boston lettuce leaves**

1. Cut each tomato into four slices. In a shallow bowl, mix flour, cornmeal and salt. Pour milk into a separate shallow bowl. Dip tomato slices in milk, then in flour mixture, patting to help coating adhere.
2. In a large skillet, heat oil over medium-high heat. Add tomato slices; cook until golden brown, 3-5 minutes on each side.
3. Mix salad dressing, green onions and dill. Layer roll bottoms with bacon, lettuce and tomatoes. Spoon the dressing mixture over tomatoes; add roll tops.

1 sandwich: 623 cal., 37g fat (7g sat. fat), 26mg chol., 1329mg sod., 52g carb. (11g sugars, 4g fiber), 18g pro.

TEST KITCHEN TIP

Turn this into a hearty salad by skipping the bun and serving over torn greens. Top with crumbled bacon. Try the doctored-up ranch dressing as a spread for burgers or deli sandwiches.

FAVORITE FISH CHOWDER

I grew up during the Depression, and fish was plentiful and affordable—that's how we began eating this dish. When meat was rationed in World War II, this chowder again became a staple in our household. Fortunately, my family loved it!

—Fran Gustafson, Bethesda, MD

Prep: 10 min. • **Cook:** 25 min.
Makes: 16 servings (4 qt.)

- **1 large onion, chopped**
- **½ cup butter, cubed**
- **4 cups water**
- **6 cups cubed peeled potatoes**
- **2 lbs. cod fillets, cut into large chunks**
- **3 Tbsp. lemon juice**
- **2 cups milk**
- **2 cans (12 oz. each) evaporated milk**
- **2½ tsp. salt**
- **2 tsp. pepper**
- **Minced fresh parsley**

In a Dutch oven, saute onion in butter. Add water and bring to a boil. Add potatoes; cook for 10 minutes. Add fish and lemon juice; reduce heat and simmer for 10 minutes. Add milk, evaporated milk, salt and pepper. Sprinkle with parsley.

1 cup: 192 cal., 8g fat (5g sat. fat), 48mg chol., 496mg sod., 16g carb. (5g sugars, 1g fiber), 12g pro.

FAST FIX

TURKEY GUACAMOLE WRAPS

PICTURED ON P. 47

Tuck smoked turkey and this creamy avocado spread into warm tortillas. The dash of hot sauce adds a little kick.

—Margee Berry, White Salmon, WA

Takes: 15 min. • **Makes:** 2 servings

- **1 small ripe avocado, peeled**
- **2 Tbsp. mayonnaise**
- **1½ tsp. lime juice**
- **¼ tsp. minced garlic**
- **⅛ tsp. Louisiana-style hot sauce**
- **2 flour tortillas (10 in.), room temperature**
- **¼ lb. sliced deli smoked turkey**
- **½ cup chopped red onion**
- **1 cup torn romaine**

Place the first five ingredients in a food processor; process until smooth. Spread over the tortillas. Top with turkey, onion and lettuce; roll up.

1 wrap: 506 cal., 27g fat (5g sat. fat), 21mg chol., 1045mg sod., 46g carb. (5g sugars, 8g fiber), 20g pro.

FAST FIX

ITALIAN VEGETABLE SOUP

Here's a dish that will warm you up fast. After just 25 minutes, you can sit down and begin sipping on this delicious and comforting soup.

—Janet Frieman, Kenosha, WI

Takes: 25 min.
Makes: 8 servings (2 qt.)

- **1 lb. bulk Italian sausage**
- **1 medium onion, sliced**
- **1½ cups water**
- **1 can (15 oz.) garbanzo beans or chickpeas, rinsed and drained**
- **1 can (14½ oz.) diced tomatoes, undrained**
- **1 can (14½ oz.) beef broth**
- **2 medium zucchini, cut into ¼-in. slices**
- **½ tsp. dried basil**
- **Grated Parmesan cheese**

1. In a large saucepan, cook sausage and onion over medium heat until meat is no longer pink; drain. Stir in the water, beans, tomatoes, broth, zucchini and basil.
2. Bring to a boil. Reduce heat and simmer until the zucchini is tender, about 5 minutes. Garnish with cheese.

1 cup: 173 cal., 9g fat (3g sat. fat), 23mg chol., 620mg sod., 14g carb. (5g sugars, 3g fiber), 10g pro.

ITALIAN VEGETABLE SOUP

FRESH VEGGIE POCKETS

FAST FIX

FRESH VEGGIE POCKETS

One summer I worked at a health food store that sold sandwiches. We were close to a college campus, so I made lots of these fresh filled pitas for the students. With vegetables and nutty sunflower kernels, they're a fast-to-fix meal for when you're on the go.
—Linda Reeves, Cloverdale, IN

Takes: 15 min. • **Makes:** 4 servings

- **1 carton (8 oz.) spreadable cream cheese**
- **¼ cup sunflower kernels**
- **1 tsp. seasoned salt or salt-free seasoning blend**
- **4 whole wheat pita breads (6 in.), halved**
- **1 medium tomato, thinly sliced**
- **1 medium cucumber, thinly sliced**
- **1 cup sliced fresh mushrooms**
- **1 ripe avocado, peeled and sliced**

In a large bowl, combine cream cheese, sunflower kernels and seasoned salt; spread about 2 Tbsp. on the inside of each pita half. Layer with the tomato, cucumber, mushrooms and avocado.

2 filled pita halves: 434 cal., 23g fat (9g sat. fat), 37mg chol., 571mg sod., 48g carb. (6g sugars, 8g fiber), 14g pro.

* HEALTH TIP * If you're looking for more protein, add some chicken, or keep it meatless by adding garbanzo beans.

SPICY THAI COCONUT CHICKEN SOUP

SPICY THAI COCONUT CHICKEN SOUP

For national soup month, I came up with a soup recipe for every day, and this was my favorite. It's so easy and it has just a touch of special Thai flavors. I used whole coconut milk, not light. It made a big difference.
—Diane Nemitz, Ludington, MI

Prep: 20 min. • **Cook:** 40 min.
Makes: 6 servings (2 qt.)

- **1 lb. boneless skinless chicken breasts, cut into ¾-in. cubes**
- **3 Tbsp. cornstarch**
- **3 Tbsp. peanut or canola oil, divided**
- **1 large onion, chopped**
- **1 small jalapeno pepper, seeded and minced**
- **2 garlic cloves, minced**
- **2 tsp. red curry powder**
- **1 tsp. ground ginger**
- **¾ tsp. salt**
- **½ tsp. ground turmeric**
- **1 tsp. Sriracha Asian hot chili sauce**
- **1 can (13.66 oz.) coconut milk**
- **1 carton (32 oz.) chicken broth**
- **2 cups thinly sliced Chinese or napa cabbage**
- **1 cup thinly sliced fresh snow peas**
- **Thinly sliced green onions**
- **Lime wedges**

1. Toss chicken with cornstarch. In a 6-qt. stockpot, heat 2 Tbsp. oil over medium-high heat; saute chicken until lightly browned, 2-3 minutes. Remove from pot.
2. In same pan, saute onion, jalapeno and garlic in remaining oil over medium-high heat until onion is tender, 3-4 minutes. Stir in seasonings, chili sauce, coconut milk and broth; bring to a boil. Reduce heat; simmer, covered, for 20 minutes.
3. Stir in cabbage, snow peas and chicken; cook, uncovered, just until the cabbage is crisp-tender and the chicken is cooked through, 3-4 minutes. Serve with green onions and lime wedges.

1⅓ cups: 244 cal., 14g fat (5g sat. fat), 45mg chol., 1017mg sod., 11g carb. (4g sugars, 2g fiber), 17g pro.

TEST KITCHEN TIP

You can substitute regular cabbage for Chinese cabbage; just cook it a bit longer to make sure it's tender. Julienned sugar snap peas can be used in place of the snow peas.

Don't be tempted to add lime juice to the soup instead of serving it with wedges, as directed. Lime juice will turn the snow peas and cabbage an unattractive olive green color. Serving it with wedges adds the lime flavor, but doesn't give the acid time to change the color of the green vegetables in the soup.

FAST FIX

BASIL-TOMATO GRILLED CHEESE

Keep the taste of summer going past September with this easy Italian-style grilled cheese sandwich. It tastes fresh and comforting all in one bite, and is super fast to make for those busy days.
—Sylvia Schmitt, Sun City, AZ

Takes: 20 min. • **Makes:** 4 servings

- **8 slices Italian bread (¾ in. thick)**
- **8 slices part-skim mozzarella cheese**
- **2 large plum tomatoes, sliced**
- **2 Tbsp. minced fresh basil**
- **2 tsp. balsamic vinegar**
- **Salt and pepper to taste**
- **¼ cup olive oil**
- **3 Tbsp. grated Parmesan cheese**
- **¼ tsp. garlic powder**

1. On four slices of bread, layer the mozzarella cheese and tomatoes; sprinkle with basil, vinegar, salt and pepper. Top with the remaining bread.
2. In a small bowl, combine oil, Parmesan cheese and garlic powder; brush over the outsides of each sandwich.
3. In a skillet over medium heat, toast sandwiches until golden brown on both sides and the cheese is melted.

1 sandwich: 467 cal., 27g fat (9g sat. fat), 34mg chol., 723mg sod., 34g carb. (4g sugars, 2g fiber), 23g pro.

GROUND BEEF VEGGIE STEW

EAT SMART | FAST FIX

GROUND BEEF VEGGIE STEW

This is a wonderful, filling stew to help use up all the late-summer veggies from your garden. I like that it's filling enough to make a meal, and it's good for you too!
—Courtney Stultz, Weir, KS

Takes: 30 min. • **Makes:** 6 servings

- **1 lb. lean ground beef (90% lean)**
- **1 Tbsp. olive oil**
- **1 small yellow summer squash, chopped**
- **1 small zucchini, chopped**
- **1 small sweet red pepper, chopped**
- **2 cans (15 oz. each) diced tomatoes**
- **1 cup water**
- **1 tsp. salt**
- **¼ tsp. pepper**
- **3 Tbsp. minced fresh cilantro**
- **Reduced-fat sour cream, optional**

1. In a large saucepan, cook beef over medium-high heat until no longer pink, 5-7 minutes, breaking into crumbles; drain. Remove from pan; set aside.
2. In the same saucepan, add oil, squash, zucchini and red pepper; cook and stir 5-7 minutes or until crisp-tender. Add the beef, tomatoes, water, salt and pepper; bring to a boil. Reduce to a simmer; cook, stirring occasionally, until the vegetables are tender, 5-8 minutes. Stir in cilantro to serve. If desired, top with sour cream.

1¼ cups: 180 cal., 9g fat (3g sat. fat), 47mg chol., 663mg sod., 9g carb. (6g sugars, 3g fiber), 16g pro. **Diabetic exchanges:** 2 lean meat, 1 vegetable, ½ fat.

TEST KITCHEN TIP

This dish is a cross between a brothy soup and a chunky stew. It's hearty but it feels super fresh with all the veggies. If you're not a fan of cilantro, add some parsley. Chopped fresh chives would also make a flavorful addition.

FAST FIX

GOLDEN SQUASH SOUP

This delectable soup feels like fall! Its golden color and rich, satisfying flavor make it a favorite of mine—which is amazing, because I was convinced I didn't like squash until I tried this recipe.
—Becky Ruff, McGregor, IA

Takes: 30 min.
Makes: 6 servings (1½ qt.)

- **5 medium leeks (white portion only), sliced**
- **2 Tbsp. butter**
- **4 cups cubed peeled butternut squash**
- **4 cups chicken broth**
- **¼ tsp. dried thyme**
- **¼ tsp. pepper**
- **1¾ cups shredded cheddar cheese**
- **¼ cup sour cream**
- **1 green onion, thinly sliced**

1. In a large saucepan, saute leeks in butter until tender. Stir in squash, broth, thyme and pepper. Bring to a boil. Reduce heat; cover and simmer until squash is tender, 10-15 minutes. Cool slightly.
2. In a blender, cover and process the squash mixture in small batches until smooth; return all to the pan. Bring to a boil. Reduce heat to low. Add cheese; stir until the soup is heated through and the cheese is melted. Garnish with sour cream and onion.

1 cup: 294 cal., 18g fat (10g sat. fat), 48mg chol., 922mg sod., 26g carb. (7g sugars, 4g fiber), 11g pro.

GRILLED EGGPLANT PANINI WITH BASIL AIOLI

PICTURED ON P. 47

I love being able to use fresh herbs and vegetables from my garden for summer meals. This sandwich is loaded with veggies and has a satisfying crunch. Melty provolone finishes things off perfectly.
—Joseph Sciascia, San Mateo, CA

Prep: 25 min. • **Grill:** 20 min.
Makes: 4 servings

- **¾ cup mayonnaise**
- **⅓ cup chopped fresh basil**
- **3 Tbsp. grated Parmesan cheese**
- **2 Tbsp. minced fresh chives**
- **1 Tbsp. lemon juice**
- **2 garlic cloves, minced**
- **½ tsp. salt**
- **½ tsp. pepper**
- **1 large eggplant, cut into 8 slices**
- **2 large sweet red peppers, cut into large pieces**
- **2 Tbsp. olive oil**
- **4 ciabatta rolls, split**
- **8 slices provolone cheese**

1. For aioli, place first eight ingredients in a blender or food processor; cover and process until smooth.
2. Brush vegetables with oil. Place in broiling pan and broil 3-4 in. from heat, or grill, covered, over medium heat until tender, 4-5 minutes per side. Chop the red peppers when cool enough to handle.
3. Spread the cut sides of each roll with 2 Tbsp. aioli; top each with cheese. Layer the bottoms with eggplant and peppers. Replace tops.
4. In a panini press, grill the sandwiches until the cheese is melted, 5-7 minutes. Serve the remaining aioli with sandwiches or save for another use.

1 sandwich: 732 cal., 38g fat (11g sat. fat), 33mg chol., 1116mg sod., 83g carb. (12g sugars, 9g fiber), 23g pro.

GOLDEN SQUASH SOUP

FAST FIX

SPICY ASIAN HAM SANDWICHES

Our family loves these sandwiches made with ham, but you can use leftover cooked pork instead if you prefer.
—Janice Elder, Charlotte, NC

Takes: 15 min. • **Makes:** 4 servings

- **2 French bread demi baguettes (4 oz. each)**
- **¼ cup reduced-fat mayonnaise**
- **1 Tbsp. sweet chili sauce**
- **2 tsp. Thai red chili paste**
- **¼ lb. thinly sliced deli ham**
- **1 cup thinly sliced English cucumber**
- **½ cup shredded carrots**
- **2 cups spring mix salad greens**
- **2 Tbsp. fresh basil leaves**
- **2 Tbsp. fresh mint leaves**

1. Preheat broiler. Cut baguettes in half lengthwise; cut crosswise in half. Place bread on a baking sheet, cut side up. Broil 4-6 in. from heat until lightly browned, 1-2 minutes.
2. In a small bowl, mix mayonnaise, chili sauce and chili paste; spread over cut sides of baguettes. Layer baguette bottoms with ham, cucumber, carrots, salad greens, basil and mint; cover with tops.

1 sandwich: 271 cal., 8g fat (2g sat. fat), 22mg chol., 962mg sod., 38g carb. (5g sugars, 2g fiber), 11g pro.

TEST KITCHEN TIP

This is a simplified version of a banh mi sandwich. Banh mi is the Vietnamese term for the light bread used in the classic recipe. You can find sweet chili sauce in the Asian foods aisle. Common brands are Sun Luck and Mae Ploy.

5 INGREDIENTS | EAT SMART

ROASTED TOMATO SOUP WITH FRESH BASIL

Roasting brings out tomatoes' rich, sweet flavor and makes this soup a step above other tomato soups. Fresh summertime basil is the classic companion.
—Marie Forte, Raritan, NJ

Prep: 20 min. • **Bake:** 25 min.
Makes: 6 servings (1½ qt.)

- **3½ lbs. tomatoes (about 11 medium), halved**
- **1 small onion, quartered**
- **2 garlic cloves, peeled and halved**
- **2 Tbsp. olive oil**
- **2 Tbsp. fresh thyme leaves**
- **1 tsp. salt**
- **¼ tsp. pepper**
- **12 fresh basil leaves**
- **Salad croutons and thinly sliced fresh basil, optional**

1. Preheat oven to 400°. Place tomatoes, onion and garlic in a greased 15x10x1-in. baking pan; drizzle with oil. Sprinkle with thyme, salt and pepper; toss to coat. Roast until tender, 25-30 minutes, stirring once. Cool slightly.
2. Process the tomato mixture and basil leaves in batches in a blender until smooth. Transfer to a large saucepan; heat through. If desired, top with croutons and sliced basil.

1 cup: 107 cal., 5g fat (1g sat. fat), 0 chol., 411mg sod., 15g carb. (9g sugars, 4g fiber), 3g pro. **Diabetic exchanges:** 1 starch, 1 fat.

EAT SMART | FAST FIX

APPLE-SWISS TURKEY SANDWICHES

Honey mustard adds a sweet tang to this hearty concoction. Apple slices, Swiss cheese, cucumber and turkey are layered between slices of nutritious multigrain bread.
—Gloria Updyke, Front Royal, VA

Takes: 15 min. • **Makes:** 4 sandwiches

- **2 medium apples, thinly sliced**
- **8 slices multigrain bread, toasted**
- **3 Tbsp. honey mustard**
- **8 oz. thinly sliced cooked turkey breast**
- **½ cup thinly sliced cucumber**
- **8 slices reduced-fat Swiss cheese**

1. Place apples on a microwave-safe plate; microwave, uncovered, on high 1 minute or until slightly softened.
2. Lightly spread toasted bread with mustard. Layer half of the toast with turkey, cucumber, cheese and apples; top with the remaining toast.

1 sandwich: 415 cal., 13g fat (5g sat. fat), 88mg chol., 412mg sod., 41g carb. (15g sugars, 6g fiber), 38g pro. **Diabetic exchanges:** 3 lean meat, 2 starch, 1 fat, ½ fruit.

SPICY ASIAN HAM SANDWICHES

FAST FIX

COPY CAT CHICKEN SALAD

I made this to imitate the great chicken salad at Chick-fil-A. It's incredibly easy to make, and your family will love it. Sweet pickle relish gives it a distinctive taste. I like to use a thick, crusty oat bread.
—Julie Peterson, Crofton, MD

Takes: 20 min. • **Makes:** 2 servings

- **½ cup reduced-fat mayonnaise**
- **⅓ cup sweet pickle relish**
- **⅓ cup finely chopped celery**
- **½ tsp. sugar**
- **¼ tsp. salt**
- **¼ tsp. pepper**
- **1 hard-boiled large egg, cooled and minced**
- **2 cups chopped cooked chicken breast**
- **4 slices whole wheat bread, toasted**
- **2 romaine leaves**

Mix first seven ingredients; stir in chicken. Line two slices of toast with lettuce. Top with chicken salad and remaining toast.

1 sandwich: 651 cal., 29g fat (5g sat. fat), 222mg chol., 1386mg sod., 45g carb. (18g sugars, 4g fiber), 51g pro.

TEST KITCHEN TIP

Double the chicken mixture for lunch during the week—use it in sandwiches, serve over salad greens or spread it on crackers. If you're cooking your own bird for this recipe, you'll need roughly half a pound of raw chicken for every cup of cooked chopped breast meat.

DILL CHICKEN SOUP

EAT SMART | FAST FIX

DILL CHICKEN SOUP

If I could eat soup for every meal of the day, all year long, I would. I particularly like dill and spinach—they add brightness to this light and healthy soup.
—Robin Haas, Jamaica Plain, MA

Takes: 30 min. • **Makes:** 6 servings (2 qt.)

- **1 Tbsp. canola oil**
- **2 medium carrots, chopped**
- **1 small onion, coarsely chopped**
- **2 garlic cloves, minced**
- **½ cup uncooked whole wheat orzo pasta**
- **1½ cups coarsely shredded rotisserie chicken**
- **6 cups reduced-sodium chicken broth**
- **1½ cups frozen peas (about 6 oz.)**
- **8 oz. fresh baby spinach (about 10 cups)**
- **2 Tbsp. chopped fresh dill or 1 Tbsp. dill weed**
- **2 Tbsp. lemon juice**
- **Coarsely ground pepper, optional**

1. In a 6-qt. stockpot, heat oil over medium heat. Add carrots, onion and garlic; saute until carrots are tender, 4-5 minutes.
2. Stir in the orzo, chicken and broth; bring to a boil. Reduce heat; simmer, uncovered, for 5 minutes. Stir in peas, spinach and dill; return to a boil. Reduce heat; simmer, uncovered, until the orzo is tender, 3-4 minutes. Stir in lemon juice. If desired, top each serving with coarsely ground pepper.

1⅓ cups: 198 cal., 6g fat (1g sat. fat), 31mg chol., 681mg sod., 20g carb. (4g sugars, 5g fiber), 18g pro. **Diabetic exchanges:** 2 lean meat, 1 starch, 1 vegetable, ½ fat.

FAST FIX

EASY TORTELLINI SPINACH SOUP

This is the easiest soup you will ever make—take it from me! I always keep the ingredients on hand so if I'm feeling under the weather or just plain busy, I can throw together this soup in a flash.
—Angela Lively, Conroe, TX

Takes: 20 min. • **Makes:** 8 servings (3 qt.)

- **16 frozen fully cooked Italian meatballs (about 1 lb.)**
- **1 can (14½ oz.) fire-roasted diced tomatoes, undrained**
- **¼ tsp. Italian seasoning**
- **¼ tsp. pepper**
- **2 cartons (32 oz. each) chicken stock**
- **2 cups frozen cheese tortellini (about 8 oz.)**
- **3 oz. fresh baby spinach (about 4 cups)**
- **Shredded Parmesan cheese, optional**

1. Place first five ingredients in a 6-qt. stockpot; bring to a boil. Reduce heat; simmer, covered, for 10 minutes.
2. Return to a boil. Add tortellini; cook, uncovered, until the meatballs are heated through and the tortellini are tender, 3-5 minutes, stirring occasionally. Stir in spinach until wilted. Serve immediately. If desired, top with cheese.

1½ cups: 177 cal., 8g fat (4g sat. fat), 18mg chol., 949mg sod., 14g carb. (3g sugars, 1g fiber), 12g pro.

TEST KITCHEN TIP

Fully cooked Italian sausage, cut into half-moon slices, can be substituted for the meatballs. One 9-ounce package refrigerated cheese tortellini may be substituted for 2 cups frozen tortellini.

FREEZE IT | FAST FIX

BARBECUE CHICKEN SLIDERS

Thanks to rotisserie chicken, these cheesy, smoky sliders are a snap to make on a busy day. The special barbecue sauce really takes it up a notch.
—Nancy Heishman, Las Vegas, NV

Takes: 25 min. • **Makes:** 4 servings

- **¾ cup beer or reduced-sodium chicken broth**
- **½ cup barbecue sauce**
- **1 Tbsp. bourbon**
- **1 tsp. hot pepper sauce**
- **¼ tsp. seasoned salt**
- **¼ tsp. ground mustard**
- **2 cups shredded rotisserie chicken**
- **8 slider buns, split**
- **1½ cups shredded smoked cheddar cheese**

1. Preheat broiler. In a large saucepan, mix first six ingredients; bring to a boil. Reduce heat; simmer, uncovered, until slightly thickened, 8-10 minutes, stirring occasionally. Stir in chicken; heat through.
2. Place buns on a baking sheet, cut side up. Broil 3-4 in. from heat until lightly toasted, 30-60 seconds.
3. Remove the tops of the buns from the baking sheet. Spoon chicken mixture onto the bottoms; sprinkle with cheese. Broil 3-4 in. from heat until cheese is melted, 1-2 minutes. Replace bun tops.

Freeze option: Freeze cooled chicken mixture in freezer containers. To use, partially thaw in refrigerator overnight. Heat through, stirring occasionally; add water if necessary. Toast buns and prepare sliders as directed.

2 sliders: 529 cal., 23g fat (10g sat. fat), 106mg chol., 1023mg sod., 42g carb. (15g sugars, 1g fiber), 36g pro.

CABBAGE & BEEF SOUP

When I was a little girl, I helped my parents work the fields of their farm. Lunchtime was always a treat when Mother picked fresh vegetables from her garden and simmered them in her big soup pot.
—Ethel Ledbetter, Canton, NC

Prep: 10 min. • **Cook:** 70 min.
Makes: 12 servings (3 qt.)

- **1 lb. lean ground beef (90% lean)**
- **½ tsp. garlic salt**
- **¼ tsp. garlic powder**
- **¼ tsp. pepper**
- **2 celery ribs, chopped**
- **1 can (16 oz.) kidney beans, rinsed and drained**
- **½ medium head cabbage, chopped**
- **1 can (28 oz.) diced tomatoes, undrained**
- **3½ cups water**
- **4 tsp. beef bouillon granules**
- **Minced fresh parsley**

1. In a Dutch oven, cook the beef over medium heat until no longer pink; drain. Stir in the remaining ingredients except the parsley.
2. Bring to a boil. Reduce heat; cover and simmer for 1 hour. Garnish with parsley.

1 cup: 116 cal., 3g fat (1g sat. fat), 19mg chol., 582mg sod., 11g carb. (3g sugars, 3g fiber), 11g pro.

FAST FIX

EGG-TOPPED AVOCADO TOAST

We always have avocados on hand, so it's easy to make this quick and tasty breakfast toast for my husband and me.
—Kallee Krong-McCreery, Escondido, CA

Takes: 20 min. • **Makes:** 2 servings

- **2 slices multigrain bread, toasted**
- **2 tsp. butter**
- **½ medium ripe avocado, peeled and thinly sliced**
- **4 thin slices tomato**
- **2 thin slices red onion**
- **2 large eggs**
- **⅛ tsp. seasoned salt**
- **2 Tbsp. shredded cheddar cheese**
- **2 bacon strips, cooked and crumbled**

1. Spread each slice of toast with butter; place on a plate. Top with the avocado; mash gently with a fork. Top with tomato and onion.
2. To poach each egg, place ½ cup of water in a small microwave-safe bowl or glass measuring cup; break an egg into the water. Microwave, covered, on high for 1 minute. Microwave in 10-second intervals until the white is set and the yolk begins to thicken; let stand 1 minute. Using a slotted spoon, place an egg on each sandwich.
3. Sprinkle eggs with seasoned salt. Top with cheese and bacon.

1 open-faced sandwich: 313 cal., 21g fat (7g sat. fat), 211mg chol., 492mg sod., 18g carb. (4g sugars, 5g fiber), 15g pro.

* HEALTH TIP * Skip the cheese and bacon to reduce the saturated fat and start your morning on a healthier note.

TEST KITCHEN TIP

For a buttery texture and flavor, be sure to use a ripe avocado. To speed its ripening, place it in a brown paper bag along with an apple or kiwifruit. If an avocado is ripe before you need it, refrigerate it and it'll stay at its peak a few days longer. To store leftover avocado, sprinkle the cut surface with lemon juice and wrap it tightly in plastic; use within a day.

EGG-TOPPED AVOCADO TOAST

DILLY TURKEY MELT

FAST FIX
DILLY TURKEY MELT
This grilled sandwich has a distinctive combination of ingredients. The pickle slices add a bit of fun, and the barbecue sauce adds a hint of sweetness.
—Henry Mujica, North Riverside, IL

Takes: 25 min. • **Makes:** 4 servings

- **2 medium onions, sliced**
- **4 Tbsp. butter, divided**
- **4 Tbsp. barbecue sauce**
- **8 slices sourdough bread**
- **8 slices Monterey Jack cheese**
- **8 slices Canadian bacon**
- **8 thin slices cooked turkey**
- **Dill pickle slices**

1. In a large skillet, saute onions in 1 Tbsp. butter until tender; remove and set aside. Spread the barbecue sauce on four slices of bread. Layer each with one slice of cheese, two slices each bacon and turkey, pickle slices, onions and another slice of cheese. Cover with the remaining slices of bread.
2. In the same skillet over medium-low heat, melt the remaining butter. Cook sandwiches on both sides until golden brown and cheese is melted (cover the skillet during the last few minutes to help melt cheese, if necessary).

1 sandwich: 628 cal., 34g fat (19g sat. fat), 137mg chol., 1359mg sod., 42g carb. (11g sugars, 2g fiber), 39g pro.

SAVORY LEEK SOUP
This rich and creamy soup is spring comfort in a bowl. The mashed potatoes are the secret to its velvety texture, while the leeks and green onions give it loads of fresh flavor.
—Eleanor Davis, Pittsburgh, PA

Prep: 10 min. • **Cook:** 25 min.
Makes: 10 servings (2½ qt.)

- **¼ cup butter, cubed**
- **4 medium leeks (white portion only), sliced (about 4 cups)**
- **½ cup minced fresh chives**
- **2 cups mashed potatoes (prepared with milk and butter)**
- **2 Tbsp. minced fresh savory or 2 tsp. dried savory**
- **4 cups chicken broth**
- **3 cups half-and-half cream**
- **Salt and pepper to taste**

1. In a large saucepan, heat butter over medium-high heat; saute leeks and chives until tender. Stir in mashed potatoes, savory and broth; bring to a boil. Reduce heat; simmer, uncovered, until flavors are blended, 8-10 minutes.
2. Puree soup using an immersion blender or cool slightly and puree soup in batches in a blender; return to pan. Stir in cream, salt and pepper; heat through.

1 cup: 213 cal., 14g fat (9g sat. fat), 55mg chol., 605mg sod., 15g carb. (5g sugars, 1g fiber), 4g pro.

CREAMY CHICKEN GNOCCHI SOUP
I tasted a similar soup at Olive Garden and wanted to make my own version. After some experimenting at home, this was the delicious result! It's wonderful on a cool evening.
—Jaclynn Robinson, Shingletown, CA

Prep: 25 min. • **Cook:** 15 min.
Makes: 8 servings (2 qt.)

- **1 lb. boneless skinless chicken breasts, cut into ½-in. pieces**
- **⅓ cup butter, divided**
- **1 small onion, chopped**
- **1 medium carrot, shredded**
- **1 celery rib, chopped**
- **2 garlic cloves, minced**
- **⅓ cup all-purpose flour**
- **3½ cups 2% milk**
- **1½ cups heavy whipping cream**
- **1 Tbsp. reduced-sodium chicken bouillon granules**
- **¼ tsp. coarsely ground pepper**
- **1 pkg. (16 oz.) potato gnocchi**
- **½ cup chopped fresh spinach**

1. In a Dutch oven, brown chicken in 2 Tbsp. butter. Remove and keep warm. In the same pan, saute the onion, carrot, celery and garlic in the remaining butter until tender.
2. Whisk in flour until blended; gradually stir in milk, cream, bouillon and pepper. Bring to a boil. Reduce heat; cook and stir until thickened, about 2 minutes.
3. Add the gnocchi and spinach; cook until the spinach is wilted, 3-4 minutes. Add the chicken. Cover and simmer until heated through (do not boil), about 10 minutes.

1 cup: 482 cal., 28g fat (17g sat. fat), 125mg chol., 527mg sod., 36g carb. (10g sugars, 2g fiber), 21g pro.

CREAMY CHICKEN GNOCCHI SOUP

FAST FIX

GRILLED CHICKEN BURGERS

Tart apples mixed right into the patties and a cranberry-mayo spread take these chicken burgers up several levels of flavor!
—Debbie Gauthier, Timmins, ON

Takes: 30 min. • **Makes:** 4 servings

1 medium tart apple, peeled and finely chopped
1 small onion, finely chopped
1 celery rib, finely chopped
¼ tsp. salt
¼ tsp. poultry seasoning
Dash pepper
1 lb. ground chicken
¼ cup whole-berry cranberry sauce
1 Tbsp. mayonnaise
4 hamburger buns, split
Bibb lettuce leaves, optional

1. In a large bowl, combine the first six ingredients. Crumble chicken over mixture and mix well. Shape into four patties.
2. Cook patties on an indoor grill until a thermometer reads 165°, 10-12 minutes.
3. Combine cranberry sauce and mayonnaise. Serve burgers on buns with cranberry spread and, if desired, lettuce.

1 burger: 345 cal., 14g fat (3g sat. fat), 76mg chol., 450mg sod., 34g carb. (11g sugars, 2g fiber), 22g pro.

FAST FIX

SAUSAGE & SPINACH CALZONES

These calzones are perfect for quick meals—or even a midnight snack. My co-workers always ask me to make them when it's my turn to bring in lunch.
—Kourtney Williams, Mechanicsville, VA

Takes: 30 min. • **Makes:** 4 servings

½ lb. bulk Italian sausage
3 cups fresh baby spinach
1 tube (13.8 oz.) refrigerated pizza crust
¾ cup shredded part-skim mozzarella cheese
½ cup part-skim ricotta cheese
¼ tsp. pepper
Pizza sauce, optional

1. Preheat oven to 400°. In a large skillet, cook and crumble sausage over medium heat until no longer pink, 4-6 minutes; drain. Add spinach; cook and stir until wilted. Remove from heat.
2. On a lightly floured surface, unroll and pat dough into a 15x11-in. rectangle. Cut into four rectangles. Sprinkle mozzarella cheese on one half of each rectangle to within 1 in. of edges.
3. Stir ricotta cheese and pepper into sausage mixture; spoon over mozzarella cheese. Fold dough over filling; press edges with a fork to seal. Place on a greased baking sheet.
4. Bake until calzones are light golden brown, 10-15 minutes. If desired, serve with pizza sauce.

1 calzone: 489 cal., 22g fat (9g sat. fat), 54mg chol., 1242mg sod., 51g carb. (7g sugars, 2g fiber), 23g pro.

FAST FIX

WEEKNIGHT TURKEY TORTILLA SOUP

This is my family's most requested soup. You can spice it up by adding smoked sausage or andouille and Cajun seasoning.
—Gail Lucas, Olive Branch, MS

Takes: 30 min. • **Makes:** 8 servings (3 qt.)

1 Tbsp. olive oil
1 large onion, chopped
1 garlic clove, minced
6 cups reduced-sodium chicken broth
1 can (15 oz.) diced tomatoes, undrained
1 can (4 oz.) chopped green chilies
1 reduced-sodium taco seasoning
2 cups cubed cooked turkey
2 cups frozen corn (about 10 oz.), thawed
⅓ cup minced fresh cilantro
Optional toppings: tortilla strips, shredded Monterey Jack cheese, sliced avocado and lime wedges

In a Dutch oven, heat oil over medium-high heat. Add onion; cook and stir until tender, 1-2 minutes. Add garlic; cook 1 minute longer. Add broth, tomatoes, chilies and taco seasoning; bring to a boil. Reduce heat; simmer 5 minutes. Add turkey and corn; heat through. Stir in cilantro before serving. Serve with toppings of your choice.

1½ cups: 144 cal., 3g fat (1g sat. fat), 35mg chol., 846mg sod., 16g carb. (6g sugars, 2g fiber), 14g pro.

WEEKNIGHT TURKEY TORTILLA SOUP

FAST FIX

SUN-DRIED TOMATO GRILLED CHEESE SANDWICH

Grilled cheese is a classic quick and easy meal. I love experimenting with different combinations. This is one of my favorites.
—Jessie Apfe, Berkeley, CA

Takes: 30 min. • **Makes:** 4 servings

- **½ cup oil-packed sun-dried tomatoes**
- **¼ cup grated Parmesan cheese**
- **¼ cup chopped fresh basil**
- **2 Tbsp. olive oil**
- **1 tsp. balsamic vinegar**
- **1 garlic clove, crushed**
- **⅛ tsp. salt**
- **⅛ tsp. pepper**
- **8 slices sourdough bread**
- **1¼ cups shredded part-skim mozzarella cheese**
- **½ cup crumbled goat cheese**
- **¼ cup fresh arugula**
- **2 Tbsp. chopped roasted sweet red pepper**
- **3 Tbsp. butter, melted**

1. Place the first eight ingredients in a food processor; process until blended.
2. Spread over each of four bread slices; top with cheeses, arugula, red pepper and remaining bread. Brush the outsides of the sandwiches with butter.
3. On a griddle, toast sandwiches over medium heat until golden brown and cheese is melted, 3-4 minutes per side.

1 sandwich: 491 cal., 31g fat (14g sat. fat), 67mg chol., 942mg sod., 37g carb. (4g sugars, 3g fiber), 19g pro.

SUN-DRIED TOMATO GRILLED CHEESE SANDWICH

FAST FIX

COBB SALAD WRAPS

It's smiles all around when I make these wraps for dinner! They're an easy meal on a summer night. And even better, I don't have to turn on my oven!
—Bonnie Hawkins, Elkhorn, WI

Takes: 25 min. • **Makes:** 2 servings

- **¼ cup blue cheese salad dressing**
- **2 spinach or whole wheat tortillas (8 in.)**
- **1 cup shredded cooked chicken**
- **1 cup spring mix salad greens**
- **1 medium tomato, halved and sliced**
- **4 cooked bacon strips**
- **½ medium ripe avocado, peeled and sliced**
- **1 Tbsp. sliced ripe olives**
- **1 Tbsp. crumbled blue cheese**

Spread dressing over tortillas to within ½ in. of edges. Layer with remaining ingredients. Roll up tortillas.

1 wrap: 610 cal., 37g fat (8g sat. fat), 91mg chol., 880mg sod., 36g carb. (3g sugars, 5g fiber), 33g pro.

FAST FIX

TURKEY-TARRAGON NOODLE SOUP

I've always thought tarragon and turkey were a flavor match made in heaven. This recipe proves it!
—Carolyn Ketchum, Wakefield, MA

Takes: 30 min. • **Makes:** 6 servings (2 qt.)

- **6 cups chicken broth**
- **2 medium carrots, thinly sliced**
- **1 celery rib, thinly sliced**
- **2 Tbsp. lemon juice**
- **1 bay leaf**
- **½ tsp. salt**
- **¼ tsp. pepper**
- **3 cups uncooked medium egg noodles**
- **3 cups coarsely chopped cooked turkey**
- **2 Tbsp. torn fresh tarragon leaves**
- **Additional fresh tarragon leaves, optional**

1. In a large saucepan, combine the first seven ingredients; bring to a boil. Reduce heat; cover and simmer until vegetables are tender, 8-10 minutes.
2. Return to a boil; add noodles. Cook until noodles are tender, 5-6 minutes longer. Stir in turkey and tarragon; heat through. Discard bay leaf. If desired, top servings with additional tarragon.

1⅓ cups: 219 cal., 5g fat (1g sat. fat), 74mg chol., 1250mg sod., 17g carb. (3g sugars, 1g fiber), 25g pro.

CHICKEN CUCUMBER PITAS

WINTER COUNTRY SOUP

My soup will warm up your family on the chilliest winter nights! Featuring smoked sausage, beans and vegetables, it's a satisfying lunch all by itself or a perfect way to start a meal.
—Jeannette Sabo, Lexington Park, MD

Prep: 15 min. • **Cook:** 40 min.
Makes: 12 servings (3 qt.)

- **1 Tbsp. butter**
- **1 pkg. (14 oz.) smoked sausage, cut into ¼-in. slices**
- **1 large sweet red pepper, cut into ½-in. pieces**
- **8 shallots, chopped**
- **8 cups chopped fresh kale**
- **3 cups frozen corn (about 15 oz.)**
- **1 can (15½ oz.) great northern beans, rinsed and drained**
- **½ tsp. cayenne pepper**
- **¼ tsp. pepper**
- **8 cups vegetable broth**
- **¾ cup uncooked orzo pasta**

1. In a Dutch oven, heat butter over medium-high heat; saute sausage with pepper and shallots until browned.
2. Add kale; cook, covered, until the kale is wilted, 2-3 minutes. Stir in all remaining ingredients except the orzo; bring to a boil. Reduce heat; simmer, uncovered, 20 minutes.
3. Return to a boil. Stir in orzo. Cook until the pasta is tender, 8-10 minutes, stirring occasionally.

1 cup: 258 cal., 11g fat (4g sat. fat), 25mg chol., 1067mg sod., 32g carb. (5g sugars, 4g fiber), 10g pro.

FAST FIX

CHICKEN CUCUMBER PITAS

I wanted a good recipe for pita stuffing. Seeing the large stack of garden-fresh cucumbers on my counter, I decided to improvise and create my own recipe. It was a huge hit.
—Sheena Wellard, Nampa, ID

Takes: 25 min. • **Makes:** 6 servings

- **2 cups cubed cooked chicken breast**
- **1 large cucumber, quartered, seeded and sliced**
- **1 can (2¼ oz.) sliced ripe olives, drained**
- **1 medium tomato, seeded and chopped**
- **1 small sweet red pepper, chopped**
- **½ cup cubed cheddar cheese**
- **¼ cup chopped red onion**

DRESSING

- **½ cup ranch salad dressing**
- **¼ cup mayonnaise**
- **1 Tbsp. Italian salad dressing**
- **¼ tsp. garlic powder**
- **¼ tsp. pepper**
- **12 pita pocket halves**

In a large bowl, combine the first seven ingredients. In a small bowl, combine the ranch dressing, mayonnaise, Italian dressing, garlic powder and pepper; pour over the chicken mixture and toss to coat. Fill each pita half with a scant ½ cup of the chicken mixture.

2 filled pita halves: 445 cal., 22g fat (5g sat. fat), 49mg chol., 747mg sod., 37g carb. (4g sugars, 2g fiber), 22g pro.

* HEALTH TIP * Substitute reduced-fat mayo and dressings to save 60 calories and 8 grams of fat per serving.

TEST KITCHEN TIP

Warm the pitas in the microwave for a few seconds to make them more pliable and easier to fill without ripping. For a meatless sandwich, replace the chicken with a can of garbanzo beans.

FAST FIX

CHICKEN TACO POCKETS

We love these easy taco-flavored sandwiches made with crescent dough. Paired with a bowl of soup or a crisp salad, they make a quick and easy lunch or supper. I also like to cut them into smaller servings for parties.
—Donna Gribbins, Shelbyville, KY

Takes: 25 min. • **Makes:** 8 servings

- **2 tubes (8 oz. each) refrigerated crescent rolls**
- **½ cup salsa, plus more for serving**
- **½ cup sour cream**
- **2 Tbsp. taco seasoning**
- **1 cup shredded rotisserie chicken**
- **1 cup shredded cheddar cheese**
- **Shredded lettuce, guacamole and additional sour cream, optional**

1. Preheat oven to 375°. Unroll one tube of crescent dough and separate it into two rectangles; press the perforations to seal. Repeat with the second tube. In a bowl, combine the salsa, sour cream and taco seasoning. Spoon chicken onto the left side of each rectangle; top with the salsa mixture. Sprinkle with cheese. Fold dough over filling; pinch edges to seal.
2. Place on an ungreased baking sheet. Bake until golden brown, 13-15 minutes. Cut each in half. Serve with salsa and desired toppings.

½ pocket: 393 cal., 24g fat (7g sat. fat), 47mg chol., 896mg sod., 29g carb. (7g sugars, 0 fiber), 16g pro.

TEST KITCHEN TIP

Take extra care when pressing the crescent dough to seal the perforations. Patch any thin spots to prevent the filling from leaking while they bake. Make these more fun and delicious with a dipping sauce. Try salsa, guacamole, sour cream or ranch dressing.

EAT SMART | FAST FIX

WATERMELON GAZPACHO

My refreshing gazpacho is a delightfully simple, elegant dish. Serve as a side or with pita and hummus for a meal.
—Nicole Deelah, Nashville, TN

Takes: 25 min. • **Makes:** 4 servings (1 qt.)

- **4 cups cubed watermelon, seeded, divided**
- **2 Tbsp. lime juice**
- **1 Tbsp. grated lime zest**
- **1 tsp. minced fresh gingerroot**
- **1 tsp. salt**
- **1 cup chopped tomato**
- **½ cup chopped cucumber**
- **½ cup chopped green pepper**
- **¼ cup minced fresh cilantro**
- **2 Tbsp. chopped green onion**
- **1 Tbsp. finely chopped seeded jalapeno pepper**
- **Watermelon wedges, optional**

1. Puree 3 cups of the watermelon in a blender. Cut the remaining watermelon into ½-in. pieces; set aside.
2. In a large bowl, combine watermelon puree, lime juice, lime zest, ginger and salt. Stir in the tomato, cucumber, green pepper, cilantro, onion, jalapeno and the cubed watermelon. Chill until serving. If desired, serve with a wedge of watermelon.

Note: Wear disposable gloves when cutting hot peppers; the oils can burn skin. Avoid touching your face.

1 cup: 58 cal., 0 fat (0 sat. fat), 0 chol., 599mg sod., 18g carb. (15g sugars, 2g fiber), 1g pro.
Diabetic exchanges: 1 fruit.

WATERMELON GAZPACHO

Give Me Five or Fewer

With a great recipe, you can make an amazing meal with only a handful of items. All of these recipes can be made with five or fewer ingredients (not including water, salt, pepper and oil).

Garlic-Butter Steak (p. 72) **Aloha Pizza** (p. 79) **Honey Lemon Schnitzel** (p. 75) **Slow-Cooker Turkey Breast** (p. 77) **Asian Salmon Tacos** (p. 78)

LEMON BASIL SALMON

5 INGREDIENTS | EAT SMART | FAST FIX

LEMON BASIL SALMON

We eat a lot of salmon, and my husband likes trying different herbs and spices. He came up with this easy, foil-packet recipe for flaky, fork-tender salmon. This makes a tasty campfire meal, too!
—Marianne Bauman, Modesto, CA

Takes: 20 min. • **Makes:** 2 servings

2 salmon fillets (5 oz. each)
1 Tbsp. butter, melted
1 Tbsp. minced fresh basil
1 Tbsp. lemon juice
⅛ tsp. salt
⅛ tsp. pepper
Lemon wedges, optional

1. Prepare grill for medium heat. Place each fillet, skin side down, on a piece of heavy-duty foil (about 12 in. square). Mix melted butter, basil, lemon juice, salt and pepper; spoon over salmon. Fold foil around fish, sealing tightly.

2. Cook in covered grill until the fish just begins to flake easily with a fork, 10-15 minutes. Open foil carefully to allow the steam to escape. If desired, serve with lemon wedges.

1 fillet: 223 cal., 13g fat (3g sat. fat), 71mg chol., 219mg sod., 1g carb. (0 sugars, 0 fiber), 24g pro. **Diabetic exchanges:** 4 lean meat, 1½ fat.

5 INGREDIENTS | EAT SMART | FAST FIX

GRILLED STEAK & MUSHROOM SALAD

My husband loves this—he feels as if he's eating a healthy salad and getting his steak, too! I always serve it with some homemade bread.
—Julie Cashion, Sanford, FL

Takes: 30 min. • **Makes:** 6 servings

6 Tbsp. olive oil, divided
2 Tbsp. Dijon mustard, divided
½ tsp. salt
¼ tsp. pepper
1 beef top sirloin steak (1½ lbs.)
1 lb. sliced fresh mushrooms
¼ cup red wine vinegar
1 medium bunch romaine, torn

1. In a small bowl, whisk 1 Tbsp. oil, 1 Tbsp. mustard and the salt and pepper; set aside.

2. Grill steak, covered, over medium-hot heat for 4 minutes. Turn; spread with the mustard mixture. Grill 4 minutes longer or until the meat reaches desired doneness (for medium-rare, a thermometer should read 135°; for medium, 140°; for medium-well, 145°).

3. Meanwhile, in a large skillet, cook mushrooms in 1 Tbsp. oil until tender. Stir in the vinegar and the remaining oil and mustard.

4. Thinly slice steak across the grain; add to the mushroom mixture. Serve over romaine.

1 serving: 299 cal., 20g fat (4g sat. fat), 63mg chol., 378mg sod., 6g carb. (1g sugars, 2g fiber), 25g pro.

5 INGREDIENTS | FAST FIX

FIESTA RAVIOLI

I adapted this recipe to suit our love for spicy food. The ravioli taste like mini enchiladas! I serve them with a Mexican-inspired salad and pineapple sherbet for dessert.

—Debbie Purdue, Westland, MI

Takes: 20 min. • **Makes:** 6 servings

1 pkg. (25 oz.) frozen beef ravioli
1 can (10 oz.) enchilada sauce
1 cup salsa
2 cups shredded Monterey Jack cheese
1 can (2¼ oz.) sliced ripe olives, drained

1. Cook the ravioli according to package directions. Meanwhile, in a large skillet, combine the enchilada sauce and salsa. Cook and stir over medium heat until heated through.
2. Drain the ravioli; add to sauce and gently stir to coat. Top with cheese and olives. Cover and cook over low heat until the cheese is melted, 3-4 minutes.

1 serving: 470 cal., 20g fat (9g sat. fat), 74mg chol., 1342mg sod., 48g carb. (4g sugars, 6g fiber), 23g pro.

5 INGREDIENTS | EAT SMART | FAST FIX

CURRY SHRIMP LINGUINE

Curry, cilantro and coconut milk make this dish exciting and different. It's also delicious prepared with Thai rice noodles or spaghetti.

—Jana Rippee, Casa Grande, AZ

Takes: 25 min. • **Makes:** 6 servings

1 pkg. (16 oz.) linguine
3 tsp. curry powder
1 can (13.66 oz.) light coconut milk
½ tsp. salt
¼ tsp. pepper
1¼ lbs. uncooked medium shrimp, peeled and deveined
⅓ cup minced fresh cilantro

1. Cook linguine according to package directions. Meanwhile, in a large skillet over medium heat, toast curry powder for 2 minutes, stirring frequently. Stir in the milk, salt and pepper.
2. Bring to a boil. Add shrimp; cook until shrimp turn pink, 5-6 minutes. Drain the linguine; toss with shrimp mixture and fresh cilantro.

1½ cups: 406 cal., 8g fat (4g sat. fat), 115mg chol., 313mg sod., 58g carb. (4g sugars, 3g fiber), 26g pro.

FIESTA RAVIOLI

5 INGREDIENTS | FAST FIX

SIMPLE SWEET & TANGY PORK CHOPS

Just a few ingredients are all that's needed for these tender chops. Whenever I serve these to company, they get rave reviews and I get recipe requests.

—Jami Ouellette, Houston, TX

Takes: 30 min. • **Makes:** 2 servings

¼ cup beer or beef broth
4 tsp. ketchup
1 Tbsp. brown sugar
2 bone-in center-cut pork loin chops (¾ in. thick and 7 oz. each)
⅛ tsp. salt
Dash pepper
1 Tbsp. canola oil

1. Mix beer, ketchup and brown sugar. Sprinkle pork chops with salt and pepper.
2. In a large skillet, heat oil over medium heat; brown chops on both sides. Add beer mixture to pan; bring to a boil. Reduce heat; simmer, uncovered, until a thermometer inserted in pork reads 145°, 1-2 minutes. Remove chops from pan; keep warm.
3. Return sauce to a boil; cook and stir until slightly thickened. Serve over pork.

1 pork chop: 432 cal., 25g fat (7g sat. fat), 111mg chol., 353mg sod., 11g carb. (10g sugars, 0 fiber), 36g pro.

5 INGREDIENTS | EAT SMART | FAST FIX

PORK CHOPS WITH DIJON SAUCE

This dish tastes rich but isn't high in fat. It's easy for weeknights and the creamy sauce makes it special enough for weekends.
—Bonnie Brown-Watson, Houston, TX

Takes: 25 min. • **Makes:** 4 servings

- **4 boneless pork loin chops (6 oz. each)**
- **¼ tsp. salt**
- **¼ tsp. pepper**
- **2 tsp. canola oil**
- **⅓ cup reduced-sodium chicken broth**
- **2 Tbsp. Dijon mustard**
- **⅓ cup half-and-half cream**

1. Sprinkle pork chops with salt and pepper. In a large skillet coated with cooking spray, brown chops in oil until a thermometer reads 145°, 4-5 minutes on each side or. Remove and keep warm.

2. Stir broth into the skillet, scraping up any browned bits. Stir in mustard and half-and-half. Bring to a boil. Reduce the heat; simmer, uncovered, until thickened, 5-6 minutes, stirring occasionally. Serve with pork chops.

1 pork chop: 283 cal., 14g fat (5g sat. fat), 92mg chol., 432mg sod., 1g carb. (1g sugars, 0 fiber), 34g pro. **Diabetic exchanges:** 5 lean meat, 2 fat.

5 INGREDIENTS | EAT SMART | FAST FIX

FIVE-SPICE TUNA

Add Asian flair to tuna steaks with delightful results! If you want a bolder taste, marinate the tuna for 30 minutes.
—Linda Murray, Allenstown, NH

Takes: 30 min. • **Makes:** 4 servings

- **1 Tbsp. sugar**
- **1 Tbsp. reduced-sodium soy sauce**
- **1 Tbsp. sesame oil**
- **½ tsp. Chinese five-spice powder**
- **½ tsp. salt**
- **¼ tsp. pepper**
- **4 tuna steaks (1 in. thick and 6 oz. each)**

1. In a large bowl or shallow dish, combine the first six ingredients. Add tuna and turn to coat. Refrigerate for 15 minutes.

2. Drain tuna, discarding the marinade. Place tuna on a broiler pan coated with cooking spray. Broil 3-4 in. from the heat until the fish flakes easily with a fork, 3-5 minutes on each side.

1 serving: 230 cal., 5g fat (1g sat. fat), 77mg chol., 509mg sod., 4g carb. (3g sugars, 0 fiber), 40g pro. **Diabetic exchanges:** 5 lean meat, ½ fat.

PORK CHOPS WITH DIJON SAUCE

5 INGREDIENTS | FAST FIX

GARLIC-BUTTER STEAK

PICTURED ON P. 69

This quick and easy skillet entree is definitely restaurant quality and sure to become a staple at your house, too!
—Lily Julow, Lawrenceville, GA

Takes: 20 min. • **Makes:** 2 servings

- **2 Tbsp. butter, softened, divided**
- **1 tsp. minced fresh parsley**
- **½ tsp. minced garlic**
- **¼ tsp. reduced-sodium soy sauce**
- **1 beef flat iron steak or boneless top sirloin steak (¾ lb.)**
- **⅛ tsp. salt**
- **⅛ tsp. pepper**

1. Mix 1 Tbsp. butter, parsley, garlic and soy sauce.

2. Sprinkle steak with salt and pepper. In a large skillet, heat the remaining butter over medium heat. Add steak; cook until the meat reaches desired doneness (for medium-rare, a thermometer should read 135°; for medium, 140°, for medium-well, 145°), 4-7 minutes per side. Serve with garlic butter.

1 serving: 316 cal., 20g fat (10g sat. fat), 124mg chol., 337mg sod., 0 carb. (0 sugars, 0 fiber), 32g pro.

5 INGREDIENTS

LAVENDER CHICKEN

The lavender in this recipe gives off an amazing aroma while the chicken is grilling. The subtle flavor will win over even those leery of cooking with flowers!
—Colleen Duffley, Santa Rosa Beach, FL

Prep: 15 min. + marinating • **Grill:** 30 min.
Makes: 6 servings

- **⅔ cup barbecue sauce**
- **¼ cup dried lavender flowers**
- **¼ cup olive oil**
- **2 garlic cloves, minced**
- **1 broiler/fryer chicken (3 to 4 lbs.), cut up**

1. In a large bowl or shallow dish, combine the barbecue sauce, lavender, oil and garlic. Add the chicken and turn to coat. Refrigerate for up to 4 hours.
2. Drain chicken, discarding the marinade. Place the chicken skin side down on grill rack. Grill, covered, over medium heat for 20 minutes. Turn; grill until juices run clear, 10-15 minutes longer.
1 serving: 315 cal., 20g fat (5g sat. fat), 88mg chol., 243mg sod., 3g carb. (2g sugars, 0 fiber), 28g pro.

SMOKY SPANISH CHICKEN

5 INGREDIENTS | FAST FIX

REUBEN PIZZA

We do a lot of experimenting for Friday pizza nights so we don't have the same thing every week. This pizza is so easy, and it tastes like a Reuben sandwich!
—Nicole German, Hutchinson, MN

Takes: 25 min. • **Makes:** 6 servings

- **1 prebaked 12-in. pizza crust**
- **⅔ cup Thousand Island salad dressing**
- **½ lb. sliced deli corned beef, cut into strips**
- **1 can (14 oz.) sauerkraut, rinsed and well drained**
- **2 cups shredded Swiss cheese**

Preheat oven to 400°. Place the crust on an ungreased or parchment-lined baking sheet. Spread with salad dressing. Top with corned beef, sauerkraut and cheese. Bake until the cheese is melted, 12-15 minutes.
1 slice: 480 cal., 27g fat (10g sat. fat), 57mg chol., 1527mg sod., 36g carb. (6g sugars, 3g fiber), 23g pro.

5 INGREDIENTS | FAST FIX

SMOKY SPANISH CHICKEN

After enjoying a similar dish at a Spanish tapas restaurant, my husband and I were eager to make our own version at home. If I want to make it extra healthy, I remove the skin from the chicken after browning.
—Ryan Haley, San Diego, CA

Takes: 30 min. • **Makes:** 4 servings

- **3 tsp. smoked paprika**
- **½ tsp. salt**
- **¼ tsp. pepper**
- **1 Tbsp. water**
- **4 bone-in chicken thighs**
- **1½ cups baby portobello mushrooms, quartered**
- **1 cup chopped green onions, divided**
- **1 can (14½ oz.) fire-roasted diced tomatoes, undrained**

1. Mix the first four ingredients; rub over the chicken.
2. Place a large skillet over medium heat. Add chicken, skin side down. Cook until browned, 4-5 minutes per side; remove from pan. Remove all but 1 Tbsp. of the drippings from the pan.
3. In the drippings, saute mushrooms and ½ cup green onions over medium heat until tender, 1-2 minutes. Stir in tomatoes. Add chicken; bring to a boil. Reduce heat; simmer, covered, until a thermometer inserted in the chicken reads 170°, 10-12 minutes. Top with the remaining green onions.
1 serving: 272 cal., 15g fat (4g sat. fat), 81mg chol., 646mg sod., 10g carb. (4g sugars, 2g fiber), 25g pro.

TEST KITCHEN TIP

Baby portobello (or crimini) mushrooms have a firmer texture and a deeper, earthier flavor than white mushrooms Smoked paprika is made from peppers that are dried over wood fires, giving it a rich, smoky flavor. Take advantage of the flavorful sauce and serve this with a starchy side like couscous or rice.

WEEKNIGHT LAZY LASAGNA

5 INGREDIENTS | EAT SMART | FAST FIX

WEEKNIGHT LAZY LASAGNA

On hectic nights, who has time to layer up lasagna? My version cuts down on prep, but keeps all the cheesy, saucy, noodle-y goodness that makes lasagna a favorite.
—Nancy Foust, Stoneboro, PA

Takes: 30 min. • **Makes:** 6 servings

- **8 oz. uncooked lasagna noodles, broken into 2-in. pieces**
- **1 cup part-skim ricotta cheese**
- **1 cup shredded part-skim mozzarella cheese, divided**
- **⅓ cup grated Parmesan cheese**
- **1 jar (24 oz.) pasta sauce with meat**

1. Preheat oven to 400°. Cook lasagna noodles according to package directions. Meanwhile, in a large bowl, mix ricotta cheese, ½ cup mozzarella cheese and the Parmesan cheese. Drain noodles well; stir into the cheese mixture.
2. Spread 1 cup pasta sauce into a greased 11x7-in. baking dish. Layer with half the noodle mixture and 1 cup sauce; layer with the remaining noodle mixture and sauce. Sprinkle with remaining cheese.
3. Cover with greased foil; bake until heated through, 10-15 minutes.
1 serving: 332 cal., 10g fat (5g sat. fat), 29mg chol., 901mg sod., 45g carb. (11g sugars, 3g fiber), 17g pro.

5 INGREDIENTS | FAST FIX

HONEY LEMON SCHNITZEL

PICTURED ON P. 69

These pork cutlets are coated in a sweet sauce with honey, lemon juice and butter. They're good enough for company, but perfect for a quick weeknight meal, too.
—Carole Fraser, North York, ON

Takes: 20 min. • **Makes:** 4 servings

- **3 Tbsp. all-purpose flour**
- **¾ tsp. salt**
- **¾ tsp. pepper**
- **4 pork sirloin cutlets (4 oz. each)**
- **2 Tbsp. butter**
- **¼ cup lemon juice**
- **¼ cup honey**

1. Mix flour, salt and pepper; sprinkle over both sides of cutlets. In a large skillet, heat butter over medium heat. Add the pork; cook until a thermometer reads 145°, 2-3 minutes per side. Remove from pan.
2. Add lemon juice and honey to skillet; cook and stir over medium heat until thickened, about 3 minutes. Add pork; heat through.
1 serving: 291 cal., 10g fat (5g sat. fat), 87mg chol., 561mg sod., 23g carb. (18g sugars, 0 fiber), 26g pro.

CHEESY BLACK BEAN NACHOS

5 INGREDIENTS | FAST FIX

CHEESY BLACK BEAN NACHOS

We're trying to go meatless once a week, and this dish helps make those meals fun, quick and super delicious. It's also a smart way to use beans and canned tomatoes from your pantry.
—Cynthia Nelson, Saskatoon, SK

Takes: 20 min. • **Makes:** 4 servings

- **1 can (15 oz.) black beans, rinsed and drained**
- **1 can (14½ oz.) diced tomatoes, well drained**
- **3 to 4 jalapeno peppers, seeded and sliced**
- **4 cups multigrain tortilla chips**
- **1 cup shredded cheddar cheese**

Optional toppings: sour cream, chopped fresh cilantro and additional jalapeno slices

1. Preheat oven to 350°. Mix beans, tomatoes and jalapenos. Arrange chips in an even layer in a 15x10x1-in. pan. Top with the bean mixture and cheese.
2. Bake, uncovered, until the cheese is melted, 10-12 minutes. Serve immediately with toppings as desired.
Note: Wear disposable gloves when cutting hot peppers; the oils can burn exposed skin. Avoid touching your face.
1 serving: 371 cal., 17g fat (6g sat. fat), 28mg chol., 672mg sod., 42g carb. (6g sugars, 7g fiber), 15g pro.

TEST KITCHEN TIP

The multigrain tortilla chips in this dish make it a little healthier; you could use regular tortilla chips instead. Spreading out the ingredients in a large pan helps the chips stay crunchy and evenly coated with toppings.

CRISPY DILL TILAPIA

5 INGREDIENTS | EAT SMART

SIMPLE ASIAN SALMON

We try to eat healthy, and fish is one of our favorite proteins. I find different ways to make salmon to give our meals variety; this dish came about as a way to do just that.
—Jennifer Berry, Lexington, OH

Prep: 15 min. + marinating • **Bake:** 15 min.
Makes: 4 servings

- **1 cup sesame ginger salad dressing, divided**
- **4 green onions, chopped**
- **2 Tbsp. minced fresh cilantro**
- **4 salmon fillets (4 oz. each)**

1. In a large bowl or shallow dish, combine ⅔ cup dressing, onions and cilantro. Add salmon and turn to coat. Refrigerate for 30 minutes.
2. Preheat oven to 375°. Drain salmon and discard marinade. Place salmon in a greased 8-in. square baking dish. Bake, uncovered, 10 minutes. Baste with the remaining dressing. Bake until fish flakes easily with a fork, 5-10 minutes longer. Drizzle with pan juices before serving.
1 fillet: 234 cal., 15g fat (3g sat. fat), 57mg chol., 208mg sod., 4g carb. (3g sugars, 0 fiber), 19g pro. **Diabetic exchanges:** 3 lean meat, 2 fat.

5 INGREDIENTS | EAT SMART | FAST FIX

CRISPY DILL TILAPIA

Every week I try to serve a new fish dish. With its fresh dill and delicious panko bread crumb herb crust, this recipe with mild tilapia is a winner.
—Tamara Huron, New Market, AL

Takes: 20 min. • **Makes:** 4 servings

- **1 cup panko (Japanese) bread crumbs**
- **2 Tbsp. olive oil**
- **2 Tbsp. snipped fresh dill**
- **¼ tsp. salt**
- **⅛ tsp. pepper**
- **4 tilapia fillets (6 oz. each)**
- **1 Tbsp. lemon juice**
- **Lemon wedges**

1. Preheat oven to 400°. Toss together the first five ingredients.
2. Place tilapia in a 15x10x1-in. baking pan coated with cooking spray; brush with lemon juice. Top with the crumb mixture, patting to help it adhere.
3. Bake, uncovered, on an upper oven rack until the fish just begins to flake easily with a fork, 12-15 minutes. Serve with the lemon wedges.
1 fillet: 256 cal., 9g fat (2g sat. fat), 83mg chol., 251mg sod., 10g carb. (1g sugars, 1g fiber), 34g pro. **Diabetic exchanges:** 5 lean meat, 1½ fat, ½ starch.

TEST KITCHEN TIP

This breading would complement most types of fish—try it on salmon or cod if you prefer. If you don't have fresh dill, a bit of fresh thyme would be great. Tossing the bread crumbs with a bit of oil helps the coating crisp up in the short amount of time it takes to cook the fish.

SLOW COOKER | 5 INGREDIENTS | EAT SMART

SLOW-COOKER TURKEY BREAST

PICTURED ON P. 69

Here's an easy recipe to try when you're craving turkey. It uses ingredients that most cooks already have in their pantries, which is handy.
—Maria Juco, Milwaukee, WI

Prep: 10 min. • **Cook:** 5 hours
Makes: 14 servings

- 1 **bone-in turkey breast (6 to 7 lbs.), skin removed**
- 1 **Tbsp. olive oil**
- 1 **tsp. dried minced garlic**
- 1 **tsp. seasoned salt**
- 1 **tsp. paprika**
- 1 **tsp. Italian seasoning**
- 1 **tsp. pepper**
- ½ **cup water**

Brush turkey with oil. Combine the garlic, seasoned salt, paprika, Italian seasoning and pepper; rub over turkey. Transfer to a 6-qt. slow cooker; add water. Cover and cook on low for 5-6 hours or until tender.
4 oz. cooked turkey: 174 cal., 2g fat (0 sat. fat), 101mg chol., 172mg sod., 0 carb. (0 sugars, 0 fiber), 37g pro. **Diabetic exchanges:** 4 lean meat.
Lemon-Garlic Turkey Breast: Combine ¼ cup minced fresh parsley, 8 minced garlic cloves, 4 tsp. grated lemon zest, 2 tsp. salt-free lemon-pepper seasoning and 1½ tsp. salt; rub over turkey breast. Add water and cook as directed.

SLOW COOKER | 5 INGREDIENTS

MEXICAN BUBBLE PIZZA

This tasty pizza offers a new way to experience Mexican cuisine. Serve it at your next party and watch it disappear before your eyes.
—Jackie Hannahs, Cedar Springs, MI

Prep: 15 min. • **Cook:** 3 hours
Makes: 6 servings

- 1½ **lbs. ground beef**
- 1 **can (10¾ oz.) condensed tomato soup, undiluted**
- ¾ **cup water**
- 1 **envelope taco seasoning**
- 1 **tube (16.3 oz.) large refrigerated buttermilk biscuits**
- 2 **cups shredded cheddar cheese**

Optional toppings: shredded lettuce, chopped tomatoes, salsa, sliced ripe olives, sour cream and thinly sliced green onions

1. Line a 6-qt. slow cooker with a double thickness of heavy-duty foil. Coat with cooking spray.
2. In a large skillet, cook the beef over medium heat until meat is no longer pink, 6-8 minutes, breaking into crumbles; drain. Stir in the soup, water and taco seasoning. Bring to a boil. Reduce heat; simmer, uncovered, until mixture is slightly thickened, 3-5 minutes.
3. Cut each biscuit into four pieces; gently stir into the beef mixture. Transfer to slow cooker. Cook, covered, on low 3-4 hours or until dough is cooked through. Sprinkle with cheese. Cook, covered, until cheese is melted, about 5 minutes longer. Serve with toppings of your choice.
1 serving: 643 cal., 35g fat (15g sat. fat), 109mg chol., 1870mg sod., 46g carb. (8g sugars, 2g fiber), 35g pro.

★★★★★ **READER REVIEW**

"A wonderful, quick and delicious idea! It was a nice lunch for a small, unexpected crowd."

ROSEMARY TASTEOFHOME.COM

MEXICAN BUBBLE PIZZA

SLOW COOKER | 5 INGREDIENTS

TENDER BARBECUED CHICKEN

After a long day at work, a slow-cooked meal is a big help. One family favorite is this moist, slow-simmered chicken. Just choose your favorite barbecue sauce and have at it!

—Jacqueline Blanton, Gaffney, SC

Prep: 15 min. • **Cook:** 4 hours
Makes: 4 servings

- **1 broiler/fryer chicken (3 to 4 lbs.), cut up**
- **1 Tbsp. canola oil**
- **1 medium onion, thinly sliced**
- **1 medium lemon, thinly sliced**
- **1 bottle (18 oz.) barbecue sauce**
- **¾ cup cola**

In a large skillet, brown chicken in oil in batches. Transfer to a 3-qt. slow cooker. Top with the onion and lemon slices. Combine the barbecue sauce and cola; pour over the chicken. Cover and cook on low for 4-5 hours or until the chicken is tender. If desired, skim the fat and thicken cooking juices; serve with chicken.

1 serving: 533 cal., 27g fat (6g sat. fat), 131mg chol., 1157mg sod., 26g carb. (22g sugars, 3g fiber), 44g pro.

*** HEALTH TIP *** Most of the sodium in this dish comes from the generous amount of prepared barbecue sauce. To reduce the salt content, use half the called-for amount of sauce and cola.

TENDER BARBECUED CHICKEN

5 INGREDIENTS

BAKED PORK CHOPS WITH APPLE SLICES

A friend who raises pork shared this recipe with me. The lightly breaded chops with simple glazed apples on the side make a mouthwatering meal.

—Burlin Jones, Beloit, WI

Prep: 15 min. • **Bake:** 1 hour
Makes: 6 servings

- **3 Tbsp. all-purpose flour**
- **1½ tsp. salt**
- **½ tsp. pepper**
- **6 bone-in pork loin chops (1½ in. thick and 8 oz. each)**
- **¼ cup water**
- **1 jar (12 oz.) currant jelly**
- **3 to 4 medium tart apples, thinly sliced**

1. Preheat the oven to 350°. In a shallow bowl, combine flour, salt and pepper. Coat pork chops. Place in a greased 15x10x1-in. baking pan. Add water to the pan. Bake, uncovered, until a thermometer reads 145°, about 1 hour. Let stand 5 minutes.
2. In a large skillet, melt jelly. Add apples. Cook over low heat until the apples are tender, 5-7 minutes, turning occasionally. Serve with pork chops.

1 serving: 250 cal., 3g fat (1g sat. fat), 19mg chol., 603mg sod., 50g carb. (42g sugars, 2g fiber), 7g pro.

5 INGREDIENTS | EAT SMART | FAST FIX

ASIAN SALMON TACOS

PICTURED ON P. 69

This Asian-Mexican fusion dish is ready in minutes. If the salmon begins to stick, just add 2 to 3 tablespoons of water and continue cooking.

—Marisa Raponi, Vaughan, ON

Takes: 20 min. • **Makes:** 4 servings

- **1 lb. salmon fillet, skin removed, cut into 1-in. cubes**
- **2 Tbsp. hoisin sauce**
- **1 Tbsp. olive oil**
- **Shredded lettuce**
- **8 corn tortillas (6 in.), warmed**
- **1½ tsp. black sesame seeds**
- **Mango salsa, optional**

1. Toss salmon with hoisin sauce. In a large nonstick skillet, heat oil over medium-high heat. Cook salmon until it begins to flake easily with a fork, turning gently to brown all sides, 3-5 minutes.
2. Serve salmon and lettuce in tortillas; sprinkle with sesame seeds. If desired, top with salsa.

2 tacos: 335 cal., 16g fat (3g sat. fat), 57mg chol., 208mg sod., 25g carb. (3g sugars, 3g fiber), 22g pro. **Diabetic exchanges:** 3 lean meat, 2 starch, 1 fat.

TEST KITCHEN TIP

Look for thick center pieces of salmon so your cubes will be consistently sized for even cooking.

Hoisin sauce is used as both a sauce and a condiment in Chinese and Vietnamese cooking. The flavor of hoisin sauce varies quite a bit between brands, so feel free to adjust the amount used.

Black sesame seeds have a slightly nuttier flavor than white ones. If you don't have them, use toasted white sesame seeds instead.

5 INGREDIENTS | EAT SMART | FAST FIX

BLACK BEAN & BEEF TOSTADAS

Just a handful of ingredients add up to one of our family's favorites. The recipe is also easy to double for company.
—Susan Brown, Kansas City, KS

Takes: 30 min. • **Makes:** 4 servings

- **½ lb. lean ground beef (90% lean)**
- **1 can (10 oz.) diced tomatoes and green chilies, undrained**
- **1 can (15 oz.) black beans, rinsed and drained**
- **1 can (16 oz.) refried beans, warmed**
- **8 tostada shells**
- **Optional toppings: shredded reduced-fat Mexican cheese blend, shredded lettuce, salsa and sour cream**

1. In a large skillet, cook and crumble beef over medium-high heat until no longer pink, 4-6 minutes. Stir in tomatoes; bring to a boil. Reduce heat; simmer, uncovered, until the liquid is almost evaporated, 6-8 minutes. Stir in black beans; heat through.
2. To serve, spread refried beans over tostada shells. Top with the beef mixture; add toppings as desired.

2 tostadas: 392 cal., 14g fat (4g sat. fat), 35mg chol., 1011mg sod., 46g carb. (2g sugars, 10g fiber), 23g pro. **Diabetic exchanges:** 3 starch, 3 lean meat.

5 INGREDIENTS | FAST FIX

ALOHA PIZZA

PICTURED ON P. 69

This pizza came together when I had to take something to a gathering but had no time to shop. I raided the pantry and fridge and discovered this happy combo!
—Wendy Huffman, Bloomington, IL

Takes: 30 min. • **Makes:** 6 pieces

- **1 tube (8 oz.) refrigerated crescent rolls**
- **½ cup honey barbecue sauce**
- **1 pkg. (6 oz.) ready-to-use grilled chicken breast strips**
- **1 cup pineapple tidbits**
- **1½ cups shredded Mexican cheese blend**

1. Preheat oven to 375°. Unroll crescent dough into a greased 13x9-in. baking pan; seal the seams and perforations. Bake until golden brown, 6-8 minutes.
2. Spread barbecue sauce over the crust. Top with the chicken, pineapple and cheese. Bake until the cheese is melted, 12-15 minutes longer.

1 piece: 351 cal., 18g fat (8g sat. fat), 44mg chol., 985mg sod., 29g carb. (14g sugars, 0 fiber), 15g pro.

TEST KITCHEN TIP

If you have leftover chicken on hand, use 1½ to 2 cups of cubed or shredded meat instead of the grilled strips. Shredded Monterey Jack or mozzarella cheese would also be delicious on this pizza.

BLACK BEAN & BEEF TOSTADAS

30-Minute Dinners

Need a scrumptious meal on the table—fast? Whether you're planning a weeknight dinner or fitting a meal into a jam-packed weekend, these recipes will be finished in a flash...and eaten even faster!

Maple Pork Chops (p. 88) **Savory Steak Salad** (p. 83) **Lemony Scallops with Angel Hair Pasta** (p. 84) **Garlic Salmon Linguine** (p. 82) **Spanish Noodles & Ground Beef** (p. 104)

FAST FIX

EASY SWEET & SPICY CHICKEN

Tangy pineapple and peppers, tender chicken and sweet marmalade make a delicious combo. The chili powder and picante sauce add zip.
—Cassandra Corridon, Frederick, MD

Takes: 20 min. • **Makes:** 6 servings

- **1 can (20 oz.) unsweetened pineapple chunks, undrained**
- **1⅓ cups orange marmalade**
- **1 cup picante sauce**
- **1 tsp. chili powder, divided**
- **1¼ lbs. boneless skinless chicken breasts, cut into strips**
- **1 large green pepper, cut into 1-in. pieces**
- **1 medium onion, chopped**
- **1 Tbsp. canola oil**
- **Hot cooked rice**
- **Minced fresh cilantro**

1. In a bowl, combine the pineapple, marmalade, picante sauce and ½ tsp. chili powder; set aside. Sprinkle the remaining chili powder over chicken.
2. In a large skillet, saute the chicken, green pepper and onion in oil until the chicken juices run clear. Reduce heat; add the pineapple mixture. Cook until heated through, 2-3 minutes. Serve with rice; garnish with cilantro.

1 cup: 378 cal., 5g fat (1g sat. fat), 52mg chol., 393mg sod., 65g carb. (57g sugars, 2g fiber), 21g pro.

FAST FIX

GARLIC SALMON LINGUINE

PICTURED ON P. 81

This garlicky pasta is so nice to make on busy weeknights because I usually have everything I need already on hand. I serve mine with asparagus, rolls and fruit.
—Theresa Hagan, Glendale, AZ

Takes: 20 min. • **Makes:** 6 servings

- **1 pkg. (16 oz.) linguine**
- **⅓ cup olive oil**
- **3 garlic cloves, minced**
- **1 can (14¾ oz.) salmon, drained, bones and skin removed**
- **¾ cup chicken broth**
- **¼ cup minced fresh parsley**
- **½ tsp. salt**
- **⅛ tsp. cayenne pepper**

1. Cook the linguine according to package directions; drain.
2. Meanwhile, in a large skillet, heat oil over medium heat. Add garlic; cook and stir until tender, about 1 minute (do not allow to brown). Stir in the remaining ingredients; heat through. Add linguine; toss gently to combine.

1 serving: 489 cal., 19g fat (3g sat. fat), 31mg chol., 693mg sod., 56g carb. (3g sugars, 3g fiber), 25g pro.

ASPARAGUS BEEF SAUTE

FAST FIX

ASPARAGUS BEEF SAUTE

I love filet mignon but not its price, so I came up with a recipe that uses more affordable beef tenderloin tail. Now I cook it once a week—plus my husband loves taking the leftovers to work.
—Linda Flynn, Ellicott City, MD

Takes: 30 min. • **Makes:** 4 servings

- **1 lb. beef tenderloin or top sirloin steak, cut into ¾-in. cubes**
- **½ tsp. salt**
- **¼ tsp. pepper**
- **1 Tbsp. canola oil**
- **2 garlic cloves, minced**
- **1 green onion, sliced**
- **¼ cup butter, cubed**
- **1 lb. fresh asparagus, trimmed and cut into 2-in. pieces**
- **½ lb. sliced fresh mushrooms**
- **1 Tbsp. reduced-sodium soy sauce**
- **1½ tsp. lemon juice**
- **Hot cooked rice**

1. Sprinkle beef with salt and pepper. In a large skillet, heat oil over medium-high heat; saute beef 2 minutes. Add garlic and green onion; cook and stir until the beef is browned, 2-3 minutes. Remove from pan.
2. In the same skillet, heat butter over medium-high heat; saute asparagus and mushrooms until the asparagus is crisp-tender. Add beef, soy sauce and lemon juice; heat through, tossing to combine. Serve with rice.

1¼ cups beef mixture: 328 cal., 22g fat (10g sat. fat), 80mg chol., 540mg sod., 5g carb. (2g sugars, 2g fiber), 28g pro.

EAT SMART | FAST FIX

PAN-SEARED SALMON WITH CUCUMBER-DILL SAUCE

This is one of my husband's favorite recipes. Salmon is a go-to for busy nights because it cooks so quickly and goes with so many different flavors. The creamy dill sauce tastes light and fresh, and gets a nice crunch from the cucumber.

—Angela Spengler, Tampa, FL

Takes: 25 min. • **Makes:** 4 servings

- 1 **Tbsp. canola oil**
- 4 **salmon fillets (6 oz. each)**
- 1 **tsp. Italian seasoning**
- ¼ **tsp. salt**
- ½ **cup reduced-fat plain yogurt**
- ¼ **cup reduced-fat mayonnaise**
- ¼ **cup finely chopped cucumber**
- 1 **tsp. snipped fresh dill**

1. In a large skillet, heat oil over medium-high heat. Sprinkle salmon with Italian seasoning and salt. Place in skillet, skin side down. Reduce heat to medium. Cook until fish just begins to flake easily with a fork, about 5 minutes on each side.
2. Meanwhile, in a small bowl, combine yogurt, mayonnaise, cucumber and dill. Serve with the salmon.

1 salmon fillet with ¼ cup sauce: 366 cal., 25g fat (4g sat. fat), 92mg chol., 349mg sod., 4g carb. (3g sugars, 0 fiber), 31g pro. **Diabetic exchanges:** 4 lean meat, 2½ fat.

* **HEALTH TIP** * This nutritious dish provides about 2 grams of omega-3 fatty acids. Salmon is one of the best sources for this healthy fat.

TEST KITCHEN TIP

Keep an eye on the salmon. If the skillet gets too hot, the outside will get too dark before it's cooked through.

PAN-SEARED SALMON WITH CUCUMBER-DILL SAUCE

FAST FIX

SAVORY STEAK SALAD

PICTURED ON P. 81

Caramelized onion and sirloin steak seasoned with a cinnamon rub make this main dish salad different from typical versions. It's easy to toss together with packaged greens, blue cheese, dried cranberries and store-bought vinaigrette.

—*Taste of Home* Test Kitchen

Takes: 30 min. • **Makes:** 4 servings

- 2 **Tbsp. brown sugar, divided**
- 1 **tsp. salt**
- ¾ **tsp. ground cinnamon**
- ¼ **tsp. cayenne pepper**
- ¼ **tsp. pepper**
- 1 **beef top sirloin steak (1 in. thick and 1 lb.)**
- ¾ **cup balsamic vinaigrette, divided**
- 1 **medium onion, sliced**
- 2 **Tbsp. butter**
- 1 **pkg. (5 oz.) spring mix salad greens**
- ½ **cup dried cranberries**
- ¼ **cup crumbled blue cheese**

1. In a small bowl, combine 1 Tbsp. of the brown sugar, the salt, cinnamon, cayenne and pepper. Rub over both sides of steak. Brush with ¼ cup vinaigrette.
2. Place the steak on a broiler pan. Broil 4 in. from heat 5-6 minutes on each side or until meat reaches desired doneness (for medium-rare, a thermometer should read 135°; for medium, 140°; medium-well, 145°).
3. Meanwhile, in a large skillet, saute onion in butter until tender, about 10 minutes. Add the remaining brown sugar; cook and stir over medium heat until onion is browned, 5-10 minutes.
4. Cut the steak across the grain into thin slices. In a large bowl, combine greens, cranberries, blue cheese, onion and beef. Drizzle with the remaining vinaigrette; toss to coat.

1½ cups: 407 cal., 21g fat (8g sat. fat), 85mg chol., 1200mg sod., 30g carb. (24g sugars, 3g fiber), 24g pro.

* **HEALTH TIP** * With the added salt, prepared salad dressing and blue cheese, this salad is high in sodium. Decrease the salt to ¼ teaspoon and save more than 400 milligrams of sodium per serving.

PO'BOY TACOS

FAST FIX

PO'BOY TACOS

Once, when I intended to make tostadas, I misread a couple of ingredients and had to use what I had on hand. I put my own twist on a po'boy recipe and ended up with something even better.
—Cynthia Nelson, Saskatoon, SK

Takes: 30 min. • **Makes:** 4 servings

- **¼ cup mayonnaise**
- **2 Tbsp. seafood cocktail sauce**
- **½ tsp. Buffalo wing sauce**
- **½ medium ripe avocado, peeled**
- **1 Tbsp. lime juice**
- **½ cup all-purpose flour**
- **½ cup cornmeal**
- **2 Tbsp. Creole seasoning**
- **1 lb. uncooked shrimp (26-30 per lb.), peeled and deveined**
- **2 Tbsp. canola oil**
- **8 flour tortillas (6 in.)**
- **1 medium tomato, chopped**
- **2 Tbsp. minced fresh cilantro**

1. Combine mayonnaise, cocktail sauce and wing sauce; set aside. In another bowl, mash the avocado with the lime juice until combined; set aside.
2. In a shallow bowl, mix flour, cornmeal and Creole seasoning. Add shrimp, a few pieces at a time, and toss to coat; shake off excess. In a large skillet, heat oil over medium-high heat. Add shrimp; cook and stir until the shrimp turn pink, 4-6 minutes.
3. Spread the reserved avocado mixture over tortillas. Top with shrimp, the reserved mayonnaise mixture, tomato and cilantro.

2 tacos: 551 cal., 29g fat (5g sat. fat), 139mg chol., 977mg sod., 47g carb. (3g sugars, 5g fiber), 25g pro.

EAT SMART | FAST FIX

LEMONY SCALLOPS WITH ANGEL HAIR PASTA

PICTURED ON P. 81

This delicate dish tastes so bright with a touch of lemon. Serve with crusty whole grain bread, and you've got an impressive dinner that comes together in a flash.
—Thomas Faglon, Somerset, NJ

Takes: 25 min. • **Makes:** 4 servings

- **8 oz. uncooked multigrain angel hair pasta**
- **3 Tbsp. olive oil, divided**
- **1 lb. sea scallops, patted dry**
- **2 cups sliced radishes (about 1 bunch)**
- **2 garlic cloves, sliced**
- **½ tsp. crushed red pepper flakes**
- **6 green onions, thinly sliced**
- **½ tsp. kosher salt**
- **1 Tbsp. grated lemon zest**
- **¼ cup lemon juice**

1. In a 6-qt. stockpot, cook the pasta according to package directions; drain and return to pot.
2. Meanwhile, in a large skillet, heat 2 Tbsp. oil over medium-high heat; sear scallops in batches until opaque and edges are golden brown, about 2 minutes per side. Remove from skillet; keep warm.
3. In the same skillet, saute radishes, garlic and pepper flakes in the remaining oil until the radishes are tender, 2-3 minutes. Stir in green onions and salt; cook 1 minute. Add to pasta; toss to combine. Sprinkle with lemon zest and juice. Top with the scallops to serve.

1½ cups: 404 cal., 13g fat (2g sat. fat), 27mg chol., 737mg sod., 48g carb. (4g sugars, 6g fiber), 25g pro.

FAST FIX

YELLOW SQUASH TURKEY SALAD

With a wonderful mix of flavors, colors and textures, this salad can be made in minutes for lunch with friends or as a lovely light dinner on busy weeknights.
—Mildred Sherrer, Fort Worth, TX

Takes: 10 min. • **Makes:** 2 servings

- **4 cups spring mix salad greens**
- **¼ lb. thinly sliced deli smoked turkey, cut into 1-in. strips**
- **1 small yellow summer squash, halved lengthwise and sliced**
- **1 small pear, chopped**
- **½ cup dried cranberries**
- **⅓ cup honey-roasted sliced almonds**
- **¼ cup cubed cheddar cheese**
- **⅓ cup red wine vinaigrette**

In a large bowl, combine the first seven ingredients. Drizzle with vinaigrette and toss to coat. Serve immediately.

2 cups: 490 cal., 17g fat (3g sat. fat), 37mg chol., 1170mg sod., 61g carb. (48g sugars, 7g fiber), 22g pro.

FAST FIX

THAI PEANUT CHICKEN & NOODLES

This versatile chicken recipe is very similar to Pad Thai but easier to make. Instead of rice noodles, you can use mung bean noodles or any type of egg noodles.
—Kristina Segarra, Yonkers, NY

Takes: 30 min. • **Makes:** 4 servings

- **½ cup water**
- **¼ cup soy sauce**
- **2 Tbsp. rice vinegar**
- **2 Tbsp. creamy peanut butter**
- **3 garlic cloves, minced**
- **1 to 2 tsp. Sriracha Asian hot chili sauce**
- **1 tsp. sesame oil**
- **1 tsp. molasses**
- **1 pkg. (6.75 oz.) thin rice noodles**
- **2 Tbsp. peanut oil, divided**
- **1 lb. chicken tenderloins, cut into ¾-in. pieces**
- **1 medium onion, chopped**
- **Halved cucumber slices and chopped peanuts, optional**

1. For the sauce, whisk together the first eight ingredients. Bring a large saucepan of water to a boil; remove from heat. Add noodles; let stand until noodles are tender but firm, 3-4 minutes. Drain; rinse with cold water and drain well.
2. In a large skillet, heat 1 Tbsp. of peanut oil over medium-high heat; saute chicken until no longer pink, 5-7 minutes. Remove from pan.
3. In the same pan, saute onion in the remaining oil over medium-high heat until tender, 2-3 minutes. Stir in sauce; cook and stir over medium heat until slightly thickened. Add noodles and chicken; heat through, tossing to combine. If desired, top with cucumber and chopped peanuts. Serve immediately.

2 cups: 444 cal., 13g fat (2g sat. fat), 56mg chol., 1270mg sod., 48g carb. (6g sugars, 2g fiber), 34g pro.

TEST KITCHEN TIP

These noodles are lightly coated with sauce. For more peanut flavor or creamier sauce, increase the peanut butter by 1 to 2 tablespoons.

If you don't have molasses, the same amount of honey or brown sugar can be used instead.

THAI PEANUT CHICKEN & NOODLES

EAT SMART | FAST FIX

BAVARIAN APPLE-SAUSAGE HASH

This awesome recipe reflects my German roots. In the cooler months, nothing is as comforting as a hearty hash. Serve this versatile recipe as a side dish at a holiday meal or as a brunch entree over cheddar grits or topped with a fried egg.

—Crystal Schlueter, Babbitt, MN

Takes: 30 min. • **Makes:** 4 servings

- **2 Tbsp. canola oil**
- **½ cup chopped onion**
- **4 fully cooked apple chicken sausages or flavor of your choice, sliced**
- **1½ cups thinly sliced Brussels sprouts**
- **1 large tart apple, peeled and chopped**
- **1 tsp. caraway seeds**
- **¼ tsp. salt**
- **⅛ tsp. pepper**
- **2 Tbsp. finely chopped walnuts**
- **1 Tbsp. brown sugar**
- **1 Tbsp. whole grain mustard**
- **1 Tbsp. cider vinegar**

1. In a large skillet, heat oil over medium-high heat; saute the onion until tender, 1-2 minutes. Add sausages, Brussels sprouts, apple and seasonings; saute until lightly browned, 6-8 minutes.
2. Stir in walnuts, brown sugar, mustard and vinegar; cook and stir 2 minutes.

1 cup: 310 cal., 17g fat (3g sat. fat), 60mg chol., 715mg sod., 25g carb. (19g sugars, 3g fiber), 16g pro.

RASPBERRY BALSAMIC SMOKED PORK CHOPS

FAST FIX

RASPBERRY BALSAMIC SMOKED PORK CHOPS

Smoked chops are so delicious and so easy to make. They are my husband's favorite meal.

—Lynn Moretti, Oconomowoc, WI

Takes: 30 min. • **Makes:** 4 servings

- **2 large eggs**
- **¼ cup 2% milk**
- **1 cup panko (Japanese) bread crumbs**
- **1 cup finely chopped pecans**
- **4 smoked bone-in pork chops (7½ oz. each)**
- **¼ cup all-purpose flour**
- **⅓ cup balsamic vinegar**
- **2 Tbsp. brown sugar**
- **2 Tbsp. seedless raspberry jam**
- **1 Tbsp. thawed frozen orange juice concentrate**

1. Preheat oven to 425°. In a shallow bowl, whisk together eggs and milk. In another shallow bowl, toss bread crumbs with the pecans.
2. Coat pork chops with flour; shake off excess. Dip in egg mixture, then in crumb mixture, patting to help adhere. Place on a baking sheet coated with cooking spray.
3. Bake pork chops until golden brown, 15-20 minutes. Meanwhile, place the remaining ingredients in a small saucepan; bring to a boil. Cook and stir until slightly thickened, 6-8 minutes. Serve with chops.

1 pork chop with 1 Tbsp. glaze: 579 cal., 36g fat (10g sat. fat), 106mg chol., 1374mg sod., 36g carb. (22g sugars, 3g fiber), 32g pro.

TEST KITCHEN TIP

If you can't find smoked pork chops or want a lower-sodium alternative, this recipe will work with fresh chops, too. Season the meat with salt and pepper before coating, and cook the chops to at least 145°.

This recipe also will work with a variety of nuts, so feel free to try other ones. Hazelnuts and almonds would both be tasty.

AST FIX

SMOTHERED CHICKEN

You can't go wrong serving up my quick skillet specialty. I top tender chicken breasts with mushrooms, bacon, green onions and cheese. Add a side salad, and dinner's done!
—Penny Walton, Westerville, OH

Takes: 20 min. • **Makes:** 4 servings

- **4 boneless skinless chicken breast halves (5 oz. each)**
- **¼ tsp. seasoned salt**
- **¼ tsp. garlic powder**
- **3 tsp. canola oil, divided**
- **1 cup sliced fresh mushrooms**
- **1 cup shredded Mexican cheese blend**
- **4 green onions, chopped**
- **6 bacon strips, cooked and chopped**

1. Pound chicken breasts to ¼-in. thickness. Sprinkle with seasonings.
2. In a large nonstick skillet, heat 1 tsp. oil over medium-high heat; saute mushrooms until tender, 2-3 minutes. Remove from the pan.
3. In the same pan, cook chicken in the remaining oil until bottom is browned, about 4 minutes. Turn chicken; top with mushrooms and remaining ingredients. Cook, covered, until the chicken is no longer pink, 4-5 minutes.

1 chicken breast half: 363 cal., 21g fat (7g sat. fat), 116mg chol., 555mg sod., 3g carb. (1g sugars, 1g fiber), 40g pro.

FLANK STEAK WITH COUSCOUS

FLANK STEAK WITH COUSCOUS

It takes just minutes to broil this nicely seasoned flank steak. For the most tender results, slice the meat on an angle across the grain. You can substitute a pound of sirloin steak for the flank steak.
—*Taste of Home* Test Kitchen

Takes: 25 min. • **Makes:** 4 servings

- **1 garlic clove, minced**
- **1 tsp. olive oil**
- **½ tsp. Italian seasoning**
- **¼ tsp. pepper**
- **⅛ tsp. salt**
- **1 beef flank steak (1 lb.)**
- **2 pkg. (5.8 oz. each) roasted garlic and olive oil couscous**
- **¾ cup diced roasted sweet red pepper, drained**
- **½ cup Italian salad dressing**

1. Preheat broiler. Mix first the five ingredients; rub over the steak. Place on a broiler pan.
2. Broil 2-3 in. from heat until the meat reaches desired doneness (for medium-rare, a thermometer should read 135°), 6-8 minutes per side. Let stand 5 minutes.
3. Meanwhile, cook couscous according to package directions. Stir in red pepper. Slice steak thinly across the grain; drizzle with dressing. Serve with couscous.

1 serving: 587 cal., 21g fat (5g sat. fat), 54mg chol., 1445mg sod., 61g carb. (5g sugars, 3g fiber), 34g pro.

* **HEALTH TIP** * Nix the couscous mix to cut almost 750 milligrams of sodium per serving. Instead, cook plain couscous in water; add roasted garlic and a drizzle of olive oil.

MOROCCAN FLATBREADS

FAST FIX

MOROCCAN FLATBREADS

My family loves these flatbreads with Middle Eastern seasoning and lots of vegetables. You can also use ground turkey or beef instead of lamb, if you prefer.
—Arlene Erlbach, Morton Grove, IL

Takes: 25 min. • **Makes:** 6 servings

- **1½ lbs. ground lamb**
- **1½ cups chopped zucchini**
- **1¼ cups medium salsa**
- **2 cups julienned carrots, divided**
- **½ cup dried apricots, coarsely chopped**
- **2 Tbsp. apricot preserves**
- **1 Tbsp. grated lemon zest**
- **1 Tbsp. Moroccan seasoning (ras el hanout)**
- **½ tsp. garlic powder**
- **3 naan flatbreads**
- **⅓ cup crumbled feta cheese**
- **2 Tbsp. chopped fresh mint**

1. In a large skillet over medium-high heat, cook lamb 8 minutes or until no longer pink, breaking up into crumbles; drain. Add zucchini, salsa, 1 cup of the carrots, the apricots, preserves, lemon zest, Moroccan seasoning and garlic powder. Cook and stir until heated through and zucchini is crisp-tender, about 7 minutes.
2. Spoon the lamb mixture over naan. Top with the remaining carrots, the feta and mint. Cut into wedges.

½ flatbread: 423 cal., 19g fat (8g sat. fat), 81mg chol., 677mg sod., 39g carb. (15g sugars, 3g fiber), 24g pro.

FAST FIX

SALMON CAKES

Salmon was a special treat for us on Sundays when we were growing up. We ate these cakes fast as Mama could fry them—she couldn't get them off the griddle fast enough!
—Imogene Hutton, Brownwood, TX

Takes: 30 min. • **Makes:** 3 servings

- **2 large eggs**
- **¼ cup heavy whipping cream**
- **¼ cup cornmeal**
- **2 Tbsp. sliced green onions**
- **2 Tbsp. all-purpose flour**
- **¼ tsp. baking powder**
- **Pinch pepper**
- **½ tsp. salt, optional**
- **1 can (14¾ oz.) salmon, drained, bones and skin removed**
- **1 to 2 Tbsp. butter**

1. In a small bowl, beat eggs. Stir in the cream, cornmeal, green onions, flour, baking powder, pepper and, if desired, salt. Flake salmon into bowl; blend gently.
2. Melt butter in a large nonstick skillet or griddle over medium heat. Drop the salmon mixture by ⅓ cupfuls into butter. Fry in batches for 5 minutes on each side or until lightly browned. Serve warm.

2 patties: 451 cal., 25g fat (10g sat. fat), 267mg chol., 694mg sod., 16g carb. (1g sugars, 1g fiber), 39g pro.

FAST FIX

MAPLE PORK CHOPS

PICTURED ON P. 81

Tender pork chops are cooked in a maple glaze that makes every bite absolutely succulent.
—*Taste of Home* Test Kitchen

Takes: 30 min. • **Makes:** 4 servings

- **4 boneless pork loin chops (1 in. thick and 6 oz. each)**
- **1 tsp. minced fresh thyme or ¼ tsp. dried thyme**
- **½ tsp. salt**
- **½ tsp. pepper**
- **1 Tbsp. olive oil**
- **½ cup brewed coffee**
- **¼ cup maple syrup**
- **1 Tbsp. Dijon mustard**
- **2 tsp. Worcestershire sauce**

1. Sprinkle pork chops with thyme, salt and pepper. In a large skillet, brown the chops in oil. Remove and keep warm.
2. Add the remaining ingredients to skillet. Bring to a boil; cook until liquid is reduced by half.
3. Return the pork chops to the skillet. Reduce heat; cover and simmer until the meat is tender, 10-12 minutes, turning once. Serve with sauce.

1 pork chop: 316 cal., 13g fat (4g sat. fat), 82mg chol., 463mg sod., 15g carb. (12g sugars, 0 fiber), 33g pro.

FAST FIX

SAUSAGE-STUFFED ACORN SQUASH

Acorn squash gets the sweet and savory treatment when stuffed with sausage, onion, spinach and cranberries.
—*Taste of Home* Test Kitchen

Takes: 30 min. • **Makes:** 4 servings

- **2 medium acorn squash**
- **1 lb. bulk spicy pork sausage**
- **½ cup chopped onion**
- **1 cup fresh spinach, finely chopped**
- **½ cup dried cranberries**
- **1½ cups soft bread crumbs**
- **1 large egg**
- **2 Tbsp. 2% milk**

1. Halve squash lengthwise; discard seeds. Place squash in a microwave-safe dish, cut side down. Microwave, covered, on high until tender, 10-12 minutes.
2. Meanwhile, in a large skillet, cook and crumble sausage with onion over medium heat until no longer pink, 5-7 minutes; drain. Remove from heat; stir in spinach, cranberries and bread crumbs. In a small bowl, whisk together egg and milk; add to sausage mixture and toss until moistened.
3. Turn over squash; fill with sausage mixture. Microwave, covered, until a thermometer inserted in stuffing reads 165°, 2-3 minutes.

Note: To make soft bread crumbs, tear bread into pieces and place in a food processor or blender. Cover and pulse until crumbs form. One slice of bread yields ½-¾ cup crumbs.

1 stuffed squash half: 485 cal., 23g fat (8g sat. fat), 133mg chol., 843mg sod., 49g carb. (18g sugars, 5g fiber), 25g pro.

FAST FIX

BREADED TURKEY BREASTS

These cutlets seasoned with Parmesan cheese and Italian herbs prove turkey's not just for Thanksgiving. The thin slices take only a few minutes on the stovetop, so be careful not to overcook them.
—Rhonda Knight, Hecker, IL

Takes: 20 min. • **Makes:** 4 servings

- **1 cup dry bread crumbs**
- **¼ cup grated Parmesan cheese**
- **2 tsp. Italian seasoning**
- **1 cup whole milk**
- **8 turkey breast cutlets (2 oz. each)**
- **¼ cup olive oil**

1. In a shallow bowl, combine the bread crumbs, Parmesan cheese and Italian seasoning. Pour milk into another shallow bowl. Dip turkey in the milk, then roll in the crumbs.
2. In a large skillet, cook the turkey in oil over medium heat for 4-5 minutes on each side or until juices run clear. Drain on paper towels.

2 cutlets: 303 cal., 19g fat (4g sat. fat), 21mg chol., 363mg sod., 23g carb. (4g sugars, 1g fiber), 11g pro.

★★★★★ **READER REVIEW**

"This recipe is great! So quick, simple...and the kids loved it!"

RENEEBAILEY TASTEOFHOME.COM

SAUSAGE-STUFFED ACORN SQUASH

FAST FIX

SALMON WITH TARRAGON SAUCE

Here's a fast and foolproof microwave method for tender salmon steaks covered with a distinctive and flavorful sauce.

—Agnes Ward, Stratford, ON

Takes: 20 min. • **Makes:** 4 servings

- **4 salmon fillets (6 oz. each)**
- **¼ tsp. salt**
- **¼ tsp. white pepper**
- **2 Tbsp. white wine or chicken broth**
- **1 Tbsp. butter**
- **1 green onion, finely chopped**
- **1 Tbsp. all-purpose flour**
- **1 tsp. Dijon mustard**
- **½ tsp. dried tarragon**
- **⅔ cup 2% milk**

1. Place salmon in a greased 2-qt. microwave-safe dish; sprinkle with salt and pepper. Pour wine over top. Cover and microwave on high for 4-6 minutes or until fish flakes easily with a fork. Remove salmon and keep warm.
2. Add the butter and green onion to the pan juices; cover and microwave on high for 1 minute. Stir in the flour, mustard and tarragon until blended; gradually stir in milk. Cook, uncovered for 1-2 minutes or until thickened; stirring every 30 seconds. Serve with salmon.

1 piece: 372 cal., 22g fat (6g sat. fat), 111mg chol., 319mg sod., 4g carb. (2g sugars, 0 fiber), 36g pro.

FAST FIX

TZATZIKI CHICKEN

I like to make classic chicken recipes for my family but add a fresh twist. This spin using a famous Greek sauce fits the bill!

—Kristen Heigl, Staten Island, NY

Takes: 30 min. • **Makes:** 4 servings

- **1½ cups finely chopped peeled English cucumber**
- **1 cup plain Greek yogurt**
- **2 garlic cloves, minced**
- **1½ tsp. chopped fresh dill**
- **1½ tsp. olive oil**
- **⅛ tsp. salt**

CHICKEN

- **⅔ cup all-purpose flour**
- **1 tsp. pepper**
- **1 tsp. salt**
- **¼ tsp. baking powder**
- **1 large egg**
- **⅓ cup 2% milk**
- **4 boneless skinless chicken breast halves (6 oz. each)**
- **¼ cup canola oil**
- **¼ cup crumbled feta cheese**
- **Lemon wedges, optional**

1. For sauce, mix the first six ingredients; refrigerate until serving.
2. In a shallow bowl, whisk together flour, salt, pepper and baking powder. In another bowl, whisk together egg and milk. Pound chicken breasts with a meat mallet to ½-in. thickness. Dip in flour mixture to coat both sides; shake off excess. Dip in egg mixture, then again in flour mixture.
3. In a large skillet, heat oil over medium heat. Cook chicken until breading is golden brown and chicken is no longer pink, 5-7 minutes per side. Top with cheese. Serve with sauce and lemon wedges if desired.

1 chicken breast half with ⅓ cup sauce: 482 cal., 27g fat (7g sat. fat), 133mg chol., 737mg sod., 17g carb. (4g sugars, 1g fiber), 41g pro.

*** HEALTH TIP *** Save more than 100 calories and half the fat by browning the chicken in just 1 tablespoon of oil and baking it in the oven to finish it, and switch to fat-free plain yogurt in the sauce.

TEST KITCHEN TIP

English cucumber works well in this recipe because it's seedless and doesn't thin the sauce. Or you can use a regular cucumber—just seed it before chopping.

Make the sauce before preparing the rest of the recipe so the garlic mellows and the flavors meld.

Serve with lemon wedges for a pop of bright citrus flavor.

TZATZIKI CHICKEN

FAST FIX

PEANUT CHICKEN STIR-FRY

Peanut butter is one of my husband's favorite foods. I love that I can use it to make a delicious, savory meal.
—Diane Kelly, Puyallup, WA

Takes: 30 min. • **Makes:** 4 servings

- **½ cup plus 1 Tbsp. water, divided**
- **¼ cup peanut butter**
- **3 Tbsp. soy sauce**
- **1 Tbsp. brown sugar**
- **2 to 3 garlic cloves, minced**
- **2 Tbsp. canola oil**
- **1 lb. boneless skinless chicken breasts, cubed**
- **3 cups fresh broccoli florets**
- **1 Tbsp. cornstarch**
- **Hot cooked rice or noodles**

1. In a small bowl, combine ½ cup water, peanut butter, soy sauce and brown sugar until smooth; set aside. In a skillet or wok, stir-fry the garlic in oil for 30 seconds. Add the chicken; stir-fry for 5 minutes or until no longer pink. Add the broccoli; stir-fry for 5 minutes.
2. Stir in the peanut butter mixture; cook and stir for 2-3 minutes or until the sauce is smooth and the broccoli is crisp-tender. Combine cornstarch and remaining water until smooth; gradually add to skillet. Bring to a boil; cook and stir for 2 minutes or until thickened. Serve with rice or noodles.

Note: Reduced-fat peanut butter is not recommended for this recipe.

1 cup: 322 cal., 18g fat (3g sat. fat), 63mg chol., 835mg sod., 12g carb. (6g sugars, 3g fiber), 30g pro.

FAST FIX

HERBED ARTICHOKE CHEESE TORTELLINI

Vegetarians as well as meat-and-potato lovers both rave about this flavorful meatless recipe with tomatoes, black olives and artichoke hearts tossed with tender cheese tortellini.
—Karen Anzelc, Peoria, AZ

Takes: 30 min. • **Makes:** 8 servings

- **2 cans (14½ oz. each) Italian diced tomatoes**
- **2 jars (6½ oz. each) marinated quartered artichoke hearts**
- **½ cup olive oil**
- **2 medium onions, chopped**
- **½ cup minced fresh parsley**
- **2 to 4 Tbsp. minced fresh basil or 2 to 4 tsp. dried basil**
- **½ tsp. dried oregano**
- **2 garlic cloves, minced**
- **⅛ tsp. crushed red pepper flakes**
- **2 pkg. (9 oz. each) refrigerated cheese tortellini**
- **1 can (2¼ oz.) sliced ripe olives, drained**
- **½ tsp. salt**
- **¼ cup shredded Parmesan cheese**

1. Drain tomatoes, reserving ⅔ cup of the juice. Drain artichoke hearts, reserving ¾ cup of the marinade; chop artichokes.
2. In a Dutch oven, heat oil over medium-high heat. Add onions, herbs, garlic and pepper flakes; cook and stir until the onion is tender, 4-5 minutes. Stir in tomatoes and the reserved tomato juice and artichoke marinade; bring to a boil. Reduce heat; simmer, uncovered, until slightly thickened, 10-12 minutes. Meanwhile, cook the tortellini according to the package directions.
3. Drain the tortellini; add to the tomato mixture. Gently stir in olives, salt and artichoke hearts; heat through. Sprinkle with cheese.

1¼ cups: 474 cal., 28g fat (7g sat. fat), 29mg chol., 975mg sod., 45g carb. (12g sugars, 3g fiber), 11g pro.

HERBED ARTICHOKE CHEESE TORTELLINI

BLACK BEAN
BULGUR SALAD

EAT SMART | FAST FIX

BLACK BEAN BULGUR SALAD

The only cooking required for this easy bulgur salad is heating the broth in the microwave. You can adapt the recipe as you wish; if you want to add chopped, cooked chicken, use chicken broth instead of vegetable broth.
—Carole Resnick, Cleveland, OH

Takes: 30 min. • **Makes:** 4 servings

- **1 cup bulgur**
- **2 cups vegetable broth**
- **¼ cup orange juice**
- **¼ cup lime juice**
- **1 jalapeno pepper, seeded and minced**
- **2 Tbsp. olive oil**
- **¼ tsp. ground cumin**
- **1 cup shredded carrots**
- **3 Tbsp. minced fresh cilantro**
- **1 can (15 oz.) black beans, rinsed and drained**
- **1 cup frozen corn, thawed**
- **¾ cup shredded Monterey Jack cheese**
- **Sliced jalapeno pepper, optional**

1. Place bulgur and broth in a small saucepan; bring to a boil. Reduce heat; simmer, covered, until tender, 12-15 minutes. Transfer to a large bowl; cool slightly.
2. For the dressing, whisk together the citrus juices, minced jalapeno, oil and cumin. Add ⅓ cup of the dressing to the bulgur; stir in carrots and cilantro.
3. To serve, divide the bulgur mixture among four bowls. Top with beans, corn, cheese and, if desired, sliced jalapeno. Drizzle with the remaining dressing.

1 serving: 402 cal., 14g fat (5g sat. fat), 19mg chol., 688mg sod., 56g carb. (6g sugars, 10g fiber), 16g pro.

TEST KITCHEN TIP

Bulgur— sometimes called cracked wheat—is a whole grain that's been boiled, dried and ground. Since bulgur is precooked, it cooks up faster than most whole grains.

EASY STUFFED POBLANOS

FAST FIX

EASY STUFFED POBLANOS

My partner adores these saucy stuffed peppers—and I love how quickly they come together. Top with low-fat sour cream and your favorite salsa.
—Jean Erhardt, Portland, OR

Takes: 25 min. • **Makes:** 4 servings

- **½ lb. Italian turkey sausage links, casings removed**
- **½ lb. lean ground beef (90% lean)**
- **1 pkg. (8.8 oz.) ready-to-serve Spanish rice**
- **4 large poblano peppers**
- **1 cup enchilada sauce**
- **½ cup shredded Mexican cheese blend**
- **Minced fresh cilantro, optional**

1. Preheat the broiler. In a large skillet, cook turkey and beef over medium heat until no longer pink, 5-7 minutes, breaking into crumbles; drain.
2. Prepare the rice according to package directions. Add to the meat mixture.
3. Cut peppers lengthwise in half; remove seeds. Place on a foil-lined 15x10x1-in. baking pan, cut side down. Broil 4 in. from heat until skins blister, about 5 minutes. With tongs, turn peppers.
4. Fill peppers with turkey mixture; top with enchilada sauce and sprinkle with cheese. Broil 1-2 minutes longer or until cheese is melted. If desired, top with cilantro.

2 stuffed pepper halves: 312 cal., 13g fat (4g sat. fat), 63mg chol., 1039mg sod., 27g carb. (5g sugars, 2g fiber), 22g pro.

TEST KITCHEN TIP

Prepared Spanish rice adds lots of flavor with so little effort! If you're using up leftover rice, use about 2 cups cooked rice for the filling. Bell peppers would also work in this recipe.

FAST FIX
STEAK & FRIES SALAD

This is a very popular dish at restaurants in central Pennsylvania. One taste, and you'll understand why!
—Nancy Collins, Clearfield, PA

Takes: 30 min. • **Makes:** 2 servings

- **3 Tbsp. sugar**
- **2 Tbsp. canola oil**
- **1 to 2 Tbsp. malt vinegar**
- **1½ tsp. water**
- **1 cup frozen french-fried potatoes**
- **½ lb. beef top sirloin steak**
- **3 cups torn iceberg lettuce**
- **⅓ cup chopped tomato**
- **¼ cup chopped red onion**
- **½ cup shredded part-skim mozzarella cheese**

1. For the dressing, whisk the first four ingredients until sugar is dissolved. Cook potatoes according to package directions.
2. Meanwhile, place a skillet coated with cooking spray over medium heat. Add steak; cook until the meat reaches the desired doneness (for medium-rare, a thermometer should read 135°; medium, 140°), 5-6 minutes per side. Remove from heat; let stand 5 minutes before slicing.
3. Divide lettuce, tomato and onion between two plates; top with potatoes, steak and cheese. Drizzle with dressing.

1 serving: 513 cal., 26g fat (7g sat. fat), 64mg chol., 429mg sod., 34g carb. (22g sugars, 2g fiber), 33g pro.

EAT SMART | FAST FIX
SALMON WITH TOMATO-GOAT CHEESE COUSCOUS

This is a really simple, healthy and quick meal that tastes like it took much more time and trouble than it does. And it's easily adjusted for any number of people.
—Toni Roberts, La Canada Flintridge, CA

Takes: 30 min. • **Makes:** 4 servings

- **4 salmon fillets (5 oz. each)**
- **¼ tsp. salt**
- **¼ tsp. garlic salt**
- **¼ tsp. pepper**
- **1 Tbsp. olive oil**
- **1 cup chicken stock**
- **¾ cup uncooked whole wheat couscous**
- **2 plum tomatoes, chopped**
- **4 green onions, chopped**
- **¼ cup crumbled goat cheese**

1. Sprinkle the salmon with salt, garlic salt and pepper. Heat oil in a large skillet over medium-high heat; add salmon, skin side up, and cook 3 minutes. Turn fish and cook an additional 4 minutes or until the fish flakes easily with a fork. Remove from heat and keep warm.
2. In a large saucepan, bring stock to a boil. Stir in couscous. Remove from heat; let stand, covered, until stock is absorbed, about 5 minutes. Stir in tomatoes, green onions and goat cheese. Serve with the salmon.

1 fillet with 1 cup couscous mixture: 414 cal., 19g fat (4g sat. fat), 80mg chol., 506mg sod., 31g carb. (2g sugars, 6g fiber), 32g pro.
Diabetic exchanges: 4 lean meat, 2 starch, 1 fat.

TEST KITCHEN TIP

If you can't find small pieces of salmon, just buy a large fillet and cut it up into 5-ounce portions.

No chicken stock on hand? vegetable stock would be a good substitute.

SALMON WITH TOMATO-GOAT CHEESE COUSCOUS

¼ cup raisins
1 Tbsp. cider vinegar
2 cups hot cooked rice
Fresh cilantro leaves, optional

In a large skillet, cook and crumble beef with pepper and onion over medium-high heat until no longer pink, 5-7 minutes. Stir in tomato sauce, olives, raisins and vinegar; bring to a boil. Reduce heat; simmer, uncovered, until raisins are softened, 5-6 minutes. Serve with rice. If desired, top with fresh cilantro.

1 cup beef mixture with ½ cup rice: 363 cal., 13g fat (4g sat. fat), 71mg chol., 683mg sod., 36g carb. (7g sugars, 2g fiber), 26g pro. **Diabetic exchanges:** 3 lean meat, 2½ starch, 1 fat.

FAST FIX

SHRIMP MONTEREY

When company's coming, this delicious seafood dish makes a lasting impression. You'll be surprised at how fast you can prepare it. A mild, fresh-tasting sauce and Monterey Jack cheese complement the shrimp. I serve it over pasta or rice.
—Jane Birch, Edison, NJ

Takes: 25 min. • **Makes:** 6 servings

2 Tbsp. butter
2 lbs. uncooked shrimp (31-40 per lb.), peeled and deveined
2 garlic cloves, minced
½ cup white wine or chicken broth
2 cups shredded Monterey Jack cheese
2 Tbsp. minced fresh parsley
Hot cooked linguine, optional

1. Preheat oven to 350°. In a large skillet, heat butter over medium-high heat; saute shrimp and garlic just until shrimp turn pink, 3-5 minutes. Using a slotted spoon, transfer to a greased 11x7-in. baking dish.
2. Add wine to skillet; bring to a boil. Cook until liquid is reduced by half; pour over the shrimp.
3. Sprinkle with cheese and parsley. Bake, uncovered, until the cheese is melted, 8-10 minutes. If desired, serve over linguine.

1 cup shrimp mixture: 321 cal., 17g fat (10g sat. fat), 228mg chol., 437mg sod., 2g carb. (0 sugars, 0 fiber), 34g pro.

TURKEY BISCUIT SKILLET

FAST FIX

TURKEY BISCUIT SKILLET

My mother made this dish while we were growing up. Now I make it for my own husband and kids. I prefer the smaller-size biscuits, as they brown up nicely. I'll often add mushrooms to this recipe. My family loves mushrooms!
—Keri Boffeli, Monticello, IA

Takes: 30 min. • **Makes:** 6 servings

1 Tbsp. butter
⅓ cup chopped onion
¼ cup all-purpose flour
1 can (10½ oz.) condensed chicken broth, undiluted
¼ cup fat-free milk
⅛ tsp. pepper
2 cups cubed cooked turkey breast
2 cups frozen peas and carrots (about 10 oz.), thawed
1 tube (12 oz.) refrigerated buttermilk biscuits, quartered

1. Preheat oven to 400°. Melt butter in a 10-in. ovenproof skillet over medium-high heat. Add onion; cook and stir until tender, 2-3 minutes.
2. In a small bowl, mix the flour, broth, milk and pepper until smooth; stir into pan. Bring to a boil, stirring constantly; cook and stir until thickened, 1-2 minutes. Add the turkey and frozen vegetables; heat through. Arrange the biscuits over stew. Bake until the biscuits are golden brown, 15-20 minutes.

1 serving: 319 cal., 10g fat (4g sat. fat), 43mg chol., 878mg sod., 36g carb. (4g sugars, 2g fiber), 22g pro.

EAT SMART | FAST FIX

EASY CUBAN PICADILLO

My girlfriend gave me this delicious recipe years ago. Ever since, I've made it for family and friends. According to my daughter, it's the best dish I make—she loves to take leftovers to school for lunch the next day.
—Marie Wielgus, Wayne, NJ

Takes: 25 min. • **Makes:** 4 servings

1 lb. lean ground beef (90% lean)
1 small green pepper, chopped
¼ cup chopped onion
1 can (8 oz.) tomato sauce
½ cup sliced pimiento-stuffed olives

QUICK CARBONARA

FAST FIX
QUICK CARBONARA

Carbonara is a dinnertime classic, but my version cuts down on the time it takes to make. Loaded up with ham, bacon, olives, garlic and Parmesan, it certainly doesn't skimp on flavor.
—Carole Martin, Tallahassee, FL

Takes: 30 min. • **Makes:** 6 servings

- **12 oz. uncooked spaghetti**
- **3 Tbsp. butter**
- **3 Tbsp. canola oil**
- **2 garlic cloves, minced**
- **3 cups cubed fully cooked ham**
- **8 bacon strips, cooked and crumbled**
- **2 Tbsp. minced fresh parsley**
- **¾ cup sliced ripe or pimiento-stuffed olives**
- **½ cup grated Parmesan cheese**

1. Cook spaghetti according to package directions; drain.
2. In a large skillet, heat butter and oil over medium heat; saute garlic 1 minute. Stir in ham and bacon; heat through. Add spaghetti and parsley; toss to combine.
3. Remove from heat. Stir in olives and cheese.

1 serving: 513 cal., 24g fat (8g sat. fat), 73mg chol., 1333mg sod., 45g carb. (2g sugars, 2g fiber), 28g pro.

* HEALTH TIP * Most of the sodium comes from the generous portion of ham. Use just 1½ cups ham and skip the Parmesan to bring sodium below 800 milligrams per serving.

FAST FIX
CHICKEN & MANGO TORTILLA BOWLS

Crisp tortilla bowls transform fruity chicken salad into an eye-catching dish, suitable for a special lunch or party. What a fun, convenient way to make a salad into a meal!
—Ronna Farley, Rockville, MD

Takes: 30 min. • **Makes:** 6 servings

- **3 cups shredded cabbage**
- **½ cup sour cream**
- **½ cup salsa**
- **⅓ cup frozen corn, thawed**
- **⅓ cup chopped green pepper**
- **6 flour tortillas (8 in.), warmed**
- **Cooking spray**
- **2 pkg. (6 oz. each) ready-to-use grilled chicken breast strips**
- **½ tsp. chili powder**
- **2 tsp. butter**
- **1 medium mango, peeled and cubed**
- **¼ cup minced fresh cilantro**

1. Preheat oven to 425°. In a large bowl, combine the cabbage, sour cream, salsa, corn and green pepper. Chill until serving.
2. Place six 10-oz. ramekins or custard cups upside down in a 15x10x1-in. baking pan. Lightly spray warm tortillas on both sides with cooking spray. Place over prepared ramekins, pinching sides to form bowl shapes.
3. Bake the tortillas on ramekins for 8-10 minutes or until crisp. Remove from ramekins to wire racks to cool.
4. In a large skillet, saute the chicken and chili powder in butter until heated through. Spoon the chilled cabbage mixture into the tortilla bowls; top with chicken, mango and cilantro. Serve immediately.

1 serving: 313 cal., 9g fat (4g sat. fat), 50mg chol., 672mg sod., 38g carb. (7g sugars, 2g fiber), 20g pro.

FAST FIX
KOREAN SALMON SKEWERS WITH RICE SLAW

This easy dinner is light and lovely with so many delicious flavors and textures all in one stunning dish. It's so impressive that I often serve it to guests.
—Janice Elder, Charlotte, NC

Takes: 30 min. • **Makes:** 4 servings

- **1 can (20 oz.) unsweetened pineapple chunks**
- **3 Tbsp. honey**
- **2 Tbsp. gochujang (Korean red pepper paste), divided**
- **2 cups broccoli coleslaw mix**
- **2 cups hot cooked brown rice**
- **¼ cup dried cranberries**
- **¼ cup slivered almonds, toasted**
- **1 lb. salmon fillet, skin removed, cut into 1-in. cubes**

1. Preheat broiler. Drain pineapple, reserving juice. For glaze, whisk together honey, 1 Tbsp. gochujang and ½ cup of the pineapple juice. For slaw, mix the remaining pineapple juice and gochujang until smooth; toss with the coleslaw mix, rice, cranberries and almonds. Let stand, covered, until serving.
2. On eight metal or soaked wooden skewers, alternately thread salmon and pineapple chunks. Place on a foil-lined 15x10x1-in. pan.
3. Broil skewers 4-5 in. from heat until fish just begins to flake easily with a fork, 5-6 minutes; brush frequently with glaze during the last 2 minutes. Brush skewers with remaining glaze; serve with slaw.

2 skewers: 533 cal., 15g fat (3g sat. fat), 57mg chol., 310mg sod., 74g carb. (42g sugars, 6g fiber), 26g pro.

FAST FIX
FIVE-SPICE GLAZED SMOKED CHOPS

I started out fixing another recipe but didn't have all the ingredients, so I came up with this one! The five-spice powder gives it a flavorful kick. You can make your own by combining cloves, cinnamon, anise, nutmeg and pepper. I love that you can make this on the stovetop or the grill.
—Jill Thomas, Washington, IN

Takes: 25 min. • **Makes:** 4 servings

- **¼ cup unsweetened apple juice**
- **¼ cup grape jelly**
- **2 Tbsp. cider vinegar**
- **½ tsp. Chinese five-spice powder**
- **½ tsp. minced fresh gingerroot**
- **¼ tsp. crushed red pepper flakes**
- **1 Tbsp. butter**
- **4 smoked bone-in pork chops (7½ oz. each)**

1. For glaze, place the first six ingredients in a small saucepan; bring just to a boil. Reduce heat; simmer, uncovered, for 10 minutes.
2. In a 12-in. skillet, heat butter over medium-high heat. Add pork chops; cook until bottoms are browned, 4-5 minutes. Turn chops; spoon glaze over top. Cook, uncovered, until chops are glazed and heated through, 3-4 minutes.

1 pork chop: 363 cal., 22g fat (10g sat. fat), 77mg chol., 1345mg sod., 16g carb. (15g sugars, 0 fiber), 27g pro.

TEST KITCHEN TIP

Many grocery stores carry only one type of smoked pork chop. If yours sells only boneless chops, feel free to use them in place of bone-in.

FIVE-SPICE GLAZED SMOKED CHOPS

FAST FIX

SAUSAGE RICE SKILLET

Flavorful pork sausage, fresh zucchini and instant rice make this stovetop sensation a family favorite.
—Connie Putnam, Clayton, NC

Takes: 30 min. • **Makes:** 4 servings

- **1 lb. bulk pork sausage**
- **2 medium zucchini, halved and sliced**
- **1 small onion, chopped**
- **½ cup chopped green pepper**
- **1 tsp. dried oregano**
- **½ tsp. garlic salt or garlic powder**
- **1 can (11½ oz.) V8 juice**
- **⅔ cup uncooked instant rice**

1. In a large skillet, cook sausage until no longer pink; drain. Add vegetables, oregano and garlic salt; cook and stir until onion is tender, about 5 minutes. Stir in the V8 juice; bring to a boil. Reduce heat; cover and simmer for 10-14 minutes or until the vegetables are tender.
2. Return to a boil. Stir in the rice; cover and remove from the heat. Let stand for 5-7 minutes or until rice is tender. Fluff with a fork.

1¼ cups: 381 cal., 25g fat (8g sat. fat), 61mg chol., 1153mg sod., 24g carb. (6g sugars, 3g fiber), 16g pro.

*** HEALTH TIP *** Decrease the sodium to 700 milligrams per serving by using reduced-sodium V8 juice and replacing half the sausage with plain ground pork. Sprinkler in extra oregano and garlic powder for a flavor boost.

CREAMY LENTILS WITH KALE ARTICHOKE SAUTE

EAT SMART | FAST FIX

CREAMY LENTILS WITH KALE ARTICHOKE SAUTE

I've been trying to eat more meatless meals, so I experimented with this hearty saute and served it over brown rice. Even the non-kale lovers gobbled it up!
—Teri Rasey, Cadillac, MI

Takes: 30 min. • **Makes:** 4 servings

- **½ cup dried red lentils, rinsed and sorted**
- **¼ tsp. dried oregano**
- **⅛ tsp. pepper**
- **1¼ cups vegetable broth**
- **¼ tsp. sea salt, divided**
- **1 Tbsp. olive oil or grapeseed oil**
- **16 cups chopped fresh kale (about 12 oz.)**
- **1 can (14 oz.) water-packed artichoke hearts, drained and chopped**
- **3 garlic cloves, minced**
- **½ tsp. Italian seasoning**
- **2 Tbsp. grated Romano cheese**
- **2 cups hot cooked brown or basmati rice**

1. Place the first four ingredients and ⅛ tsp. salt in a small saucepan; bring to a boil. Reduce heat; simmer, covered, until the lentils are tender and the liquid is almost absorbed, 12-15 minutes. Remove from heat.
2. In a 6-qt. stockpot, heat the oil over medium heat. Add kale and the remaining salt; cook, covered, until the kale is wilted, 4-5 minutes, stirring occasionally. Add the artichoke hearts, garlic and Italian seasoning; cook and stir for 3 minutes.
3. Remove from heat; stir in cheese. Serve lentils and kale mixture over rice.

1 serving: 321 cal., 6g fat (2g sat. fat), 1mg chol., 661mg sod., 53g carb. (1g sugars, 5g fiber), 15g pro.

TEST KITCHEN TIP

Lentils don't require soaking, but they should be rinsed and sifted through to look for stones before cooking.

Of all varieties, red lentils cook the fastest, mainly because they're split during processing. Red lentils break down while cooking and don't hold their shape like brown lentils do. The lentil mixture becomes almost a sauce in this dish.

FAST FIX

GNOCCHI WITH SPINACH & CHICKEN SAUSAGE

Dinner's easy when I can use ingredients typically found in my fridge and pantry!
—Laura Miller, Lake Ann, MI

Takes: 25 min. • **Makes:** 4 servings

- **1 pkg. (16 oz.) potato gnocchi**
- **2 Tbsp. olive oil**
- **1 pkg. (12 oz.) fully cooked Italian chicken sausage links, halved and sliced**
- **2 shallots, finely chopped**
- **2 garlic cloves, minced**
- **1 cup white wine or chicken broth**
- **1 Tbsp. cornstarch**
- **½ cup reduced-sodium chicken broth**
- **3 cups fresh baby spinach**
- **½ cup heavy whipping cream**
- **¼ cup shredded Parmesan cheese**

1. Cook gnocchi according to the package directions. Meanwhile, in a large skillet, heat oil over medium-high heat; cook the sausage and shallots until the sausage is browned and the shallots are tender. Add garlic; cook 1 minute longer.
2. Stir in wine. Bring to a boil; cook until the liquid is reduced by half, 3-4 minutes. In a small bowl, mix cornstarch and broth until smooth; stir into the sausage mixture. Return to a boil, stirring constantly; cook and stir until thickened, 1-2 minutes. Add spinach and cream; cook and stir until the spinach is wilted.
3. Drain gnocchi; add to the pan and heat through. Sprinkle with cheese.

Note: Look for potato gnocchi in the pasta or frozen foods section.

1 cup: 604 cal., 28g fat (12g sat. fat), 119mg chol., 1226mg sod., 58g carb. (3g sugars, 4g fiber), 27g pro.

GNOCCHI WITH SPINACH & CHICKEN SAUSAGE

EAT SMART | FAST FIX

CHICKEN & SPINACH PASTA SALAD

We love pasta salads, but usually they have too much mayonnaise or oily dressing. Using hummus gives this dish a great taste and texture, while also increasing its nutritional profile. Adding chicken (store-bought rotisserie chicken works well), makes this pasta salad a complete meal.
—Jenny Lynch, Rock Island, IL

Takes: 25 min. • **Makes:** 6 servings

- **8 oz. uncooked whole wheat rotini**
- **½ cup hummus**
- **3 Tbsp. Italian salad dressing**
- **¼ tsp. salt**
- **⅛ tsp. pepper**
- **4 cups fresh baby spinach**
- **1 cup cubed cooked chicken breast**
- **2 cups cherry tomatoes, halved**
- **1 can (2¼ oz.) sliced ripe olives, drained**
- **¼ cup crumbled feta cheese**

1. Cook pasta according to the package directions for al dente. Drain and rinse with cold water.
2. Combine hummus, salad dressing, salt and pepper in a large bowl. Add the pasta; toss to coat. Stir in spinach, chicken, tomatoes and olives. Sprinkle with feta. Serve immediately.

1½ cups: 263 cal., 6g fat (1g sat. fat), 20mg chol., 405mg sod., 35g carb. (3g sugars, 7g fiber), 16g pro. **Diabetic exchanges:** 2 starch, 1 lean meat, 1 fat.

★★★★★ **READER REVIEW**

"I love this recipe! My family are not hummus fans but I was able to sneak it into this and they all loved it. The feta makes it so special... this is a keeper!"

BONITO15 TASTEOFHOME.COM

EAT SMART | FAST FIX

GINGERED PEPPER STEAK

This tender steak is a treat even for folks who aren't watching their diet. When my mother-in-law shared the recipe, she said it cooks up in no time...and she was right!
—Susan Adair, Somerset, KY

Takes: 20 min. • **Makes:** 4 servings

- **2 tsp. cornstarch**
- **2 tsp. sugar**
- **¼ tsp. ground ginger**
- **¼ cup reduced-sodium soy sauce**
- **1 Tbsp. cider or white wine vinegar**
- **1 lb. beef flank steak, cut into ¼-in.-thick strips**
- **2 tsp. canola oil, divided**
- **2 medium green peppers, julienned**
- **Hot cooked rice, optional**

1. Mix the first five ingredients until smooth. Add beef; toss to coat.
2. In a skillet, heat 1 tsp. oil over medium-high heat; stir-fry peppers until crisp-tender, 2-3 minutes. Remove from pan.
3. In the same pan, heat the remaining oil over medium-high heat; stir-fry beef until browned, 2-3 minutes. Stir in peppers. If desired, serve over rice.

1 cup stir-fry: 224 cal., 11g fat (4g sat. fat), 54mg chol., 644mg sod., 7g carb. (4g sugars, 1g fiber), 23g pro. **Diabetic exchanges:** 3 lean meat, 1 vegetable, ½ fat.

FAST FIX

CREAMY PROSCIUTTO PASTA

I'm always looking for dinners that I can put together quickly. I re-created a favorite pasta dish from an Italian restaurant by using grocery store products. All you need is crusty bread and a salad to make it a complete meal.
—Christine Ward, Austin, TX

Takes: 25 min. • **Makes:** 4 servings

- **1 pkg. (9 oz.) refrigerated fettuccine or linguine**
- **1 Tbsp. butter**
- **½ lb. sliced fresh mushrooms**
- **1 small onion, chopped**
- **10 oz. fresh baby spinach (about 12 cups)**
- **1 jar (15 oz.) Alfredo sauce**
- **¼ lb. thinly sliced prosciutto, coarsely chopped**
- **Coarsely ground pepper, optional**

1. Cook fettuccine according to the package directions; drain.
2. Meanwhile, in a large skillet, heat the butter over medium-high heat; saute the mushrooms and onion until tender. Stir in spinach just until wilted.
3. Stir in Alfredo sauce; cook until heated through, 1-2 minutes, stirring occasionally. Add prosciutto and fettuccine; toss to combine. If desired, top with freshly ground pepper to serve.

1½ cups: 454 cal., 20g fat (12g sat. fat), 100mg chol., 1065mg sod., 48g carb. (3g sugars, 5g fiber), 24g pro.

FAST FIX

NORTH CAROLINA SHRIMP SAUTE

Seafood is very popular in my state. I altered this recipe several times and now it's truly a family favorite.
—Teresa Hildreth, Stoneville, NC

Takes: 25 min. • **Makes:** 4 servings

- **8 oz. uncooked linguine or spaghetti**
- **4 Tbsp. butter, divided**
- **½ lb. sliced fresh mushrooms**
- **1 small green pepper, chopped**
- **½ tsp. salt**
- **¼ tsp. pepper**
- **1 lb. uncooked shrimp (31-40 per lb.), peeled and deveined**
- **3 garlic cloves, minced**
- **½ cup grated Romano cheese**
- **Chopped fresh parsley**

1. Cook linguini according to the package directions; drain and keep warm.
2. In a large skillet, heat 2 Tbsp. butter over medium-high heat; saute mushrooms and green pepper until tender. Stir in salt and pepper; remove from pan.
3. In same pan, saute shrimp in remaining butter over medium-high heat 2 minutes. Add garlic; cook and stir until the shrimp turn pink, 1-2 minutes. Stir in mushroom mixture; heat through. Serve over linguini. Sprinkle with cheese and parsley.

1 serving: 481 cal., 19g fat (11g sat. fat), 171mg chol., 752mg sod., 46g carb. (3g sugars, 3g fiber), 34g pro.

NORTH CAROLINA SHRIMP SAUTE

MUSHROOM & BROWN RICE HASH WITH POACHED EGGS

FAST FIX

TORTELLINI WITH TOMATO SPINACH CREAM SAUCE

I enjoy all things pasta, and tortellini is my favorite. The flavor of this dish is amazing. Even my husband, who hates pasta of any kind, loves it!
—Jenny Dubinsky, Inwood, WV

Takes: 30 min. • **Makes:** 6 servings

- **1 Tbsp. olive oil**
- **1 small onion, chopped**
- **3 garlic cloves, minced**
- **1 can (14½ oz.) petite diced tomatoes, undrained**
- **5 oz. frozen chopped spinach, thawed and squeezed dry (about ½ cup)**
- **1 tsp. dried basil**
- **¾ tsp. salt**
- **½ tsp. pepper**
- **1 cup heavy whipping cream**
- **1 pkg. (19 oz.) frozen cheese tortellini**
- **½ cup grated Parmesan cheese**

1. In a large skillet, heat oil over medium-high heat. Add onion; cook and stir until tender, 2-3 minutes. Add the garlic; cook 1 minute longer. Add tomatoes, spinach and seasonings. Cook and stir over medium heat until liquid is absorbed, about 3 minutes.
2. Stir in cream; bring to a boil. Reduce heat; simmer, uncovered, until thickened, about 10 minutes. Meanwhile, cook the tortellini according to package directions; drain. Stir into sauce. Sprinkle with cheese.

1 cup: 404 cal., 22g fat (13g sat. fat), 80mg chol., 810mg sod., 38g carb. (6g sugars, 4g fiber), 13g pro.

EAT SMART | FAST FIX

MUSHROOM & BROWN RICE HASH WITH POACHED EGGS

I made my mother's famous (but decadent) roast beef hash healthier by using mushrooms instead of beef, and brown rice instead of potatoes. Now it's ideal for a light main dish.
—Lily Julow, Lawrenceville, GA

Takes: 30 min. • **Makes:** 4 servings

- **2 Tbsp. olive oil**
- **1 lb. sliced baby portobello mushrooms**
- **½ cup chopped sweet onion**
- **1 pkg. (8.8 oz.) ready-to-serve brown rice**
- **1 large carrot, grated**
- **2 green onions, thinly sliced**
- **½ tsp. salt**
- **¼ tsp. pepper**
- **¼ tsp. caraway seeds**
- **4 large eggs**

1. In a large skillet, heat oil over medium-high heat; saute mushrooms until lightly browned, 5-7 minutes. Add sweet onion; cook 1 minute. Add rice and carrot; cook and stir until the vegetables are tender, 4-5 minutes. Stir in green onions, salt, pepper and caraway seeds; heat through.
2. Meanwhile, place 2-3 in. of water in a large saucepan or skillet with high sides. Bring to a boil; adjust heat to maintain a gentle simmer. Break cold eggs, one at a time, into a small bowl; holding bowl close to surface of water, slip egg into water.
3. Cook, uncovered, for 3-5 minutes or until egg whites are completely set and the yolks begin to thicken but are not hard. Using a slotted spoon, lift the eggs out of the water. Serve over the rice mixture.

1 serving: 282 cal., 13g fat (3g sat. fat), 186mg chol., 393mg sod., 26g carb. (4g sugars, 3g fiber), 13g pro. **Diabetic exchanges:** 1½ starch, 1½ fat, 1 medium-fat meat.

* HEALTH TIP * This is a great dinner or brunch option for anyone following a gluten-free diet.

TEST KITCHEN TIP

This recipe is a delicious way to use up leftover rice, quinoa or roasted potatoes you may have. You'll need about 2 cups to substitute for the package of ready-to-serve rice.

White button mushrooms can be used in place of baby portobellos, but the baby portobellos add a richer, earthier flavor.

BEEF SKILLET SUPPER

FAST FIX

BEEF SKILLET SUPPER

Sometimes I'll make extra of this comforting, noodle-y supper to guarantee leftovers for work or school the next day. You can trim calories by substituting ground turkey for the beef and using low-fat cheese.
—Tabitha Allen, Cypress, TX

Takes: 30 min. • **Makes:** 8 servings

- **8 oz. uncooked medium egg noodles (about 4 cups)**
- **1½ lbs. ground beef**
- **1 medium onion, chopped**
- **½ tsp. salt**
- **¼ tsp. pepper**
- **1 can (8 oz.) tomato sauce**
- **½ cup water**
- **1 can (11 oz.) Mexicorn, drained**
- **1 cup shredded cheddar cheese**

1. Cook noodles according to package directions; drain.
2. Meanwhile, in a large skillet, cook and crumble beef with onion over medium-high heat until no longer pink, 6-8 minutes. Stir in the salt, pepper, tomato sauce and water; bring to a boil. Reduce the heat; simmer, covered, for 10 minutes.
3. Stir in corn and noodles; heat through. Sprinkle with cheese; let stand, covered, until cheese is melted.

1 serving: 368 cal., 16g fat (7g sat. fat), 90mg chol., 548mg sod., 30g carb. (4g sugars, 2g fiber), 24g pro.

FAST FIX

CHICKEN WITH ARTICHOKES & SHRIMP

Besides adding color to the dish, the shrimp complement the flavor of the chicken. The recipe has recently become one of our family favorites.
—Rebecca Baird, Salt Lake City, UT

Takes: 30 min. • **Makes:** 2 servings

- **¼ cup all-purpose flour**
- **¼ tsp. salt, optional**
- **¼ tsp. pepper**
- **2 boneless skinless chicken breast halves (4 oz. each)**
- **2 tsp. canola oil**
- **8 uncooked medium shrimp, peeled and deveined**
- **1 can (14 oz.) water-packed artichoke hearts, rinsed, drained and chopped**
- **1 plum tomato, chopped**
- **2 garlic cloves, minced**
- **⅓ cup reduced-sodium chicken broth**
- **1 Tbsp. minced fresh basil**
- **1 Tbsp. minced fresh parsley**
- **1 Tbsp. butter**
- **3 Tbsp. shredded Parmesan cheese**

1. In a large resealable plastic bag, combine the flour, salt if desired and pepper; add chicken and shake to coat.
2. In a large skillet, cook the chicken in oil over medium heat for 5-6 minutes on each side or until a thermometer reads 170°. Remove and keep warm.
3. Add the shrimp, artichokes, tomato and garlic to the skillet; cook for 4 minutes. Add the broth, basil, parsley and butter; heat through. Pour over chicken and sprinkle with cheese.

1 serving: 433 cal., 16g fat (6g sat. fat), 146mg chol., 878mg sod., 28g carb. (1g sugars, 1g fiber), 42g pro.

★★★★★ **READER REVIEW**

"One of our kids looked skeptical about the artichokes, but he ended up going back for more. The flavors blend beautifully."

MAYBAKE TASTEOFHOME.COM

FAST FIX

MEAT LOVER'S PIZZA RICE SKILLET

My son named this after I made a quick dinner from some ingredients I had in the fridge and the pantry. It's good with other pizza toppings, too—I'll often use black olives or mushrooms.
—Teri Rasey, Cadillac, MI

Takes: 25 min. • **Makes:** 6 servings

- **1 lb. bulk Italian sausage**
- **1 can (14½ oz.) diced tomatoes with basil, oregano and garlic**
- **1 can (15½ oz.) cannellini beans, rinsed and drained**
- **1½ cups water**
- **1½ cups uncooked instant rice**
- **¼ cup grated Parmesan cheese**
- **½ cup (2 oz.) sliced mini pepperoni**
- **Additional grated Parmesan cheese, optional**
- **Chopped fresh basil, optional**

1. In a large skillet, cook sausage over medium heat for 5-7 minutes or until no longer pink, breaking into crumbles; drain. Return to skillet with next four ingredients. Bring to a boil; cover and remove from heat. Let stand 5 minutes.
2. Fluff with a fork; stir in cheese. Top with pepperoni and, if desired, additional Parmesan cheese and basil.

11/4 cups: 390 cal., 20g fat (6g sat. fat), 48mg chol., 906mg sod., 35g carb. (2g sugars, 4g fiber), 15g pro.

EAT SMART | FAST FIX

SHRIMP PUTTANESCA

I throw together these bold ingredients for a feisty and flavorful seafood pasta sauce. If you think you don't like anchovies, think again—they make this dish rich and savory, without standing out. Serve with spaghetti or the pasta of your choice. You can control the heat by using more or less red pepper flakes.
—Lynda Balslev, Sausalito, CA

Takes: 30 min. • **Makes:** 4 servings

- **2 Tbsp. olive oil, divided**
- **1 lb. uncooked shrimp (31-40 per lb.), peeled and deveined**
- **¾ to 1 tsp. crushed red pepper flakes, divided**
- **¼ tsp. salt**
- **1 small onion, chopped**
- **2 to 3 anchovy fillets, finely chopped**
- **3 garlic cloves, minced**
- **2 cups grape tomatoes or small cherry tomatoes**
- **½ cup dry white wine or vegetable broth**
- **⅓ cup pitted Greek olives, coarsely chopped**
- **2 tsp. drained capers**
- **Sugar to taste**
- **Chopped fresh Italian parsley**
- **Hot cooked spaghetti, optional**

1. In a large skillet, heat 1 Tbsp. oil; saute shrimp with ½ tsp. red pepper flakes until the shrimp turn pink, 2-3 minutes. Stir in salt; remove from pan.
2. In the same pan, heat the remaining oil over medium heat; saute onion until tender, about 2 minutes. Add anchovies, garlic and the remaining pepper flakes; cook and stir until fragrant, about 1 minute. Stir in tomatoes, wine, olives and capers; bring to a boil. Reduce heat; simmer, uncovered, until tomatoes are softened and mixture is thickened, 8-10 minutes.
3. Stir in the shrimp and sugar to taste; sprinkle with parsley. If desired, serve with spaghetti.

1 cup shrimp mixture: 228 cal., 12g fat (2g sat. fat), 140mg chol., 579mg sod., 8g carb. (3g sugars, 1g fiber), 20g pro.
Diabetic exchanges: 3 lean meat, 2 fat, ½ starch.

SHRIMP PUTTANESCA

TEQUILA LIME SHRIMP ZOODLES

EAT SMART | FAST FIX

TEQUILA LIME SHRIMP ZOODLES

This tangy shrimp is a great way to cut carbs without sacrificing flavor. If you don't have a spiralizer, use thinly julienned zucchini.
—Brigette Schroeder, Yorkville, IL

Takes: 30 min. • **Makes:** 4 servings

- **3 Tbsp. butter, divided**
- **1 shallot, minced**
- **2 garlic cloves, minced**
- **¼ cup tequila**
- **1½ tsp. grated lime zest**
- **2 Tbsp. lime juice**
- **1 Tbsp. olive oil**
- **1 lb. uncooked shrimp (31-40 per lb.), peeled and deveined**
- **2 medium zucchini, spiralized (about 6 cups)**
- **½ tsp. salt**
- **¼ tsp. pepper**
- **¼ cup minced fresh parsley**
- **Additional grated lime zest**

1. In a large skillet, heat 2 Tbsp. butter over medium heat. Add shallot and garlic; cook 1-2 minutes. Remove from heat; stir in tequila, lime zest and lime juice. Cook over medium heat until the liquid is almost evaporated, 2-3 minutes.
2. Add olive oil and the remaining butter; stir in shrimp and zucchini. Sprinkle with salt and pepper. Cook and stir until the shrimp begin to turn pink and the zucchini is crisp-tender, 4-5 minutes. Sprinkle with parsley and additional lime zest.

1¼ cups: 246 cal., 14g fat (6g sat. fat), 161mg chol., 510mg sod., 7g carb. (3g sugars, 1g fiber), 20g pro. **Diabetic exchanges:** 3 lean meat, 3 fat, 1 vegetable.

FAST FIX

SPANISH NOODLES & GROUND BEEF

PICTURED ON P. 81

Bacon adds flavor to this comforting stovetop supper. My mom made this when we were growing up; I'm happy to share it with my family now.
—Kelli Jones, Peris, CA

Takes: 30 min. • **Makes:** 2 servings

- **½ lb. lean ground beef (90% lean)**
- **¼ cup chopped green pepper**
- **2 Tbsp. chopped onion**
- **1½ cups uncooked medium egg noodles**
- **¾ cup canned diced tomatoes**
- **½ cup water**
- **2 Tbsp. chili sauce**
- **¼ tsp. salt**
- **Dash pepper**
- **2 bacon strips, cooked and crumbled**

In a large skillet, cook and crumble beef with green pepper and onion over medium-high heat until no longer pink, 4-6 minutes. Stir in all the remaining ingredients except bacon; bring to a boil. Reduce heat; simmer, covered, until the noodles are tender, 15-20 minutes, stirring occasionally. Top with bacon.

Note: This recipe was tested with Heinz chili sauce.

1¼ cups: 371 cal., 14g fat (5g sat. fat), 103mg chol., 887mg sod., 31g carb. (7g sugars, 3g fiber), 30g pro.

FAST FIX

SWEET POTATO-CRUSTED CHICKEN NUGGETS

I came up with this recipe when I was looking for ways to spice up traditional chicken nuggets. The chips add flavor and crunchy texture while the meat stays juicy and tender on the inside.
—Kristina Segarra, Yonkers, NY

Takes: 30 min. • **Makes:** 4 servings

- **Oil for deep-fat frying**
- **1 cup sweet potato chips**
- **¼ cup all-purpose flour**
- **1 tsp. salt, divided**
- **½ tsp. coarsely ground pepper**
- **¼ tsp. baking powder**
- **1 Tbsp. cornstarch**
- **1 lb. chicken tenderloins, cut into 1½-in. pieces**

1. In an electric skillet or deep fryer, heat oil to 350°. Place chips, flour, ½ tsp. salt, pepper and baking powder in a food processor; pulse until ground. Transfer to a shallow dish.
2. Mix cornstarch and the remaining salt; toss with the chicken. Toss chicken with the potato chip mixture, pressing gently to coat.
3. Fry nuggets, a few at a time, until golden brown, 2-3 minutes. Drain on paper towels.

1 serving: 308 cal., 17g fat (1g sat. fat), 56mg chol., 690mg sod., 12g carb. (1g sugars, 1g fiber), 28g pro.

TEST KITCHEN TIP

Fry in small batches to maintain consistent oil temperature.

To reuse frying oil, cool and strain it to remove any food particles. Store, covered, in the refrigerator.

SWEET POTATO-CRUSTED
CHICKEN NUGGETS

LEMON PORK WITH MUSHROOMS

EAT SMART | FAST FIX

LEMON PORK WITH MUSHROOMS

This is a go-to healthy dish you wouldn't guess is good for you. A little squeeze of lemon gives these crispy, seasoned chops a bright boost.

—Christine Datian, Las Vegas, NV

Takes: 30 min. • **Makes:** 4 servings

- **1 large egg, lightly beaten**
- **1 cup seasoned bread crumbs**
- **8 boneless thin pork loin chops (2 oz. each)**
- **¼ tsp. salt**
- **⅛ tsp. pepper**
- **1 Tbsp. olive oil**
- **1 Tbsp. butter**
- **½ lb. sliced fresh mushrooms**
- **2 garlic cloves, minced**
- **2 tsp. grated lemon zest**
- **1 Tbsp. lemon juice**
- **Lemon wedges, optional**

1. Place egg and bread crumbs in separate shallow bowls. Sprinkle pork chops with salt and pepper; dip in the egg, then coat with crumbs, pressing to adhere.
2. In a large skillet, heat oil over medium heat. In batches, cook pork until golden brown, 2-3 minutes per side. Remove from pan; keep warm.
3. Wipe skillet clean. In the same skillet, heat butter over medium heat; saute mushrooms until tender, 2-3 minutes. Stir in garlic, lemon zest and lemon juice; cook and stir 1 minute. Serve over pork. If desired, serve with lemon wedges.

2 pork chops: 331 cal., 15g fat (5g sat. fat), 109mg chol., 601mg sod., 19g carb. (2g sugars, 1g fiber), 28g pro. **Diabetic exchanges:** 3 lean meat, 1½ fat, 1 starch.

EAT SMART | FAST FIX

SAUCY MEDITERRANEAN CHICKEN WITH RICE

The hints of Mediterranean flavor in this chicken dish make it a family favorite in our house.

—Tabitha Alloway, Edna, KS

Takes: 30 min. • **Makes:** 4 servings

- **¾ cup water**
- **3 Tbsp. tomato paste**
- **2 Tbsp. lemon juice**
- **¾ tsp. salt**
- **1 tsp. chili powder**
- **½ tsp. garlic powder**
- **½ tsp. ground ginger**
- **¼ tsp. ground fennel seed**
- **¼ tsp. ground turmeric**
- **1 tsp. ground coriander, optional**
- **3 Tbsp. olive oil**
- **1 medium onion, chopped**
- **1 lb. boneless skinless chicken breasts, cut into 1-in. cubes**
- **3 cups hot cooked rice**
- **Minced fresh parsley, optional**

1. In a small bowl, mix the water, tomato paste, lemon juice, salt, chili powder, garlic powder, ginger, fennel seed, turmeric and, if desired, coriander until smooth.
2. In a large skillet, heat oil over medium-high heat. Add onions; cook and stir until tender. Stir in chicken; brown 3-4 minutes. Pour tomato paste mixture into the pan.
3. Bring to a boil. Reduce heat; simmer, uncovered, until the chicken is no longer pink, 8-10 minutes. Serve with rice. If desired, top with parsley.

¾ cup chicken mixture with ¾ cup rice: 394 cal., 13g fat (2g sat. fat), 63mg chol., 527mg sod., 40g carb. (3g sugars, 2g fiber), 27g pro. **Diabetic exchanges:** 3 lean meat, 2½ starch, 2 fat.

TEST KITCHEN TIP

Freeze leftover tomato paste on a waxed paper-lined baking sheet in 1-tablespoon mounds. Transfer frozen tomato paste to a zip-top freezer bag.

Long grain rice triples when cooked and instant rice doubles. So you'll need 1 cup of uncooked long grain or 1½ cups of uncooked instant to yield about 3 cups of hot cooked rice.

FAST FIX

PIEROGI BEEF SKILLET

Hearty and thick with beef, veggies and potatoes, this is a complete meal in one.
—*Taste of Home* Test Kitchen

Takes: 25 min. • **Makes:** 4 servings

- **1 lb. ground beef**
- **½ cup chopped onion**
- **¼ cup all-purpose flour**
- **½ tsp. Italian seasoning**
- **½ tsp. pepper**
- **⅛ tsp. salt**
- **1 can (14½ oz.) beef broth**
- **1 pkg. (16 oz.) frozen cheese and potato pierogies, thawed**
- **2 cups frozen mixed vegetables (about 10 oz.), thawed and drained**
- **½ cup shredded cheddar cheese**

1. In a large cast-iron or other heavy skillet, cook and crumble beef with onion over medium heat until no longer pink, 5-7 minutes. Drain, reserving 3 Tbsp. of the drippings in the pan. Stir in flour and seasonings until blended. Gradually stir in broth; bring to a boil. Cook and stir until thickened, 1-2 minutes.
2. Stir in pierogies and vegetables. Cook, uncovered, until heated through, about 5 minutes, stirring occasionally. Sprinkle with cheese.

1¾ cups: 654 cal., 31g fat (12g sat. fat), 102mg chol., 1157mg sod., 57g carb. (12g sugars, 7g fiber), 34g pro.

PIEROGI BEEF SKILLET

EAT SMART | FAST FIX

COLORFUL VEGETARIAN LINGUINE

My bright pasta dish is a satisfying supper that takes advantage of the flavor of fresh mushrooms, zucchini, tomatoes and basil.
—Jane Bone, Cape Coral, FL

Takes: 30 min. • **Makes:** 6 servings

- **6 oz. uncooked linguine**
- **2 medium zucchini, thinly sliced**
- **½ lb. fresh mushrooms, sliced**
- **2 green onions, chopped**
- **1 garlic clove, minced**
- **2 Tbsp. butter**
- **1 Tbsp. olive oil**
- **1 large tomato, chopped**
- **2 tsp. minced fresh basil**
- **½ tsp. salt**
- **¼ tsp. pepper**
- **4 oz. reduced-fat provolone cheese, shredded**
- **3 Tbsp. shredded Parmesan cheese**

1. Cook linguine according to package directions. Meanwhile, in a large skillet, saute the zucchini, mushrooms, onions and garlic in butter and oil for 3-5 minutes. Add the tomato, basil, salt and pepper; cover and simmer for 3 minutes.
2. Drain the linguine; add to the vegetable mixture. Sprinkle with cheeses and toss to coat.

1½ cups: 243 cal., 11g fat (5g sat. fat), 22mg chol., 417mg sod., 26g carb. (4g sugars, 3g fiber), 12g pro. **Diabetic exchanges:** 2 lean meat, 1 starch, 1 vegetable, 1 fat.

FAST FIX

SHRIMP POMODORO

This shrimp with garlic, tomatoes and pasta is a fast meal with special-occasion appeal—a must for hectic schedules!
—Catherine Jensen, Blytheville, AR

Takes: 20 min. • **Makes:** 4 servings

- **8 oz. uncooked thin spaghetti**
- **1 Tbsp. olive oil**
- **¾ lb. uncooked shrimp (26-30 per lb.), peeled and deveined**
- **2 cloves garlic, minced**
- **¼ to ½ tsp. crushed red pepper flakes**
- **1 can (14½ oz.) petite diced tomatoes, undrained**
- **10 fresh basil leaves, torn**
- **½ tsp. salt**
- **⅛ tsp. pepper**
- **¼ cup grated Parmesan cheese**

1. Cook thin spaghetti according to the package directions.
2. In a large skillet, heat oil over medium-high heat. Add shrimp; cook until shrimp begin to turn pink, 1-2 minutes. Add garlic and pepper flakes; cook 1 minute longer.
3. Add the tomatoes; bring to a boil. Reduce heat; simmer, uncovered, until shrimp turn pink, 2-3 minutes, stirring occasionally. Remove from heat; stir in basil, salt and pepper. Serve with spaghetti and cheese.

¾ cups shrimp mixture with 1 cup cooked spaghetti: 357 cal., 7g fat (2g sat. fat), 108mg chol., 653mg sod., 49g carb. (5g sugars, 4g fiber), 24g pro.

FAST FIX
THAI PEANUT NAAN PIZZAS

I'm a fan of Thai food, but don't always have time to make it at home. To get my fix, I top fluffy naan bread with a ginger-peanut sauce, fresh veggies, a sprinkle of cilantro and a spicy squiggle of Sriracha.
—Rachel Bernhard Seis, Milwaukee, WI

Takes: 25 min. • **Makes:** 4 servings

- **¼ cup creamy peanut butter**
- **3 Tbsp. sesame ginger salad dressing**
- **1 Tbsp. water**
- **1 tsp. soy sauce**
- **2 naan flatbreads**
- **1 cup shredded part-skim mozzarella cheese**
- **1 small sweet red pepper, julienned**
- **½ cup julienned carrot**
- **½ cup sliced baby portobello mushrooms**
- **¼ cup chopped fresh cilantro**
- **Sriracha Asian hot chili sauce, optional**

1. Preheat oven to 425°. For sauce, mix the first four ingredients until blended. Place naan on a baking sheet; spread with sauce. Top with cheese and vegetables.
2. Bake until the cheese is melted and the crust is golden brown, 8-10 minutes. Top with cilantro and, if desired, drizzle with chili sauce.

½ pizza: 316 cal., 19g fat (6g sat. fat), 21mg chol., 698mg sod., 25g carb. (8g sugars, 2g fiber), 13g pro.

FAST FIX
CHICKEN & SHRIMP WITH LEMON CREAM SAUCE

My kids love this creamy pasta. Whenever I make it, I know that they will happily clean their plates.
—Joe Milholland, Smelterville, ID

Takes: 30 min. • **Makes:** 6 servings

- **10 oz. uncooked fettuccine**
- **1 lb. fresh asparagus, trimmed and cut into 2-in. pieces**
- **1 lb. boneless skinless chicken breasts, cubed**
- **½ tsp. garlic salt**
- **1 Tbsp. olive oil**
- **½ lb. uncooked shrimp (31-40 per lb.), peeled and deveined**
- **1 cup heavy whipping cream**
- **2 tsp. grated lemon zest**
- **3 Tbsp. lemon juice**
- **½ tsp. salt**
- **⅛ tsp. pepper**

1. In a Dutch oven, cook fettuccine according to package directions, adding asparagus during the last 3 minutes.
2. Meanwhile, sprinkle chicken with garlic salt. In a large skillet, heat oil over medium heat. Add chicken; cook until chicken is no longer pink, 8-10 minutes.
3. Stir in shrimp and cream; cook, covered, until shrimp turn pink, 2-3 minutes. Stir in lemon zest, lemon juice, salt and pepper. Drain fettuccine and return to pan. Add sauce; toss to coat.

1 cup: 443 cal., 20g fat (10g sat. fat), 133mg chol., 472mg sod., 37g carb. (3g sugars, 3g fiber), 30g pro.

TEST KITCHEN TIP

You might find this size shrimp labeled as medium shrimp.

One medium lemon is all you need for the lemon zest and juice called for in this recipe.

CHICKEN & SHRIMP WITH LEMON CREAM SAUCE

EAT SMART | FAST FIX

QUICK GINGER PORK

For empty nesters, it's a challenge learning to cook for just two again. Recipes like this give my husband and me delicious scaled-down dinners.
—Esther Johnson Danielson, Lawton, PA

Takes: 20 min. • **Makes:** 2 servings

- **½ lb. pork tenderloin, cut into thin strips**
- **1 Tbsp. canola oil**
- **1 garlic clove, minced**
- **2 Tbsp. reduced-sodium soy sauce**
- **¼ tsp. sugar**
- **⅛ to ¼ tsp. ground ginger**
- **½ cup cold water**
- **1½ tsp. cornstarch**
- **Hot cooked rice, optional**
- **Thinly sliced green onions and toasted sesame seeds, optional**

1. In a large skillet or wok, stir-fry pork in oil until no longer pink. Add garlic; cook 1 minute longer.

2. In a small bowl, combine the soy sauce, sugar and ginger; add to skillet. Combine water and cornstarch until smooth; add to the skillet. Bring to a boil; cook and stir for 2 minutes or until thickened. If desired, serve with rice and top with green onions and sesame seeds.

1 serving: 216 cal., 11g fat (2g sat. fat), 64mg chol., 621mg sod., 4g carb. (1g sugars, 0 fiber), 24g pro. **Diabetic exchanges:** 3 lean meat, 1½ fat, ½ starch.

* **HEALTH TIP** * Cuts of pork with loin in the name are lean—pork tenderloin, pork loin roast and pork loin chops.

TASTY TACO CHOPPED SALAD

FAST FIX

TASTY TACO CHOPPED SALAD

My friends and I love Mexican food, but we also try to eat healthy. My mom taught me how to make this tasty taco salad for my friends.
—Matthew Smith, Knippa, TX

Takes: 25 min. • **Makes:** 6 servings

- **1 lb. lean ground beef (90% lean)**
- **1 envelope reduced-sodium taco seasoning**
- **⅔ cup water**
- **1 can (15 oz.) Ranch Style beans (pinto beans in seasoned tomato sauce)**
- **1 head iceberg lettuce, chopped (about 8 cups)**
- **1 cup shredded Colby-Monterey Jack cheese**
- **1 large tomato, chopped**
- **2 cups corn chips**
- **½ cup Catalina salad dressing**

1. In a large skillet, cook the beef over medium heat 6-8 minutes or until no longer pink, breaking into crumbles; drain. Stir in taco seasoning, water and beans; bring to a boil. Reduce heat; simmer, uncovered, 3-4 minutes or until thickened, stirring occasionally.

2. Place the remaining ingredients in separate bowls; combine with the beef mixture as desired.

1 serving: 471 cal., 25g fat (9g sat. fat), 64mg chol., 1193mg sod., 37g carb. (12g sugars, 5g fiber), 24g pro.

* **HEALTH TIP** * Add more veggies, swap spinach for iceberg, skip the cheese, and top with baked chips for a healthier salad.

TEST KITCHEN TIP

Try this salad over tortilla chips instead of corn chips.

For a hearty appetizer, arrange the salad on one large serving platter and serve with extra chips.

MANGO SALSA CHICKEN WITH VEGGIE HASH

FAST FIX

MANGO SALSA CHICKEN WITH VEGGIE HASH

This hash has the fresh flavors of spring. And precooked grilled chicken strips make it a snap to get on the table quickly. Bonus: The veggies make it pretty, too!
—Lori McLain, Denton, TX

Takes: 30 min. • **Makes:** 4 servings

- **1 Tbsp. canola oil**
- **2 cups chopped red potatoes (2-3 medium)**
- **1 small sweet yellow pepper, chopped**
- **½ cup chopped red onion**
- **1½ cups cut fresh asparagus (1-in. pieces)**
- **12 oz. frozen grilled chicken breast strips, partially thawed (about 2 cups)**
- **1½ cups mango salsa, divided**
- **1 Tbsp. chopped fresh cilantro Additional cilantro**

1. In a large skillet, heat oil over medium-high heat; saute potatoes, pepper and onion until potatoes are lightly browned, 6-8 minutes. Add asparagus; cook and stir until potatoes are tender, 2-3 minutes. Stir in chicken strips, ¾ cups of the salsa and 1 Tbsp. cilantro; heat through, stirring mixture occasionally.
2. Sprinkle with additional cilantro. Serve with remaining salsa.

1½ cups: 237 cal., 6g fat (1g sat. fat), 51mg chol., 1025mg sod., 20g carb. (3g sugars, 2g fiber), 24g pro.

TEST KITCHEN TIP

We used half a pound of untrimmed fresh asparagus to yield 1½ cups of cut asparagus.

For a meatless version, skip the chicken and serve topped with a fried egg.

Red potatoes work well in hash because they hold their shape and add nice color. Leaving the skin on also adds fiber and saves prep time.

FAST FIX

THAI LIME SHRIMP & NOODLES

The flavors just keep popping in this quick dinner! Use as much lime zest and chili paste as you like. My family is into spicy foods, but I kept the heat moderate in this version.
—Teri Rasey, Cadillac, MI

Takes: 25 min. • **Makes:** 6 servings

- **1 cup minced fresh basil**
- **3 Tbsp. lime juice**
- **4 tsp. Thai red chili paste**
- **1 garlic clove, minced**
- **1 tsp. minced fresh gingerroot**
- **1½ lbs. uncooked shrimp (26-30 per lb.), peeled and deveined**
- **12 oz. uncooked angel hair pasta**
- **4 tsp. olive oil, divided**
- **1 can (14½ oz.) chicken broth**
- **1 can (13.66 oz.) coconut milk**
- **1 tsp. salt**
- **1 Tbsp. cornstarch**
- **2 Tbsp. cold water**
- **2 Tbsp. grated lime zest**

1. Place the first five ingredients in a blender; cover and process until blended. Remove 1 Tbsp. mixture; toss with shrimp.
2. Cook pasta according to package directions. Meanwhile, in a large nonstick skillet, heat 2 tsp. oil over medium-high heat. Add half of the shrimp mixture; stir-fry 2-4 minutes or until the shrimp turn pink. Remove from skillet; keep warm. Repeat with the remaining oil and shrimp mixture.
3. Add broth, coconut milk, salt and remaining basil mixture to same pan. In a small bowl, mix cornstarch and water until smooth. Stir into broth mixture. Bring to a boil; cook and stir 1-2 minutes or until slightly thickened. Stir in lime zest.
4. Drain pasta; add pasta and shrimp to sauce, tossing to coat.

1 serving: 486 cal., 20g fat (13g sat. fat), 141mg chol., 865mg sod., 49g carb. (3g sugars, 2g fiber), 28g pro.

FAST FIX

EASY SWEDISH MEATBALLS

My recipe relies on ingredients we always have on hand in the kitchen. While these tender homemade meatballs cook in the microwave, make your favorite noodles on the stovetop to get this meal on the table in minutes.

—Sheryl Ludeman, Kenosha, WI

Takes: 30 min. • **Makes:** 4 servings

- **1 small onion, chopped**
- **1 large egg**
- **¼ cup seasoned bread crumbs**
- **2 Tbsp. 2% milk**
- **½ tsp. salt**
- **⅛ tsp. pepper**
- **1 lb. ground beef**

SAUCE

- **1 can (10¾ oz.) condensed cream of mushroom soup, undiluted**
- **½ cup sour cream**
- **¼ cup 2% milk**
- **1 Tbsp. dried parsley flakes**
- **¼ tsp. ground nutmeg, optional**
- **Hot cooked noodles**
- **Minced fresh parsley, optional**

1. In a large bowl, combine the onion, egg, bread crumbs, milk, salt and pepper. Crumble beef over mixture and mix well. Shape into 1-in. meatballs, about 24.
2. Place meatballs in a shallow 1½-qt. microwave-safe dish. Cover; microwave on high until the meat is no longer pink, 7½ minutes; drain.
3. Combine the soup, sour cream, milk, parsley and, if desired, nutmeg; pour over the meatballs. Cover and cook on high until heated through, 5-6 minutes. Serve with noodles and, if desired, top with minced parsley.

6 meatballs with sauce: 366 cal., 21g fat (10g sat. fat), 135mg chol., 1055mg sod., 15g carb. (4g sugars, 1g fiber), 26g pro.

EASY SWEDISH MEATBALLS

FAST FIX

JAMAICAN JERK PORK CHOPS

These sweet, spicy chops can be thrown together in minutes, but definitely don't taste like it. Serve it with a side of jasmine rice and it's like a tropical vacation.

—Allison Ulrich, Frisco, TX

Takes: 25 min. • **Makes:** 2 servings

- **3 Tbsp. butter, divided**
- **¼ cup peach preserves**
- **4 boneless thin-cut pork loin chops (2 to 3 oz. each)**
- **3 tsp. Caribbean jerk seasoning**
- **½ tsp. salt**
- **¼ tsp. pepper**
- **½ medium sweet orange pepper**
- **½ medium sweet yellow pepper**
- **½ medium sweet red pepper**
- **Hot cooked rice, optional**

1. Soften 1 Tbsp. butter; mix with the peach preserves.
2. Sprinkle chops with seasonings. In a large skillet, heat 1 Tbsp. butter over medium-high heat; brown chops, 2-3 minutes per side. Remove from pan.
3. Cut peppers into thin strips. In same pan, saute peppers in the remaining butter over medium-high heat until crisp-tender and lightly browned, 5-6 minutes. Add chops; top with the preserves mixture. Cook, uncovered, until heated through, 30-60 seconds. If desired, serve with rice.

1 serving: 470 cal., 26g fat (14g sat. fat), 114mg chol., 1190mg sod., 32g carb. (28g sugars, 2g fiber), 28g pro.

*** HEALTH TIP *** Use reduced-sodium or salt-free Jamaican jerk seasoning to significantly reduce the amount of sodium in this dish.

NO-FUSS PORK CHOPS

FAST FIX

NO-FUSS PORK CHOPS

These tender chops taste like sweet-and-sour pork! I make them whenever time is tight but I still want a scrumptious meal.
—Sally Jones, Lancaster, NH

Takes: 30 min. • **Makes:** 4 servings

- **½ cup pineapple juice**
- **2 Tbsp. brown sugar**
- **2 Tbsp. cider vinegar**
- **½ tsp. salt**
- **2 Tbsp. olive oil, divided**
- **4 boneless pork loin chops (5 oz. each)**
- **2 medium onions, chopped**
- **Hot cooked noodles and sliced green onions, optional**

1. Mix the first four ingredients. In a large skillet, heat 1 Tbsp. oil over medium heat; brown pork chops on both sides. Remove from pan.
2. In the same pan, saute onions in the remaining oil over medium heat until tender. Add the juice mixture; bring to a boil. Reduce heat; simmer, covered, for 10 minutes. Add chops; cook, covered, until a thermometer inserted in pork reads 145°, 2-3 minutes. Let stand, covered, 5 minutes before serving. If desired, serve over noodles and top with green onions.

1 pork chop: 315 cal., 15g fat (4g sat. fat), 68mg chol., 340mg sod., 16g carb. (12g sugars, 1g fiber), 28g pro.

FAST FIX

BOW TIES WITH GORGONZOLA SAUCE

The name may sound fancy, but this pasta dish is comforting and simple to prepare. A green salad makes it a complete meal.
—Nadine Mesch, Mount Healthy, OH

Takes: 30 min. • **Makes:** 8 servings

- **1 pkg. (16 oz.) bow tie pasta**
- **1 pkg. (16 oz.) bulk pork sausage**
- **2 Tbsp. butter**
- **2 Tbsp. all-purpose flour**
- **1½ cups half-and-half cream**
- **¾ cup crumbled Gorgonzola cheese**
- **¾ tsp. salt**
- **½ tsp. lemon-pepper seasoning**
- **4 cups fresh spinach, lightly packed**
- **3 Tbsp. minced fresh basil**

1. Cook pasta according to the package directions. Drain; return to pot.
2. In a large skillet, cook sausage over medium heat until no longer pink, 4-6 minutes, breaking the meat into crumbles; drain.
3. In a small saucepan, melt butter over medium heat. Stir in flour until smooth; gradually whisk in cream. Bring to a boil, stirring constantly; cook and stir until thickened, 1-2 minutes. Remove from heat. Stir in cheese, salt and lemon pepper.
4. Add cheese sauce, sausage and spinach to hot pasta; toss to combine. Sprinkle with basil.

1¼ cups: 475 cal., 24g fat (11g sat. fat), 70mg chol., 813mg sod., 46g carb. (3g sugars, 3g fiber), 18g pro.

EAT SMART | FAST FIX

STOVETOP ORANGE-GLAZED CHICKEN

I love a recipe that can put dinner on the table quickly and not sacrifice flavor. This sweet and saucy dish does that with ingredients you probably already have on hand!
—Kallee Krong-McCreery, Escondido, CA

Takes: 25 min. • **Makes:** 2 servings

- ¼ cup orange juice
- 1 Tbsp. reduced-sodium soy sauce
- ½ tsp. cornstarch
- ½ tsp. Dijon mustard
- 2 Tbsp. orange marmalade
- 2 boneless skinless chicken breast halves (6 oz. each)
- ¼ tsp. garlic salt
- 1 Tbsp. olive oil

1. For glaze, whisk together the first four ingredients in a microwave-safe bowl; stir in marmalade. Microwave, covered, on high until mixture thickens, 2½-3 minutes, stirring occasionally.
2. Pound chicken breasts to ½-in. thickness; sprinkle with garlic salt. In a large skillet, heat oil over medium heat; cook chicken until a thermometer reads 165°, 5-6 minutes per side. Top with glaze.

1 chicken breast half with about 2 Tbsp. sauce: 314 cal., 11g fat (2g sat. fat), 94mg chol., 656mg sod., 18g carb. (15g sugars, 0 fiber), 35g pro. **Diabetic exchanges:** 5 lean meat, 1½ fat, 1 starch.

FAST FIX

SKILLET BEEF & MACARONI

I found this recipe years ago on a can label. I made some tweaks, and my family loved it. It's a real timesaver for people with super busy schedules.
—Maxine Neuhauser, Arcadia, CA

Takes: 30 min. • **Makes:** 6 servings

- 1½ lb. ground beef
- ½ cup chopped onion
- 2 cans (8 oz. each) tomato sauce
- 1 cup water
- 1 pkg. (7 oz.) macaroni
- ½ cup chopped green pepper
- 2 Tbsp. Worcestershire sauce
- 1 tsp. salt
- ¼ tsp. pepper

In a large skillet over medium-high heat, cook beef and onion until the meat is no longer pink; drain. Stir in the remaining ingredients; bring to a boil. Reduce heat; simmer, covered, until macaroni is tender, stirring occasionally, 20-25 minutes. Add more water if needed.

1 cup: 317 cal., 11g fat (5g sat. fat), 56mg chol., 700mg sod., 29g carb. (3g sugars, 2g fiber), 25g pro.

EAT SMART | FAST FIX

QUICK MOROCCAN SHRIMP SKILLET

When my niece was attending West Point, she was sent to Morocco for five months. I threw her a going-away party with Moroccan decorations, costumes and cuisine, including this shrimp dish. Now, whenever I make it, I think of her.
—Barbara Lento, Houston, PA

Takes: 25 min. • **Makes:** 4 servings

- 1 Tbsp. canola oil
- 1 small onion, chopped
- ¼ cup pine nuts
- 1 lb. uncooked shrimp (16-20 per lb.), peeled and deveined
- 1 cup uncooked pearl (Israeli) couscous
- 2 Tbsp. lemon juice
- 3 tsp. Moroccan seasoning (ras el hanout)
- 1 tsp. garlic salt
- 2 cups hot water
- Minced fresh parsley, optional

1. In a large skillet, heat oil over medium-high heat; saute onion and pine nuts until onion is tender, 2-3 minutes. Stir in all of the remaining ingredients except parsley; bring just to a boil. Reduce heat; simmer, covered, until the shrimp turn pink, 4-6 minutes.
2. Remove from heat; let stand 5 minutes. If desired, top with parsley.

1 cup: 335 cal., 11g fat (1g sat. fat), 138mg chol., 626mg sod., 34g carb. (1g sugars, 1g fiber), 24g pro.

SKILLET BEEF & MACARONI

EAT SMART | FAST FIX

CHICKEN PARMESAN WITH SPAGHETTI SQUASH

I grow spaghetti squash and herbs in my garden every year, so this recipe is the perfect way to make the most of them.
—Kristina Krummel, Elkins, AR

Takes: 30 min. • **Makes:** 4 servings

- **1 medium spaghetti squash**
- **4 boneless skinless chicken breast halves (6 oz. each)**
- **2 Tbsp. minced fresh parsley, plus more for topping**
- **1 Tbsp. minced fresh oregano or ¾ tsp. dried oregano**
- **1 Tbsp. minced fresh basil or ¾ tsp. dried basil**
- **2 Tbsp. olive oil**
- **1 jar (14 oz.) pasta sauce**
- **½ cup shredded mozzarella cheese**
- **¼ cup grated Parmesan cheese**

1. Halve squash lengthwise; discard seeds. Place squash on a microwave-safe plate, cut side down; microwave on high until tender, about 15 minutes. Cool slightly.
2. Meanwhile, sprinkle the chicken with parsley, oregano and basil. In a large skillet, heat oil over medium heat. Add chicken; cook 7-9 minutes on each side or until a thermometer reads 165°. Stir in pasta sauce; sprinkle with cheeses. Cover and cook until cheese is melted, 3-5 minutes.
3. Separate strands of squash with a fork. Serve with chicken and sauce. If desired, top with chopped parsley.

1 chicken breast half with ¾ cup squash and ½ cup sauce: 501 cal., 19g fat (5g sat. fat), 109mg chol., 704mg sod., 43g carb. (8g sugars, 9g fiber), 43g pro.

FAST FIX

ITALIAN SAUSAGE & SUN-DRIED TOMATO PASTA

Sausage and sun-dried tomatoes pack this simple pasta dish with flavor. I have a feeling that once you try this, it'll become a new favorite.
—Dawn Singleton, Eighty Four, PA

Takes: 30 min. • **Makes:** 8 servings

- **1 pkg. (16 oz.) uncooked penne pasta**
- **1½ lbs. bulk Italian sausage**
- **⅔ cup julienned soft sun-dried tomatoes (not packed in oil)**
- **3 garlic cloves, thinly sliced**
- **2 tsp. fennel seed**
- **¼ tsp. crushed red pepper flakes**
- **½ cup dry red wine or reduced-sodium chicken broth**
- **½ cup heavy whipping cream**
- **1 pkg. (9 oz.) fresh spinach**
- **¾ cup shredded Romano cheese, divided**
- **⅔ cup crushed seasoned salad croutons**

1. Cook the pasta according to package directions for al dente.
2. Meanwhile, in a Dutch oven, cook the sausage over medium-high heat until no longer pink, 5-6 minutes, breaking into crumbles. Stir in the tomatoes, garlic, fennel seed and pepper flakes; cook 1 minute longer.
3. Add wine. Bring to a boil; cook until liquid is almost evaporated, 1-2 minutes. Stir in cream; cook 1 minute longer. Add spinach; cook and stir just until the spinach is wilted.
4. Drain pasta; add to sausage mixture. Stir in ½ cup of the Romano cheese. Sprinkle with the crushed croutons and remaining cheese.

Note: This recipe was tested with ready-to-use sun-dried tomatoes (packed in oil). When using other sun-dried tomatoes, cover with boiling water and let stand until soft. Drain before using.

1½ cups: 617 cal., 33g fat (13g sat. fat), 83mg chol., 949mg sod., 53g carb. (6g sugars, 5g fiber), 24g pro.

ITALIAN SAUSAGE & SUN-DRIED TOMATO PASTA

EASY SWEET-AND-SOUR MEATBALLS

FAST FIX

EASY SWEET-AND-SOUR MEATBALLS

Prepared meatballs help jump-start supper on a busy night, but you can always use homemade!
—Ruth Andrewson, Leavenworth, WA

Takes: 30 min. • **Makes:** 6 servings

- **1 can (20 oz.) unsweetened pineapple chunks**
- **1 pkg. (12 oz.) frozen fully cooked homestyle or Swedish meatballs, thawed**
- **1 large green pepper, cut into 1-in. pieces**
- **3 Tbsp. cornstarch**
- **⅓ cup cold water**
- **3 Tbsp. cider vinegar**
- **1 Tbsp. soy sauce**
- **½ cup packed brown sugar**
- **Hot cooked rice, optional**
- **Thinly sliced green onions, optional**

1. Drain pineapple, reserving the juice. Set pineapple aside. Add enough water to the juice (if needed) to measure 1 cup. In a large skillet over medium heat, cook the meatballs, green pepper and the juice mixture until heated through.
2. In a small bowl, combine cornstarch, cold water, vinegar and soy sauce until smooth. Add brown sugar and reserved pineapple chunks to the pan; stir in the cornstarch mixture. Bring to a boil; cook and stir for 2 minutes or until thickened. If desired, serve with rice and top with green onions.

1 serving: 330 cal., 15g fat (7g sat. fat), 24mg chol., 572mg sod., 40g carb. (31g sugars, 2g fiber), 9g pro.

FAST FIX

BROCCOLI BEEF STIR-FRY

My family frequently requests this tasty combination of tender beef and nutritious vegetables. It's delicious year-round, but especially in the summer when I use the broccoli and onions from my garden.
—Ruth Stahl, Shepherd, MT

Takes: 25 min. • **Makes:** 4 servings

- **½ tsp. garlic powder**
- **3 Tbsp. cornstarch, divided**
- **2 Tbsp. plus ½ cup water, divided**
- **1 lb. boneless beef top round steak, cut into thin 2-in. strips**
- **¼ cup soy sauce**
- **2 Tbsp. brown sugar**
- **1 tsp. ground ginger**
- **2 Tbsp. canola oil, divided**
- **4 cups fresh broccoli florets**
- **1 small onion, cut into thin wedges**
- **Hot cooked rice**

1. Mix garlic powder and 2 Tbsp. each of cornstarch and water; toss with beef. In a small bowl, mix soy sauce, brown sugar, ginger and the remaining cornstarch and water until smooth.
2. In a large skillet, heat 1 Tbsp. oil over medium-high heat; stir-fry beef until browned, 2-3 minutes. Remove from pan.
3. In the same pan, stir-fry broccoli and onion in the remaining oil over medium-high heat until crisp-tender, 4-5 minutes. Stir the soy sauce mixture; add to the pan. Cook and stir until thickened, 1-2 minutes. Return beef to the pan; heat through. Serve with rice.

1 cup stir-fry: 291 cal., 11g fat (2g sat. fat), 63mg chol., 974mg sod., 18g carb. (9g sugars, 2g fiber), 30g pro.

* HEALTH TIP * A simple swap to reduced-sodium soy sauce saves 350 milligrams of sodium per serving.

FAST FIX

ASIAN BEEF NOODLE TOSS

If you're in the mood for Far East fare, try this recipe. It's a cinch to prepare and gives you a satisfying blend of flavors.
—Sue Livangood, Waukesha, WI

Takes: 30 min. • **Makes:** 4 servings

- **1 lb. ground beef**
- **2 pkg. (3 oz. each) Oriental ramen noodles**
- **1 pkg. (16 oz.) frozen stir-fry vegetable blend**
- **2 cups water**
- **4 to 5 Tbsp. soy sauce**
- **¼ tsp. ground ginger**
- **3 Tbsp. thinly sliced green onions**

1. In a large skillet, cook beef over medium heat until no longer pink; drain. Stir in the contents of one noodle seasoning packet; set aside and keep warm.
2. Break the noodles; place in a large saucepan. Add the contents of the second seasoning packet, the vegetables, water, soy sauce and ginger. Bring to a boil. Reduce heat; cover and simmer for 6-10 minutes or until the vegetables and noodles are tender. Stir in the beef and onions.

1½ cups: 208 cal., 9g fat (4g sat. fat), 37mg chol., 978mg sod., 13g carb. (3g sugars, 2g fiber), 17g pro.

Casseroles & Oven Entrees

These homey, savory recipes are perfect when the weather turns cold and rich, satisfying comfort food is the best thing going. But don't hold back—you can enjoy these delicious oven-baked treats any time of year!

Cheesy Fiesta Beef Casserole (p. 122) **Smoked Sausage & Veggie Sheet-Pan Supper** (p. 120) **Chicken Florentine Casserole** (p. 123) **Breaded Curry Chicken Drummies** (p. 121) **Shrimp & Crab Casserole** (p. 128)

FAST FIX

CHICKEN CORDON BLEU PIZZA

This recipe is a combination of my two favorite foods: pizza and chicken cordon bleu. I have made this for my family and also the teachers at my school. Now my teachers often ask me to make it for them for lunch!

—Justin Rippel, Colgate, WI

Takes: 30 min. • **Makes:** 6 servings

- **1 tube (13.8 oz.) refrigerated pizza crust**
- **½ cup Alfredo sauce**
- **¼ tsp. garlic salt**
- **1 cup shredded Swiss cheese**
- **1½ cups cubed fully cooked ham**
- **10 breaded chicken nuggets, thawed, cut into ½-in. pieces**
- **1 cup shredded part-skim mozzarella cheese**

1. Preheat oven to 425°. Unroll and press the pizza dough onto bottom of a greased 15x10x1-in. pan, pinching edges to form a rim if desired. Bake until edges are light brown, 8-10 minutes.
2. Spread crust with Alfredo sauce; sprinkle with garlic salt. Top with the remaining ingredients. Bake until crust is golden brown and cheese is melted, 8-10 minutes.

1 serving: 438 cal., 20g fat (9g sat. fat), 65mg chol., 1386mg sod., 39g carb. (5g sugars, 2g fiber), 27g pro.

SASSY SOUTHWEST STUFFED SHELLS

When I was a child, my mom made this dish quite often. When I came across her recipe on an index card, I quickly copied it. Over the years, I have made very few changes because I wanted to retain that taste-of-home memory.

—Kellie Braddell, West Point, CA

Prep: 45 min. • **Bake:** 35 min.
Makes: 8 servings

- **24 uncooked jumbo pasta shells**
- **½ lb. lean ground beef (90% lean)**
- **½ lb. lean ground pork**
- **1 large carrot, shredded**
- **3 green onions, chopped**
- **3 garlic cloves, minced**
- **2 cans (4 oz. each) chopped green chilies**
- **2 cups shredded Mexican cheese blend, divided**
- **1 can (6 oz.) french-fried onions, divided**
- **¼ cup minced fresh cilantro**
- **1 jar (16 oz.) picante sauce**
- **2 cans (8 oz. each) tomato sauce**
- **1 cup water**

1. Preheat oven to 350°. Cook pasta according to package directions for al dente. Drain and rinse in cold water.
2. Meanwhile, in a large skillet, cook beef and pork over medium heat until no longer pink, breaking into crumbles, 8-10 minutes; drain. Add carrot, green onions and garlic; cook 1 minute longer. Stir in chilies, 1 cup cheese, half of the fried onions and the cilantro. In a bowl, combine picante sauce, tomato sauce and water; stir 1 cup picante mixture into pan.
3. Spread 1 cup remaining picante mixture into a greased 13x9-in. baking dish. Fill pasta shells with meat mixture; place in baking dish, overlapping ends slightly. Top with remaining sauce. Cover and bake 30 minutes. Uncover; top with remaining cheese and remaining fried onions. Bake until the cheese is melted, 5-10 minutes.

3 stuffed shells: 487 cal., 26g fat (10g sat. fat), 59mg chol., 1181mg sod., 41g carb. (5g sugars, 3g fiber), 22g pro.

SASSY SOUTHWEST STUFFED SHELLS

DIJON PORK CHOPS WITH CABBAGE & FENNEL

gained a new appreciation for cabbage after traveling through France's Alsace-Lorraine region, an area renowned for the best sauerkraut and classic cabbage, pork, sausage and potato dishes. Fennel complements cabbage beautifully, and juniper berries tease out a special flavor. Both are in this recipe, with two varieties of cabbage.

—Grace Voltolina, Westport, CT

Prep: 35 min. • **Bake:** 55 min.
Makes: 6 servings

- **1 small head green cabbage (about 1½ lbs.)**
- **1 small head red cabbage (about 1½ lbs.)**
- **4 Tbsp. whole grain Dijon mustard, divided**
- **2 Tbsp. light brown sugar**
- **3 tsp. kosher salt, divided**
- **2½ tsp. pepper, divided**
- **3 cups chicken stock**
- **2 Tbsp. olive oil, divided**
- **1 large onion, halved and thinly sliced**
- **4 garlic cloves, thinly sliced**
- **3 large Granny Smith apples, quartered**
- **1 fennel bulb, cored and cut into ¼-in. slices**
- **3 tsp. rubbed sage**
- **6 center-cut pork rib chops (1 in. thick and 8 oz. each)**
- **2 Tbsp. all-purpose flour**

1. Preheat oven to 375°. Core and cut each cabbage into six wedges. In a bowl, mix 2 Tbsp. mustard, brown sugar, 1½ tsp. salt, 1 tsp. pepper and stock.
2. In a large Dutch oven, heat 1 Tbsp. oil over medium-high heat; saute onion until lightly browned, 4-6 minutes. Add garlic; cook and stir 1 minute. Remove from heat; add the apples, fennel and cabbage. Pour mustard mixture over top. Bake, covered, until cabbage is tender, 45-60 minutes.
3. Meanwhile, mix sage and the remaining salt and pepper; rub onto both sides of the pork chops. Dust with flour; shake off excess. In a large skillet, heat the remaining oil over medium-high heat. Brown chops in batches, 4-6 minutes per side; remove from pan.
4. Spread the tops of pork chops with the remaining mustard; place over vegetables in Dutch oven. Bake, uncovered, until a thermometer inserted in the pork reads 145°, 8-10 minutes.

1 pork chop with 2 cups vegetables: 435 cal., 16g fat (5g sat. fat), 72mg chol., 1533mg sod., 42g carb. (25g sugars, 10g fiber), 36g pro.

TEST KITCHEN TIP

If your store doesn't have rib chops, feel free to substitute bone-in pork loin chops.

We used a Dutch oven large enough to accommodate all the vegetables. The veggies will cook down, allowing room for the pork chops, which need to be cooked for just a short time after browning them.

Whole-grain mustard is prepared mustard with whole mustard seeds, lending texture and robust flavor to many foods.

DIJON PORK CHOPS WITH CABBAGE & FENNEL

GREEK SPINACH BAKE

This delicious bake features the flavors of spinach and feta, a classic combination in traditional Greek cuisine. This dish works well as a side dish or a meatless main.

—Sharon Olney, Galt, CA

Prep: 10 min. • **Bake:** 1 hour
Makes: 6 servings

- **2 cups 4% cottage cheese**
- **1 pkg. (10 oz.) frozen chopped spinach, thawed and squeezed dry**
- **8 oz. crumbled feta cheese**
- **6 Tbsp. all-purpose flour**
- **½ tsp. pepper**
- **¼ tsp. salt**
- **4 large eggs, lightly beaten**

1. Preheat oven to 350°. In a large bowl, combine the cottage cheese, spinach and feta cheese. Stir in the flour, pepper and salt. Add eggs and mix well.
2. Spoon into a greased 9-in. square baking dish. Bake, uncovered, until a thermometer reads 160°, about 1 hour.

1 serving: 262 cal., 13g fat (7g sat. fat), 178mg chol., 838mg sod., 14g carb. (4g sugars, 3g fiber), 21g pro.

TURKEY & BROCCOLI PASTRY BRAID

FAST FIX

TURKEY & BROCCOLI PASTRY BRAID

This meal in one is an easy way to get kids—and adults—to eat broccoli. The puff pastry that wraps up turkey, cheese and veggies is pure, flaky goodness.
—Jenelle Fender, Steinbach, MB

Takes: 30 min. • **Makes:** 4 servings

- **1 cup finely chopped cooked turkey (about 5 oz.)**
- **½ cup finely chopped fresh broccoli**
- **½ cup finely chopped sweet red pepper**
- **½ cup shredded cheddar cheese**
- **¼ cup Miracle Whip**
- **¼ tsp. dill weed**
- **1 sheet frozen puff pastry, thawed**

1. Preheat oven to 400°. For the filling, mix the first six ingredients.
2. Unfold the pastry onto a lightly floured surface; roll into a 15x10-in. rectangle. Transfer to a baking sheet. Spoon filling down the center third of the rectangle. On each long side, cut eight strips about 3 in. into the center. Starting at one end, fold alternating strips over the filling, pinching ends to join.
3. Bake until golden brown and filling is heated through, 20-25 minutes.

1 piece: 463 cal., 26g fat (7g sat. fat), 50mg chol., 435mg sod., 38g carb. (2g sugars, 5g fiber), 18g pro.

FAST FIX

SMOKED SAUSAGE & VEGGIE SHEET-PAN SUPPER

PICTURED ON P. 117

This recipe is tasty and quick, and it can easily be doubled for last-minute guests. Cook it in the oven or on the grill, and add the veggies of your choice.
—Judy Batson, Tampa, FL

Takes: 30 min. • **Makes:** 4 servings

- **1 pkg. (13½ oz.) smoked sausage, cut into ½-in. slices**
- **8 fresh Brussels sprouts, thinly sliced**
- **1 large sweet onion, halved and sliced**
- **1 medium yellow summer squash, halved and sliced**
- **1 medium zucchini, halved and sliced**
- **1 medium sweet yellow pepper, chopped**
- **1 medium green pepper, chopped**
- **1 medium tomato, chopped**
- **¾ cup sliced fresh mushrooms**
- **½ cup Greek vinaigrette**

Preheat oven to 400°. Place the first nine ingredients into a greased 15x10x1-in. baking pan. Drizzle with vinaigrette; toss to coat. Bake, uncovered, 15 minutes. Remove pan from oven; preheat broiler. Broil the sausage mixture 3-4 in. from heat until the vegetables are lightly browned, 3-4 minutes.

2 cups: 491 cal., 37g fat (13g sat. fat), 64mg chol., 1430mg sod., 22g carb. (13g sugars, 5g fiber), 18g pro.

BREADED CURRY CHICKEN DRUMMIES

PICTURED ON P. 117

These drumsticks are crispy with just the right amount of zing to get your mouth watering for more. They're baked rather than fried, so they save on fat but not flavor. Boneless, skinless chicken breasts or assorted parts can also be used instead of all drumsticks.
—Lynn Kaufman, Mount Morris, IL

Prep: 20 min. • **Bake:** 45 min.
Makes: 8 servings

- **1½ cups seasoned bread crumbs**
- **1½ tsp. kosher salt**
- **1½ tsp. onion powder**
- **1½ tsp. garlic powder**
- **1 tsp. curry powder**
- **1 tsp. smoked paprika**
- **1 tsp. dried parsley flakes**
- **½ tsp. ground turmeric**
- **¼ tsp. pepper**
- **⅛ tsp. cayenne pepper**
- **½ cup butter, cubed**
- **3 Tbsp. lemon juice**
- **16 chicken drumsticks (about 4 lbs.)**

1. Preheat oven to 375°. In a shallow bowl, mix bread crumbs and seasonings. In a microwave, melt butter with lemon juice. Brush drumsticks with the butter mixture, then coat with the crumb mixture. Place on greased racks in two 15x10x1-in. pans.
2. Bake drumsticks until golden brown and a thermometer reads 170°-175°, 45-55 minutes. Rotate the pans halfway through baking.

2 drumsticks: 380 cal., 24g fat (11g sat. fat), 125mg chol., 535mg sod., 9g carb. (1g sugars, 1g fiber), 31g pro.

TEST KITCHEN TIP

This coating would work well on chicken wings. Just substitute 4 pounds of wing sections or wingettes for the chicken drumsticks.

The drumsticks are great on their own, but if you'd like to serve with a dip or sauce, make raita, which is a simple combination of plain yogurt, chopped and seeded cucumber, cilantro and salt.

THAI PEANUT CHICKEN CASSEROLE

I used traditional pizza sauce and toppings in this recipe for years. After becoming a fan of Thai peanut chicken pizza, I used those flavors instead. Serve with stir-fried vegetables or a salad with sesame dressing on the side for a delicious meal.
—Katherine Wollgast, Troy, MO

Prep: 30 min. • **Bake:** 30 min.
Makes: 10 servings

- **2 tubes (12 oz. each) refrigerated buttermilk biscuits**
- **3 cups shredded cooked chicken**
- **1 cup sliced fresh mushrooms**
- **1 bottle (11½ oz.) Thai peanut sauce, divided**
- **2 cups shredded mozzarella cheese, divided**
- **½ cup chopped sweet red pepper**
- **½ cup shredded carrot**
- **4 green onions, sliced**
- **¼ cup honey-roasted peanuts, coarsely chopped**

1. Preheat oven to 350°. Cut each biscuit into four pieces. Place biscuit pieces in a greased 13x9-in. baking pan.
2. In a large bowl, combine the chicken, mushrooms and 1 cup of the peanut sauce; spread over biscuits. Top with 1 cup of cheese, the red pepper, carrot and green onions. Sprinkle top with the remaining cheese.
3. Bake until the topping is set, the cheese is melted and biscuits have cooked all the way through, about 40 minutes. Sprinkle with peanuts and serve with the remaining peanut sauce.

1 serving: 490 cal., 25g fat (8g sat. fat), 55mg chol., 1013mg sod., 43g carb. (13g sugars, 1g fiber), 26g pro.

THAI PEANUT CHICKEN CASSEROLE

CHEESY FIESTA BEEF CASSEROLE

PICTURED ON P. 117

Over the years I have tweaked this recipe to end up with a wonderful and quick weeknight meal. Feel free to spice it up a bit with jalapenos, if you prefer a little heat.

—Joan Hallford, North Richland Hills, TX

Prep: 25 min. • **Cook:** 15 min.
Makes: 8 servings

- **1 lb. ground beef**
- **1 medium onion, chopped**
- **1 can (15 oz.) black beans, rinsed and drained**
- **1 cup picante sauce**
- **½ tsp. chili powder**
- **1 can (10½ oz.) reduced-fat reduced-sodium condensed cream of chicken soup, undiluted**
- **1 can (10 oz.) diced tomatoes and green chilies, undrained**
- **1 can (4 oz.) chopped green chilies**
- **1 pkg. (9¾ oz.) nacho-flavored tortilla chips or plain tortilla chips, crushed**
- **1 cup shredded sharp cheddar cheese**
- **1 cup shredded Monterey Jack cheese**
- **Cubed avocado and sour cream, optional**

1. In a large skillet, cook beef and onion over medium heat until beef is no longer pink, 6-8 minutes, breaking up beef into crumbles; drain. Stir in the beans, picante sauce and chili powder.
2. In a bowl, combine soup and tomatoes and green chilies. In a lightly greased 2½-qt. microwave-safe baking dish, layer half the chips, beef mixture, soup mixture and cheeses. Repeat layers.
3. Microwave casserole on medium-high, uncovered, until heated through and cheese is melted, about 12 minutes. If desired, top with avocado and sour cream.

1¼ cups: 477 cal., 26g fat (9g sat. fat), 63mg chol., 1119mg sod., 37g carb. (4g sugars, 5g fiber), 23g pro.

TEST KITCHEN TIP

Nacho-flavored tortilla chips add some fabulous flavor to this casserole without a lot of effort. You can also increase the heat by using medium picante sauce and diced jalapenos instead of green chilies.

PLEASING POTATO PIZZA

I first heard of this distinctive pizza when a friend tried it at a restaurant. It sounded fantastic, so I experimented to create my own recipe. The way the slices disappear, there's not a doubt in my mind that this recipe is a success.

—Barbara Zimmer, Wanless, MB

Prep: 30 min. • **Bake:** 30 min.
Makes: 8 servings

- **1 lb. bacon strips, chopped**
- **1 large onion, chopped**
- **½ cup chopped sweet red pepper**
- **2 lbs. potatoes (about 3 large), peeled and cut into 1-in. cubes**
- **1 tube (13.8 oz.) refrigerated pizza crust**
- **¼ cup 2% milk**
- **¼ tsp. salt**
- **1½ cups shredded cheddar cheese**
- **1½ cups shredded part-skim mozzarella cheese**
- **Minced fresh chives and sour cream, optional**

1. Preheat oven to 350°. In a large skillet, cook the bacon over medium heat until partially cooked but not crisp, stirring occasionally. Add onion and pepper; cook and stir until bacon is crisp. Drain well.
2. Place potatoes and water to cover in a large saucepan; bring to a boil. Reduce the heat; cook, uncovered, until tender, 10-15 minutes.
3. Meanwhile, unroll and press pizza crust onto an ungreased 14-in. pizza pan; prick several times with a fork. Bake until lightly browned, about 15 minutes. Increase oven setting to 375°.
4. Drain potatoes; return to pan. Mash potatoes, gradually adding milk and salt. Spread over crust. Top with the bacon mixture and cheeses.
5. Bake until the cheese is melted, 15-20 minutes. If desired, sprinkle with chives and serve with sour cream.

1 slice: 456 cal., 22g fat (10g sat. fat), 51mg chol., 1012mg sod., 43g carb. (6g sugars, 2g fiber), 21g pro.

PLEASING POTATO PIZZA

FARMERS MARKET ENCHILADAS

CHICKEN FLORENTINE CASSEROLE

PICTURED ON P. 117

Creamy and comforting, this chicken and spinach bake is sure to be a hit at dinnertime. The toasty bread crumb topping delivers a bit of a crunch.
—Dori Jackson, Gulf Breeze, FL

Prep: 20 min. • **Bake:** 40 min.
Makes: 6 servings

- **2 cups uncooked elbow macaroni**
- **3 cups shredded cooked chicken**
- **1 can (10¾ oz.) condensed cream of mushroom soup, undiluted**
- **2 cups shredded Swiss cheese**
- **1 pkg. (10 oz.) frozen creamed spinach, thawed**
- **½ cup mayonnaise**
- **¼ cup loosely packed minced fresh basil**
- **1 tsp. garlic powder**
- **½ tsp. dried thyme**
- **½ tsp. pepper**
- **½ cup seasoned bread crumbs**
- **2 Tbsp. butter, melted**

1. Preheat oven to 350°. Cook macaroni according to package directions.
2. Meanwhile, in a large bowl, combine chicken, soup, cheese, spinach, mayonnaise, basil, garlic powder, thyme and pepper.
3. Drain macaroni; gently stir into chicken mixture. Transfer to an ungreased 2½-qt. baking dish. Toss the bread crumbs and butter; sprinkle over casserole.
4. Bake the casserole, uncovered, until bubbly, 40-45 minutes.

1½ cups: 539 cal., 36g fat (13g sat. fat), 111mg chol., 1006mg sod., 17g carb. (4g sugars, 2g fiber), 36g pro.

★★★★★ **READER REVIEW**

"A huge success at our house, which includes some picky eaters! Feeding the kids spinach without complaints is a real accomplishment."

JNFRHRRS TASTEOFHOME.COM

FARMERS MARKET ENCHILADAS

These pretty vegetarian enchiladas use a lot of garden favorites in a quick weeknight meal. Feel free to make substitutions—yellow summer squash, eggplant and corn all taste excellent here, too. Roasting the veggies before making the enchiladas takes more time, but adds so much flavor!
—Elisabeth Larsen, Pleasant Grove, UT

Prep: 20 min. • **Bake:** 45 min.
Makes: 7 servings

- **3 medium zucchini, quartered lengthwise and cut into ¼-in. pieces**
- **1 poblano pepper, seeded and chopped**
- **8 oz. sliced fresh mushrooms**
- **8 oz. cherry tomatoes**
- **1 Tbsp. olive oil**
- **1 tsp. ground cumin**
- **½ tsp. salt**
- **¼ tsp. cayenne pepper**
- **2 cups shredded Monterey Jack cheese**
- **1 cup queso fresco or crumbled feta cheese, divided**
- **½ cup minced fresh cilantro, divided**
- **2 Tbsp. lime juice**
- **14 corn tortillas (6 in.) warmed**
- **1 can (15 oz.) enchilada sauce**

1. Preheat oven to 400°. In a large bowl, combine zucchini, poblano, mushrooms and tomatoes; drizzle with oil and sprinkle with cumin, salt and cayenne. Toss to coat.
2. Divide vegetable mixture between two lightly greased 15x10x1-in. baking pans. Roast for 15 minutes; rotate pans top to bottom. Roast an additional 10 minutes or until vegetables are tender.
3. Return to bowl and cool slightly. Stir in Monterey Jack cheese, ½ cup queso fresco, ¼ cup cilantro and lime juice. Place a scant ½ cup vegetable mixture off center on each tortilla. Roll up and place in a greased 13x9-in. baking dish, seam side down. Top with enchilada sauce; sprinkle with remaining queso fresco.
4. Bake, uncovered, until heated through and cheese is melted, about 20 minutes. Top with remaining cilantro.

2 enchiladas: 346 cal., 17g fat (9g sat. fat), 40mg chol., 780mg sod., 33g carb. (5g sugars, 5g fiber), 18g pro.

SHEET-PAN PINEAPPLE CHICKEN FAJITAS

EAT SMART

SHEET-PAN PINEAPPLE CHICKEN FAJITAS

I combined chicken and pineapple for a new fajita flavor. Just a little sweet, it's a sheet of happiness right out of the oven!

—Nancy Heishman, Las Vegas, NV

Prep: 20 min. • **Cook:** 20 min.
Makes: 6 servings

- **2 Tbsp. coconut oil, melted**
- **3 tsp. chili powder**
- **2 tsp. ground cumin**
- **1 tsp. garlic powder**
- **¾ tsp. kosher salt**
- **1½ lbs. chicken tenderloins, halved lengthwise**
- **1 large red or sweet onion, halved and sliced (about 2 cups)**
- **1 large sweet red pepper, cut into ½-in. strips**
- **1 large green pepper, cut into ½-in. strips**
- **1 Tbsp. minced seeded jalapeno pepper**
- **2 cans (8 oz. each) unsweetened pineapple tidbits, drained**
- **2 Tbsp. honey**
- **2 Tbsp. lime juice**
- **12 corn tortillas (6 in.), warmed**
- **Optional toppings: pico de gallo, sour cream, shredded Mexican cheese blend and sliced avocado**
- **Lime wedges, optional**

1. Preheat oven to 425°. In a large bowl, mix the first five ingredients; stir in the chicken. Add onion, peppers, pineapple, honey and lime juice; toss to combine. Spread evenly in two greased 15x10x1-in. baking pans.
2. Roast for 10 minutes, rotating pans halfway through cooking. Remove pans from oven; preheat broiler.
3. Broil the chicken mixture, one pan at a time, 3-4 in. from heat until the vegetables are lightly browned and the chicken is no longer pink, 3-5 minutes. Serve in tortillas, with toppings and lime wedges as desired.

2 fajitas: 359 cal., 8g fat (4g sat. fat), 56mg chol., 372mg sod., 45g carb. (19g sugars, 6g fiber), 31g pro. **Diabetic exchanges:** 3 starch, 3 lean meat, 1 fat.

CHEESY SEAFOOD ENCHILADAS

CHEESY SEAFOOD ENCHILADAS

Quick-cooking seafood and mildly spicy chilies and salsa make this dish a flavor adventure that my family loves. I've made this with chicken instead of fish, and it's a huge winner. Just increase the saute time to 10-12 minutes.

—Trisha Kruse, Eagle, ID

Prep: 30 min. • **Bake:** 20 min.
Makes: 6 servings

- **1 Tbsp. butter**
- **1 small onion, chopped**
- **½ lb. uncooked shrimp (31-40 per lb.), peeled, deveined and chopped**
- **½ lb. red snapper fillet or other firm whitefish, cut into 1-in. chunks**
- **1½ cups salsa verde**
- **1 pkg. (8 oz.) cream cheese, cubed**
- **1 can (4 oz.) chopped green chilies**
- **½ tsp. salt**
- **2 cups shredded Monterey Jack cheese, divided**
- **12 corn tortillas (6 in.)**
- **Fresh cilantro leaves or jalapeno pepper slices**

1. Preheat oven to 350°. In a large skillet, heat butter over medium-high heat. Add onion; cook and stir until crisp-tender, 3-4 minutes. Add shrimp and snapper; cook until shrimp turn pink, 5-7 minutes. Remove from pan.
2. In the same pan, cook and stir salsa, cream cheese, chilies and salt over medium heat just until cream cheese is melted. Stir in 1 cup shredded cheese; remove from heat.
3. Spread 1 cup of the cheese sauce into a greased 13x9-in. baking dish. Gently stir the remaining cheese sauce into the shrimp mixture. Place ⅓ cup of the shrimp mixture off center on each tortilla. Roll up the tortillas and place in the prepared dish, seam side down. Sprinkle the remaining cheese on top.
4. Cover and bake until heated through and cheese is melted, 20-25 minutes. Sprinkle with cilantro before serving.

2 enchiladas: 481 cal., 29g fat (16g sat. fat), 136mg chol., 1055mg sod., 30g carb. (5g sugars, 4g fiber), 28g pro.

FAST FIX

SPINACH FETA TURNOVERS

These quick and easy turnovers are a favorite with my wife, who says they are delicious and melt in your mouth.
—David Baruch, Weston, FL

Takes: 30 min. • **Makes:** 4 servings

- **2 large eggs**
- **1 pkg. (10 oz.) frozen leaf spinach, thawed, squeezed dry and chopped**
- **¾ cup crumbled feta cheese**
- **2 garlic cloves, minced**
- **¼ tsp. pepper**
- **1 tube (13.8 oz.) refrigerated pizza crust**
- **Refrigerated tzatziki sauce, optional**

1. Preheat oven to 425°. Whisk eggs; set aside 1 Tbsp. of eggs. Combine spinach, feta cheese, garlic, pepper and remaining beaten eggs.
2. Unroll pizza dough; roll into a 12-in. square. Cut into four 3-in. squares; top each with ⅓ cup spinach mixture. Fold into a triangle; pinch the edges to seal. Cut slits in top; brush with the reserved egg.
3. Place on a greased baking sheet. Bake until golden brown, for 10-12 minutes. If desired, serve with tzatziki sauce.

1 turnover: 361 cal., 9g fat (4g sat. fat), 104mg chol., 936mg sod., 51g carb. (7g sugars, 4g fiber), 17g pro.

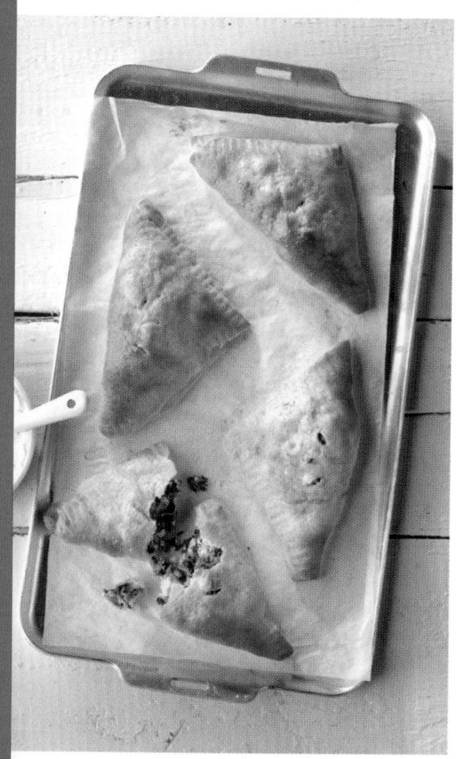

BAKED CHICKEN WITH BACON-TOMATO RELISH

EAT SMART | FAST FIX

BAKED CHICKEN WITH BACON-TOMATO RELISH

We eat chicken for dinner often, and I always try to do something just a little different with it. My children love the crispness of this chicken and my husband and I love the flavorful relish—you can't go wrong with bacon!
—Elisabeth Larsen, Pleasant Grove, UT

Takes: 30 min. • **Makes:** 4 servings

- **1 cup panko (Japanese) bread crumbs**
- **2 Tbsp. plus 1 tsp. minced fresh thyme, divided**
- **½ tsp. salt, divided**
- **½ tsp. pepper, divided**
- **⅓ cup all-purpose flour**
- **1 large egg, beaten**
- **1 lb. chicken tenderloins**
- **4 bacon strips, cut into ½-in. pieces**
- **1½ cups grape tomatoes, halved**
- **1 Tbsp. red wine vinegar**
- **1 Tbsp. brown sugar**

1. Preheat oven to 425°. In a shallow bowl, mix bread crumbs, 2 Tbsp. thyme and ¼ tsp. each salt and pepper. Place flour and egg in separate shallow bowls. Dip chicken in flour; shake off excess. Dip in egg, then in crumb mixture, patting to help coating adhere.
2. Place the chicken on a greased rack in a 15x10x1-in. baking pan. Bake until a thermometer reads 165°, about 15 minutes.
3. Meanwhile, in a large skillet, cook bacon over medium heat until crisp, stirring occasionally, about 5 minutes. Remove with a slotted spoon; drain on paper towels. Discard the drippings, reserving 2 Tbsp. in pan.
4. Add tomatoes, vinegar, sugar and remaining salt and pepper to drippings; cook and stir until tomatoes are tender, 2-3 minutes. Stir in the bacon and the remaining thyme. Serve with chicken.

2 chicken tenders with ¼ cup relish: 326 cal., 13g fat (4g sat. fat), 95mg chol., 602mg sod., 19g carb. (6g sugars, 2g fiber), 34g pro. **Diabetic exchanges:** 4 lean meat, 2 fat, 1 starch.

TEST KITCHEN TIP

Using chicken tenders instead of chicken breast halves speeds along the bake time to make this a quick dinner. Baking on a rack helps the coating on the underside of the chicken stay crunchy, but it isn't a must if you don't have a rack that fits into your pan.

DELUXE MEAT LOAF

This is not only my family's favorite meat loaf when I serve it hot for supper—it's also the highlight of our lunch when I slice cold leftovers for sandwiches.
—Ruth Fisher, Kingston, ON

Prep: 10 min. • **Bake:** 1 hour 20 min.
Makes: 10 servings

- **2 lbs. lean ground beef**
- **2 large eggs, beaten**
- **1 cup dry bread crumbs**
- **⅔ cup whole milk**
- **½ cup chopped onion**
- **3 Tbsp. horseradish**
- **1 tsp. prepared mustard**
- **1 tsp. salt**
- **⅛ tsp. pepper**
- **½ cup chili sauce**

Preheat oven to 350°. In a large bowl, combine the first nine ingredients and mix well. Press into a 9x5-in. loaf pan. Bake for 1 hour. Remove from oven; drain. Spoon chili sauce over loaf. Return to oven and bake until no pink remains, about 20 minutes longer.

1 serving: 224 cal., 9g fat (4g sat. fat), 100mg chol., 579mg sod., 13g carb. (4g sugars, 0 fiber), 21g pro.

CHICKEN PARMESAN STUFFED SHELLS

When chicken Parmesan meets stuffed shells, the result is amazingly good. The chicken texture holds up in a deliciously creamy, cheesy mixture.
—Cyndy Gerken, Naples, FL

Prep: 45 min. • **Bake:** 40 min.
Makes: 12 servings

- **1 pkg. (12 oz.) uncooked jumbo pasta shells**
- **2 Tbsp. olive oil**

FILLING

- **1 lb. boneless skinless chicken breasts, cut into ½-in. cubes**
- **1½ tsp. Italian seasoning**
- **1 tsp. salt, divided**
- **½ tsp. pepper, divided**
- **1 Tbsp. olive oil**
- **2 Tbsp. butter**
- **⅓ cup seasoned bread crumbs**
- **3 cups part-skim ricotta cheese**
- **1 cup shredded part-skim mozzarella cheese**
- **½ cup grated Parmesan cheese**
- **½ cup 2% milk**
- **¼ cup chopped fresh Italian parsley**

ASSEMBLY

- **4 cups meatless pasta sauce**
- **¼ cup grated Parmesan cheese**
- **8 oz. fresh mozzarella cheese, thinly sliced and halved**

1. Preheat oven to 375°. Cook the shells according to the package directions for al dente; drain. Toss with oil; spread in an even layer on a baking sheet.
2. For filling, toss the chicken with Italian seasoning, ½ tsp. salt and ¼ tsp. pepper. In a large skillet, heat oil over medium-high heat; saute the chicken just until lightly browned, about 2 minutes. Reduce heat to medium; stir in butter until melted. Stir in bread crumbs; cook until the crumbs are slightly toasted, 2-3 minutes, stirring occasionally. Cool slightly.
3. In a large bowl, mix cheeses, milk, parsley and the remaining salt and pepper. Fold in the chicken.
4. Spread 2 cups of pasta sauce into a greased 13x9-in. baking dish. Fill each shell with 2½ Tbsp. of the ricotta mixture; place over sauce. Top with the remaining sauce and cheeses (dish will be full).
5. Cover with greased foil; bake shells for 30 minutes. Uncover; bake until heated through, 10-15 minutes longer.

1 serving: 431 cal., 19g fat (10g sat. fat), 71mg chol., 752mg sod., 36g carb. (8g sugars, 2g fiber), 28g pro.

TEST KITCHEN TIP

Avoid overcooking pasta. Shells are easier to stuff when al dente. To fill shells easily, spoon the filling into a plastic storage bag. Cut a 1-inch hole in the corner and pipe the filling into the shells.

Coat the foil with cooking spray to keep it from sticking to the cheese.

CHICKEN PARMESAN STUFFED SHELLS

EAT SMART | FAST FIX

CREAMY SKINNY PASTA CASSEROLE

Baked pasta is a favorite potluck dish, so I altered some of the ingredients in this recipe to make it lower in calories.

—Andrea Bolden, Unionville, TN

Takes: 30 min. • **Makes:** 6 servings

- **12 oz. uncooked whole wheat penne pasta**
- **1 lb. lean ground chicken**
- **1 small onion, finely chopped**
- **1 tsp. garlic powder, divided**
- **1 tsp. Italian seasoning**
- **½ tsp. salt**
- **¼ tsp. pepper**
- **1 can (14½ oz.) diced tomatoes, undrained**
- **3 oz. reduced-fat cream cheese**
- **½ cup reduced-fat sour cream**
- **1 cup shredded part-skim mozzarella cheese, divided**
- **Minced fresh parsley and crushed red pepper flakes, optional**

1. Preheat oven to 400°. Cook pasta according to package directions for al dente. Drain, reserving ⅓ cup of the pasta water; return all to pot.
2. Meanwhile, in a large skillet, cook and crumble chicken with onion, ½ tsp. garlic powder and remaining seasonings over medium-high heat until no longer pink, 5-7 minutes. Stir in tomatoes; bring to a boil. Add to pasta; toss to combine. Transfer to a 13x9-in. baking dish coated with cooking spray.
3. Mix cream cheese, sour cream, ½ cup mozzarella cheese and remaining garlic powder. Drop mixture by tablespoonfuls over pasta. Sprinkle with the remaining mozzarella cheese.
4. Bake, uncovered, until cheese is melted, 8-10 minutes. If desired, sprinkle with parsley and pepper flakes.

1⅔ cups: 445 cal., 13g fat (6g sat. fat), 78mg chol., 559mg sod., 49g carb. (6g sugars, 7g fiber), 33g pro.

CREAMY SKINNY PASTA CASSEROLE

*** HEALTH TIP *** Whole wheat pasta is an effective way to get whole grains into your daily diet. If the flavor is too strong for your family, try using half whole wheat and half regular pasta.

SHRIMP & CRAB CASSEROLE

PICTURED ON P. 117

This quick and easy recipe delivers delicious flavors and melt-in-your mouth textures that are satisfying yet elegant. And it lends itself to making in advance. Let the sauce cool slightly before adding the seafood, then cover and refrigerate. Take it out of the fridge 30 minutes before baking.

—Jan Bartley, Evergreen, NC

Prep: 25 min. • **Bake:** 40 min.
Makes: 8 servings

- **2 pkg. (8.8 oz. each) ready-to-serve long grain and wild rice**
- **¼ cup butter, cubed**
- **2 celery ribs, chopped**
- **1 medium onion, chopped**
- **3 Tbsp. all-purpose flour**
- **1½ cups half-and-half cream**
- **1 tsp. seafood seasoning**
- **¾ tsp. salt**
- **½ tsp. hot pepper sauce**
- **¼ tsp. pepper**
- **1½ lbs. uncooked shrimp (31-40 per lb.), peeled and deveined**
- **2 cans (6 oz. each) lump crabmeat, drained**
- **1 cup shredded Colby-Monterey Jack cheese**

1. Preheat oven to 350°. Spread rice into a greased 13x9-in. baking dish. In a large skillet, heat butter over medium-high heat. Add the celery and onion; cook and stir until tender, 6-8 minutes. Stir in flour until blended; gradually whisk in cream. Bring to a boil, stirring constantly; cook and stir 1-2 minutes or until thickened.
2. Stir in seafood seasoning, salt, pepper sauce and pepper. Fold in shrimp and crab. Spoon over the rice. Sprinkle with cheese. Bake, covered until the shrimp turn pink, 40-45 minutes. Let stand 5 minutes.

1 serving: 376 cal., 17g fat (10g sat. fat), 195mg chol., 1127mg sod., 24g carb. (3g sugars, 1g fiber), 29g pro.

APPLE-GLAZED STUFFED PORK CHOPS

CREAMY HAM & MACARONI

The original comfort food, macaroni and cheese gets a makeover with the addition of cubed ham and grated Parmesan. Kids won't be able to stop talking about it!
—Christy Looper, Colorado Springs, CO

Prep: 20 min. • **Bake:** 20 min.
Makes: 6 servings

- **2 cups uncooked elbow macaroni**
- **¼ cup butter, cubed**
- **¼ cup all-purpose flour**
- **2 cups 2% milk**
- **4 tsp. chicken bouillon granules**
- **¼ tsp. pepper**
- **2 cups shredded cheddar cheese, divided**
- **1½ cups cubed fully cooked ham**
- **¼ cup grated Parmesan cheese**

1. Cook macaroni according to package directions; drain and set aside. In a large saucepan, melt butter over low heat; whisk in flour until smooth. Whisk in the milk, bouillon and pepper. Bring to a boil; cook and stir for 2 minutes or until thickened. Remove from the heat. Stir in 1 cup of cheddar cheese, ham, Parmesan cheese and macaroni.
2. Transfer to a greased 2-qt. baking dish. Sprinkle with remaining cheddar cheese. Bake, uncovered, at 350° until bubbly, 20-25 minutes. Let stand for 5 minutes before serving.

1 cup: 434 cal., 26g fat (16g sat. fat), 93mg chol., 1414mg sod., 29g carb. (5g sugars, 1g fiber), 22g pro.

APPLE-GLAZED STUFFED PORK CHOPS

I've served these for many dinner parties, paired with a veggie and a green salad. Once prepared, they can be baked later in the day.
—Judy Wilson, Sun City West, AZ

Prep: 25 min. • **Bake:** 35 min.
Makes: 4 servings

- **3 cups seasoned stuffing cubes**
- **1 medium Granny Smith apple, peeled and diced**
- **1 celery rib, diced**
- **⅓ cup raisins**
- **2½ cups apple juice, divided**
- **¼ cup butter, melted**
- **4 center-cut pork rib chops (1½ in. thick and 12 oz. each)**
- **½ tsp. salt**
- **¼ tsp. coarsely ground pepper**
- **⅓ cup packed brown sugar**

1. Preheat oven to 350°. Place the first four ingredients in a large bowl. Add ¾ cup juice and the melted butter; toss until combined.
2. Cut a pocket in each pork chop by slicing horizontally to the bone. Fill each pocket with about ½ cup stuffing; place chops on a rack in a roasting pan. Sprinkle with salt and pepper. Add 1½ cups apple juice to the pan. Cover tightly with foil; bake until a thermometer inserted in the pork reads at least 145°, 35-45 minutes.
3. Place the remaining stuffing in a greased 8-in. baking dish. Bake, covered, until heated through, 20-25 minutes.
4. Meanwhile, for glaze, place the brown sugar and the remaining ¼ cup apple juice in a small saucepan; bring to a boil, stirring to dissolve the sugar. Reduce the heat; simmer, uncovered, until the mixture is reduced by half, about 5 minutes.
5. To serve, brush chops with the glaze. Serve with additional stuffing.

1 stuffed pork chop with ½ cup stuffing: 750 cal., 28g fat (13g sat. fat), 139mg chol., 1000mg sod., 77g carb. (45g sugars, 3g fiber), 48g pro.

TEST KITCHEN TIP

Bone-in pork loin chops may also be used, but rib chops will give you more room to make a pocket. Let the apple juice mixture simmer to thicken it to a perfect glaze consistency.

ROASTED SALMON WITH SAUTEED BALSAMIC SPINACH

FOIL PACKET SHRIMP & SAUSAGE JAMBALAYA

This hearty, satisfying dinner has all the flavors of authentic jambalaya but is ready in minutes. The packets can be prepared a day ahead and cooked right before serving. These are also good on the grill!
—Allison Stroud, Oklahoma City, OK

Prep: 20 min. • **Bake:** 25 min.
Makes: 6 servings

- **12 oz. fully cooked andouille sausage links, cut into ½-in. slices**
- **12 oz. uncooked shrimp (31-40 per lb.), peeled and deveined**
- **1 medium green pepper, chopped**
- **1 medium onion, chopped**
- **2 celery ribs, chopped**
- **3 garlic cloves, minced**
- **2 tsp. Creole seasoning**
- **1 can (14½ oz.) fire-roasted diced tomatoes, drained**
- **1 cup uncooked instant rice**
- **1 can (8 oz.) tomato sauce**
- **½ cup chicken broth**

Preheat oven to 425°. In a large bowl, combine all ingredients. Divide mixture among six greased 18x12-in. pieces of heavy-duty foil. Fold foil around mixture and crimp edges to seal, forming packets; place on a baking sheet. Bake until the shrimp turn pink and the rice is tender, 20-25 minutes.

1 packet: 287 cal., 12g fat (4g sat. fat), 143mg chol., 1068mg sod., 23g carb. (3g sugars, 2g fiber), 23g pro.

TEST KITCHEN TIP

Make sure to use instant rice. If you use long grain or converted rice, the shrimp will be done long before the rice. Wear oven mitts when opening the packets to protect hands from the escaping steam.

EAT SMART | FAST FIX

ROASTED SALMON WITH SAUTEED BALSAMIC SPINACH

This is my favorite way to eat salmon. It is healthy, affordable, fast and delicious.
—Susan Hall, Sparks, MD

Takes: 30 min. • **Makes:** 4 servings

- **3 tsp. olive oil, divided**
- **4 salmon fillets (6 oz. each)**
- **1½ tsp. reduced-sodium seafood seasoning**
- **¼ tsp. pepper**
- **1 garlic clove, sliced**
- **Dash crushed red pepper flakes**
- **10 cups fresh baby spinach (about 10 oz.)**
- **6 small tomatoes, seeded and cut into ½-in. pieces**
- **½ cup balsamic vinegar**

1. Preheat oven to 450°. Rub 1 tsp. oil over both sides of salmon; sprinkle with seafood seasoning and pepper. Place in a greased 15x10x1-in. baking pan; roast until fish just begins to flake easily with a fork, 10-12 minutes.
2. Meanwhile, place the remaining oil, the garlic and pepper flakes in a 6-qt. stockpot; heat over medium-low heat until the garlic is softened, 3-4 minutes. Increase heat to medium-high. Add spinach; cook and stir until wilted, 3-4 minutes. Stir in tomatoes; heat through. Divide mixture among four serving dishes.
3. In a small saucepan, bring vinegar to a boil. Cook until the vinegar is reduced by half, 2-3 minutes. Immediately remove from heat.
4. To serve, place the salmon fillets over the spinach mixture. Drizzle salmon with the balsamic glaze.

1 serving: 348 cal., 19g fat (4g sat. fat), 85mg chol., 333mg sod., 12g carb. (9g sugars, 2g fiber), 31g pro. **Diabetic exchanges:** 3 lean meat, 2 vegetable, 1 fat.

MEAT & PEPPER CORNBREAD

It suits me to be able to brown and bake this delicious cornbread in the same cast-iron-skillet—such convenience!
—Rita Carlson, Idaho Falls, ID

Prep: 15 min. • **Bake:** 20 min.
Makes: 6 servings

- 1 lb. ground beef
- 1 cup chopped green pepper
- 1 cup chopped onion
- 2 cans (8 oz. each) tomato sauce
- 1½ tsp. chili powder
- ½ tsp. salt
- ¼ tsp. pepper
- 1 cup all-purpose flour
- ¾ cup cornmeal
- ¼ cup sugar
- 1 Tbsp. baking powder
- ½ tsp. salt
- 1 large egg, beaten
- 1 cup whole milk
- ¼ cup canola oil

1. In a 10-in. cast-iron or other ovenproof skillet, lightly brown ground beef, green pepper and onion; drain. Add the tomato sauce, chili powder, salt and pepper; simmer for 10-15 minutes.
2. Meanwhile, combine dry ingredients. In a second bowl, combine egg, milk and oil; stir into the dry ingredients just until moistened. Pour over the beef mixture.
3. Bake at 400° for 20-25 minutes or until golden. Serve in skillet, or cool briefly, then run a knife around edge of skillet and invert on a serving plate; cut into wedges.

1 serving: 432 cal., 18g fat (5g sat. fat), 87mg chol., 839mg sod., 46g carb. (13g sugars, 3g fiber), 22g pro.

CREAMY GREEN CHILI CHICKEN COBBLER

This dish, which combines shredded chicken with diced green chilies, green enchilada sauce, creams and cheeses, is a family go-to that everyone raves about.
—Johnna Johnson, Scottsdale, AZ

Prep: 25 min. • **Bake:** 45 min.
Makes: 8 servings

- 2 cups all-purpose flour
- ½ cup grated Parmesan cheese
- 2 tsp. baking powder
- 6 Tbsp. cold butter, cubed
- ¾ cup plus 2 Tbsp. heavy whipping cream
- 3 oz. cream cheese, softened
- ½ cup sour cream
- 1 can (10½ oz.) condensed cream of chicken soup, undiluted
- 1 can (10 oz.) green enchilada sauce
- 2 cans (4 oz. each) chopped green chilies
- 2½ cups shredded rotisserie chicken (about 10 oz.)
- 1½ cups shredded Colby-Monterey Jack cheese

1. Preheat oven to 450°. For the crumb topping, whisk together flour, cheese and baking powder. Cut in butter until mixture resembles coarse crumbs. Add cream; stir just until moistened. On a lightly greased 15x10x1-in. pan, crumble mixture into ½- to 1-in. pieces.
2. Bake on an upper oven rack until light golden brown, 8-10 minutes. Reduce oven setting to 350°.
3. In a large bowl, mix cream cheese and sour cream until smooth. Stir in soup, enchilada sauce, green chilies and chicken. Transfer mixture to an 11x7-in. baking dish; sprinkle with cheese. Add crumb topping (dish will be full).
4. Place dish on a baking sheet. Bake, uncovered, on a lower oven rack until the topping is deep golden brown and the filling is bubbly, 35-40 minutes.

1¼ cups: 581 cal., 39g fat (22g sat. fat), 132mg chol., 1076mg sod., 33g carb. (3g sugars, 2g fiber), 25g pro.

TEST KITCHEN TIP

An average 2-pound rotisserie chicken will yield about 3 cups of meat. If you don't have an 11x7-inch baking dish, a 13x9-inch or other shallow dish that holds at least 2½ quarts will work.

CREAMY GREEN CHILI CHICKEN COBBLER

On the Lighter Side

Healthy eating doesn't mean you have to give up fresh, delicious, even decadent-tasting meals. All the recipes in these pages are good for you—but you'd never guess by tasting!

Dijon-Crusted Fish (p. 150) **Maple-Glazed Pork Tenderloin** (p. 147)
Split-Second Shrimp (p. 155) **Lentil Burritos** (p. 146) **Strawberry-Turkey Spinach Salad** (p. 150)

EASY CARIBBEAN CHICKEN

EAT SMART | FAST FIX

LEMON-CAPER PORK MEDALLIONS

Looking for an elegant but easy dinner you can put together in a twinkling for guests or unexpected visitors? These lightly breaded medallions are truly something special!
—*Taste of Home* Test Kitchen

Takes: 30 min. • **Makes:** 4 servings

- **1 pork tenderloin (1 lb.), cut into 12 slices**
- **½ cup all-purpose flour**
- **½ tsp. salt**
- **¼ tsp. pepper**
- **1 Tbsp. butter**
- **1 Tbsp. olive oil**
- **1 cup reduced-sodium chicken broth**
- **¼ cup white wine or additional reduced-sodium chicken broth**
- **1 garlic clove, minced**
- **1 Tbsp. capers, drained**
- **1 Tbsp. lemon juice**
- **½ tsp. dried rosemary, crushed**

1. Flatten pork slices to ¼-in. thickness. In a large shallow dish, combine the flour, salt and pepper. Add the pork, a few pieces at a time, and turn to coat.
2. In a large nonstick skillet over medium heat, cook the pork in butter and oil in batches until juices run clear. Remove and keep warm.
3. Add broth, wine and garlic to the pan, stirring to loosen browned bits. Bring to a boil; cook until the liquid is reduced by half. Stir in the capers, lemon juice and rosemary; heat through. Serve with pork.

3 medallions: 232 cal., 10g fat (4g sat. fat), 71mg chol., 589mg sod., 7g carb. (1g sugars, 0 fiber), 24g pro. **Diabetic exchanges:** 3 lean meat, 1½ fat, ½ starch.

EAT SMART | FAST FIX

EASY CARIBBEAN CHICKEN

This simple recipe uses easy-to-find ingredients. Serve with steamed vegetables for a complete meal. For a change, try using cubes of pork or even shrimp instead of the chicken.
—Courtney Stultz, Weir, KS

Takes: 20 min. • **Makes:** 4 servings

- **1 Tbsp. olive oil**
- **1 lb. boneless skinless chicken breasts, cut into 1-in. pieces**
- **2 tsp. garlic-herb seasoning blend**
- **1 can (14½ oz.) fire-roasted diced tomatoes**
- **1 can (8 oz.) unsweetened pineapple chunks**
- **¼ cup barbecue sauce**
- **Hot cooked rice**
- **Fresh cilantro leaves, optional**

In large nonstick skillet, heat oil over medium-high heat. Add chicken and seasoning; saute until the chicken is lightly browned and no longer pink, about 5 minutes. Add tomatoes, pineapple and barbecue sauce. Bring to a boil; cook and stir until the flavors are blended and the chicken is cooked through, 5-7 minutes. Serve with rice and, if desired, cilantro.

1 cup chicken mixture: 242 cal., 6g fat (1g sat. fat), 63mg chol., 605mg sod., 20g carb. (15g sugars, 1g fiber), 24g pro. **Diabetic exchanges:** 3 lean meat, 1 starch, ½ fat.

TEST KITCHEN TIP

The flavors of this dish will remind you of a pineapple barbecue chicken pizza. You can use fresh pineapple instead of canned; use about 1 cup.

FREEZE IT | EAT SMART | FAST FIX

QUINOA UNSTUFFED PEPPERS

This deconstructed stuffed pepper dish packs a wallop of flavor. I make it all the time, and I always make sure my freezer's stocked with single-serve portions to take to work.
—Rebecca Ende, Phoenix, NY

Takes: 30 min. • **Makes:** 4 servings

1½ cups vegetable stock
¾ cup quinoa, rinsed
1 lb. Italian turkey sausage links, casings removed
1 medium sweet red pepper, chopped
1 medium green pepper, chopped
¾ cup chopped sweet onion
1 garlic clove, minced
¼ tsp. garam masala
¼ tsp. pepper
⅛ tsp. salt

1. In a small saucepan, bring the stock to a boil. Add quinoa. Reduce heat; simmer, covered, until the liquid is absorbed, 12-15 minutes. Remove from heat.

2. In a large skillet, cook and crumble sausage with peppers and onion over medium-high heat until no longer pink, 8-10 minutes. Add garlic and seasonings; cook and stir 1 minute. Stir in quinoa.

Freeze option: Place cooled quinoa mixture in freezer containers. To use, partially thaw in refrigerator overnight. Microwave, covered, on high in a microwave-safe dish until heated through, stirring occasionally.

1 cup: 261 cal., 9g fat (2g sat. fat), 42mg chol., 760mg sod., 28g carb. (3g sugars, 4g fiber), 17g pro. **Diabetic exchanges:** 2 starch, 2 medium-fat meat.

TEST KITCHEN TIP

This dish is a fusion of flavors. The garam masala and Italian flavors in the sausage work together with the hint of cinnamon for a unique blend of balanced flavor.

If you don't have vegetable stock on hand, use chicken or beef stock instead. You could use broth, but think of stock like a blank canvas where you get to layer on the flavors. Broth is already seasoned.

QUINOA UNSTUFFED PEPPERS

EAT SMART | FAST FIX

PEPPER STEAK

When I need a speedy skillet supper, this pepper steak comes to my rescue. The tender meat is slightly sweet, with a hint of brown sugar and molasses.
—Monica Williams, Burleson, TX

Takes: 25 min. • **Makes:** 6 servings

2 Tbsp. cornstarch
2 Tbsp. brown sugar
2 Tbsp. minced fresh gingerroot
¾ tsp. garlic powder
1 can (14½ oz.) beef broth
3 Tbsp. reduced-sodium soy sauce
1 Tbsp. molasses
1½ lbs. beef top sirloin steak, cut into ¼-in. strips
1 Tbsp. canola oil
2 large green peppers, cut into ½-in. strips
1½ cups sliced celery
3 green onions, chopped
4 tsp. lemon juice
Hot cooked noodles, optional

1. In a bowl, combine the cornstarch, brown sugar, ginger and garlic powder. Stir in broth until smooth. Add soy sauce and molasses; set aside.

2. In a nonstick skillet or wok, stir-fry steak in oil for 4-5 minutes; remove and keep warm. Stir-fry peppers, celery and onions until crisp-tender, about 5 minutes. Stir broth mixture and add it to the vegetables. Return the meat to the pan. Bring to a boil; cook and stir until thickened, 2 minutes. Stir in lemon juice. Serve over hot noodles if desired.

¾ cup: 233 cal., 7g fat (2g sat. fat), 46mg chol., 672mg sod., 14g carb. (9g sugars, 2g fiber), 26g pro. **Diabetic exchanges:** 3 lean meat, 1 vegetable, ½ starch, ½ fat.

EAT SMART | FAST FIX

GLAZED ROSEMARY PORK

Savory honey-glazed pork tenderloin feels sophisticated, but it's super easy, too—ideal for weekend dinner parties and weeknight suppers alike.
—Barbara Sistrunk, Fultondale, AL

Takes: 30 min. • **Makes:** 6 servings

- **¼ cup reduced-sodium chicken broth**
- **3 Tbsp. honey**
- **1 Tbsp. minced fresh rosemary or 1 tsp. dried rosemary, crushed**
- **1 Tbsp. Dijon mustard**
- **1 tsp. balsamic vinegar**
- **⅛ tsp. salt**
- **⅛ tsp. pepper**
- **2 pork tenderloins (1 lb. each)**
- **2 Tbsp. olive oil, divided**
- **4 garlic cloves, minced**

1. Whisk together the first seven ingredients. Cut the tenderloins crosswise into 1-in. slices; pound each with a meat mallet to ½-in. thickness.
2. In a large nonstick skillet, heat 1 Tbsp. oil over medium-high heat. In batches, cook the pork until a thermometer reads 145°, 3-4 minutes per side. Remove from the pan.
3. In the same skillet, heat the remaining 1 Tbsp. oil over medium heat; saute garlic until tender, about 1 minute. Stir in the broth mixture; bring to a boil, stirring to loosen browned bits from pan. Add pork, turning to coat; heat through.

4 oz. cooked pork: 255 cal., 10g fat (2g sat. fat), 85mg chol., 194mg sod., 10g carb. (9g sugars, 0 fiber), 31g pro. **Diabetic exchanges:** ½ starch, 4 lean meat, 1 fat.

EAT SMART | FAST FIX

ASPARAGUS SPINACH SALAD WITH CHICKEN

This salad is one of our favorites because it packs in so many of the summer fruits and vegetables we love so much!
—Joan Hallford, North Richland Hills, TX

Takes: 30 min. • **Makes:** 6 servings

- **1 lb. fresh asparagus, trimmed and cut into 1-in. pieces**
- **2 Tbsp. water**
- **¼ cup prepared poppy seed salad dressing**
- **1 Tbsp. orange juice**
- **1 Tbsp. honey**
- **1 tsp. grated orange zest**
- **½ tsp. Dijon mustard**
- **8 cups fresh baby spinach**
- **3 cups shredded rotisserie chicken**
- **2 cups sliced fresh strawberries or fresh blueberries**
- **¼ cup sliced almonds, toasted**
- **2 Tbsp. sesame seeds, toasted**

1. In a microwave-safe bowl, combine asparagus and water. Microwave, covered, on high until crisp-tender, 2-4 minutes; drain. Remove asparagus and immediately drop into ice water. Drain and pat dry.
2. In a small bowl, whisk the dressing, orange juice, honey, orange zest and mustard until blended.
3. In a large bowl, combine the spinach, chicken, strawberries, almonds, sesame seeds and asparagus. Add the dressing and toss to coat.

2 cups: 267 cal., 13g fat (3g sat. fat), 66mg chol., 151mg sod., 14g carb. (9g sugars, 3g fiber), 24g pro. **Diabetic exchanges:** 3 lean meat, 2 vegetable, 2 fat.

TEST KITCHEN TIP

If spinach isn't your favorite, try this salad with spring mix or a baby kale blend. If you don't have almonds or sesame seeds, try toasted pecans or walnuts, sunflower seeds, or even wonton strips to add some crunch.

ASPARAGUS SPINACH SALAD WITH CHICKEN

EAT SMART | FAST FIX

TURKEY ALFREDO PIZZA

A longtime family favorite, we love this thin-crusted pizza for its nutrition and flavor—and as an excellent way to use up leftover turkey during the holidays. Served with a bowl of vegetable soup or rustic green salad, it's also a perfect busy weeknight meal solution!
—Edie DeSpain, Logan, UT

Takes: 25 min. • **Makes:** 6 servings

- **1 prebaked 12-in. thin pizza crust**
- **1 garlic clove, peeled and halved**
- **¾ cup reduced-fat Alfredo sauce, divided**
- **1 pkg. (10 oz.) frozen chopped spinach, thawed and squeezed dry**
- **2 tsp. lemon juice**
- **¼ tsp. salt**
- **⅛ tsp. pepper**
- **2 cups shredded cooked turkey breast**
- **¾ cup shredded Parmesan cheese**
- **½ tsp. crushed red pepper flakes**

1. Place the crust on a baking sheet; rub with cut sides of garlic. Discard garlic. Spread ½ cup Alfredo sauce over crust.
2. In a small bowl, combine the spinach, lemon juice, salt and pepper; spoon evenly over sauce. Top with turkey; drizzle with remaining ¼ cup Alfredo sauce. Sprinkle with cheese and pepper flakes.
3. Bake at 425° until heated through and the cheese is melted, 11-13 minutes.

1 piece: 300 cal., 9g fat (4g sat. fat), 60mg chol., 823mg sod., 27g carb. (2g sugars, 2g fiber), 25g pro. **Diabetic exchanges:** 3 lean meat, 2 starch, ½ fat.

TURKEY ALFREDO PIZZA

EAT SMART | FAST FIX

TOMATO-BASIL BAKED FISH

This recipe can be made with different kinds of fish as desired, and I usually have the rest of the ingredients on hand. Baked fish is wonderful, and I fix this healthy dish often.
—Annie Hicks, Zephyrhills, FL

Takes: 15 min. • **Makes:** 2 servings

- **1 Tbsp. lemon juice**
- **1 tsp. olive oil**
- **8 oz. orange roughy, red snapper, cod or haddock fillets**
- **¼ tsp. dried basil**
- **⅛ tsp. salt**
- **⅛ tsp. pepper**
- **2 plum tomatoes, thinly sliced**
- **2 tsp. grated Parmesan cheese**

1. In a shallow bowl, combine the lemon juice and oil. Add the fish fillets; turn to coat. Place in a greased 9-in. pie plate. Sprinkle with half of the basil, salt and pepper. Arrange tomatoes over top; sprinkle with Parmesan cheese and the remaining seasonings.
2. Cover and bake at 400° for 10-12 minutes or until the fish flakes easily with a fork.

1 serving: 121 cal., 4g fat (1g sat. fat), 24mg chol., 256mg sod., 4g carb. (2g sugars, 1g fiber), 18g pro. **Diabetic exchanges:** 3 lean meat, 1 vegetable, ½ fat.

EAT SMART | FAST FIX

SAUSAGE PASTA WITH VEGETABLES

I made this for our pastor one night. He loved it so much we nicknamed it "Jason's Pasta." It's a sneaky (and successful!) way to get our kids to eat more veggies.
—Suzie Foutty, Mansfield, OH

Takes: 25 min. • **Makes:** 4 servings

- **2 cups uncooked whole wheat penne pasta**
- **1 lb. Italian turkey sausage links, casings removed**
- **1¾ cups sliced fresh mushrooms**
- **1 can (14½ oz.) fire-roasted diced tomatoes with garlic, undrained**
- **6 oz. fresh baby spinach (about 8 cups)**
- **¼ cup shredded part-skim mozzarella cheese**

1. In a 6-qt. stockpot, cook the pasta according to the package directions; drain and return to the pot.
2. Meanwhile, in a large skillet, cook and crumble sausage with mushrooms over medium-high heat until no longer pink, 5-7 minutes. Stir in tomatoes; bring to a boil. Stir in spinach until wilted.
3. Add to pasta; heat through. Sprinkle with cheese; remove from the heat. Let stand, covered, until cheese is melted.

1½ cups: 392 cal., 10g fat (3g sat. fat), 46mg chol., 825mg sod., 51g carb. (4g sugars, 8g fiber), 26g pro.

EAT SMART | FAST FIX

PORK CHOPS WITH CRANBERRY SAUCE

Moist and tender pork chops are treated to a sweet, light cranberry glaze in this weeknight-friendly entree. It's one of my husband's favorites and quite suitable for company, too.

—Stephanie Homme, Baton Rouge, LA

Takes: 30 min. • **Makes:** 6 servings

- **6 boneless pork loin chops (4 oz. each)**
- **¾ tsp. salt**
- **¼ tsp. coarsely ground pepper**
- **2 tsp. cornstarch**
- **1 cup cranberry-apple juice**
- **2 tsp. honey**
- **¾ cup dried cranberries**
- **1 Tbsp. minced fresh tarragon**
- **1 Tbsp. minced fresh parsley**
- **3 cups hot cooked brown rice**

1. Sprinkle the pork chops with salt and pepper. In a large skillet coated with cooking spray, brown the chops over medium heat, 3-5 minutes per side. Remove from pan.
2. In same pan, mix cornstarch, juice and honey until smooth; stir in cranberries and herbs. Bring to a boil, stirring to loosen any browned bits from pan; cook until thickened and bubbly, about 2 minutes.
3. Add chops. Reduce heat; simmer, covered, until a thermometer inserted in pork reads 145°, 4-5 minutes. Let stand 5 minutes before serving. Serve with rice.

1 pork chop with ½ cup rice: 374 cal., 8g fat (3g sat. fat), 55mg chol., 333mg sod., 52g carb. (23g sugars, 3g fiber), 25g pro.

EAT SMART | FAST FIX

SEASONED TILAPIA FILLETS

This restaurant-quality dish relies on everyday spices for big flavor. It's delicous, healthy, simple to make, and so good!

—Dana Alexander, Lebanon, MO

Takes: 25 min. • **Makes:** 2 servings

- **2 tilapia fillets (6 oz. each)**
- **1 Tbsp. butter, melted**
- **1 tsp. Montreal steak seasoning**
- **½ tsp. dried parsley flakes**
- **¼ tsp. paprika**
- **¼ tsp. dried thyme**
- **⅛ tsp. onion powder**
- **⅛ tsp. salt**
- **⅛ tsp. pepper**
- **Dash garlic powder**

1. Preheat oven to 425°. Place tilapia in a greased 11x7-in. baking dish; drizzle with butter. In a small bowl, mix the remaining ingredients; sprinkle over fillets.
2. Bake, covered, 10 minutes. Uncover; bake until the fish just begins to flake easily with a fork, 5-8 minutes.

1 fillet: 193 cal., 7g fat (4g sat. fat), 98mg chol., 589mg sod., 1g carb. (0 sugars, 0 fiber), 32g pro. **Diabetic exchanges:** 5 lean meat, 1½ fat.

BEEF FILETS WITH PORTOBELLO SAUCE

EAT SMART | FAST FIX

BEEF FILETS WITH PORTOBELLO SAUCE

We enjoy these tasty, mushroom-topped fillets with crusty French bread, mixed salad and a light lemon dessert.

—Christel Stein, Tampa, FL

Takes: 20 min. • **Makes:** 2 servings

- **2 beef tenderloin steaks (4 oz. each)**
- **1¾ cups sliced baby portobello mushrooms (about 4 oz.)**
- **½ cup dry red wine or reduced-sodium beef broth**
- **1 tsp. all-purpose flour**
- **½ cup reduced-sodium beef broth**
- **1 tsp. ketchup**
- **1 tsp. steak sauce**
- **1 tsp. Worcestershire sauce**
- **½ tsp. ground mustard**
- **¼ tsp. pepper**
- **⅛ tsp. salt**
- **1 Tbsp. minced fresh chives, optional**

1. Place a large skillet coated with cooking spray over medium-high heat; brown the steaks on both sides. Remove from pan.
2. Add mushrooms and wine to pan; bring to a boil over medium heat, stirring to loosen browned bits from pan. Cook until liquid is reduced by half, 2-3 minutes. Mix flour and broth until smooth; stir into pan. Stir in all remaining ingredients except the chives; bring to a boil.
3. Return steaks to pan; cook, uncovered, until meat reaches desired doneness (for medium-rare, a thermometer should read 135°; medium, 140°), 1-2 minutes per side. If desired, sprinkle with chives.

1 serving: 247 cal., 7g fat (3g sat. fat), 51mg chol., 369mg sod., 7g carb. (3g sugars, 1g fiber), 27g pro. **Diabetic exchanges:** 3 lean meat, 1 vegetable.

EAT SMART | FAST FIX

LEMON CHICKEN & RICE

On our busy ranch, we often need to put meals on the table in a hurry. We find this all-in-one chicken dish, with its delicate lemon flavor, fits the bill. It's inexpensive to boot!

—Kat Thompson, Prineville, OR

Takes: 30 min. • **Makes:** 4 servings

- **2 Tbsp. butter**
- **1 lb. boneless skinless chicken breasts, cut into strips**
- **1 medium onion, chopped**
- **1 large carrot, thinly sliced**
- **2 garlic cloves, minced**
- **1 Tbsp. cornstarch**
- **1 can (14½ oz.) chicken broth**
- **2 Tbsp. lemon juice**
- **¼ tsp. salt**
- **1 cup frozen peas**
- **1½ cups uncooked instant rice**

1. In a large cast-iron or other heavy skillet, heat butter over medium-high heat; saute chicken, onion, carrot and garlic until the chicken is no longer pink, 5-7 minutes.
2. In a small bowl, mix the cornstarch, broth, lemon juice and salt until smooth. Gradually add to skillet; bring to a boil. Cook and stir until thickened, 1-2 minutes.
3. Stir in peas; return to a boil. Stir in rice. Remove from heat; let stand, covered, 5 minutes.

1 serving: 370 cal., 9g fat (4g sat. fat), 80mg chol., 746mg sod., 41g carb. (4g sugars, 3g fiber), 29g pro. **Diabetic exchanges:** 3 starch, 3 lean meat, 1½ fat.

EAT SMART

EGGPLANT SALAD WITH TOMATO & GOAT CHEESE

Tender, grilled eggplant helps make this light summer salad a meal. The balsamic dressing adds depth and a burst of bright flavor.

—Susan Leiser, Hammonton, NJ

Prep: 25 min. • **Grill:** 10 min.
Makes: 8 servings

- **1 large eggplant, cut into 8 slices**
- **¼ cup extra virgin olive oil, divided**
- **1¼ tsp. salt, divided**
- **½ tsp. pepper, divided**
- **4 plum tomatoes, chopped**
- **¼ cup chopped red onion**
- **2 Tbsp. chopped fresh basil**
- **2 Tbsp. chopped fresh parsley**
- **4 tsp. balsamic vinegar**
- **4 cups fresh arugula or baby spinach**
- **½ cup crumbled goat cheese**

1. Brush both sides of the eggplant slices with 2 Tbsp. of the oil. Sprinkle with ¾ tsp. salt and ¼ tsp. pepper.
2. Broil eggplant 3-4 in. from heat or grill, covered, over medium heat, until tender, 4-5 minutes per side.
3. Meanwhile, in a small bowl, combine tomatoes, onion, basil, parsley, vinegar, 1 Tbsp. oil and the remaining ½ tsp. salt and ¼ tsp. pepper. Toss arugula with the remaining 1 tbsp. oil and divide among eight plates. Top each with an eggplant slice, tomato mixture, and goat cheese.

1 serving: 115 cal., 9g fat (2g sat. fat), 9mg chol., 410mg sod., 8g carb. (5g sugars, 3g fiber), 3g pro. **Diabetic exchanges:** 2 fat, 1 vegetable.

TEST KITCHEN TIP

Try this salad with portobello mushrooms instead of eggplant.

EGGPLANT SALAD WITH TOMATO & GOAT CHEESE

EAT SMART | FAST FIX

PINEAPPLE-GINGER CHICKEN STIR-FRY

I found the original recipe for this dish on a can of pineapple slices in the 1980s. I lightened it up and adapted it to a quick skillet meal. My family gave it a big thumbs-up, and we've enjoyed it this way ever since!
—Sue Gronholz, Beaver Dam, WI

Takes: 30 min. • **Makes:** 4 servings

1 can (20 oz.) unsweetened pineapple chunks
1 Tbsp. cornstarch
3 Tbsp. reduced-sodium soy sauce
2 Tbsp. honey
¼ tsp. ground cinnamon
2 Tbsp. canola oil, divided
1 lb. boneless skinless chicken breasts, cut into 1-in. cubes
1 small onion, chopped
1 Tbsp. minced fresh gingerroot
2 garlic cloves, minced
Hot cooked brown rice
Minced fresh cilantro

1. Drain pineapple, reserving juice. Mix cornstarch, soy sauce, honey, cinnamon and reserved juice until smooth. In a skillet, heat 1 Tbsp. oil over medium-high heat; saute chicken until lightly browned, 4-6 minutes. Remove from pan.
2. In same pan, saute onion, ginger and garlic in the remaining 1 Tbsp. oil until crisp-tender, about 2 minutes. Stir the cornstarch mixture; add to pan with the chicken and pineapple chunks. Bring to a boil, stirring constantly; cook and stir until sauce is thickened and chicken is cooked through, 5-7 minutes.
3. Serve with rice. If desired, sprinkle with cilantro.

1 cup chicken mixture: 316 cal., 10g fat (1g sat. fat), 63mg chol., 487mg sod., 31g carb. (26g sugars, 1g fiber), 25g pro. **Diabetic exchanges:** 3 lean meat, 1½ starch, 1½ fat, ½ fruit.

EAT SMART | FAST FIX

CITRUS COD

We enjoy fish frequently, and this baked version has a tempting mild orange flavor. It comes out of the oven flaky and moist.
—Jacquelyn Dixon, La Porte City, IA

Takes: 25 min. • **Makes:** 4 servings

4 cod fillets (4 oz. each)
2 Tbsp. butter
½ cup chopped onion
1 garlic clove, minced
1 tsp. grated orange zest
⅓ cup orange juice
1 Tbsp. lemon juice
⅛ tsp. pepper
1 Tbsp. minced fresh parsley

1. Preheat oven to 375°. Place cod fillets in an 11x7-in. baking dish coated with cooking spray.
2. In a skillet, heat butter over medium-high heat; saute the onion and garlic until tender. Spoon over the fish. Mix orange zest and citrus juices; drizzle over the fish.
3. Bake, uncovered, until fish just begins to flake easily with a fork, 15-20 minutes. Sprinkle with pepper and parsley.

1 cod fillet: 153 cal., 6g fat (4g sat. fat), 58mg chol., 108mg sod., 5g carb. (3g sugars, 0 fiber), 18g pro. **Diabetic exchanges:** 3 lean meat, 1½ fat.

CITRUS COD

SPICY SAUSAGE & RICE SKILLET

EAT SMART | FAST FIX

SPICY SAUSAGE & RICE SKILLET

The spicy sausage in this quick skillet dish gives it a kick, and the sliced apples are a pleasant and tart surprise.

—Jamie Jones, Madison, GA

Takes: 30 min. • **Makes:** 6 servings

- **1 pkg. (12 oz.) fully cooked spicy chicken sausage links, halved lengthwise and cut into ½-in. slices**
- **1 Tbsp. olive oil**
- **2 medium yellow summer squash, chopped**
- **2 medium zucchini, chopped**
- **1 large sweet red pepper, chopped**
- **1 medium onion, chopped**
- **1 medium tart apple, cut into ¼-in. slices**
- **1 garlic clove, minced**
- **½ tsp. salt**
- **1 pkg. (8.8 oz.) ready-to-serve brown rice**
- **1 can (15 oz.) black beans, rinsed and drained**
- **¼ to ½ cup water**

1. In a large nonstick skillet, cook the sausage over medium-high heat, turning occasionally, until lightly browned. Remove from skillet.
2. In the same skillet, heat olive oil over medium-high heat. Saute squash, zucchini, pepper, onion, apple, garlic and salt until until vegetables are tender, 5-7 minutes. Add rice, beans, ¼ cup water and sausage; cook and stir until heated through, about 5 minutes, adding more water if needed.

1⅓ cups: 285 cal., 8g fat (2g sat. fat), 43mg chol., 668mg sod., 34g carb. (9g sugars, 6g fiber), 17g pro. **Diabetic exchanges:** 2 starch, 2 lean meat, 1 vegetable, ½ fat.

*

TEST KITCHEN TIP

If making rice from scratch, you'll need about 2 cups cooked rice. For a meatless version, skip the sausage and add more beans.

EAT SMART

ISLAND CHICKEN WITH MANGO SLAW & CURRY SAUCE

The fresh mango slaw is what makes this dish pop. But it wouldn't be complete without my sauce using yogurt, orange marmalade and curry powder.

—Evelyn Cleare, Miami, FL

Prep: 30 min. + marinating
Cook: 10 min. • **Makes:** 4 servings

- **¼ cup orange juice**
- **3 Tbsp. canola oil, divided**
- **2 tsp. Caribbean jerk seasoning**
- **1 tsp. garlic powder**
- **4 boneless skinless chicken breast halves (5 oz. each)**

SAUCE

- **⅓ cup plain yogurt**
- **2 Tbsp. plus 2 tsp. orange marmalade**
- **¾ tsp. curry powder**

SLAW

- **1 medium mango, peeled, cut into thin strips**
- **2 cups fresh baby spinach, cut into strips**
- **1 large sweet red pepper, cut into thin strips**
- **1 Tbsp. honey**
- **1 Tbsp. lime juice**
- **1 Tbsp. minced fresh gingerroot**
- **¼ tsp. crushed red pepper flakes**

1. In a large bowl or dish, combine orange juice, 2 Tbsp. oil, jerk seasoning and garlic powder. Flatten chicken breasts to ½-in. thickness; add to marinade. Turn to coat; refrigerate for 2 hours.
2. Whisk sauce ingredients until blended. Cover and refrigerate until serving.
3. Drain chicken; discard marinade. In a large skillet, cook chicken in remaining 1 Tbsp. oil for 5-6 minutes on each side or until no longer pink.
4. Meanwhile, in a large bowl, combine the mango, spinach and red pepper. Whisk remaining slaw ingredients until blended. Drizzle over mango mixture; toss to coat. Serve with chicken and sauce.

1 chicken breast half with 1 cup slaw and 2 Tbsp. sauce: 293 cal., 7g fat (2g sat. fat), 81mg chol., 205mg sod., 28g carb. (23g sugars, 2g fiber), 31g pro. **Diabetic exchanges:** 4 lean meat, 1½ starch.

PORK TENDERLOIN WITH THREE-BERRY SALSA

EAT SMART

PORK TENDERLOIN WITH THREE-BERRY SALSA

My husband came home from a work event raving about the meal they'd served—pork with a spicy blueberry salsa. It took several tries, but I came up with my own delicious rendition based on his description.
—Angie Phillips, Tarzana, CA

Prep: 30 min. + standing • **Cook:** 25 min.
Makes: 6 servings

- **1¼ cups fresh or frozen blackberries (about 6 oz.), thawed and drained**
- **1¼ cups fresh or frozen raspberries (about 6 oz.), thawed and drained**
- **1 cup fresh or frozen blueberries (about 6 oz.), thawed**
- **1 medium sweet red pepper, finely chopped**
- **1 jalapeno pepper, seeded and minced**
- **½ medium red onion, finely chopped**
- **¼ cup lime juice**
- **3 Tbsp. minced fresh cilantro**
- **¼ tsp. salt**

PORK

- **2 pork tenderloins (¾ lb. each), cut into ¾-in. slices**
- **1 tsp. salt**
- **½ tsp. pepper**
- **2 Tbsp. olive oil, divided**
- **½ cup white wine or chicken broth**
- **2 shallots, thinly sliced**
- **½ cup chicken stock**

1. Place the first five ingredients in a bowl; toss lightly to combine. Remove 1 cup of the berry mixture; reserve for sauce. For salsa, gently stir onion, lime juice, cilantro and salt into the remaining mixture; let stand 30 minutes.
2. Meanwhile, sprinkle the pork with salt and pepper. In a large skillet, heat 1 Tbsp. oil over medium-high heat. Add half the pork slices and cook until a thermometer inserted in meat reads 145°, 2-4 minutes on each side. Remove from pan. Repeat with the remaining pork and oil.
3. In the same pan, add the wine, shallots and the reserved berry mixture, stirring to loosen browned bits from pan. Bring to a boil; cook until liquid is reduced to 1 Tbsp., 4-6 minutes. Stir in stock; cook 5 minutes longer or until the shallots are tender, stirring occasionally. Return pork to pan; heat through. Serve with salsa.

QUICKPEA CURRY

3 oz. cooked pork with ⅔ cup salsa and 3 Tbsp. sauce: 239 cal., 9g fat (2g sat. fat), 64mg chol., 645mg sod., 15g carb. (7g sugars, 5g fiber), 25g pro. **Diabetic exchanges:** 3 lean meat, ½ starch, ½ fruit.

EAT SMART

QUICKPEA CURRY

This colorful curry is a nice change of pace for a busy weeknight. I like to substitute fresh peas for the frozen when they are in season.
—Beth Fleming, Downers Grove, IL

Prep: 15 min. • **Cook:** 35 min.
Makes: 6 servings

- **1 Tbsp. canola oil**
- **1 medium onion, finely chopped**
- **2 garlic cloves, minced**
- **1 Tbsp. curry powder**
- **2 cans (14½ oz. each) diced tomatoes, undrained**
- **2 cans (15 oz. each) chickpeas or garbanzo beans, rinsed and drained**
- **2 cups cubed peeled sweet potato (about 1 medium)**
- **1 cup light coconut milk**
- **2 tsp. sugar**
- **¼ tsp. crushed red pepper flakes**
- **1 cup uncooked whole wheat pearl (Israeli) couscous**
- **1½ cups frozen peas (about 6 oz.)**
- **¼ tsp. salt**
- **Chopped fresh parsley**
- **Plain yogurt, optional**

1. In a large skillet, heat oil over medium heat; saute onion and garlic with curry powder until tender, 3-4 minutes. Stir in tomatoes, chickpeas, sweet potato, coconut milk, sugar and pepper flakes; bring to a boil. Reduce heat; simmer, uncovered, until mixture is thickened and potatoes are tender, 25-30 minutes, stirring occasionally.
2. Meanwhile, prepare the couscous and peas separately according to their package directions. Stir salt into peas.
3. To serve, divide the couscous among six bowls. Top with the chickpea mixture, peas, parsley and, if desired, yogurt.

1 serving: 390 cal., 8g fat (2g sat. fat), 0 chol., 561mg sod., 68g carb. (14g sugars, 13g fiber), 13g pro.

TEST KITCHEN TIP

Leftover coconut milk can be frozen or stirred into oatmeal or herbal tea, or even added to whisked eggs before scrambling them for a soft and fluffy version. No pearl couscous on hand? Regular couscous can be substituted.

EAT SMART | FAST FIX

CHORIZO SPAGHETTI SQUASH SKILLET

Get your noodle fix minus the pasta with this spiced-up meal that comes together in one skillet. It's a fill-you-up dinner that's low in calories—a weeknight winner!
—Sherrill Oake, Springfield, MA

Takes: 30 min. • **Makes:** 4 servings

- **1 small spaghetti squash (about 2 lbs.)**
- **1 Tbsp. canola oil**
- **1 pkg. (12 oz.) fully cooked chorizo chicken sausage links or flavor of choice, sliced**
- **1 medium sweet yellow pepper, chopped**
- **1 medium sweet onion, halved and sliced**
- **1 cup sliced fresh mushrooms**
- **1 can (14½ oz.) no-salt-added diced tomatoes, undrained**
- **1 Tbsp. reduced-sodium taco seasoning**
- **¼ tsp. pepper**
- **Chopped green onions, optional**

1. Halve squash lengthwise; discard seeds. Place squash on a microwave-safe plate, cut side down; microwave on high until tender, about 15 minutes. Cool slightly.
2. Meanwhile, in a large skillet, heat 1 Tbsp. oil over medium-high heat; saute the sausage, yellow pepper, onion and mushrooms until the onion is tender, about 5 minutes.
3. Separate strands of squash with a fork; add to skillet. Stir in the tomatoes and seasonings; bring to a boil. Reduce heat; simmer, uncovered, until flavors are blended, about 5 minutes. If desired, top with green onions.

1½ cups: 299 cal., 12g fat (3g sat. fat), 65mg chol., 725mg sod., 34g carb. (12g sugars, 6g fiber), 18g pro. **Diabetic exchanges:** 2 starch, 2 lean meat, 1 vegetable, 1 fat.

TEST KITCHEN TIP

An 8-oz. container of sliced mushrooms contains about 3½ cups. If you want to avoid leftovers, get 1 cup from the grocery store salad bar.

ITALIAN TURKEY CUTLETS

EAT SMART | FAST FIX

ITALIAN TURKEY CUTLETS

With their lovely herbed tomato sauce, these cutlets taste so good that my son often requests them for his birthday dinner. But they're easy enough to make any time, even when there's no special reason to celebrate.
—Janet Bumb, Beallsville, MD

Takes: 30 min. • **Makes:** 4 servings

- **2 tsp. plus 1 Tbsp. olive oil, divided**
- **1 small onion, finely chopped**
- **2 garlic cloves, minced**
- **1 can (14½ oz.) Italian stewed tomatoes, undrained**
- **1 Tbsp. minced fresh basil or 1 tsp. dried basil**
- **1 tsp. dried oregano**
- **½ tsp. dried rosemary, crushed**
- **1 pkg. (17.6 oz.) turkey breast cutlets**
- **½ tsp. salt**
- **⅛ tsp. pepper**
- **2 Tbsp. shredded Parmesan cheese**

1. In a large saucepan, heat 2 tsp. oil; saute onion until tender. Add garlic; cook and stir for 1 minute. Stir in tomatoes and herbs; bring to a boil. Reduce heat; cook, uncovered, over medium heat until the sauce is thickened, about 10 minutes.
2. Meanwhile, sprinkle both sides of the turkey with salt and pepper. In a large nonstick skillet, heat remaining 1 Tbsp. oil over medium-high heat. In batches, cook turkey until no longer pink, turning once. Serve with sauce. Sprinkle with cheese.

1 serving: 242 cal., 8g fat (2g sat. fat), 73mg chol., 700mg sod., 9g carb. (4g sugars, 1g fiber), 32g pro. **Diabetic exchanges:** 4 lean meat, 1 vegetable, 1 fat.

EAT SMART | FAST FIX

CHICKEN WITH CREAMY JALAPENO SAUCE

My sister Amy came up with this recipe that does an amazing job of making boring old chicken breasts a lot more exciting. My husband and I just love the wonderful sauce!

—Molly Cappone, Lewis Center, OH

Takes: 25 min.
Makes: 4 servings (2 cups sauce)

- **4 boneless skinless chicken breast halves (4 oz. each)**
- **¼ tsp. salt**
- **1 Tbsp. canola oil**
- **2 medium onions, chopped**
- **½ cup reduced-sodium chicken broth**
- **2 jalapeno peppers, seeded and minced**
- **2 tsp. ground cumin**
- **3 oz. reduced-fat cream cheese, cubed**
- **¼ cup reduced-fat sour cream**
- **3 plum tomatoes, seeded and chopped**
- **2 cups hot cooked rice**

1. Sprinkle chicken with salt. In a large nonstick skillet over medium-high heat, brown chicken in oil on both sides.
2. Add the onions, broth, jalapenos and cumin. Bring to a boil. Reduce heat; cover and simmer until a thermometer reads 165°, 5-7 minutes. Remove chicken and keep warm.
3. Stir cream cheese and sour cream into the onion mixture until blended. Stir in tomatoes; heat through. Serve with chicken and rice.

Note: Wear disposable gloves when cutting hot peppers; the oils can burn exposed skin. Avoid touching your face.

1 serving: 376 cal., 13g fat (5g sat. fat), 83mg chol., 389mg sod., 34g carb. (8g sugars, 3g fiber), 30g pro. **Diabetic exchanges:** 3 lean meat, 2 vegetable, 2 fat, 1½ starch.

CHICKEN WITH CREAMY JALAPENO SAUCE

EAT SMART | FAST FIX

BAJA SHRIMP AVOCADO SALAD

This Mexican-style shrimp cocktail's bright, fresh flavors and colors entice even my little ones. I serve it alongside a scoop of lime-cilantro rice for a light meal.

—Carly Terrell, Granbury, TX

Takes: 20 min. • **Makes:** 6 servings

- **2 medium ripe avocados, peeled and cut into ½-in. pieces**
- **1½ lbs. peeled and deveined cooked shrimp (31-40 per lb.), tails removed**
- **1 cup pico de gallo**
- **½ cup Clamato juice, chilled**
- **2 Tbsp. lime juice**
- **¼ tsp. kosher salt**
- **¼ tsp. ground cumin**
- **⅛ to ¼ tsp. hot pepper sauce**
- **Dash pepper**
- **Lime wedges, optional**

Combine all ingredients in a large bowl, stirring gently to combine. Divide among serving bowls. Garnish with lime wedges if desired.

1 cup: 209 cal., 9g fat (1g sat. fat), 172mg chol., 329mg sod., 8g carb. (1g sugars, 3g fiber), 24g pro. **Diabetic exchanges:** 3 lean meat, 2 fat.

*** HEALTH TIP *** This dinner clocks in at just 8g carbs per serving. If you're not on a low-carb diet, serve it with whole grain crackers or French bread.

TEST KITCHEN TIP

This salad can be made ahead. Combine everything except the avocado; cover and refrigerate for up to four hours. Add the avocado just before serving.

EAT SMART | FAST FIX

MONGOLIAN BEEF

My family just loves this meal-in-one—even my husband, a meat-and-potatoes kind of guy. The dish uses inexpensive ingredients to offer big flavor in a small amount of time.

—Heather Blum, Coleman, WI

Takes: 25 min. • **Makes:** 4 servings

- **1 Tbsp. cornstarch**
- **¾ cup reduced-sodium chicken broth**
- **2 Tbsp. reduced-sodium soy sauce**
- **1 Tbsp. hoisin sauce**
- **2 tsp. sesame oil**
- **1 lb. beef top sirloin steak, cut into thin strips**
- **1 Tbsp. olive oil, divided**
- **5 green onions, cut into 1-in. pieces**
- **2 cups hot cooked rice**

1. In a small bowl, combine cornstarch and broth until smooth. Stir in the soy sauce, hoisin sauce and sesame oil; set aside. In a large nonstick skillet or wok, stir-fry beef in 1½ tsp. hot olive oil until no longer pink. Remove and keep warm.
2. In the same skillet, stir-fry the onions in the remaining 1½ tsp. olive oil until just crisp-tender, 3-4 minutes. Stir cornstarch mixture and add it to the pan. Bring to a boil; cook and stir until thickened, about 2 minutes. Reduce heat; add beef and heat through. Serve with rice.

1 serving: 328 cal., 11g fat (3g sat. fat), 46mg chol., 529mg sod., 28g carb. (2g sugars, 1g fiber), 28g pro. **Diabetic exchanges:** 3 lean meat, 2 starch, 1 fat.

MONGOLIAN BEEF

EAT SMART | FAST FIX

LENTIL BURRITOS

PICTURED ON P. 133

I'm constantly trying to incorporate healthy but tasty meals into our menu. Both kids and adults love these mildly spiced burritos that combine filling lentils with crisp zucchini.

—Pam Masters, Wickenburg, AZ

Takes: 30 min. • **Makes:** 8 burritos

- **2 cups water**
- **1 cup dried brown lentils**
- **2 Tbsp. dried minced onion**
- **½ tsp. dried minced garlic**
- **½ tsp. ground cumin**
- **⅛ tsp. hot pepper sauce**
- **1 small zucchini, chopped**
- **1 cup taco sauce**
- **1 cup shredded part-skim mozzarella cheese**
- **8 flour tortillas (8 in.), warmed**

1. Place the first six ingredients in a large saucepan; bring to a boil. Reduce heat; simmer, covered, until the lentils are tender, 15-20 minutes. Drain if necessary.
2. Stir zucchini, taco sauce and cheese into lentils. To serve, place about ½ cup lentil mixture on each tortilla and roll up.

1 burrito: 313 cal., 7g fat (3g sat. fat), 9mg chol., 452mg sod., 47g carb. (4g sugars, 5g fiber), 14g pro. **Diabetic exchanges:** 3 starch, 2 lean meat, 1 fat.

EAT SMART | FAST FIX

LIGHT CHICKEN & BROCCOLI BAKE

Cheesy chicken and broccoli bakes are the ultimate comfort food, but I wanted to give the classic casserole a healthier spin. Mine cuts down on fat and calories but keeps the same cozy flavor.

—Jenny Dubinsky, Inwood, WV

Takes: 30 min. • **Makes:** 4 servings

- **2 large eggs**
- **1 cup fat-free milk**
- **½ cup reduced-fat biscuit/baking mix**
- **½ tsp. salt**
- **¼ tsp. pepper**
- **4 cups frozen broccoli florets (about 9 oz.), thawed and drained**
- **1 cup shredded rotisserie chicken**
- **1 small onion, chopped**
- **½ cup shredded cheddar cheese, divided**

1. Preheat oven to 400°. In a large bowl, whisk together the first five ingredients. Stir in broccoli, chicken, onion and ¼ cup cheddar cheese. Transfer to a greased 9-in. pie plate. Sprinkle with the remaining ¼ cup cheese.
2. Bake until golden brown and a knife inserted in the center comes out clean, 15-20 minutes. Let stand for 10 minutes before serving.

1 serving: 274 cal., 11g fat (4g sat. fat), 139mg chol., 667mg sod., 20g carb. (7g sugars, 3g fiber), 22g pro. **Diabetic exchanges:** 3 lean meat, 1½ fat, 1 starch, 1 vegetable.

BROILED GREEK FISH FILLETS

EAT SMART | FAST FIX

BROILED GREEK FISH FILLETS

Olives, onion, dill and feta cheese combine in this tangy, Greek-inspired topping to boost the flavor of tilapia or your favorite whitefish. I usually serve it with a side of rice.
—Jennifer Maslowski, NY, NY

Takes: 25 min. • **Makes:** 8 servings

- **1 small red onion, finely chopped**
- **¼ cup plain yogurt**
- **2 Tbsp. butter, melted**
- **1 Tbsp. lime juice**
- **1 tsp. dill weed**
- **½ tsp. paprika**
- **¼ tsp. garlic powder**
- **8 tilapia fillets (4 oz. each)**
- **¼ tsp. salt**
- **¼ tsp. pepper**
- **½ cup crumbled feta cheese**
- **½ cup pitted Greek olives, sliced**

Preheat broiler. Mix first seven ingredients. Place tilapia on a 15x10x1-in. pan; sprinkle with salt and pepper. Spread the onion mixture down the center of the fillets; top with cheese and olives. Broil 3-4 in. from heat until the fish just begins to flake easily with a fork, 6-9 minutes.

1 serving: 169 cal., 7g fat (3g sat. fat), 68mg chol., 353mg sod., 3g carb. (1g sugars, 1g fiber), 23g pro. **Diabetic exchanges:** 3 lean meat, 1½ fat.

EAT SMART | FAST FIX

MAPLE-GLAZED PORK TENDERLOIN

PICTURED ON P. 133

My husband and I think this roasted pork tenderloin tastes like a fancy restaurant dish, but it couldn't be simpler to make at home. The glaze makes it extra-special.
—Colleen Mercier, Salmon Arm, BC

Takes: 30 min. • **Makes:** 4 servings

- **¾ tsp. salt**
- **¾ tsp. rubbed sage**
- **½ tsp. pepper**
- **2 pork tenderloins (¾ lb. each)**
- **1 tsp. butter**
- **¼ cup maple syrup**
- **3 Tbsp. cider vinegar**
- **1¾ tsp. Dijon mustard**

1. Preheat oven to 425°. Mix seasonings; sprinkle over pork. In a large nonstick skillet, heat butter over medium heat; brown the tenderloins on all sides. Transfer to a 15x10x1-in. pan lined with foil. Roast for 10 minutes.
2. Meanwhile, for glaze, in same skillet, mix syrup, vinegar and mustard; bring to a boil, stirring to loosen browned bits from pan. Cook and stir until slightly thickened, 1-2 minutes; remove from heat.
3. Brush 1 Tbsp. of the glaze over pork; continue roasting until a thermometer inserted in pork reads 145°, 7-10 minutes, brushing halfway through with remaining glaze. Let stand 5 minutes before slicing.

5 oz. cooked pork: 264 cal., 7g fat (3g sat. fat), 98mg chol., 573mg sod., 14g carb. (12g sugars, 0 fiber), 34g pro. **Diabetic exchanges:** 5 lean meat, 1 starch.

EAT SMART | FAST FIX

BEEF BARLEY SKILLET

Made with quick-cooking barley, this versatile dish goes together fast. You can make it with ground turkey or chicken, substituting any color bell pepper you have on hand.

—Irene Tetreault, South Hadley, MA

Takes: 30 min. • **Makes:** 4 servings

- **1 lb. lean ground beef (90% lean)**
- **1 small onion, chopped**
- **¼ cup chopped celery**
- **¼ cup chopped green pepper**
- **1 can (14½ oz.) diced tomatoes, undrained**
- **1½ cups water**
- **¾ cup quick-cooking barley**
- **½ cup chili sauce**
- **1 tsp. Worcestershire sauce**
- **½ tsp. dried marjoram**
- **⅛ tsp. pepper**
- **Chopped parsley, optional**

In a large skillet, cook beef, onion, celery and green pepper over medium-high heat until the beef is no longer pink and the vegetables are tender, breaking up beef into crumbles, 5-7 minutes; drain. Stir in the remaining ingredients. Bring to a boil; reduce heat. Simmer, uncovered, until barley is tender, 5-10 minutes. If desired, top with chopped parsley.

1½ cups: 362 cal., 10g fat (4g sat. fat), 71mg chol., 707mg sod., 41g carb. (11g sugars, 8g fiber), 27g pro. **Diabetic exchanges:** 3 lean meat, 2 starch, 1 vegetable.

TUSCAN FISH PACKETS

EAT SMART | FAST FIX

TUSCAN FISH PACKETS

My husband does a lot of fishing and I'm always looking for different ways to serve his catch. A professional chef was kind enough to share this recipe with me, and I played around with different veggie combinations until I found the one my family liked best.

—Kathy Morrow, Hubbard, OH

Takes: 30 min. • **Makes:** 4 servings

- **1 can (15 oz.) great northern beans, rinsed and drained**
- **4 plum tomatoes, chopped**
- **1 small zucchini, chopped**
- **1 medium onion, chopped**
- **1 garlic clove, minced**
- **¼ cup white wine**
- **¾ tsp. salt, divided**
- **¼ tsp. pepper, divided**
- **4 tilapia fillets (6 oz. each)**
- **1 medium lemon, cut into 8 thin slices**

1. Preheat oven to 400°. In a bowl, combine beans, tomatoes, zucchini, onion, garlic, wine, ½ tsp. salt and ⅛ tsp. pepper.

2. Rinse fish and pat dry. Place each fillet on a piece of 18x12-in. heavy-duty foil; season with the remaining ¼ tsp. salt and ⅛ tsp. pepper. Spoon bean mixture over fish; top with lemon slices. Fold foil around fish and crimp edges to seal. Transfer the packets to a baking sheet.

3. Bake until fish just begins to flake easily with a fork and the vegetables are tender, 15-20 minutes. Be careful of escaping steam when opening packet.

1 packet: 270 cal., 2g fat (1g sat. fat), 83mg chol., 658mg sod., 23g carb. (4g sugars, 7g fiber), 38g pro. **Diabetic exchanges:** 5 lean meat, 1 starch, 1 vegetable.

TEST KITCHEN TIP

Great northern beans are small, tender white beans; navy beans or cannellini beans are good substitutes.

If you hate to open a bottle of wine just for ¼ cup, look for wine in single-portion bottles or boxes.

EAT SMART | FAST FIX

TENDERLOIN WITH HERB SAUCE

Tender pork is treated to a rich and creamy sauce with a slight red-pepper kick. This simple and hearty dish is always a dinnertime winner.
—Monica Shipley, Tulare, CA

Takes: 25 min. • **Makes:** 6 servings

- 2 **pork tenderloins (1 lb. each)**
- ½ **tsp. salt**
- 4 **tsp. butter**
- ⅔ **cup half-and-half cream**
- 2 **Tbsp. minced fresh parsley**
- 2 **tsp. herbes de Provence**
- 2 **tsp. reduced-sodium soy sauce**
- 1 **tsp. beef bouillon granules**
- ½ **to ¾ tsp. crushed red pepper flakes**

1. Cut each tenderloin into 12 slices; sprinkle with salt. In a large nonstick skillet, heat butter over medium heat; brown the pork in batches, 3-4 minutes per side. Return all pork to pan.
2. Mix the remaining ingredients; pour over the pork. Cook, uncovered, over low heat until the sauce is thickened and a thermometer inserted in pork reads 145°, 2-3 minutes, stirring occasionally. Let stand for 5 minutes before serving.

4 oz. cooked pork: 238 cal., 10g fat (5g sat. fat), 104mg chol., 495mg sod., 2g carb. (1g sugars, 0 fiber), 31g pro. **Diabetic exchanges:** 4 lean meat, 1 fat.

TENDERLOIN WITH HERB SAUCE

EAT SMART | FAST FIX

CHICKEN & BROCCOLI WITH DILL SAUCE

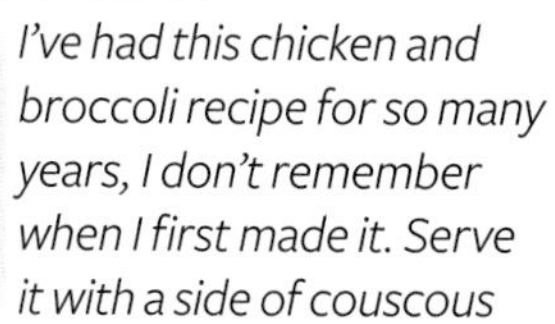

I've had this chicken and broccoli recipe for so many years, I don't remember when I first made it. Serve it with a side of couscous or rice for a complete meal, or add some sliced mushrooms or carrots.
—Kallee Krong-McCreery, Escondido, CA

Takes: 30 min. • **Makes:** 4 servings

- 4 **boneless skinless chicken breast halves (6 oz. each)**
- ½ **tsp. garlic salt**
- ¼ **tsp. pepper**
- 1 **Tbsp. olive oil**
- 4 **cups fresh broccoli florets**
- 1 **cup chicken broth**
- 1 **Tbsp. all-purpose flour**
- 1 **Tbsp. snipped fresh dill**
- 1 **cup 2% milk**

1. Sprinkle chicken with garlic salt and pepper. In a large skillet, heat oil over medium heat; brown the chicken on both sides. Remove from pan.
2. Add broccoli and broth to the same skillet; bring to a boil. Reduce heat; simmer, covered, until the broccoli is just tender, 3-5 minutes. Using a slotted spoon, remove the broccoli from pan, reserving the broth. Keep broccoli warm.
3. In a small bowl, mix flour, dill and milk until smooth; stir into the broth in pan. Bring to a boil, stirring constantly; cook and stir until thickened, 1-2 minutes. Add chicken; cook, covered, over medium heat until a thermometer inserted in the chicken reads 165°, 10-12 minutes. Serve with broccoli.

1 serving: 274 cal., 9g fat (2g sat. fat), 100mg chol., 620mg sod., 8g carb. (4g sugars, 2g fiber), 39g pro. **Diabetic exchanges:** 5 lean meat, 1 vegetable, 1 fat.

*

TEST KITCHEN TIP

If you buy whole broccoli stalks, don't throw out the stems! Peel away the tough outer portion and chop the center to use in soups and stir-fries or add to salads and slaws.

EAT SMART | FAST FIX

BLACK BEAN BURRITOS

My neighbor and I discovered these fabulous low-fat burritos a few years ago. On nights my husband or I have a meeting, we can have a satisfying supper on the table in minutes.

—Angela Studebaker, Goshen, IN

Takes: 10 min. • **Makes:** 4 servings

- **1 Tbsp. canola oil**
- **3 Tbsp. chopped onion**
- **3 Tbsp. chopped green pepper**
- **1 can (15 oz.) black beans, rinsed and drained**
- **4 flour tortillas (8 in.), warmed**
- **1 cup shredded Mexican cheese blend**
- **1 cup shredded lettuce**
- **1 medium tomato, chopped**
- **salsa, sour cream, minced fresh cilantro, cubed avocado, optional**

In a nonstick skillet, heat oil over medium heat; saute the onion and green pepper until tender. Stir in beans; heat through. Spoon about ½ cupful off center on each tortilla. Sprinkle with the cheese, tomato and lettuce. Fold sides and ends over filling and roll up. Serve with salsa, sour cream, cilantro and avocado if desired.

1 burrito: 346 cal., 13g fat (5g sat. fat), 25mg chol., 615mg sod., 43g carb. (2g sugars, 6g fiber), 15g pro. **Diabetic exchanges:** 2½ starch, 1 lean meat, 1 vegetable, 1 fat.

EAT SMART | FAST FIX

STRAWBERRY-TURKEY SPINACH SALAD

PICTURED ON P. 133

This light, refreshing salad is a true showstopper, visually and nutritionally, with fresh strawberries and yellow pepper strips tossed with fresh baby spinach. Serve with warm whole wheat rolls or flax or bran muffins.

—*Taste of Home* Test Kitchen

Takes: 20 min. • **Makes:** 4 servings

- **5 oz. fresh baby spinach (about 6 cups)**
- **2 cups julienned cooked turkey breast**
- **2 cups sliced fresh strawberries**
- **1 small sweet yellow pepper, julienned**
- **4 green onions, sliced**

DRESSING

- **¼ cup red wine vinegar**
- **3 Tbsp. olive oil**
- **2 Tbsp. water**
- **4 tsp. honey**
- **½ tsp. dried minced onion**
- **½ tsp. salt**
- **¼ tsp. pepper**

Place the first five ingredients in a large bowl. Place dressing ingredients in a jar with a tight-fitting lid; shake well. Drizzle over salad; toss to combine. Serve immediately.

1¾ cups: 260 cal., 12g fat (2g sat. fat), 56mg chol., 397mg sod., 17g carb. (11g sugars, 3g fiber), 23g pro. **Diabetic exchanges:** 3 lean meat, 1 vegetable, ½ fruit, 2 fat.

EAT SMART | FAST FIX

DIJON-CRUSTED FISH

PICTURED ON P. 133

Dijon, Parmesan and a hint of spicy horseradish give this toasty fish lots of flavor. The preparation is so easy, it takes just a few minutes to get four servings ready for the oven.

—Scott Schmidtke, Chicago, IL

Takes: 25 min. • **Makes:** 4 servings

- **3 Tbsp. reduced-fat mayonnaise**
- **1 Tbsp. lemon juice**
- **2 tsp. Dijon mustard**
- **1 tsp. prepared horseradish**
- **2 Tbsp. grated Parmesan cheese, divided**
- **4 tilapia fillets (5 oz. each)**
- **¼ cup dry bread crumbs**
- **2 tsp. butter, melted**

1. Preheat oven to 425°. Mix the first four ingredients with 1 Tbsp. of the Parmesan cheese. Place tilapia on a baking sheet coated with cooking spray; spread evenly with the mayonnaise mixture.
2. Toss bread crumbs with melted butter and remaining 1 Tbsp. cheese; sprinkle over fillets. Bake until fish just begins to flake easily with a fork, 12-15 minutes.

1 fillet: 214 cal., 8g fat (3g sat. fat), 80mg chol., 292mg sod., 7g carb. (1g sugars, 1g fiber), 28g pro. **Diabetic exchanges:** 4 lean meat, 1½ fat, ½ starch.

* **HEALTH TIP** * Tilapia is low in calories, rich in high-quality protein and a good source of many B vitamins.

BLACK BEAN BURRITOS

EAT SMART | FAST FIX

ITALIAN SAUSAGE VEGGIE SKILLET

We love Italian sausage sandwiches, but because bread isn't diet-friendly for me, I created this recipe to satisfy my craving. If you like some heat, use hot peppers in place of the sweet.
—Tina M. Howells, Salem, OH

Takes: 30 min. • **Makes:** 6 Servings

- **4 cups uncooked whole wheat spiral pasta**
- **1 lb. Italian turkey sausage, casings removed**
- **1 medium onion, chopped**
- **1 garlic clove, minced**
- **2 medium zucchini, chopped**
- **1 large sweet red pepper, chopped**
- **1 large sweet yellow pepper, chopped**
- **1 can (28 oz.) diced tomatoes, drained**
- **¼ tsp. salt**
- **¼ tsp. pepper**

Cook pasta according to the package directions; drain. Meanwhile, in a large skillet, cook sausage and onion over medium-high heat until the sausage is no longer pink, 5-7 minutes. Add the garlic and cook 1 minute longer. Add zucchini and peppers; cook until crisp-tender, 3-5 minutes. Add tomatoes, salt and pepper. Cook and stir until the vegetables are tender and begin to release their juices, 5-7 minutes. Serve with pasta.

1⅓ cups: 251 cal., 6g fat (1g sat. fat), 28mg chol., 417mg sod., 35g carb. (4g sugars, 6g fiber), 16g pro. **Diabetic exchanges:** 2 vegetable, 2 lean meat, 1½ starch.

ASPARAGUS SHRIMP LINGUINE

EAT SMART | FAST FIX

ASPARAGUS SHRIMP LINGUINE

My family really enjoys asparagus and shrimp together. We often have this dish on busy weeknights because it's healthy and cooks quickly.
—Wannetta Ehnes, Eagle Bend, MN

Takes: 30 min. • **Makes:** 4 servings

- **6 oz. uncooked whole wheat linguine**
- **1 lb. fresh asparagus, trimmed and cut into ½-in. pieces**
- **2 Tbsp. olive oil**
- **1 medium onion, chopped**
- **1½ lbs. uncooked shrimp (26-30 per lb.), peeled and deveined**
- **4 garlic cloves, minced**
- **¼ cup reduced-sodium chicken broth**
- **4 wedges garlic-and-herb Swiss cheese**
- **2 Tbsp. lemon juice**
- **¼ tsp. salt**
- **¼ tsp. pepper**
- **¼ cup grated Parmesan cheese**

1. In a large saucepan, cook the linguine according to the package directions; add asparagus pieces during the last 3 minutes of cooking.
2. Meanwhile, in a large skillet, heat oil over medium-high heat. Add onion; cook and stir 6-8 minutes or until tender. Add shrimp and garlic; cook until the shrimp turn pink, 2-4 minutes longer. Stir in the broth; cook over medium heat until liquid is almost evaporated, 1-2 minutes. Add the Swiss cheese, lemon juice, salt and pepper; stir until the cheese is melted.
3. Drain the linguine and asparagus, reserving ¼ cup of the pasta water. Stir the linguine and asparagus into the shrimp mixture, adding enough of the reserved pasta water to moisten the pasta. Sprinkle with Parmesan cheese before serving.

Note: We used garlic-and-herb Swiss cheese from The Laughing Cow for this recipe.

2 cups: 444 cal., 16g fat (5g sat. fat), 221mg chol., 685mg sod., 41g carb. (4g sugars, 6g fiber), 38g pro. **Diabetic exchanges:** 4 lean meat, 2 starch, 2 fat, 1 vegetable.

PORK TENDERLOIN WITH WINE SAUCE

EAT SMART | FAST FIX

PORK TENDERLOIN WITH WINE SAUCE

Here's a fast and easy meal that's as big on flavor as it is low in fat and calories. I serve it with fresh green beans and mashed potatoes.

—Nancy LaVoice, Wexford, PA

Takes: 25 min. • **Makes:** 2 servings

- **1 pork tenderloin (¾ lb.)**
- **Dash pepper**
- **1 tsp. canola oil**
- **1 tsp. butter**
- **¼ cup reduced-sodium beef broth**
- **¼ cup dry red wine or additional reduced-sodium beef broth**
- **¼ tsp. Dijon mustard**
- **¼ tsp. dried thyme**
- **⅛ tsp. dried rosemary, crushed**

1. Cut pork into 2-in. slices; flatten to 1½-in. thickness. Sprinkle with pepper. In a large skillet over medium heat, cook pork in oil and butter for 5 minutes on each side or until meat is no longer pink. Remove and keep warm.

2. Add broth to the pan, scraping to loosen any browned bits. Stir in the wine, mustard, thyme and rosemary. Bring to a boil. Reduce heat; simmer, uncovered, for 3 minutes, stirring occasionally. Serve with the pork.

5 oz. cooked pork: 259 cal., 10g fat (3g sat. fat), 100mg chol., 159mg sod., 1g carb. (0 sugars, 0 fiber), 34g pro. **Diabetic exchanges:** 5 lean meat, 1 fat.

EAT SMART | FAST FIX

OLIVE & RED PEPPER LINGUINE

With 16 grandchildren, someone is always hungry. This is a quick dish to fix when I'm busy and someone needs to eat as soon as possible! Paired with garlic bread, it makes an easy meatless meal.

—Betty Carpenter, Hookstown, PA

Takes: 20 min. • **Makes:** 8 servings

- **8 oz. uncooked linguine**
- **1 medium sweet red pepper, chopped**
- **¾ cup sliced fresh mushrooms**
- **½ cup chopped onion**
- **1½ tsp. minced garlic**
- **1 Tbsp. canola oil**
- **15 pimiento-stuffed olives, sliced**
- **1 Tbsp. butter**

Cook linguine according to the package directions. Meanwhile, in a large skillet, saute the red pepper, mushrooms, onion and garlic in oil until tender. Drain linguine; add to the skillet. Stir in the olives and butter; heat through.

1 cup: 158 cal., 6g fat (1g sat. fat), 4mg chol., 223mg sod., 24g carb. (2g sugars, 2g fiber), 4g pro. **Diabetic exchanges:** 1½ starch, 1 fat.

EAT SMART | FAST FIX

EASY MOROCCAN CHICKPEA STEW

When I'm invited to a potluck, I easily double or triple this healthy vegetarian recipe to treat the crowd to an exotic dish of enticing, bold flavors.

—Heather Demeritte, Scottsdale, AZ

Takes: 30 min. • **Makes:** 4 servings

- **1 Tbsp. olive oil**
- **2 cups cubed peeled butternut squash (½-in. cubes)**
- **1 large onion, chopped**
- **1 large sweet red pepper, chopped**
- **1 tsp. ground cinnamon**
- **½ tsp. pepper**
- **¼ tsp. ground ginger**
- **¼ tsp. ground cumin**
- **¼ tsp. salt**
- **1 can (15 oz.) chickpeas or garbanzo beans, rinsed and drained**
- **1 can (14½ oz.) diced tomatoes, undrained**
- **1 cup water**
- **Chopped cilantro, optional**

1. In a Dutch oven, heat oil over medium-high heat. Add squash, onion and red pepper; cook and stir until the onion is translucent and red pepper is crisp-tender, about 5 minutes. Stir in the seasonings until blended.

2. Add the remaining ingredients; bring to a boil. Reduce heat; cover and simmer until squash is tender, about 8 minutes. If desired, top with cilantro.

1½ cups: 217 cal., 6g fat (1g sat. fat), 0 chol., 455mg sod., 38g carb. (11g sugars, 9g fiber), 7g pro.

EASY MOROCCAN CHICKPEA STEW

EAT SMART | FAST FIX

SCALLOPS WITH SNOW PEAS

Vibrant, crisp pea pods in are a nice contrast with the soft scallops. The result is a whole dish that looks and tastes bright and fresh.

—Barb Carlucci, Orange Park, FL

Takes: 30 min. • **Makes:** 4 servings

- **2 Tbsp. cornstarch**
- **2 Tbsp. reduced-sodium soy sauce**
- **⅔ cup water**
- **4 tsp. canola oil, divided**
- **1 lb. bay scallops**
- **½ lb. fresh snow peas, halved diagonally**
- **2 medium leeks (white portion only), cut into 3x½-in. strips**
- **1½ tsp. minced fresh gingerroot**
- **3 cups hot cooked brown rice**

1. Mix cornstarch, soy sauce and water. In a large nonstick skillet, heat 2 tsp. oil over medium-high heat; stir-fry scallops until firm and opaque, 1-2 minutes. Remove from pan.
2. In the same pan, heat the remaining 2 tsp. oil over medium-high heat; stir-fry snow peas, leeks and ginger until peas are just crisp-tender, 4-6 minutes. Stir the cornstarch mixture; add to pan. Cook and stir until the sauce is thickened, about 1 minute. Add scallops; heat through. Serve with rice.

1 cup stir-fry with ¾ cup rice: 378 cal., 7g fat (1g sat. fat), 27mg chol., 750mg sod., 57g carb. (4g sugars, 5g fiber), 21g pro.

TEST KITCHEN TIP

Bay scallops are the smallest of the scallops and are usually available in a 70/120 size, meaning there are about 70 to 120 scallops per pound. They are tender and have a sweet flavor but can easily become tough if overcooked.

FREEZE IT | EAT SMART | FAST FIX

CHICKEN PESTO MEATBALLS

These tender, pesto-stuffed meatballs get gobbled up at our house. They may not have many ingredients, but they are packed with flavor. I always make a double batch and freeze half, so I'll have them on hand for a busy night.

—Ally Billhorn, Wilton, IA

Takes: 30 min. • **Makes:** 4 servings

- **6 oz. uncooked whole grain spaghetti**
- **¼ cup dry bread crumbs**
- **2 Tbsp. prepared pesto**
- **2 Tbsp. grated Parmesan cheese**
- **1 tsp. garlic powder**
- **1 lb. lean ground chicken**
- **1½ cups marinara sauce**
- **¼ cup water**
- **Torn fresh basil and additional Parmesan cheese, optional**

1. Cook the spaghetti according to the package directions; drain.
2. In a large bowl, combine bread crumbs, pesto, cheese and garlic powder. Add the chicken; mix lightly but thoroughly. Shape into 1-in. balls.
3. In a large skillet, brown the meatballs over medium heat, turning occasionally. Add the sauce and water; bring to a boil. Reduce the heat; simmer, covered, until the meatballs are cooked through, about 5 minutes. Serve with spaghetti. Top with basil and additional cheese, if desired.

Freeze option: Freeze cooled meatball mixture in freezer containers. To use, partially thaw in refrigerator overnight. Heat through in a covered saucepan over low heat, stirring gently and adding a little water if necessary.

¾ cup meatball mixture with 1 cup spaghetti: 422 cal., 12g fat (3g sat. fat), 85mg chol., 706mg sod., 45g carb. (7g sugars, 7g fiber), 32g pro. **Diabetic exchanges:** 3 starch, 3 lean meat, 1½ fat.

CHICKEN PESTO MEATBALLS

EAT SMART | FAST FIX

BUFFALO CHICKEN SALAD

Delicious, and even better—quick!—this salad is a summer staple at our house. Sometimes we cook the chicken on the grill, then sprinkle the hot sauce over it with the dressing, because you've gotta have that kick!
—Cori Cooper, Boise, ID

Takes: 25 min. • **Makes:** 4 servings

- **1 Tbsp. olive oil**
- **1 lb. boneless skinless chicken breasts, cut into ¾-in. cubes**
- **2 Tbsp. Louisiana-style hot sauce**
- **¼ tsp. salt**
- **¼ tsp. pepper**
- **1 bunch romaine, chopped (about 5 cups)**
- **2 celery ribs, chopped**
- **1 cup shredded carrots**
- **½ cup fat-free ranch salad dressing**

1. In a large skillet, heat oil over medium-high heat. In batches, saute chicken until no longer pink, 3-4 minutes; remove to a bowl. Stir in hot sauce, salt and pepper.
2. On a platter, combine romaine, celery and carrots. Top with the chicken. Serve with dressing.

1 serving: 229 cal., 7g fat (1g sat. fat), 63mg chol., 644mg sod., 16g carb. (4g sugars, 3g fiber), 25g pro. **Diabetic exchanges:** 3 lean meat, 1 starch, 1 vegetable, ½ fat.

BUFFALO CHICKEN SALAD

SLOW COOKER | EAT SMART

SWEET ONION & CHERRY PORK CHOPS

When I want to jump-start supper, I opt for these tender pork chops. The sweet and savory cherry sauce makes this recipe a keeper. Try serving it with wild rice pilaf.
—Stephanie Ray, Naples, FL

Prep: 15 min. • **Cook:** 3 hours
Makes: 2 servings

- **½ cup fresh or frozen pitted tart cherries, thawed**
- **2 Tbsp. chopped sweet onion**
- **1 Tbsp. honey**
- **½ tsp. seasoned salt**
- **¼ tsp. pepper**
- **2 boneless pork loin chops (5 oz. each)**
- **1 tsp. cornstarch**
- **1 tsp. cold water**

1. In a 1½-qt. slow cooker, combine the first five ingredients; top with pork chops. Cover and cook on low for 3-4 hours or until the meat is tender.
2. Remove meat to a serving platter; keep warm. Skim fat from cooking juices; transfer to a small saucepan. Bring liquid to a boil. Combine cornstarch and water until smooth. Gradually stir into the pan. Bring to a boil; cook and stir for 2 minutes or until thickened. Serve with meat.

1 serving: 278 cal., 8g fat (3g sat. fat), 68mg chol., 425mg sod., 23g carb. (9g sugars, 1g fiber), 28g pro. **Diabetic exchanges:** 4 lean meat, 1 starch, ½ fat.

EAT SMART | FAST FIX

SPLIT-SECOND SHRIMP

PICTURED ON P. 133

I use my microwave to hurry along preparation of this super fast shrimp scampi that's buttery and full of garlic flavor. It makes an elegant entree or a special-occasion appetizer.
—Jalayne Luckett, Marion, IL

Takes: 10 min. • **Makes:** 4 servings

- **2 Tbsp. butter**
- **1 large garlic clove, minced**
- **⅛ to ¼ tsp. cayenne pepper**
- **2 Tbsp. white wine or chicken broth**
- **5 tsp. lemon juice**
- **1 Tbsp. minced fresh parsley**
- **½ tsp. salt**
- **1 lb. uncooked shrimp (26-30 per lb.), peeled and deveined**

1. Place butter, garlic and cayenne in a 9-in. microwave-safe pie plate. Microwave, covered, on high until the butter is melted, about 1 minute. Stir in wine, lemon juice, parsley and salt. Add shrimp; toss to coat.
2. Microwave, covered, on high until the shrimp turns pink, 2½-3½ minutes. Stir before serving.

3 oz. cooked shrimp: 157 cal., 7g fat (4g sat. fat), 153mg chol., 476mg sod., 2g carb. (0 sugars, 0 fiber), 19g pro. **Diabetic exchanges:** 3 lean meat, 1½ fat.

SWEET ONION & SAUSAGE SPAGHETTI

EAT SMART | FAST FIX

SWEET ONION & SAUSAGE SPAGHETTI

This wholesome pasta dish gets tossed with light cream, basil and tomatoes for a quick, fresh-tasting meal in minutes.
—Mary Relyea, Canastota, NY

Takes: 30 min. • **Makes:** 4 servings

- **6 oz. uncooked whole wheat spaghetti**
- **¾ lb. Italian turkey sausage links, casings removed**
- **2 tsp. olive oil**
- **1 sweet onion, thinly sliced**
- **1 pint cherry tomatoes, halved**
- **½ cup loosely packed fresh basil leaves, thinly sliced**
- **½ cup half-and-half cream**
- **Shaved Parmesan cheese, optional**

1. Cook spaghetti according to the package directions. Meanwhile, in a large nonstick skillet over medium heat, cook sausage in oil for 5 minutes. Add onion; cook 8-10 minutes longer or until the meat is no longer pink and onion is tender.
2. Stir in the tomatoes and basil; heat through. Add cream; bring to a boil. Drain the spaghetti; toss with the sausage mixture. Garnish with cheese if desired.

1½ cups: 334 cal., 12g fat (4g sat. fat), 46mg chol., 378mg sod., 41g carb. (8g sugars, 6g fiber), 17g pro. **Diabetic exchanges:** 2½ starch, 2 lean meat, 1 vegetable, 1 fat.

EAT SMART | FAST FIX

STOVETOP MEAT LOAVES

Who says meat loaf has to bake in the oven for hours? For this convenient recipe, all you need is your stovetop and 30 minutes.
—Emily Sund, Geneseo, IL

Takes: 30 min. • **Makes:** 2 servings

- **3 Tbsp. 2% milk**
- **2 Tbsp. quick-cooking oats**
- **1 Tbsp. chopped onion**
- **⅛ tsp. salt**
- **½ lb. lean ground beef**
- **½ tsp. cornstarch**
- **½ cup Italian tomato sauce**
- **¼ cup cold water**

1. In a small bowl, combine the milk, oats, onion and salt. Crumble beef over mixture and mix well. Shape into two loaves.
2. In a small nonstick skillet, brown loaves on all sides; drain. Combine cornstarch, tomato sauce and water until smooth. Pour over meat loaves. Bring to a boil. Reduce heat to medium-low; cover and cook for 15-20 minutes or until meat is no longer pink.

1 meat loaf: 292 cal., 13g fat (5g sat. fat), 99mg chol., 548mg sod., 10g carb. (2g sugars, 2g fiber), 33g pro. **Diabetic exchanges:** 3 lean meat, ½ starch.

EAT SMART | FAST FIX

BEEF VEGGIE SOUP

Brimming with beef, potatoes, carrots, green beans and mushrooms, this hearty soup is a meal in itself. Ready in little time, it's ideal when unexpected guests visit.
—Ruby Williams, Bogalusa, LA

Takes: 30 min.
Makes: 12 servings (3 qt.)

- **1½ lbs. potatoes (about 3 medium), peeled and cut into 1-in. cubes**
- **6 medium carrots, cut into ½-in. slices**
- **1 Tbsp. Worcestershire sauce**
- **1 tsp. ground mustard**
- **½ tsp. salt**
- **¼ tsp. pepper**
- **2 cans (14½ oz. each) beef broth**
- **3 cups cubed cooked roast beef**
- **2 cups sliced fresh mushrooms**
- **2 cups frozen cut green beans**
- **1 cup frozen peas**
- **1 can (15 oz.) tomato sauce**
- **2 Tbsp. minced fresh parsley**

1. Place the first seven ingredients in a 6-qt. stockpot; bring to a boil. Reduce heat; simmer, covered, until carrots are crisp-tender, 10-12 minutes.
2. Stir in remaining ingredients; bring to a boil. Reduce heat; simmer, uncovered, until vegetables are tender, 4-5 minutes.

1 cup: 150 cal., 3g fat (1g sat. fat), 32mg chol., 634mg sod., 16g carb. (4g sugars, 3g fiber), 16g pro. **Diabetic exchanges:** 1 starch, 2 lean meat.

EAT SMART | FAST FIX

TURKEY LO MEIN

I substituted turkey for pork in this classic Chinese recipe. It was a hit at our church potluck, and my husband and two children love it, too.
—Leigh Lundy, York, NE

Takes: 30 min. • **Makes:** 6 servings

- **1 lb. lean ground turkey**
- **2 medium carrots, thinly sliced**
- **1 medium onion, chopped**
- **½ tsp. garlic powder**
- **1½ cups water**
- **2 pkg. (3 oz. each) ramen noodles**
- **6 cups shredded cabbage**
- **1 cup frozen peas, thawed**
- **¼ cup reduced-sodium soy sauce**

1. In a large skillet, cook and crumble turkey with carrots, onion and garlic powder over medium-high heat until no longer pink, 5-7 minutes.
2. Break up noodles and add to skillet; stir in water and the contents of the seasoning packets. Bring to a boil. Reduce heat; simmer, covered, 3-5 minutes. Add remaining ingredients; cook and stir until cabbage is crisp-tender, 1-3 minutes.

1⅓ cups: 297 cal., 11g fat (4g sat. fat), 52mg chol., 580mg sod., 29g carb. (3g sugars, 4g fiber), 21g pro. **Diabetic exchanges:** 2 starch, 2 lean meat.

EAT SMART | FAST FIX

MEDITERRANEAN SHRIMP ORZO SALAD

Put this pretty crowd-pleaser on the buffet table as a tasty change-of-pace from pasta salads. I sometimes like to serve it with a from-scratch vinaigrette.
—Ginger Johnson, Pottstown, PA

Takes: 30 min. • **Makes:** 8 servings

- **1 pkg. (16 oz.) orzo pasta**
- **¾ lb. peeled and deveined cooked shrimp (31-40 per lb.), cut into thirds**
- **1 can (14 oz.) water-packed quartered artichoke hearts, rinsed and drained**
- **1 cup finely chopped green pepper**
- **1 cup finely chopped sweet red pepper**
- **¾ cup finely chopped red onion**
- **½ cup pitted Greek olives**
- **½ cup minced fresh parsley**
- **⅓ cup chopped fresh dill**
- **¾ cup Greek vinaigrette**

1. Cook orzo according to the package directions. Drain; rinse with cold water and drain well.
2. In a large bowl, combine the orzo, shrimp, vegetables, olives and herbs. Add vinaigrette; toss to coat. Refrigerate, covered, until serving.

1½ cups: 397 cal., 12g fat (2g sat. fat), 65mg chol., 574mg sod., 52g carb. (4g sugars, 3g fiber), 18g pro.

MEDITERRANEAN SHRIMP ORZO SALAD

EAT SMART | FAST FIX

TASTY TURKEY & MUSHROOMS

Sliced mushrooms star in this tender turkey recipe. It takes minimal preparation and makes a healthy main dish when served with a side of brown rice. We love it!
—Nancy Zimmerman, Cape May Court House, NJ

Takes: 15 min. • **Makes:** 2 servings

- **1 garlic clove, minced**
- **1 Tbsp. butter**
- **½ lb. boneless skinless turkey breast, cut into 2-in. strips**
- **¾ cup reduced-sodium beef broth**
- **1 Tbsp. tomato paste**
- **2 cups sliced fresh mushrooms**
- **⅛ tsp. salt**

In a large nonstick skillet, saute garlic in butter until tender. Add turkey; cook until juices run clear. Remove and keep warm. Add the broth, tomato paste, mushrooms and salt to skillet; cook for 3-5 minutes or until mushrooms are tender, stirring occasionally. Return turkey to the pan and heat through.

1 cup: 209 cal., 7g fat (4g sat. fat), 88mg chol., 435mg sod., 5g carb. (3g sugars, 1g fiber), 31g pro. **Diabetic exchanges:** 3 lean meat, 1½ fat, 1 vegetable.

EAT SMART | FAST FIX

CURRIED CHICKEN SKILLET

This protein-packed skillet dish is loaded with bright flavor. A little curry and fresh ginger make the veggies, chicken and quinoa pop.
—Ruth Hartunian-Alumbaugh, Willimantic, CT

Takes: 30 min. • **Makes:** 4 servings

- **1⅓ cups plus ½ cup reduced-sodium chicken broth, divided**
- **⅔ cup quinoa, rinsed**
- **1 Tbsp. canola oil**
- **1 medium sweet potato, diced**
- **1 medium onion, chopped**
- **1 celery rib, chopped**
- **1 cup frozen peas**
- **2 garlic cloves, minced**
- **1 tsp. minced fresh gingerroot**
- **3 tsp. curry powder**
- **¼ tsp. salt**
- **2 cups shredded cooked chicken**

1. In a small saucepan, bring 1⅓ cups broth to a boil. Add quinoa. Reduce heat; simmer, covered, until liquid is absorbed, 12-15 minutes.

2. In a large skillet, heat canola oil over medium-high heat; saute sweet potato, onion and celery until potato is tender, 10-12 minutes. Add peas, garlic, ginger and seasonings; cook and stir 2 minutes. Stir in chicken and remaining ½ cup broth; heat through. Stir in quinoa.

2 cups: 367 cal., 11g fat (2g sat. fat), 62mg chol., 450mg sod., 39g carb. (8g sugars, 6g fiber), 29g pro. **Diabetic exchanges:** 3 lean meat, 2½ starch, ½ fat.

TEST KITCHEN TIP

If you don't have cooked chicken handy, you can use 12 oz. uncooked boneless chicken. Cut it into cubes or strips and saute it before cooking the vegetables. Remove it from the pan while you saute the vegetables so it doesn't overcook.

Look for fresh ginger with smooth, even-colored skin that is not dry or wrinkled. Peel the skin with the tip of a spoon or paring knife before using.

CURRIED CHICKEN SKILLET

2. In a small bowl, combine the oats, bran flakes, golden raisins, raisins and brown sugar; spoon into the apples. Top with remaining cheese. Bake, uncovered, at 350° for 35-40 minutes or until tender.

2 filled apple halves: 181 cal., 3g fat (2g sat. fat), 6mg chol., 141mg sod., 39g carb. (27g sugars, 5g fiber), 3g pro.

STIR-FRIED SCALLOPS

EAT SMART | FAST FIX

STIR-FRIED SCALLOPS

Scallops add interest to this mild tomato-based stovetop supper. Try serving the saucy mixture over rice or pasta, and garnish with cilantro or parsley! This recipe serves two, but it's easy to double or triple it if you're serving a group.
—Stephany Gocobachi, San Rafael, CA

Takes: 15 min. • **Makes:** 2 servings

- **1 small onion, chopped**
- **3 garlic cloves, minced**
- **1 Tbsp. olive oil**
- **¾ lb. sea scallops, halved**
- **2 medium plum tomatoes, chopped**
- **2 Tbsp. lemon juice**
- **⅛ tsp. pepper**
- **Hot cooked pasta or rice, optional**

1. In a nonstick skillet or wok, stir-fry the onion and garlic in hot oil until tender. Add scallops; stir-fry until scallops turn opaque. Add tomatoes; cook and stir until heated through, 1-2 minutes longer.
2. Stir in lemon juice and pepper. Serve over pasta or rice if desired.

1 cup: 213 cal., 8g fat (1g sat. fat), 41mg chol., 672mg sod., 14g carb. (4g sugars, 2g fiber), 22g pro. **Diabetic exchanges:** 3 lean meat, 2 vegetable, 1½ fat.

EAT SMART

BAKED APPLE SURPRISE

Depending on the crowd, I'll sometimes use mild Brie cheese instead of sharper blue cheese. I bake the apples in a muffin tin so they don't roll around.
—Jessica Levinson, Nyack, NY

Prep: 10 min. • **Bake:** 35 min.
Makes: 2 servings

- **2 medium apples**
- **2 Tbsp. crumbled blue cheese, divided**
- **2 Tbsp. quick-cooking oats**
- **2 Tbsp. bran flakes**
- **1 Tbsp. golden raisins**
- **1 Tbsp. raisins**
- **1 Tbsp. brown sugar**

1. Cut apples in half lengthwise; remove cores. Place in an ungreased 8-in. square baking dish or a muffin tin. Fill each half with 1 tsp. blue cheese.

EAT SMART

GOLDEN CLAM CHOWDER

My recipe makes it easy to enjoy delicious homemade clam chowder any night. The crispy bits of bacon are traditional and make the chowder feel rich and indulgent.
—Amanda Bowyer, Caldwell, ID

Prep: 20 min. • **Cook:** 20 min.
Makes: 7 servings

- **2 celery ribs**
- **2 medium carrots**
- **1 medium onion**
- **2 tsp. olive oil**
- **4 garlic cloves, minced**
- **4 medium potatoes, peeled and diced**
- **2 cans (6½ oz. each) minced clams, undrained**
- **1 bottle (8 oz.) clam juice**
- **1 cup plus 1 Tbsp. water, divided**
- **1 tsp. dried thyme**
- **½ tsp. salt**
- **½ tsp. pepper**
- **1 can (12 oz.) evaporated milk**
- **2 tsp. cornstarch**
- **2 bacon strips, cooked and crumbled**

1. Finely chop the celery, carrots and onion. In a Dutch oven, saute vegetables in oil until tender. Add garlic; cook 1 minute longer. Stir in the potatoes, clams, clam juice, 1 cup water, thyme, salt and pepper. Bring to a boil. Reduce heat; cover and simmer for 12-15 minutes or until potatoes are tender.
2. Gradually stir in milk; heat through. Combine the cornstarch and remaining 1 Tbsp. water until smooth; stir into the chowder. Bring to a boil; cook and stir for 2 minutes or until thickened. Stir in bacon.

1 cup: 195 cal., 5g fat (3g sat. fat), 27mg chol., 574mg sod., 28g carb. (8g sugars, 2g fiber), 10g pro. **Diabetic exchanges:** 1 starch, 1 lean meat, 1 vegetable, 1 fat.

Cooking for Kids

Noodles, mash-ups and finger food—delicious recipes served up with a sense of fun—prove that kids will happily eat more than chicken nuggets at dinnertime. But because we're talking kids, we've got a fabulous chicken nugget recipe here, too!

Pizza Meat Loaf Cups (p. 173) **Beef & Tater Bake** (p. 165) **Marshmallow Pops** (p. 167) **Salsa Steak Garlic Toasts** (p. 172) **Chicken Nuggets** (p. 172)

SPAGHETTI PIE

A classic Italian combination is remade into a creamy, family-pleasing casserole in this quick and easy dish. This recipe was given to me several years ago, and my family never gets tired of it.
—Ellen Thompson, Springfield, OH

Prep: 30 min. • **Bake:** 25 min.
Makes: 6 servings

- **6 oz. uncooked spaghetti**
- **1 lb. lean ground beef (90% lean)**
- **½ cup finely chopped onion**
- **¼ cup chopped green pepper**
- **1 cup undrained canned diced tomatoes**
- **1 can (6 oz.) tomato paste**
- **1 tsp. dried oregano**
- **¾ tsp. salt**
- **½ tsp. garlic powder**
- **¼ tsp. pepper**
- **¼ tsp. sugar**
- **2 large egg whites, lightly beaten**
- **1 Tbsp. butter, melted**
- **¼ cup grated Parmesan cheese**
- **1 cup fat-free cottage cheese**
- **½ cup shredded part-skim mozzarella cheese**

1. Preheat oven to 350°. Cook spaghetti according to package directions for al dente; drain.
2. In a large skillet, cook the beef, onion and green pepper over medium heat for 5-7 minutes or until beef is no longer pink, breaking up beef into crumbles; drain. Stir in tomatoes, tomato paste, seasonings and sugar.
3. In a large bowl, whisk the egg whites, melted butter and Parmesan cheese until blended. Add the spaghetti and toss to coat. Coat a 9-in. deep-dish pie plate with cooking spray. Press spaghetti mixture onto bottom and up sides of pie plate to form a crust. Spread cottage cheese onto bottom; top with beef mixture.
4. Bake, uncovered, 20 minutes. Sprinkle with mozzarella cheese. Bake 5-10 minutes longer or until heated through. Let stand 5 minutes before serving.
1 piece: 348 cal., 10g fat (5g sat. fat), 52mg chol., 690mg sod., 33g carb. (9g sugars, 4g fiber), 29g pro. **Diabetic exchanges:** 3 lean meat, 2 vegetable, 1½ starch, 1 fat.

CALIFORNIA BURGER WRAPS

EAT SMART | FAST FIX

CALIFORNIA BURGER WRAPS

I love the way these fresh flavors and creamy sauce combine for a quick, healthy lunch. Serve the burgers on buns if you'd like, or simply speed up the process by using burger patties leftover from last night's barbecue.
—Rachelle McCalla, Atlantic, IA

Takes: 30 min. • **Makes:** 4 servings

- **1 lb. lean ground beef (90% lean)**
- **½ tsp. salt**
- **¼ tsp. pepper**
- **8 Bibb lettuce leaves**
- **⅓ cup crumbled feta cheese**
- **2 Tbsp. Miracle Whip Light**
- **½ medium ripe avocado, peeled and cut into 8 slices**
- **¼ cup chopped red onion**
- **Chopped cherry tomatoes, optional**

1. In a large bowl, combine beef, salt and pepper, mixing lightly but thoroughly. Shape into eight ½-in.-thick patties.
2. Grill burgers, covered, over medium heat or broil 3-4 in. from heat 3-4 minutes on each side or until a thermometer reads 160°. Place burgers in lettuce leaves. Combine feta and Miracle Whip; spread over burgers. Top with avocado, red onion and if desired, tomatoes.
2 wraps: 252 cal., 15g fat (5g sat. fat), 78mg chol., 518mg sod., 5g carb. (2g sugars, 2g fiber), 24g pro. **Diabetic exchanges:** 3 lean meat, 2 fat.

TEST KITCHEN TIP

Don't have any Miracle Whip on hand? You can simply substitute it with regular mayonnaise mixed with a pinch of sugar.

FAST FIX

STOVETOP CHEESEBURGER PASTA

Cheeseburgers are delicious in any form, but I'm partial to this heavenly pasta dish that tastes just like the real thing. It's weeknight comfort in a bowl.
—Tracy Avis, Peterborough, ON

Takes: 30 min. • **Makes:** 8 servings

- **1 pkg. (16 oz.) penne pasta**
- **1 lb. ground beef**
- **¼ cup butter, cubed**
- **½ cup all-purpose flour**
- **2 cups 2% milk**
- **1¼ cups beef broth**
- **1 Tbsp. Worcestershire sauce**
- **3 tsp. ground mustard**
- **2 cans (14½ oz. each) diced tomatoes, drained**
- **4 green onions, chopped**
- **3 cups shredded Colby-Monterey Jack cheese, divided**
- **⅔ cup grated Parmesan cheese, divided**

1. Cook pasta according to package directions; drain.

2. Meanwhile, in a Dutch oven, cook and crumble the beef over medium heat until no longer pink, 5-7 minutes. Remove from pan with a slotted spoon; pour off drippings.

3. In same pan, melt the butter over low heat; stir in flour until smooth. Cook and stir until lightly browned, 2-3 minutes (do not burn). Gradually whisk in milk, broth, Worcestershire sauce and mustard. Bring to a boil, stirring constantly; cook and stir until thickened, 1-2 minutes. Stir in the tomatoes; return to a boil. Reduce heat; simmer, covered, 5 minutes.

4. Stir in green onions, pasta and beef; heat through. Stir in half of the cheeses until melted. Sprinkle with remaining cheese; remove from heat. Let stand, covered, until melted.

1½ cups: 616 cal., 29g fat (17g sat. fat), 98mg chol., 727mg sod., 56g carb. (7g sugars, 3g fiber), 33g pro.

STOVETOP CHEESEBURGER PASTA

FAST FIX

BACON, LETTUCE & TOMATO PIZZA

I combine two all-time favorites with this easy recipe: pizza and BLT sandwiches! It's just perfect for kids of all ages.
—Bonnie Hawkins, Elkhorn, WI

Takes: 30 min. • **Makes:** 6 servings

- **1 tube (13.8 oz.) refrigerated pizza crust**
- **2 Tbsp. olive oil**
- **2 Tbsp. grated Parmesan cheese**
- **1 tsp. garlic salt**
- **½ cup mayonnaise**
- **2 tsp. ranch dip mix**
- **4 cups shredded romaine**
- **3 to 4 plum tomatoes, chopped**
- **½ lb. bacon strips, cooked and crumbled**

1. Preheat oven to 425°. Unroll dough. Press dough onto bottom of a greased 15x10x1-in. baking pan. Brush with olive oil; top with cheese and garlic salt. Bake until golden brown, about 15-18 minutes; cool slightly.

2. Meanwhile, combine mayonnaise and ranch mix. Spread over pizza crust; top with lettuce, tomatoes and bacon.

1 piece: 389 cal., 23g fat (5g sat. fat), 16mg chol., 1236mg sod., 34g carb. (5g sugars, 2g fiber), 11g pro.

TEST KITCHEN TIP

Amp up this pizza's flavor by adding a little torn fresh basil to the romaine.

S'MORES ON A STICK

My kids love these treats! Lucky for me, the treats are easy to make. Mini candies also make good toppings.
—Ronda Weirich, Plains, KS

Prep: 15 min. + standing • **Makes:** 2 dozen

- **1 can (14 oz.) sweetened condensed milk, divided**
- **1 cup miniature marshmallows**
- **1½ cups miniature semisweet chocolate chips, divided**
- **24 whole graham crackers, broken in half**
- **Assorted sprinkles**
- **24 wooden pop sticks**

1. In a small microwave-safe bowl, microwave ⅔ cup milk on high for 1½ minutes. Add marshmallows and 1 cup chips; stir until smooth. Drop by tablespoonfuls onto 24 graham cracker halves; spread evenly. Top with remaining graham cracker halves; press down gently.
2. Microwave the remaining milk for 1½ minutes. Add the remaining chips; stir until smooth. Drizzle over cookies; decorate with sprinkles. Let stand 2 hours before inserting a pop stick into the center of each snack.
1 serving: 177 cal., 6g fat (3g sat. fat), 6mg chol., 118mg sod., 30g carb. (20g sugars, 1g fiber), 3g pro.

EAT SMART

BLACK BEAN CHICKEN BURRITOS

I try to hide as many veggies as possible in these popular burritos. Another way I bump up the nutrition is by using thinly sliced cabbage instead of regular iceberg lettuce. The filling freezes well, so double the recipe.
—Jeni Pittard, Statham, GA

Prep: 25 min. • **Cook:** 15 min.
Makes: 8 servings

- **1 lb. ground chicken**
- **1 small green pepper, chopped**
- **1 small sweet red pepper, chopped**
- **1 small onion, chopped**
- **1 Tbsp. canola oil**
- **1 jalapeno pepper, seeded and finely chopped**
- **2 garlic cloves, minced**
- **1 can (15 oz.) black beans, rinsed and drained**
- **1 can (10 oz.) diced tomatoes and green chilies**
- **1 cup fresh or frozen corn**
- **2 tsp. chili powder**
- **1 tsp. ground cumin**
- **½ tsp. salt**
- **½ tsp. paprika**
- **¼ tsp. pepper**
- **8 flour tortillas (8 in.)**
- **Sour cream, shredded cheddar cheese, shredded lettuce and fresh cilantro leaves, optional**

1. In a large nonstick skillet, cook chicken over medium-high heat until no longer pink, breaking into crumbles, 4-6 minutes; drain and remove from skillet.
2. In the same skillet, saute the peppers and onion in oil until lightly browned and crisp-tender, 2-4 minutes. Add jalapeno pepper and garlic; saute 1 minute longer. Stir in beans, tomatoes, corn, seasonings and chicken. Bring to a boil. Reduce heat; simmer, uncovered, until the liquid is evaporated, about 5 minutes. Serve in tortillas, with optional toppings as desired.
1 burrito: 325 cal., 10g fat (2g sat. fat), 38mg chol., 678mg sod., 42g carb. (2g sugars, 5g fiber), 17g pro. **Diabetic exchanges:** 3 starch, 2 lean meat, ½ fat.

TEST KITCHEN TIP

This recipe is easy to adapt for kids. Leave out the jalapeno pepper, for instance, or mix in some avocado.

BLACK BEAN CHICKEN BURRITOS

FAST FIX

CREAMY TOMATO BASIL TORTELLINI

Tortellini is a delightful change-of-pace any night of the week. After a friend remarked about a baked tortellini dish at a restaurant, I experimented to make this for her at home.

—Cyndy Gerken, Naples, FL

Takes: 30 min. • **Makes:** 8 servings

- 1 pkg. (19 oz.) frozen cheese tortellini
- 2 Tbsp. olive oil, divided
- 1 lb. boneless skinless chicken breasts, cut into 1-in. cubes
- 2 tsp. Italian seasoning, divided
- ½ tsp. salt
- ¼ tsp. pepper
- 1 large onion, chopped
- 1 habanero pepper, seeded and finely chopped
- 3 garlic cloves, minced
- 1 can (14½ oz.) fire-roasted diced tomatoes, drained
- 2 cups heavy whipping cream
- ½ cup shredded Italian cheese blend
- ⅓ cup chopped fresh basil

1. Cook the pasta according to package directions; drain.
2. Meanwhile, heat 1 Tbsp. oil in a Dutch oven over medium-high heat. Add the chicken, 1 tsp. Italian seasoning, salt and pepper; saute until meat is no longer pink, about 5 minutes. Remove from pan.
3. In the same pan, add onion, habanero pepper, garlic and the remaining Italian seasoning and oil; reduce heat to medium. Cook and stir until onion is tender, about 5 minutes. Add tomatoes; cook and stir until slightly thickened, about 2 minutes. Stir in cream; bring to a boil. Add tortellini, chicken and cheese; heat through. Top with basil to serve.

1¼ cups: 488 cal., 31g fat (17g sat. fat), 126mg chol., 575mg sod., 30g carb. (5g sugars, 2g fiber), 22g pro.

TEST KITCHEN TIP

If you don't have fire-roasted diced tomatoes, use plain or try diced tomatoes flavored with basil, oregano and garlic.

CREAMY TOMATO BASIL TORTELLINI

BEEF & TATER BAKE

PICTURED ON P. 161

This heartwarming, all-in-one dinner is perfect for the entire family. Try it on a hectic weeknight.

—Mike Tchou, Pepper Pike, OH

Prep: 10 min. • **Bake:** 35 min.
Makes: 8 servings

- 4 cups frozen Tater Tots
- 1 lb. ground beef
- ¼ tsp. garlic powder
- ⅛ tsp. pepper
- 1 can (10¾ oz.) condensed cream of broccoli soup, undiluted
- ⅓ cup 2% milk
- 1 pkg. (16 oz.) frozen chopped broccoli, thawed
- 1 can (2.8 oz.) French-fried onions, divided
- 1 cup shredded Colby-Monterey Jack cheese, divided
- 1 medium tomato, chopped

1. Preheat oven to 400°. Spread Tater Tots evenly in an ungreased 13x9-in. baking dish. Bake, uncovered, 10 minutes.
2. Meanwhile, in a large skillet, cook and crumble beef over medium heat until no longer pink, 5-7 minutes; drain. Stir in seasonings, soup, milk, broccoli, ¾ cup onions, ½ cup cheese and tomato; heat through. Pour over potatoes.
3. Bake, covered, 20 minutes. Sprinkle with the remaining onions and cheese. Bake, uncovered, until cheese is melted, 5-10 minutes.

1 piece: 400 cal., 24g fat (9g sat. fat), 50mg chol., 805mg sod., 29g carb. (3g sugars, 4g fiber), 17g pro.

Corn, Beef & Tater Bake: Substitute 1 package frozen corn for the broccoli and 1 can cream of celery soup for the cream of broccoli soup.

Rainbow Strawberries

Dip fresh strawberries in melted candy discs to create a rainbow of color. Or get adventurous and make a unicorn. The creative possibilities are endless.

*
Consider red, white and blue candy discs for Independence Day, or use orange discs and dark chocolate for Halloween treats.

MARSHMALLOW POPS

PICTURED ON P. 161

Indulge your sweet tooth with fluffy chocolate-covered marshmallows. Kids can help decorate these cuties, easily customizable to any holiday or occasion when rolled in festive toppings. Substitute vanilla baking chips for the semisweet chocolate chips if you like.

—Marcia Porch, Winter Park, FL

Prep: 30 min. + chilling
Makes: 20 servings

- **2 cups (12 oz.) semisweet chocolate chips**
- **4½ tsp. canola oil**
- **40 large marshmallows**
- **20 wooden pop sticks**
- **Optional toppings: toasted coconut, assorted sprinkles and toasted chopped nuts**

1. In a microwave, melt the chocolate chips with oil; stir until smooth.
2. Thread two marshmallows onto each pop stick. Dip the marshmallows into melted chocolate, turning to coat; allow excess to drip off. Roll in the toppings as desired. Place on waxed paper-lined baking sheets; refrigerate until set.

1 serving: 136 cal., 6g fat (3g sat. fat), 0 chol., 13mg sod., 22g carb. (17g sugars, 1g fiber), 1g pro.

5 INGREDIENTS

AMBROSIA SALAD

Easy to prepare, with just five basic ingredients, this tropical medley makes a tempting last-minute menu addition.

—Judi Bringegar, Liberty, NC

Prep: 10 min. + chilling
Makes: 4 servings

- **1 can (11 oz.) mandarin oranges, drained**
- **1 can (8 oz.) pineapple chunks, drained**
- **1 cup miniature marshmallows**
- **1 cup sweetened shredded coconut**
- **1 cup sour cream**

In a large bowl, combine the oranges, pineapple, marshmallows and coconut. Add sour cream and toss to mix. Cover and refrigerate for several hours.

1 cup: 332 cal., 18g fat (14g sat. fat), 40mg chol., 99mg sod., 37g carb. (30g sugars, 1g fiber), 4g pro.

EVERYTHING BAGEL CHICKEN STRIPS

FAST FIX

EVERYTHING BAGEL CHICKEN STRIPS

I love the flavor profile of everything bagels, so I recreated it with traditional breaded chicken fingers. Serve them with your favorite chicken finger dip.

—Cyndy Gerken, Naples, FL

Takes: 30 min. • **Makes:** 4 servings

- **1 day-old everything bagel, torn**
- **½ cup panko (Japanese) bread crumbs**
- **½ cup grated Parmesan cheese**
- **¼ tsp. crushed red pepper flakes**
- **¼ cup butter, cubed**
- **1 lb. chicken tenderloins**
- **½ tsp. salt**

1. Preheat oven to 425°. Pulse torn bagel in a food processor until coarse crumbs form. Place ½ cup bagel crumbs in a shallow bowl; toss with panko, cheese and pepper flakes. (Save the remaining bagel crumbs for another use.)
2. In a microwave-safe shallow bowl, microwave butter until melted. Sprinkle chicken with salt. Dip in warm butter, then coat with crumb mixture, patting to help adhere. Place on a greased rack in a 15x10x1-in. pan.
3. Bake until golden brown and chicken is no longer pink, 15-17 minutes.

1 serving: 246 cal., 12g fat (7g sat. fat), 85mg chol., 593mg sod., 6g carb. (0 sugars, 0 fiber), 30g pro.

TEST KITCHEN TIP

One bagel will yield about 2 cups crumbs. Save remaining crumbs to use as a tasty topping for casseroles or to bind meat loaves and meatballs.

Baking breaded foods on a rack allows the bottom to crisp up better. If you don't have a rack that fits the pan, you can also use a broiler pan with a rack.

FAST FIX

TEX-MEX CHICKEN STRIPS

When looking for a way to up the flavor of regular chicken strips, I crushed up some leftover corn chips. It makes for a crispy, flavorful coating.
—Cyndy Gerken, Naples, FL

Takes: 30 min. • **Makes:** 4 servings

½ cup finely crushed corn chips
¼ cup panko (Japanese) bread crumbs
¼ cup dry bread crumbs
¼ cup finely shredded Mexican cheese blend
5 tsp. taco seasoning
Dash cayenne pepper
¼ cup butter, melted
1 lb. chicken tenderloins

Preheat oven to 400°. In a shallow bowl mix the first six ingredients. Place butter in a separate shallow bowl. Dip chicken in butter, then roll in crumb mixture to coat; press to adhere. Place chicken on a foil-lined 15x10x1-in. baking pan. Bake until a thermometer inserted into the chicken reads 165°, about 15 minutes, turning halfway through cooking time.
3 oz. cooked chicken: 258 cal., 14g fat (7g sat. fat), 85mg chol., 351mg sod., 7g carb. (0 sugars, 0 fiber), 28g pro.

PEPPERONI PIZZA BAKED POTATOES

EAT SMART | FAST FIX

PEPPERONI PIZZA BAKED POTATOES

These tasty taters became a spur-of-the-moment dish born of leftovers! It is a mash-up that combines two dinnertime favorites into one super fun meal for everyone at the table.
—Dawn E. Lowenstein
Huntingdon Valley, PA

Takes: 30 min. • **Makes:** 4 servings

4 medium russet potatoes (about 8 oz. each)
1 Tbsp. olive oil
1 cup sliced fresh mushrooms
1 small green pepper, chopped
1 small onion, chopped
1 garlic clove, minced
1 can (8 oz.) pizza sauce
⅓ cup mini sliced turkey pepperoni
½ cup shredded Italian cheese blend
Fresh oregano leaves or dried oregano, optional

1. Preheat oven to 400°. Scrub potatoes; place on a microwave-safe plate. Pierce several times with a fork. Microwave, uncovered, on high until fork-tender, 12-15 minutes.
2. In a large skillet, heat oil over medium-high heat; saute mushrooms, pepper and onion until tender, 6-8 minutes. Add garlic; cook and stir 1 minute. Stir in pizza sauce and pepperoni; heat through.
3. Place the potatoes on a baking sheet; cut an X in the top of each. Fluff pulp with a fork. Top with the vegetable mixture; sprinkle with cheese. Bake until cheese is melted, 5-7 minutes. If desired, sprinkle with oregano.

1 baked potato with toppings: 311 cal., 9g fat (3g sat. fat), 23mg chol., 515mg sod., 46g carb. (5g sugars, 6g fiber), 13g pro. **Diabetic exchanges:** 3 starch, 1 medium-fat meat, ½ fat.

PAPRIKA CHICKEN STROGANOFF

Chicken and noodles—the perfect comfort food! While Stroganoff is traditionally a beef dish, it can easily be adapted for other proteins, such as chicken, and customized for picky eaters.
—Leo Lo, Norfolk, VA

Prep: 20 min. • **Cook:** 30 min.
Makes: 6 servings

- **8 oz. uncooked wide egg noodles**
- **1½ lbs. boneless skinless chicken breasts, cut into ½-in.-thick strips**
- **2 tsp. paprika**
- **1½ tsp. salt, divided**
- **¾ tsp. pepper, divided**
- **1 Tbsp. olive oil**
- **1 lb. sliced baby portobello mushrooms**
- **1 Tbsp. butter**
- **1 large red onion, halved and sliced**
- **3 garlic cloves, minced**
- **2 cups chicken stock**
- **1 Tbsp. Worcestershire sauce**
- **1 Tbsp. Dijon mustard**
- **1 cup creme fraiche or sour cream**
- **1 Tbsp. minced fresh Italian parsley**

1. Cook noodles according to package directions; drain.
2. Meanwhile, toss chicken with paprika, ½ tsp. salt and ¼ tsp. pepper. In a Dutch oven, heat oil over medium-high heat. In batches, saute chicken until browned, 2-3 minutes. Remove from pan.
3. In the same pan, saute mushrooms in butter until lightly browned, 4-5 minutes. Add onion; cook and stir until softened, 3-4 minutes. Add garlic; cook and stir roughly 1 minute.
4. Add stock, stirring to loosen browned bits from pan. Add the Worcestershire sauce and mustard; bring to a boil. Cook, uncovered, until the liquid is reduced by half, 10-12 minutes. Stir in chicken; cook, uncovered, over medium-low until the chicken is no longer pink, 3-5 minutes.
5. Stir in creme fraiche, parsley and the remaining salt and pepper; remove from heat. Stir in noodles.

1⅔ cups: 505 cal., 24g fat (12g sat. fat), 133mg chol., 874mg sod., 35g carb. (4g sugars, 3g fiber), 33g pro.

FAIR-FAVORITE CORN DOGS

Bring the county fair to your kitchen with these summer-ready corn dogs. A tip for dipping: Pour the batter into a tall mason jar and dunk your dogs for even all-over coating.
—*Taste of Home* Test Kitchen

Prep: 15 min. + standing
Cook: 5 min./batch • **Makes:** 10 corn dogs

- **1 pkg. (8½ oz.) cornbread/muffin mix**
- **⅔ cup all-purpose flour**
- **1 tsp. ground mustard**
- **½ tsp. onion powder**
- **½ tsp. chili powder**
- **½ tsp. paprika**
- **⅛ tsp. ground cumin**
- **1 large egg**
- **1 cup 2% milk**
- **10 hot dogs**
- **10 wooden skewers**
- **Oil for deep-fat frying**

1. In a large bowl, combine the first seven ingredients. In another bowl, whisk milk and egg; stir into dry ingredients just until moistened. Let stand about 15 minutes. Insert wooden skewers into hot dogs; dip into batter.
2. In an electric skillet or deep-fat fryer, heat oil to 375°. Fry the corn dogs, a few at a time, for 2-3 minutes or until golden brown, turning occasionally. Drain on paper towels.

1 corn dog: 352 cal., 23g fat (7g sat. fat), 53mg chol., 682mg sod., 26g carb. (7g sugars, 1g fiber), 9g pro.

TEST KITCHEN TIP

Don't forget to let the batter stand before coating the hot dogs. It thickens a bit and clings better after 15 minutes. Make sure the oil temperature returns to 375° between batches.

PAPRIKA CHICKEN STROGANOFF

FAST FIX

SCHOOL-NIGHT SAUSAGE STROGANOFF

I found this recipe in an old church cookbook about 25 years ago and tweaked it to fit my family's tastes. It's a savory, creamy dish that's quick to fix on a busy school night.

—Kristine Chayes, Smithtown, NY

Takes: 30 min. • **Makes:** 4

- **8 oz. uncooked wide egg noodles**
- **1 lb. bulk pork sausage**
- **8 oz. sliced fresh mushrooms**
- **1 medium onion, chopped**
- **2 garlic cloves, minced**
- **¼ cup all-purpose flour**
- **¼ tsp. salt**
- **½ tsp. paprika**
- **1½ cups beef broth**
- **1 cup sour cream**
- **Chopped fresh parsley**

1. Cook noodles according to package directions. Set aside.

2. In a large skillet, cook pork sausage, mushrooms, onion and garlic over medium heat until sausage is no longer pink and vegetables are tender, 5-7 minutes. Stir in flour, salt and paprika until blended; gradually stir in broth. Bring to a boil, stirring constantly; cook and stir 1-2 minutes or until thickened. Turn off heat. Stir in sour cream. Serve with noodles and sprinkle with parsley.

1¼ cups sausage mixture with 1½ cups noodles: 675 cal., 39g fat (15g sat. fat), 123mg chol., 1204mg sod., 55g carb. (4g sugars, 3g fiber), 26g pro.

SCHOOL-NIGHT SAUSAGE STROGANOFF

FAST FIX

SPICY CHICKEN & BACON MAC

I've been working to perfect a creamy, spicy mac and cheese for years. After adding smoky bacon, chicken, jalapenos and spicy cheese, this is the ultimate! I use rotisserie chicken and precooked bacon when I'm pressed for time.

—Sarah Gilbert, Aloha, OR

Takes: 30 min. • **Makes:** 6 servings

- **1½ cups uncooked cavatappi pasta or elbow macaroni**
- **3 Tbsp. butter**
- **3 Tbsp. all-purpose flour**
- **1½ cups heavy whipping cream**
- **½ cup 2% milk**
- **1 tsp. Cajun seasoning**
- **¼ tsp. salt**
- **¼ tsp. pepper**
- **2 cups shredded pepper jack cheese**
- **2 cups shredded cooked chicken**
- **6 bacon strips, cooked and crumbled**
- **1 jalapeno pepper, seeded and chopped**
- **1 cup crushed kettle-cooked potato chips or panko (Japanese) bread crumbs**

1. Cook pasta according to package directions for al dente; drain. Preheat the broiler.

2. In a 10-in. ovenproof skillet, heat the butter over medium heat. Stir in flour until blended; cook and stir until lightly browned, 1-2 minutes (do not burn). Gradually whisk in cream, milk, Cajun seasoning, salt and pepper. Bring to a boil, stirring constantly. Reduce heat; cook and stir until thickened, about 5 minutes. Stir in cheese until melted. Add pasta, chicken, bacon and jalapeno; cook and stir until heated through. Sprinkle chips over top.

3. Broil 3-4 in. from heat until chips are browned, about 30 seconds.

1 cup: 673 cal., 50g fat (28g sat. fat), 175mg chol., 705mg sod., 26g carb. (3g sugars, 1g fiber), 32g pro.

TEST KITCHEN TIP

If your family likes spicy foods, add more Cajun seasoning or jalapeno pepper.

SHORTCUT OVEN-BAKED CHICKEN CHIMICHANGAS

SHORTCUT OVEN-BAKED CHICKEN CHIMICHANGAS

Brushing these with oil and baking them mimics the authentic crunch of a chimichanga. Our children love to have them when they get home late after school activities.
—Johnna Johnson, Scottsdale, AZ

Prep: 35 min. • **Bake:** 15 min.
Makes: 6 servings

- **¼ cup canola oil, divided**
- **1 small onion, chopped**
- **1 rotisserie chicken, skin removed, shredded (about 3½ cups)**
- **1 pkg. (8.8 oz.) ready-to-serve long grain rice**
- **1 can (15 oz.) black beans, rinsed and drained**
- **1 can (4 oz.) chopped green chilies**
- **2 tsp. minced chipotle peppers in adobo sauce**
- **¼ tsp. ground cumin**
- **¼ tsp. salt**
- **¼ tsp. pepper**
- **1½ cups shredded Mexican cheese blend**
- **⅓ cup chopped fresh cilantro**
- **6 flour tortillas (10 in.), warmed**
- **Salsa**

1. Preheat oven to 425°. Carefully place a 15x10x1-in. baking pan in the oven.
2. In a large skillet, heat 2 Tbsp. oil over medium-high heat; saute onion until lightly browned, about 5 minutes. Stir in chicken, rice, black beans, chilies, chipotle pepper, cumin, salt and pepper; cook until heated through. Remove from heat; stir in cheese and cilantro.
3. Spoon 1 cup chicken mixture across bottom third of each tortilla. Fold bottom and sides of tortilla over filling and roll up. Brush preheated baking pan with some of the remaining oil. Place chimichangas seam side down; brush tortillas with oil. Bake until crisp and golden, 15 minutes, turning halfway through baking. Serve with toppings.

1 chimichanga: 704 cal., 31g fat (9g sat. fat), 98mg chol., 1081mg sod., 62g carb. (4g sugars, 6g fiber), 41g pro.

TEST KITCHEN TIP

Use 2 cups leftover cooked rice as a substitute for ready-to-serve packaged rice.

FAST FIX

MEATBALL FLATBREAD

As amazing as this flatbread tastes, you would never know how quickly it comes together. A little hidden carrot, unnoticed by the kids, adds sweet texture. For a crispier crust, bake the flatbread in the oven until it is slightly crispy on top before applying tomato puree.
—Kimberly Berg, North Street, MI

Takes: 25 min. • **Makes:** 4 pizzas

- **1 can (15 oz.) Italian tomato sauce**
- **1 medium carrot, coarsely chopped**
- **3 fresh basil leaves**
- **1 garlic clove, halved**
- **4 naan flatbreads**
- **2 cups shredded mozzarella cheese**
- **20 frozen fully cooked Italian meatballs, thawed and halved**
- **Dash each salt, pepper, dried parsley flakes and dried oregano**

1. Preheat oven to 400°. Place the tomato sauce, carrot, basil and garlic in a food processor; cover and process until pureed. Place flatbreads on an ungreased baking sheet. Spread with tomato sauce mixture; top with cheese and meatballs. Sprinkle with seasonings.
2. Bake on a lower oven rack until cheese is melted, 12-15 minutes.

½ flatbread: 284 cal., 16g fat (8g sat. fat), 42mg chol., 993mg sod., 21g carb. (3g sugars, 2g fiber), 15g pro.

Caramel Apple Float

Kids of all ages can't get enough of this no-fuss specialty that combines the best of summer fun and fall flavors.

Top equal parts apple cider and ginger ale with vanilla ice cream. Drizzle with caramel syrup. Top with finely chopped green apple.

5 INGREDIENTS | FAST FIX

SALSA STEAK GARLIC TOASTS

PICTURED ON P. 161

These open-faced steak sandwiches play up the popular combo of steak and garlic bread. The salsa, sour cream and garnish elevate it into quick, satisfying meal. Substitute chopped green onions or chives for the cilantro if desired.
—Arlene Erlbach, Morton Grove, IL

Takes: 25 min. • **Makes:** 4 servings

- **4 slices frozen garlic Texas toast**
- **1 Tbsp. olive oil**
- **1 beef top sirloin steak (1 lb.), thinly sliced**
- **1½ cups salsa**
- **Sour cream and chopped fresh cilantro**

1. Prepare garlic toast according to the package directions.
2. Meanwhile, in a large skillet, heat oil over medium heat. Saute steak until no longer pink, 3-5 minutes; drain. Stir in salsa; cook and stir until heated through. Serve over toast. Top with sour cream and cilantro.

1 garlic toast with ¾ cup steak mixture: 375 cal., 16g fat (4g sat. fat), 52mg chol., 721mg sod., 27g carb. (5g sugars, 1g fiber), 29g pro.

EAT SMART | FAST FIX

CHICKEN NUGGETS

PICTURED ON P. 161

I like to make these chicken nuggets because they're fast and simple, and my whole family loves them. I sometimes leave the chicken breasts whole and cook them up for incredible sandwiches.
—Annette Ellyson, Carolina, WV

Takes: 30 min. • **Makes:** 8 servings

- **1 cup all-purpose flour**
- **4 tsp. seasoned salt**
- **1 tsp. poultry seasoning**
- **1 tsp. ground mustard**
- **1 tsp. paprika**
- **½ tsp. pepper**
- **2 lbs. boneless skinless chicken breasts**
- **¼ cup canola oil**

1. In a large shallow dish, combine the first six ingredients. Flatten the chicken breasts to ½-in. thickness; cut into 1½-in. pieces. Add chicken, a few pieces at a time, to dish and turn to coat.
2. In a large skillet, cook the chicken in oil in batches until meat is no longer pink, 6-8 minutes.

3 oz. cooked chicken: 212 cal., 10g fat (2g sat. fat), 63mg chol., 435mg sod., 6g carb. (0 sugars, 0 fiber), 24g pro. **Diabetic exchanges:** 3 lean meat, 1½ fat, ½ starch.

FAST FIX

PHILLY CHEESESTEAK GNOCCHI

My family loves this warm and welcoming meal. It has all the Philly cheesesteak flavor served up in a bowl!
—Lauren Wyler, Dripping Springs, TX

Takes: 30 min. • **Makes:** 6 servings

- **1 lb. ground beef**
- **1 medium green pepper, halved and sliced**
- **1 small onion, halved and thinly sliced**
- **1 jalapeno pepper, halved, seeded and thinly sliced**
- **2 Tbsp. butter**
- **2 Tbsp. all-purpose flour**
- **½ tsp. pepper**
- **¼ tsp. salt**
- **1½ cups 2% milk**
- **2 Tbsp. Worcestershire sauce**
- **2 cups shredded provolone cheese**
- **1 pkg. (16 oz.) potato gnocchi**

1. In a large skillet, cook and crumble beef with green pepper, onion and jalapeno over medium-high heat until no longer pink, 5-7 minutes. Remove from pan with a slotted spoon; pour off drippings.
2. In same skillet, melt butter over medium heat. Stir in flour, pepper and salt until smooth; cook and stir until lightly browned, 2-3 minutes. Gradually whisk in milk and Worcestershire sauce. Bring to a boil, stirring constantly; cook and stir until thickened, 5-7 minutes. Stir in cheese until melted. Stir in beef mixture; heat through.
3. Meanwhile, cook gnocchi according to package directions. Drain; add to sauce, stirring gently. Serve immediately.

1 cup: 512 cal., 25g fat (14g sat. fat), 93mg chol., 918mg sod., 40g carb. (9g sugars, 2g fiber), 31g pro.

TEST KITCHEN TIP

The Worcestershire sauce may seem odd, but don't leave it out! It adds a savory depth of flavor that balances out this dish. If left to stand and cool, the gnocchi will get sticky, so serve the final dish hot from the pan.

FREEZE IT | FAST FIX

PIZZA MEAT LOAF CUPS

Fix and freeze these moist little meat loaves that are packed with pizza flavor. Try reheating for an after-school snack or quick dinner. My family likes to drizzle extra pizza sauce on top.
—Susan Wollin, Marshall, WI

Takes: 30 min. • **Makes:** 1 dozen

- **1 large egg, lightly beaten**
- **½ cup pizza sauce**
- **¼ cup seasoned bread crumbs**
- **½ tsp. Italian seasoning**
- **1½ lbs. ground beef**
- **1½ cups shredded part-skim mozzarella cheese**
- **Additional pizza sauce and basil leaves, optional**

1. Preheat oven to 375°. In a large bowl, mix first four ingredients. Add beef; mix lightly but thoroughly. Divide into 12 portions; press each onto the bottom and up sides of a greased muffin cup. Add cheese to centers.
2. Bake until meat is cooked through, 15-18 minutes. If desired, top with additional sauce and basil before serving.
Freeze option: Freeze the cooled meat loaves in freezer containers. To use, partially thaw in refrigerator overnight. Microwave, covered, on high in a microwave-safe dish until heated through.

2 meat loaf cups: 167 cal., 10g fat (4g sat. fat), 63mg chol., 177mg sod., 3g carb. (1g sugars, 0 fiber), 16g pro.

PIZZA MEAT LOAF CUPS

Breakfast & Brunch Favorites

Make the morning special for your family—and for brunch guests, too! These yummy morning treats are perfect for a special-occasion gathering, but quick and easy enough to make on a weekday morning.

Orange Juice Spritzer (p. 179) **Feta Asparagus Frittata** (p. 177) **Hash Brown Nests with Portobellos & Eggs** (p. 180) **Cheesy Broccoli & Ham Quiche** (p. 186) **Easy Breakfast Strata** (p.185)

EAT SMART | FAST FIX

HAM MUFFINWICHES

I concocted this fun recipe when I needed to pack lunch and was out of bread, so I got creative with a box of cornbread mix.
—Jenny Wiebe, Villa Hills, KY

Takes: 30 min. • **Makes:** 4 servings

- **1 large egg, lightly beaten, room temperature**
- **⅓ cup 2% milk**
- **1 Tbsp. canola oil**
- **⅛ tsp. ground mustard**
- **1 pkg. (8½ oz.) cornbread/muffin mix**
- **1 cup chopped fully cooked ham**
- **2 green onions, thinly sliced**
- **2 Tbsp. shredded cheddar cheese**

1. Preheat oven to 400°. Whisk together first four ingredients. Add the muffin mix; stir just until moistened. Fold in the ham and green onions. Fill eight greased or paper-lined muffin cups half full.
2. Bake until a toothpick inserted in center comes out clean, 15-20 minutes. Immediately sprinkle with cheese. Cool 5 minutes before removing from pan to a wire rack. Serve warm.

2 muffins: 186 cal., 8g fat (2g sat. fat), 37mg chol., 483mg sod., 22g carb. (7g sugars, 2g fiber), 7g pro. **Diabetic exchanges:** 1½ starch, 1 lean meat, 1 fat.

RUSTIC VEGETABLE FRITTATA

EAT SMART | FAST FIX

RUSTIC VEGETABLE FRITTATA

This veggie-loaded frittata combines seriously nutritious ingredients into a filling dish I can serve as breakfast, lunch or dinner—and it's just as delicious even as leftovers!
—Deborah Jamison, Austin, TX

Takes: 30 min. • **Makes:** 4 servings

- **1 medium sweet potato, peeled and cut into ¼-in. slices**
- **2 Tbsp. water**
- **7 large eggs**
- **3 Tbsp. fat-free milk**
- **¼ tsp. salt**
- **⅛ tsp. pepper**
- **6 center-cut bacon strips, coarsely chopped**
- **1 small green pepper, chopped**
- **½ cup chopped red onion**
- **2 cups coarsely chopped fresh kale**

1. Preheat oven to 375°. Place sweet potato and water in a microwave-safe bowl; microwave, covered, on high until potato is just tender, 5-6 minutes; drain.
2. Meanwhile, whisk together eggs, milk, salt and pepper. In a 10-in. oven-safe skillet, cook bacon over medium heat until crisp, stirring occasionally. Using a slotted spoon, remove to paper towels. Remove all but 1 Tbsp. of the drippings from pan.
3. In the same pan, over medium heat, saute green pepper, onion and kale in the drippings until tender, 4-5 minutes. Reduce heat to low. Stir in egg mixture; add potato and bacon. Cook until the eggs are partially set, 1-2 minutes.
4. Transfer to oven; bake until the eggs are set, 5-7 minutes. Cut into wedges.

1 wedge: 259 cal., 14g fat (5g sat. fat), 340mg chol., 448mg sod., 16g carb. (7g sugars, 2g fiber), 17g pro. **Diabetic exchanges:** 2 medium-fat meat, 1 starch.

TEST KITCHEN TIP

Center-cut bacon has more meat and less fat per strip than regular bacon, which you can use instead.

Frittatas can also be served cold, making them easy to pack for lunch or a picnic.

FAST FIX | 5 INGREDIENTS

CRANBERRY CHIP PANCAKES

These simple pancakes taste so great, you don't even need syrup! Adding cranberries, orange juice and vanilla chips livens up a classic pancake batter.
—Aris Gonzalez, Deltona, FL

Takes: 25 min. • **Makes:** 6 pancakes

- **½ cup fresh or frozen cranberries**
- **1 cup water, divided**
- **1 cup complete pancake mix**
- **1 tsp. grated orange zest**
- **¼ cup orange juice**
- **¼ cup white baking chips**

1. In a small saucepan over medium heat, cook the cranberries and ½ cup of water until the berries pop, about 10 minutes. Meanwhile, in a large bowl, combine the pancake mix, orange zest, orange juice and remaining water just until moistened. Fold in chips. Drain cranberries; fold into batter.
2. Pour the batter by ¼ cupfuls onto a greased hot griddle; turn when bubbles form on top. Cook until the second side is golden brown.

3 pancakes: 368 cal., 9g fat (4g sat. fat), 4mg chol., 853mg sod., 66g carb. (24g sugars, 3g fiber), 8g pro.

FAST FIX

FETA ASPARAGUS FRITTATA

PICTURED ON P. 175

Asparagus and feta cheese combine to make this frittata extra special. It's perfect for a lazy Sunday or to serve with a tossed salad for a light lunch.
—Mildred Sherrer, Fort Worth, TX

Takes: 30 min. • **Makes:** 2 servings

- **12 fresh asparagus spears, trimmed**
- **6 large eggs**
- **2 Tbsp. heavy whipping cream**
- **Dash salt**
- **Dash pepper**
- **1 Tbsp. olive oil**
- **2 green onions, chopped**
- **1 garlic clove, minced**
- **½ cup crumbled feta cheese**

1. Preheat oven to 350°. Place asparagus spears in a large skillet in ½ in. of water; bring to a boil. Cook, covered, until the asparagus is crisp-tender, 3-5 minutes; drain. Cool slightly.
2. In a bowl, whisk together eggs, cream, salt and pepper. Chop 2 asparagus spears. In an 8-in. cast-iron or other ovenproof skillet, heat oil over medium heat until hot. Saute green onions, garlic and chopped asparagus for 1 minute. Stir in the egg mixture; cook, covered, over medium heat until eggs are nearly set, 3-5 minutes. Top with whole asparagus spears and cheese.
3. Bake until the eggs are completely set, 7-9 minutes.

½ frittata: 425 cal., 31g fat (12g sat. fat), 590mg chol., 1231mg sod., 8g carb. (3g sugars, 3g fiber), 27g pro.

CRANBERRY CHIP PANCAKES

Ooh la la!

For a morning treat, try a breakfast with a little French flair. These crepes are magnifique!

CREAMY STRAWBERRY CREPES

Take summer-ripe strawberries plus a creamy filling and tuck them into these delicate crepes—you'll have an elegant brunch entree.

—Kathy Kochiss, Huntington, CT

Prep: 10 min. • **Cook:** 35 min.
Makes: 14 crepes

- 4 large eggs
- 1 cup milk
- 1 cup cold water
- 2 Tbsp. butter, melted
- ¼ tsp. salt
- 2 cups all-purpose flour
- Additional butter

FILLING

- 1 pkg. (8 oz.) cream cheese, softened
- 1¼ cups confectioners' sugar
- 1 Tbsp. lemon juice
- 1 tsp. grated lemon zest
- ½ tsp. vanilla extract
- 4 cups fresh strawberries, sliced, divided
- 1 cup heavy whipping cream, whipped
- Additional confectioners' sugar, optional

2 crepes: 504 cal., 26g fat (15g sat. fat), 194mg chol., 275mg sod., 58g carb. (28g sugars, 3g fiber), 12g pro.

HOW-TO

Make Perfect Strawberry Crepes

For the batter:
In a bowl, beat the eggs, milk, water, butter and salt. Add flour; beat until smooth. Cover and refrigerate for 1 hour.

1. Pour and swirl
In an 8-in. nonstick skillet, melt 1 tsp. butter; pour 2 Tbsp. of batter into the center of the skillet. Lift and tilt pan, swirling to evenly coat the bottom.

2. Cook crepes
Cook until the top appears dry; turn and cook 15-20 seconds longer. Remove to wire rack. Repeat, adding butter as needed. Stack crepes between waxed paper or paper towels.

3. Make filling
In a bowl, beat cream cheese, confectioners' sugar, lemon juice, zest and vanilla until smooth. Fold in 2 cups berries and whipped cream.

4. Assemble
Spoon about ⅓ cup filling down the center of each of 14 crepes; roll up. Garnish with remaining berries. Freeze leftover crepes, unfilled, for another use.

5 INGREDIENTS | FAST FIX

BREAKFAST SKEWERS

These spicy-sweet kabobs make a surprising but delightful offering for brunch with friends. They're a pretty perfect companion to any egg dish.
—Bobi Raab, St. Paul, MN

Takes: 20 min. • **Makes:** 5 servings

- **1 pkg. (7 oz.) frozen fully cooked breakfast sausage links, thawed**
- **1 can (20 oz.) pineapple chunks, drained**
- **10 medium fresh mushrooms**
- **2 Tbsp. butter, melted**
- **Maple syrup**

1. Cut sausages in half; on five metal or soaked wooden skewers, alternately thread the sausages, pineapple and mushrooms. Brush with butter and syrup.
2. Grill, uncovered, over medium heat, turning and basting with syrup, for 8 minutes or until sausages are lightly browned and the fruit is heated through.

1 skewer: 246 cal., 20g fat (8g sat. fat), 37mg chol., 431mg sod., 13g carb. (12g sugars, 1g fiber), 7g pro.

5 INGREDIENTS | FAST FIX

ORANGE JUICE SPRITZER

PICTURED ON P. 175

This is a nice twist on regular orange juice. It's a treat that's not overly sweet.
—Michelle Krzmarzick, Torrance, CA

Takes: 5 min.
Makes: 8 servings (1 cup each)

- **4 cups orange juice**
- **1 liter ginger ale, chilled**
- **¼ cup maraschino cherry juice**
- **Orange wedges and maraschino cherries, optional**

In a 2-qt. pitcher, mix orange juice, ginger ale and cherry juice. Serve over ice. If desired, top servings with orange wedges and cherries.

1 cup: 103 cal., 0 fat (0 sat. fat), 0 chol., 9mg sod., 25g carb. (23g sugars, 0 fiber), 1g pro.

5 INGREDIENTS

BACON & EGG BUNDLES

This is a fun way to serve bacon and eggs all in one cute package! The recipe can be doubled easilyfor a larger group.
—Edith Landinger, Longview, TX

Prep: 20 min. • **Bake:** 15 min.
Makes: 6 servings

- **12 to 18 bacon strips**
- **1 tsp. butter**
- **6 large eggs**
- **Freshly ground pepper, optional**

1. Preheat oven to 325°. In a large skillet, cook the bacon over medium heat until partially cooked but not crisp. Drain on paper towels.
2. Lightly grease six muffin cups with 1 tsp. butter. Cut six bacon strips in half crosswise. Line the bottom of each muffin cup with two bacon halves. Line the sides of each muffin cup with one or two whole bacon strips. Break an egg into each cup.
3. Bake until the whites are completely set and the yolks begin to thicken but are not hard, 12-18 minutes. If desired, sprinkle with pepper.

1 bundle: 311 cal., 28g fat (9g sat. fat), 225mg chol., 447mg sod., 1g carb. (1g sugars, 0 fiber), 13g pro.

BACON & EGG BUNDLES

FAST FIX

STUFFED FRENCH TOAST

Kids like to help stuff the sausage and cheese into the bread. I serve this for holidays, when we have guests or on special family occasions.

—Heidi Wilcox, Lapeer, MI

Takes: 25 min. • **Makes:** 6 servings

- **6 frozen fully cooked breakfast sausage patties (about 7 oz.)**
- **6 slices Italian bread (1½ in. thick)**
- **3 slices Muenster or brick cheese, halved**
- **4 large eggs**
- **1 cup 2% milk**
- **1 Tbsp. sugar**
- **Maple syrup**

1. Cook sausage according to the package directions; cool slightly.
2. Cut a pocket in one side of each slice of bread. Fill the pockets with the sausage and cheese. In a shallow bowl, whisk together eggs, milk and sugar. Soak stuffed bread in the egg mixture, about 1 minute per side.
3. Cook bread on a greased griddle over medium heat until golden brown on both sides. Serve with syrup.

1 piece: 276 cal., 15g fat (6g sat. fat), 153mg chol., 456mg sod., 20g carb. (6g sugars, 1g fiber), 14g pro.

5 INGREDIENTS | FAST FIX

SWEET BROILED GRAPEFRUIT

I was never a fan of grapefruit until I had it broiled at a restaurant—it was so tangy and delicious!

—Terry Bray, Auburndale, FL

Takes: 15 min. • **Makes:** 2 servings

- **1 large grapefruit**
- **2 Tbsp. butter, softened**
- **2 Tbsp. sugar**
- **½ tsp. ground cinnamon**

1. Preheat broiler. Cut the grapefruit crosswise in half; if desired, cut a thin slice from the bottom of each half so they sit level. Cut around each grapefruit section to loosen the fruit. Top with butter. Mix sugar and cinnamon; sprinkle over the fruit.
2. Place on a baking sheet. Broil 4 in. from heat until the sugar is bubbly.

½ grapefruit: 203 cal., 12g fat (7g sat. fat), 31mg chol., 116mg sod., 26g carb. (24g sugars, 2g fiber), 1g pro.

STUFFED FRENCH TOAST

EAT SMART

HASH BROWN NESTS WITH PORTOBELLOS & EGGS

PICTURED ON P. 175

Hash browns make a fabulous crust for these individual egg quiches. They look fancy but are actually quite easy to make.

—Kate Meyer, Brentwood, TN

Prep: 30 min. • **Bake:** 15 min.
Makes: 1 dozen

- **2 Tbsp. butter**
- **½ lb. sliced baby portobello mushrooms, chopped**
- **¼ cup chopped shallots**
- **1 garlic clove, minced**
- **½ tsp. salt**
- **¼ tsp. pepper**
- **Dash cayenne pepper**
- **2 Tbsp. sour cream**
- **1 Tbsp. minced fresh basil or 1 tsp. dried basil**
- **4 cups frozen shredded hash brown potatoes (about 1 lb.), thawed**
- **7 large eggs, lightly beaten**
- **¼ cup shredded Swiss cheese**
- **2 bacon strips, cooked and crumbled**

1. Preheat oven to 400°. In a large skillet, heat butter over medium-high heat; saute mushrooms and shallots until tender. Add the garlic, salt, pepper and cayenne; cook and stir 1 minute. Remove from heat; stir in the sour cream and basil.
2. Press about ¼ cup of the potatoes into the bottoms and up the sides of greased muffin cups. Fill each with about 2 Tbsp. beaten eggs. Top with the mushroom mixture, cheese and bacon.
3. Bake until eggs are set, 15-18 minutes.

1 egg nest: 105 cal., 7g fat (3g sat. fat), 118mg chol., 191mg sod., 6g carb. (1g sugars, 1g fiber), 6g pro. **Diabetic exchanges:** 1 medium-fat meat, ½ starch, ½ fat.

GREEN CHILE BRUNCH BAKE

You assemble this delicious, satisfying breakfast casserole the night before—perfect for busy moms.
—Trista Thinnes, Fort Worth, TX

Prep: 30 min. + chilling • **Bake:** 45 min.
Makes: 8 servings

- **1 lb. bulk pork sausage**
- **10 cups cubed day-old French bread**
- **2 cups shredded sharp cheddar cheese**
- **1 can (4 oz.) mushroom stems and pieces, drained**
- **5 green onions, chopped**
- **6 large eggs**
- **2¾ cups half-and-half cream**
- **1 can (4 oz.) chopped green chiles, drained**
- **1½ tsp. Worcestershire sauce**
- **½ tsp. salt**
- **¼ tsp. ground mustard**
- **¼ tsp. paprika**
- **¼ tsp. pepper**
- **⅛ to ¼ tsp. hot pepper sauce**

1. In a large skillet, cook the sausage over medium heat until no longer pink, breaking into crumbles, for 5-7 minutes; drain and set aside. Place the bread cubes in a greased 13x9-in. baking dish. Top with cheese, mushrooms, green onions and cooked sausage.
2. In a large bowl, whisk the remaining ingredients. Pour over layers. Refrigerate, covered, overnight.
3. Preheat oven to 350°. Remove the casserole from refrigerator while oven heats. Bake, uncovered, until a knife inserted near the center comes out clean, 45-50 minutes. Let stand 5-10 minutes.

1 serving: 503 cal., 34g fat (16g sat. fat), 239mg chol., 1052mg sod., 22g carb. (5g sugars, 1g fiber), 24g pro.

SPIRAL OMELET SUPREME

SPIRAL OMELET SUPREME

This jelly-roll style omelet works with any combination of fillings, so fill it up with your favorites! A serrated knife works best for easy slicing.
—Debbie Morris, Hamilton, OH

Prep: 20 min. • **Bake:** 20 min.
Makes: 8 servings

- **4 oz. cream cheese, softened**
- **¾ cup 2% milk**
- **¼ cup plus 2 Tbsp. grated Parmesan cheese, divided**
- **2 Tbsp. all-purpose flour**
- **12 large eggs**
- **2 tsp. canola oil**
- **1 large green pepper, chopped**
- **1 cup sliced fresh mushrooms**
- **1 small onion, chopped**
- **1¼ tsp. Italian seasoning, divided**
- **1½ cups shredded part-skim mozzarella cheese**
- **1 plum tomato, seeded and chopped**

1. Preheat oven to 375°. Line the bottom and sides of a greased 15x10x1-in. pan with parchment; grease paper.
2. Beat cream cheese until soft; gradually beat in milk. Beat in ¼ cup Parmesan cheese and the flour. In a large bowl, beat eggs until blended. Add the cream cheese mixture; mix well. Pour into prepared pan. Bake until set, 20-25 minutes.
3. In a large skillet, heat oil over medium-high heat; saute pepper, mushrooms and onion until crisp-tender, 3-4 minutes. Stir in 1 tsp. Italian seasoning. Keep warm.
4. Remove omelet from the oven; top immediately with mozzarella, tomato and pepper mixture. Starting with a short side, roll up omelet jelly-roll style, lifting with the parchment and removing it as you roll. Transfer to a platter. Sprinkle omelet with the remaining Parmesan cheese and the Italian seasoning.

1 serving: 275 cal., 19g fat (9g sat. fat), 312mg chol., 372mg sod., 8g carb. (4g sugars, 1g fiber), 18g pro.

SWEET POTATO & EGG SKILLET

5 INGREDIENTS | FREEZE IT | FAST FIX

EGG BURRITOS

Zap one of these frozen burritos in the microwave and you'll stave off hunger all morning. This recipe is my family's favorite combo, but I'll sometimes use breakfast sausage instead of bacon.
—Audra Niederman, Aberdeen, SD

Takes: 25 min. • **Makes:** 10 burritos

- **12 bacon strips, chopped**
- **12 large eggs**
- **½ tsp. salt**
- **¼ tsp. pepper**
- **10 flour tortillas (8 in.), warmed**
- **1½ cups shredded cheddar cheese**
- **4 green onions, thinly sliced**

1. In a large cast-iron or other heavy skillet, cook the bacon until crisp; drain on paper towels. Remove all but 1-2 Tbsp. drippings from pan.
2. Whisk together eggs, salt and pepper. Pour egg mixture into the pan; cook and stir over medium heat until the eggs are thickened and no liquid egg remains; remove from heat.
3. Spoon about ¼ cup of the egg mixture onto the center of each tortilla; sprinkle with cheese, bacon and green onions. Roll into burritos.

Freeze option: Cool the eggs before making the burritos. Wrap each burrito in a paper towel and then foil; freeze in a resealable plastic freezer bag. To use, remove foil; place paper towel-wrapped burrito on a microwave-safe plate and microwave on high until heated through, turning once. Let stand 15 seconds.

1 burrito: 376 cal., 20g fat (8g sat. fat), 251mg chol., 726mg sod., 29g carb. (0 sugars, 2g fiber), 19g pro.

*** HEALTH TIP *** Breakfast burritos can be a smart choice to start the day because they include a good amount of protein. To make these healthier, use whole wheat tortillas, skip the bacon, reduce the cheese and add veggies.

EAT SMART | FAST FIX

SWEET POTATO & EGG SKILLET

I try to incorporate nutritious sweet potatoes in meals—especially breakfast—as often as possible. This recipe originated with the intention of feeding my family a healthy, hearty breakfast that they would love to eat...and it worked!.
—Jeanne Larson
Rancho Santa Margarita, CA

Takes: 25 min. • **Makes:** 4 servings

- **2 Tbsp. butter**
- **2 medium sweet potatoes, peeled and shredded (about 4 cups)**
- **1 garlic clove, minced**
- **½ tsp. salt, divided**
- **⅛ tsp. dried thyme**
- **2 cups fresh baby spinach**
- **4 large eggs**
- **⅛ tsp. coarsely ground pepper**

1. In a large cast-iron or other heavy skillet, heat butter over low heat. Add sweet potatoes, garlic, ¼ tsp. salt and the thyme; cook, covered, until the potatoes are almost tender, 4-5 minutes, stirring occasionally. Stir in spinach just until wilted, 2-3 minutes.
2. With the back of a spoon, make four wells in the potato mixture. Break an egg into each well. Sprinkle eggs with pepper and the remaining salt. Cook, covered, on medium-low until the egg whites are completely set and the yolks begin to thicken but are not hard, 5-7 minutes.

1 serving: 224 cal., 11g fat (5g sat. fat), 201mg chol., 433mg sod., 24g carb. (10g sugars, 3g fiber), 8g pro. **Diabetic exchanges:** 1½ starch, 1½ fat, 1 medium-fat meat.

TEST KITCHEN TIP

Break the eggs into a dish, then add them to the pan. It's easier to remove any shell bits. If you like your eggs sunny-side up, leave the pan uncovered.

EGG BURRITOS

5 INGREDIENTS

HABANERO APRICOT JAM

This won a blue ribbon at our county fair. I mix it with applesauce to serve with pork, with cranberry sauce for poultry and with cream cheese to spread on celery.
—Janet Eckhoff, Woodland, CA

Prep: 15 min. • **Process:** 5 min.
Makes: 11 half-pints

- **3½ lbs. fresh apricots**
- **6 Tbsp. bottled lemon juice**
- **2 to 4 habanero peppers, seeded**
- **1 pkg. (1¾ oz.) powdered fruit pectin**
- **7 cups sugar**

1. Pit and chop apricots; place in a Dutch oven. Stir in lemon juice. Place habaneros in a blender; add a small amount of the apricot mixture. Cover and process until smooth. Return to the pan.
2. Stir in pectin. Bring to a full rolling boil, stirring constantly. Stir in sugar; return to a full rolling boil. Boil for 1 minute, stirring constantly.
3. Remove from the heat; skim off foam. Carefully ladle the hot mixture into hot sterilized half-pint jars, leaving ¼-in. of headspace. Wipe the rims and adjust the lids. Process for 5 minutes in a boiling-water canner.
4. For best results, let processed jam stand at room temperature for 2 weeks to set up.

Note: When cutting hot peppers, wear disposable gloves and avoid touching your face. • The processing time is for altitudes of 1,000 feet or less. Add 1 minute of processing time for each 1,000 feet of additional altitude.

2 Tbsp.: 71 cal., 0 fat (0 sat. fat), 0 chol., 0 sod., 18g carb. (18g sugars, 0 fiber), 0 pro.

ROASTED VEGETABLE & GOAT CHEESE QUICHE

Roasting veggies in this rich, yet bright, quiche intensifies their flavors. And fresh goat cheese lends a wonderful creamy tanginess. Throw in some fresh basil if you have it, too!
—Laura Davis, Chincoteague, VA

Prep: 45 min. + chilling
Bake: 25 min. + standing
Makes: 6 servings

- **1 sheet refrigerated pie crust**
- **1 small eggplant, cut into 1-in. pieces**
- **1 poblano pepper, cut into 1-in. pieces**
- **1 medium tomato, cut into 1-in. pieces**
- **2 garlic cloves, minced**
- **1 Tbsp. olive oil**
- **2 large eggs plus 2 large egg yolks**
- **¾ cup half-and-half cream**
- **1 tsp. kosher salt**
- **½ tsp. pepper**
- **1 log (4 oz.) fresh goat cheese, crumbled**

1. Unroll pie crust into an ungreased 9-in. tart pan. Refrigerate 30 minutes.
2. Preheat oven to 450°. Line unpricked crust with a double thickness of foil. Fill with pie weights, dried beans or uncooked rice. Bake on a lower oven rack until edges are golden brown, 10-12 minutes. Remove foil and weights; bake 3-5 minutes longer or until bottom is golden brown. Cool on a wire rack.
3. In a large bowl, combine the eggplant, pepper, tomato and garlic. Add oil; toss to coat. Transfer to a greased 15x10x1-in. baking pan. Roast vegetables until tender, 15-20 minutes, stirring halfway through.
4. Reduce oven setting to 375°. Spoon roasted vegetables into crust. In a large bowl, whisk eggs, egg yolks, cream, salt and pepper until blended; pour over top. Sprinkle with goat cheese.
5. Bake on a baking sheet on a lower oven rack until a knife inserted in the center comes out clean, 25-30 minutes. Cover edges with foil if they begin to get too dark. Let stand 10 minutes before cutting.

1 piece: 219 cal., 14g fat (7g sat. fat), 83mg chol., 471mg sod., 19g carb. (2g sugars, 0 fiber), 3g pro.

TEST KITCHEN TIP

For prebaking crust without a filling, place dried beans in an oven bag on the pastry so they are easy to remove.

Freeze the goat cheese for 10-20 minutes before crumbling to make it less sticky.

ROASTED VEGETABLE & GOAT CHEESE QUICHE

FREEZE IT

EASY BREAKFAST STRATA

PICTURED ON P. 175

We start this hearty breakfast casserole the night before so it's ready to go into the oven the next day. That way, we don't have to deal with prep and dirty dishes first thing in the morning.
—Debbie Johnson, Centertown, MO

Prep: 25 min. + chilling • **Bake:** 30 min.
Makes: 12 servings

- **1 loaf (1 lb.) herb or cheese bread, cubed**
- **1 lb. bulk pork sausage**
- **1 medium green pepper, chopped**
- **1 medium onion, chopped**
- **1 cup shredded cheddar cheese**
- **6 large eggs**
- **1 tsp. ground mustard**
- **2 cups 2% milk**

1. Place bread cubes in a greased 13x9-in. baking dish. In a large skillet, cook and crumble sausage with pepper and onion over medium-high heat until meat is no longer pink, 5-7 minutes. With a slotted spoon, place sausage mixture over bread. Sprinkle with cheese.
2. In a large bowl, whisk together eggs, mustard and milk; pour over the top. Refrigerate, covered, overnight.
3. Preheat oven to 350°. Remove strata from refrigerator while oven heats.
4. Bake, uncovered, until a knife inserted in center comes out clean, 30-35 minutes. Let stand 5 minutes before cutting.

Freeze option: Cover and freeze unbaked casserole. To use, partially thaw in refrigerator overnight. Remove from refrigerator 30 minutes before baking. Preheat oven to 350°. Bake casserole as directed, increasing time as necessary to heat through and for a thermometer inserted in center to read 165°.

1 serving: 295 cal., 16g fat (6g sat. fat), 126mg chol., 555mg sod., 23g carb. (4g sugars, 2g fiber), 14g pro.

*** HEALTH TIP *** Mix and match your way to a lighter, healthier version: Use whole grain bread, reduced-fat sausage and fat-free milk.

BLUEBERRY FRENCH TOAST

BLUEBERRY FRENCH TOAST

This is the best breakfast dish I've ever tasted. With the cream cheese and berry combination, it reminds me of dessert! Luscious blueberries are tucked into the French toast and in the sauce that goes over the top. A local blueberry grower shared the recipe with me.
—Patricia Axelsen, Aurora, MN

Prep: 30 min. + chilling • **Bake:** 55 min.
Makes: 8 servings (1¾ cups sauce)

- **12 slices day-old white bread, crusts removed**
- **2 pkg. (8 oz. each) cream cheese**
- **1 cup fresh or frozen blueberries**
- **12 large eggs, lightly beaten**
- **2 cups 2% milk**
- **⅓ cup maple syrup or honey**

SAUCE

- **1 cup sugar**
- **1 cup water**
- **2 Tbsp. cornstarch**
- **1 cup fresh or frozen blueberries**
- **1 Tbsp. butter**

1. Cut bread into 1-in. cubes; place half in a greased 13x9-in. baking dish. Cut cream cheese into 1-in. cubes; place over the bread. Top with blueberries and the remaining bread cubes.
2. Whisk eggs, milk and syrup. Pour over the bread mixture. Cover and refrigerate for 8 hours or overnight.
3. Preheat oven to 350°. Remove from the refrigerator 30 minutes before baking. Bake, covered, for 30 minutes. Uncover; bake 25-30 minutes longer or until a knife inserted in center comes out clean.
4. Combine sugar, water and cornstarch until smooth in a small saucepan. Bring to a boil over medium heat; cook and stir until thickened, 3 minutes. Stir in blueberries; bring to a boil. Reduce heat; simmer until berries burst, 8-10 minutes. Remove from heat; stir in butter. Serve with French toast.

Note: If using frozen blueberries, do not thaw.

1 serving: 621 cal., 31g fat (15g sat. fat), 350mg chol., 569mg sod., 68g carb. (44g sugars, 2g fiber), 19g pro.

REUBEN & RYE STRATA

REUBEN & RYE STRATA

This make-ahead dish is wonderful for brunch, lunch, supper—or as even a potluck meal. It's so easy to prepare, and Reuben is a real crowd-pleaser. If you prefer it, substitute turkey pastrami for the corned beef.

—Mary Louise Lever, Rome, GA

Prep: 25 min. + chilling
Bake: 50 min. + standing
Makes: 10 servings

- **10 slices rye bread, cubed (about 6 cups)**
- **1¼ lbs. thinly sliced deli corned beef, chopped**
- **2 cups shredded Gruyere cheese or Swiss cheese**
- **1 cup sauerkraut, rinsed, drained and patted dry**
- **¼ cup chopped dill pickles**
- **6 large eggs**
- **2 cups 2% milk**
- **⅔ cup Thousand Island salad dressing**
- **Dash garlic powder**
- **¼ cup shredded Parmesan cheese**
- **Chopped fresh parsley**

1. Place bread cubes in a greased 13x9-in. baking dish. Top with corned beef, cheese, sauerkraut and pickles. In a large bowl, whisk the eggs, milk, dressing and garlic powder. Pour over the bread. Refrigerate, covered, overnight.
2. Preheat oven to 350°. Remove strata from refrigerator while the oven heats. Bake, uncovered, 45 minutes. Sprinkle with Parmesan. Bake until a knife inserted near the center comes out clean, 5-10 minutes longer. Let stand 10-15 minutes before cutting. Sprinkle with parsley.

1 serving: 382 cal., 22g fat (9g sat. fat), 175mg chol., 1377mg sod., 21g carb. (6g sugars, 2g fiber), 25g pro.

FAST FIX

CHEESY BROCCOLI & HAM QUICHE

PICTURED ON P. 175

Filled with cheese, ham and broccoli, this quiche features an easy crust made of frozen hash browns—and doesn't even heat up the kitchen!

—Sue Armstrong, Norman, OK

Takes: 30 min. • **Makes:** 4 servings

- **2 cups frozen shredded hash brown potatoes**
- **1 cup shredded cheddar cheese**
- **1 cup diced fully cooked ham**
- **½ cup chopped fresh broccoli**
- **4 large eggs**
- **½ cup whole milk**
- **1 tsp. dried minced onion**
- **½ tsp. garlic powder**
- **½ tsp. salt**
- **½ tsp. pepper**

1. Place hash browns in a greased 9-in. microwave-safe pie plate. Microwave, uncovered, on high for 3 minutes or until thawed. Press onto the bottom and halfway up the sides of plate. Microwave, uncovered, on high for 3 minutes. Sprinkle with cheese, ham and broccoli.
2. In a large bowl, whisk the eggs, milk and seasonings; pour over ham mixture. Cover and microwave at 70% power for 5-7 minutes or until a knife inserted in the center comes out clean. Let stand for 5 minutes before cutting.

1 piece: 283 cal., 17g fat (8g sat. fat), 238mg chol., 999mg sod., 11g carb. (3g sugars, 1g fiber), 22g pro.

BANANA CREPES

I like to serve these at parties—while they're not hard to make, they're pretty and impressive! The banana-orange flavor works for dinner or dessert, too.
—Freda Becker, Garrettsville, OH

Prep: 20 min. + standing • **Cook:** 10 min.
Makes: 12 crepes

- **2 large eggs**
- **¾ cup 2% milk**
- **½ cup all-purpose flour**
- **1 Tbsp. butter, melted**
- **1 Tbsp. sugar**
- **⅛ tsp. salt**

FILLING
- **½ cup butter, cubed**
- **⅔ cup sugar**
- **4 tsp. grated orange zest**
- **⅔ cup orange juice**
- **6 medium firm bananas, peeled and sliced**
- **Fresh raspberries, optional**

1. In a bowl, whisk together first six ingredients; let stand 20 minutes.
2. Heat a lightly greased 8-in. nonstick skillet over medium heat. Fill a ¼-cup measure halfway with batter; pour into center of pan. Quickly lift, tilt and rotate pan to coat bottom evenly. Cook crepe until top appears dry; turn over and cook until bottom is done, 15-20 seconds. Remove to a wire rack. Repeat with the remaining batter, greasing pan as needed.
3. For sauce, place butter, sugar, orange zest and orange juice in a large skillet; bring to a boil, stirring to dissolve sugar. Reduce heat to medium; add bananas to warm.
4. To serve, spoon bananas onto crepes; fold into quarters. Top with the remaining sauce and, if desired, raspberries.

2 filled crepes: 443 cal., 20g fat (12g sat. fat), 110mg chol., 226mg sod., 64g carb. (43g sugars, 3g fiber), 6g pro.

* HEALTH TIP * Try these crepes with more wholesome filling: sliced bananas, strawberries, Greek yogurt and a sprinkle of granola for crunch.

BREAKFAST LOAF

I love to make this hearty sandwich when we have weekend company. You can add sliced mushrooms and olives, too.
—Amy McCuan, Oakley, CA

Prep: 15 min. • **Bake:** 25 min.
Makes: 6 servings

- **6 large eggs**
- **¼ tsp. salt**
- **⅛ tsp. pepper**
- **1 Tbsp. butter**
- **1 round loaf (1 lb.) French bread**
- **6 oz. sliced deli ham, divided**
- **¾ cup shredded Monterey Jack cheese, divided**
- **¾ cup shredded cheddar cheese, divided**
- **½ medium sweet red pepper, thinly sliced**
- **1 medium tomato, thinly sliced**

1. Preheat oven to 350°. Whisk together eggs, salt and pepper. In a large skillet, heat butter over medium heat. Pour in the egg mixture; cook and stir until the eggs are thickened and no liquid egg remains. Remove from heat.
2. Cut one-fourth off the top of the bread loaf. Hollow out both parts, leaving a ½-in. shell (save removed bread for another use or discard).
3. Place a fourth of the ham in the bread bottom; top with half of each of the cheeses. Layer with red pepper, scrambled eggs, tomato and the remaining cheeses and ham. Press layers gently; replace bread top. Wrap tightly in foil.
4. Bake until heated through, 25-30 minutes. Let the loaf stand 10 minutes before cutting.

1 slice: 439 cal., 18g fat (9g sat. fat), 230mg chol., 1083mg sod., 42g carb. (5g sugars, 2g fiber), 26g pro.

BREAKFAST LOAF

Breads in a Jiffy

Sweet or savory, at any hour, homemade breads make the day feel special. Whether you're making yeast bread or quick bread, coffee cake or dinner rolls, these recipes prove that homemade doesn't need to be complicated—and they'll make your kitchen smell heavenly!

Kate Smith Coffee Cake (p. 199) **Sticky Cinnamon-Sugar Monkey Bread** (p. 196) **Orange Pecan Bread** (p. 200) **English Muffin Bread Loaf** (p. 195) **No-Fuss Rolls** (p. 195)

OVENEX

PARMESAN ZUCCHINI BREAD

PARMESAN ZUCCHINI BREAD

This loaf has a rugged, textured look that adds to its old-fashioned appeal. The mild Parmesan flavor complements the zucchini, which adds bits of color to every tender slice.
—Chris Wilson, Sellersville, PA

Prep: 10 min. • **Bake:** 1 hour + cooling
Makes: 1 loaf (16 slices)

- **3 cups all-purpose flour**
- **3 Tbsp. grated Parmesan cheese**
- **1 tsp. salt**
- **½ tsp. baking powder**
- **½ tsp. baking soda**
- **2 large eggs, room temperature**
- **1 cup buttermilk**
- **⅓ cup sugar**
- **⅓ cup butter, melted**
- **1 cup shredded peeled zucchini**
- **1 Tbsp. grated onion**

1. Preheat oven to 350°. In a large bowl, combine the flour, cheese, salt, baking powder and baking soda. In another bowl, whisk eggs, buttermilk, sugar and butter. Stir into the dry ingredients just until moistened. Fold in zucchini and onion.
2. Pour into a greased and floured 9x5-in. loaf pan. Bake 1 hour or until a toothpick inserted in the center comes out clean. Cool for 10 minutes before removing from pan to a wire rack.

1 slice: 156 cal., 5g fat (3g sat. fat), 35mg chol., 288mg sod., 23g carb. (5g sugars, 1g fiber), 4g pro.

FAST FIX

BLUEBERRY-ORANGE MUFFINS

This recipe was given to me years ago, and it's been a standby ever since. It's so good, it won first prize at our county fair! Blueberries are plentiful in the Midwest, and this is a fragrant and fruity way to prepare them.
—Irene Parry, Kenosha, WI

Takes: 30 min. • **Makes:** 2 dozen

- **1 cup quick-cooking oats**
- **1 cup orange juice**
- **1 tsp. grated orange zest**
- **1 cup canola oil**
- **3 large eggs, room temperature, beaten**
- **3 cups all-purpose flour**
- **1 cup sugar**
- **4 tsp. baking powder**
- **1 tsp. salt**
- **½ tsp. baking soda**
- **3 to 4 cups fresh blueberries**

TOPPING

- **½ cup finely chopped nuts**
- **3 Tbsp. sugar**
- **½ tsp. ground cinnamon**

1. Preheat oven to 400°. Mix oats, orange juice and zest. Blend in oil and eggs; set aside. Stir together flour, sugar, baking powder, salt and baking soda. Add oat mixture; mix lightly. Fold in blueberries. Spoon batter into 24 paper-lined muffin tins, filling two-thirds full. Combine topping ingredients; sprinkle over batter.
2. Bake for 15-18 minutes or until lightly browned. Cool in pans for 5 minutes before removing to a wire rack.

1 muffin: 228 cal., 12g fat (2g sat. fat), 27mg chol., 200mg sod., 28g carb. (13g sugars, 1g fiber), 4g pro.

* HEALTH TIP * For a lighter version of these muffins, replace half the all-purpose flour with whole wheat flour, and half the oil with ½ cup unsweetened applesauce.

AUTUMN PEAR BREAD

Pears give these little loaves fabulous flavor and help keep them nice and moist. Wrap loaves to give as gifts for an unexpected treat.

—Mary Lynn Wilson, Linden, TX

Prep: 15 min. • **Bake:** 35 min. + cooling
Makes: 2 mini loaves (8 slices each)

- **2 cups all-purpose flour**
- **1 cup sugar**
- **1 tsp. baking powder**
- **½ tsp. baking soda**
- **½ tsp. salt**
- **⅛ tsp. ground nutmeg**
- **½ cup cold butter**
- **2 large eggs, room temperature**
- **¼ cup buttermilk**
- **1 tsp. vanilla extract**
- **1 cup finely chopped peeled ripe pears**

1. Preheat oven to 350°. In a large bowl, combine the flour, sugar, baking powder, baking soda, salt and nutmeg; cut in butter until mixture resembles coarse crumbs. Combine eggs, buttermilk and vanilla; stir into the flour mixture just until moistened. Fold in pears.
2. Spoon into two greased 5¾x3x2-in. loaf pans. Bake for 35-40 minutes or until a toothpick inserted in the center comes out clean. Cool for 10 minutes before removing from pans to wire racks to cool completely.

1 slice: 173 cal., 7g fat (4g sat. fat), 42mg chol., 208mg sod., 26g carb. (14g sugars, 1g fiber), 3g pro.

Apple Walnut Bread: Use 1 cup finely chopped unpeeled tart apples instead of the pears. Fold in ½ cup chopped walnuts along with the apples. Bake as directed or transfer to an 8x4x2-in. loaf pan and bake at 350° for 50-65 minutes or until toothpick comes out clean.

★★★★★ **READER REVIEW**

"I loved the crusty top—so buttery and sweet. The texture is excellent, and it comes together quickly. I am not a fan of nutmeg, so I used cinnamon instead."

MISSCOFFEEPOT TASTEOFHOME.COM

JUMBO PUMPKIN PECAN MUFFINS

Perk up an autumn morning with one of these hearty muffins. You'll really enjoy the pumpkin-spice flavor and crumbly nut topping—and so will everyone else!

—Janice Christofferson, Eagle River, WI

Prep: 25 min. • **Bake:** 25 min.
Makes: 6 muffins

- **2½ cups all-purpose flour**
- **½ cup sugar**
- **¼ cup packed brown sugar**
- **2 tsp. pumpkin pie spice**
- **1 tsp. baking powder**
- **1 tsp. baking soda**
- **½ tsp. salt**
- **2 large eggs, room temperature**
- **1 cup canned pumpkin**
- **½ cup buttermilk**
- **¼ cup canola oil**
- **1 tsp. vanilla extract**
- **½ cup chopped pecans**

TOPPING

- **⅓ cup packed brown sugar**
- **⅓ cup finely chopped pecans**
- **¼ cup all-purpose flour**
- **¼ cup cold butter, cubed**

1. Preheat oven to 375°. In a large bowl, combine the first seven ingredients. In another bowl, combine eggs, pumpkin, buttermilk, oil and vanilla. Stir into dry ingredients just until moistened. Fold in pecans. Fill six greased or paper-lined jumbo muffin cups three-fourths full.
2. In a small bowl, combine the brown sugar, pecans and flour; cut in butter until crumbly. Sprinkle over batter.
3. Bake for 25-30 minutes or until a toothpick inserted in the center comes out clean. Cool for 5 minutes before removing from muffin pan to a wire rack. Serve warm.

1 muffin: 660 cal., 30g fat (7g sat. fat), 83mg chol., 619mg sod., 89g carb. (41g sugars, 4g fiber), 11g pro.

JUMBO PUMPKIN PECAN MUFFINS

A Touch of the Irish

Easy to make, dense and flavorful, Irish soda bread is the perfect complement to a hearty soup any time.

IRISH SODA BREAD

Traditional Irish soda bread can be made with an assortment of mix-ins such as dried fruit and nuts; I like it best with a handful of raisins. Bring soda bread as a change-of-pace item at your next get-together.
—Gloria Warczak, Cedarburg, WI

Prep: 15 min. • **Bake:** 30 min.
Makes: 8 servings

- **2 cups all-purpose flour**
- **2 Tbsp. brown sugar**
- **1 tsp. baking powder**
- **1 tsp. baking soda**
- **½ tsp. salt**
- **3 Tbsp. cold butter, cubed**
- **2 large eggs, room temperature, divided use**
- **¾ cup buttermilk**
- **⅓ cup raisins**

1 piece: 210 cal., 6g fat (3g sat. fat), 59mg chol., 463mg sod., 33g carb. (8g sugars, 1g fiber), 6g pro.

HOW-TO

Make Classic Irish Soda Bread

1.

2.

3.

4.

1. Preheat oven to 375°. Whisk together the first five ingredients.

2. Cut in butter until the mixture resembles coarse crumbs. In another bowl, whisk together 1 egg and buttermilk. Add to the flour mixture; stir just until moistened. Stir in raisins.

3. Turn the dough onto a lightly floured surface; knead gently 6-8 times. Shape into a 6½-in. round loaf; place on a greased baking sheet. Using a sharp knife, make a shallow cross in top of loaf.

4. Whisk the remaining egg; brush over the top of the loaf. Bake until golden brown, 30-35 minutes. Remove from pan to a wire rack. Serve warm.

CHOCOLATE CHAI MINI LOAVES

This bread is irresistible! A friend gets mad when I make it because I give her a loaf and she can't help but eat the whole thing!
—Lisa Christensen, Poplar Grove, IL

Prep: 25 min. • **Bake:** 35 min. + cooling
Makes: 3 mini loaves (6 slices each)

- **2 oz. semisweet chocolate, chopped**
- **½ cup water**
- **½ cup butter, softened**
- **1 cup packed brown sugar**
- **2 large eggs, room temperature**
- **1 tsp. vanilla extract**
- **1½ cups all-purpose flour**
- **3 Tbsp. chai tea latte mix**
- **1 tsp. baking soda**
- **½ tsp. salt**
- **½ cup sour cream**

FROSTING

- **1 cup confectioners' sugar**
- **1 Tbsp. butter, softened**
- **1 Tbsp. chai tea latte mix**
- **½ tsp. vanilla extract**
- **4 to 5 tsp. whole milk**

1. Preheat oven to 350°. In a microwave, melt chocolate with the water; stir until smooth. Cool slightly. In a large bowl, cream butter and brown sugar until light and fluffy. Add eggs, one at a time, beating well after each addition. Beat in vanilla, then the chocolate mixture.
2. Combine flour, latte mix, baking soda and salt; add to the creamed mixture alternately with sour cream.
3. Transfer to three greased 5¾x3x2-in. loaf pans. Bake for 35-40 minutes or until a toothpick inserted in the center comes out clean. Cool for 10 minutes before removing from pans to a wire rack to cool completely.
4. For frosting, combine confectioners' sugar, butter, latte mix, vanilla and enough milk to achieve desired consistency. Frost tops of loaves.

1 slice: 208 cal., 9g fat (5g sat. fat), 43mg chol., 206mg sod., 30g carb. (21g sugars, 1g fiber), 3g pro.

*** HEALTH TIP *** Skip the frosting and dust the top of these loaves with confectioners' sugar to cut calories by almost 20 percent.

CHOCOLATE CHAI MINI LOAVES

5 INGREDIENTS | FAST FIX

BERRY-FILLED DOUGHNUTS

Four ingredients are all you'll need for this sure-to-be-popular treat. Friends and family will never guess that refrigerated buttermilk biscuits are the base for these golden, jelly-filled doughnuts.
—Ginny Watson, Broken Arrow, OK

Takes: 25 min. • **Makes:** 10 servings

- **Oil for deep-fat frying**
- **2 tubes (6 oz. each) small refrigerated flaky biscuits (5 count)**
- **½ cup seedless strawberry jam**
- **¾ cup confectioners' sugar**

1. In an electric skillet or deep fryer, heat oil to 350°. Separate biscuits; press each to flatten slightly. Fry biscuits, a few at a time, until golden brown, 1 to 1¼ minutes per side. Drain on paper towels.
2. Cut a small hole in the tip of a pastry bag or corner of a food-safe plastic bag; insert a small pastry tip. Fill bag with jam. With a small knife, pierce a hole into the side of each doughnut; fill with jam.
3. Toss with confectioners' sugar. Serve warm.

1 doughnut: 190 cal., 7g fat (1g sat. fat), 0 chol., 360mg sod., 30g carb. (17g sugars, 0 fiber), 2g pro.

PUMPKIN SURPRISE MUFFINS

Filled with cream cheese and apricot preserves, these almond-topped pumpkin muffins are heavenly.
—Elizabeth Blondefield, San Jose, CA

Prep: 20 min. • **Bake:** 20 min.
Makes: 14 muffins

- **2 cups all-purpose flour**
- **1 Tbsp. baking powder**
- **1 tsp. ground cinnamon**
- **¼ tsp. salt**
- **¼ tsp. ground ginger**
- **¼ tsp. ground nutmeg**
- **½ cup plus 3 Tbsp. sugar, divided**
- **2 large eggs, room temperature**
- **1 cup canned pumpkin**
- **½ cup sour cream**
- **6 Tbsp. butter, melted**
- **7 Tbsp. apricot preserves**
- **4 oz. cream cheese, divided into 14 portions**
- **¼ cup sliced almonds**

1. Preheat oven to 400°. Whisk together first six ingredients and ½ cup sugar. In another bowl, whisk the eggs, pumpkin, sour cream, melted butter and 3 Tbsp. preserves until blended. Add to flour mixture; stir just until moistened.
2. Fill 14 greased or paper-lined muffin cups half full with batter. Place a portion of cream cheese and about ¾ tsp. apricot preserves in each muffin; cover with the remaining batter. Sprinkle with almonds and remaining sugar.
3. Bake until top springs back when touched, 20-25 minutes. Cool 5 minutes before removing from pans to a wire rack. Refrigerate leftovers.

1 muffin: 243 cal., 11g fat (6g sat. fat), 50mg chol., 228mg sod., 33g carb. (16g sugars, 1g fiber), 4g pro.

CRANBERRY CRUMBLE COFFEE CAKE

This delicious coffee cake doesn't last long! People are delighted to find the ruby cranberry sauce swirled inside.
—Jeani Robinson, Weirton, WV

Prep: 20 min. • **Bake:** 70 min. + cooling
Makes: 12 servings

- **¼ cup chopped almonds**
- **1 cup sugar**
- **½ cup butter, softened**
- **1 tsp. vanilla extract**
- **2 large eggs, room temperature**
- **2 cups all-purpose flour**
- **1¼ tsp. baking powder**
- **½ tsp. baking soda**
- **¼ tsp. salt**
- **1 cup sour cream**
- **1 cup whole-berry cranberry sauce**

TOPPING

- **¼ cup all-purpose flour**
- **¼ cup sugar**
- **¼ cup chopped almonds**
- **¼ tsp. vanilla extract**
- **2 Tbsp. cold butter**

1. Preheat oven to 350°. Sprinkle almonds over the bottom of a greased 9-in. springform pan; set aside. In a bowl, cream sugar, butter and vanilla; beat on medium for 1-2 minutes. Add eggs, one at a time, beating well after each addition.
2. Combine the dry ingredients; add to batter alternately with the sour cream. Mix well. Spread 3 cups over almonds. Spoon cranberry sauce over batter. Top with the remaining batter.
3. For the topping, combine flour, sugar, almonds and vanilla; cut in butter until crumbly. Sprinkle over batter.
4. Bake for 70-75 minutes or until a toothpick inserted in the center comes out clean. Cool in pan on a wire rack for 15 minutes; remove sides of pan. Serve warm.

1 piece: 368 cal., 17g fat (9g sat. fat), 74mg chol., 266mg sod., 49g carb. (27g sugars, 2g fiber), 5g pro.

CRANBERRY CRUMBLE COFFEE CAKE

ENGLISH MUFFIN BREAD LOAF

Many years ago, a good friend gave me her mother's recipe for this delightful bread. Toast it up for breakfast and don't forget to slather on your favorite jam.
—Jane Zielinski, Rotterdam Junction, NY

Prep: 15 min. • **Bake:** 35 min.
Makes: 2 loaves

- **5 cups all-purpose flour, divided**
- **2 pkg. (¼ oz. each) active dry yeast**
- **1 Tbsp. sugar**
- **2 tsp. salt**
- **¼ tsp. baking soda**
- **2 cups warm milk (120° to 130°)**
- **½ cup warm water (120° to 130°)**
- **Cornmeal**

1. In a large bowl, combine 2 cups flour, yeast, sugar, salt and baking soda. Add warm milk and water; beat on low speed 30 seconds, scraping bowl occasionally. Beat on high for 3 minutes.
2. Stir in the remaining flour (batter will be stiff). Do not knead. Grease two 8x4-in. loaf pans. Sprinkle pans with cornmeal. Spoon the batter into the pans and sprinkle cornmeal on top. Cover and let rise in a warm place until doubled, about 45 minutes.
3. Bake at 375° about 35 minutes or until golden brown. Remove from pans immediately and cool on wire racks. Slice and toast.

1 slice: 83 cal., 1g fat (0 sat. fat), 2mg chol., 165mg sod., 16g carb. (1g sugars, 1g fiber), 3g pro.

ENGLISH MUFFIN BREAD LOAF

GRANDMA'S OATMEAL BREAD

The aroma from this old-fashioned oat bread will draw your family to the kitchen to sample it fresh from the oven.
—Marcia Hostetter, Canton, NY

Prep: 20 min. + rising • **Bake:** 35 min.
Makes: 2 loaves (8 slices each)

- **1½ cups boiling water**
- **1 Tbsp. butter**
- **2 tsp. salt**
- **½ cup sugar**
- **1 cup old-fashioned oats**
- **2 pkg. (¼ oz. each) active dry yeast**
- **¾ cup warm water (110° to 115°)**
- **¼ cup molasses**
- **¼ cup packed brown sugar**
- **6 to 6½ cups all-purpose flour, divided**

1. In a small bowl, combine the boiling water, butter, salt and sugar. Stir in oats; cool to lukewarm. In a large bowl, dissolve yeast in warm water. Stir in the molasses, brown sugar and 1 cup flour. Beat until smooth. Stir in oat mixture and enough remaining flour to make a stiff dough.
2. Turn dough out onto a floured surface; knead until smooth and elastic, about 6-8 minutes. Place in a greased bowl, turning once to grease top. Cover and let rise in a warm place until doubled, about 1½ hours.
3. Punch dough down. Turn onto a lightly floured surface; divide in half. Shape each portion into a ball. Cover and let rest for 10 minutes; Shape into loaves. Place in two greased 9x5-in. loaf pans. Cover and let rise until nearly doubled, about 1 hour.
4. Bake at 375° for 30-35 minutes (cover loosely with foil if top browns too quickly). Remove from pans to wire racks to cool.

1 slice: 247 cal., 2g fat (1g sat. fat), 2mg chol., 307mg sod., 52g carb. (13g sugars, 2g fiber), 6g pro.

5 INGREDIENTS | **FAST FIX**

NO-FUSS ROLLS

PICTURED ON P. 189

These four-ingredient rolls are ready in hardly any time. Go sweet with jam or savory with herb butter on these rolls.
—Glenda Trail, Manchester, TN

Takes: 25 min. • **Makes:** 6 rolls

- **1 cup self-rising flour**
- **½ cup 2% milk**
- **2 Tbsp. mayonnaise**
- **½ tsp. sugar**

Preheat oven to 450°. Combine all of the ingredients. Spoon into six muffin cups coated with cooking spray. Bake until a toothpick comes out clean, 12-14 minutes. Cool 5 minutes before removing from pan to a wire rack. Serve warm.

Note: As a substitute for 1 cup of self-rising flour, place 1½ tsp. baking powder and ½ tsp. salt in a measuring cup. Add all-purpose flour to measure 1 cup.

1 roll: 111 cal., 4g fat (1g sat. fat), 3mg chol., 275mg sod., 16g carb. (1g sugars, 0 fiber), 3g pro. **Diabetic exchanges:** 1 starch, 1 fat.

FAVORITE MEXICAN CORNBREAD

FAVORITE MEXICAN CORNBREAD

I love to cook and my supportive and encouraging mom finally convinced me to submit this recipe. I often serve this cornbread with chili.
—Donna Hypes, Ramona, CA

Prep: 10 min. • **Bake:** 35 min.
Makes: 9 servings

- **1 cup yellow cornmeal**
- **1 cup all-purpose flour**
- **3 tsp. baking powder**
- **1 tsp. salt**
- **2 Tbsp. sugar**
- **1 cup buttermilk**
- **1 large egg, room temperature, beaten**
- **1 can (8¼ oz.) cream-style corn**
- **Dash hot pepper sauce**
- **¼ cup bacon drippings, melted**
- **¼ cup chopped green onions**
- **½ cup shredded cheddar cheese**
- **Honey, optional**

1. Preheat oven to 400°. In a large bowl, combine first five ingredients; set aside. In another bowl, combine buttermilk and egg; add corn and remaining ingredients. Add to the dry ingredients; stir just until combined. Pour batter into a greased 8-in. square baking pan.
2. Bake for 35 minutes or until a toothpick comes out clean. Cool for 5 minutes before cutting into squares. Serve warm. Drizzle with honey if desired.

1 piece: 235 cal., 9g fat (5g sat. fat), 38mg chol., 583mg sod., 32g carb. (5g sugars, 2g fiber), 6g pro.

STICKY CINNAMON-SUGAR MONKEY BREAD

PICTURED ON P. 189

When I make this monkey bread, I prepare the dough pieces and put all the sauce ingredients in the pan the night before so it's ready for the morning. If you like chopped nuts, sprinkle them in with the dough pieces before pouring on the sauce and baking.
—Diana Kunselman, Rimersburg, PA

Prep: 20 min. + rising • **Bake:** 20 min.
Makes: 16 servings

- **2 loaves (1 lb. each) frozen bread dough, thawed**
- **1 cup packed brown sugar**
- **¾ cup butter, cubed**
- **1 pkg. (3 oz.) cook-and-serve vanilla pudding mix**
- **2 Tbsp. 2% milk**
- **2 tsp. ground cinnamon**

1. Cut dough into 1-in. pieces; place in a greased 13x9-in. baking dish. In a large saucepan, combine the remaining ingredients; bring to a boil. Cook and stir for 1 minute; remove from heat. Pour over the dough pieces.
2. Cover loosely with parchment paper or nonstick foil; let rise in a warm place until almost doubled, about 45 minutes.
3. Bake, uncovered, at 350° until golden brown, 20-25 minutes. Immediately invert onto a serving plate.

1 serving: 247 cal., 9g fat (4g sat. fat), 18mg chol., 339mg sod., 36g carb. (16g sugars, 2g fiber), 5g pro.

CARAMEL APPLE MUFFINS

Anyone who craves caramel apples will love these muffins. Served with breakfast or just coffee, they're a lovely way to start the morning.
—Therese Puckett, Shreveport, LA

Prep: 25 min. • **Bake:** 20 min.
Makes: 12 muffins

- **2 cups all-purpose flour**
- **¾ cup sugar**
- **2 tsp. baking powder**
- **2½ tsp. ground cinnamon**
- **½ tsp. salt**
- **1 large egg, room temperature**
- **1 cup 2% milk**
- **¼ cup butter, melted**
- **2 tsp. vanilla extract**
- **½ cup chopped peeled tart apple**
- **12 caramels, chopped**

TOPPING

- **½ cup packed brown sugar**
- **¼ cup quick-cooking oats**
- **3 Tbsp. butter, melted**
- **1 tsp. ground cinnamon**

1. Preheat oven to 350°. In a large bowl, combine the flour, sugar, baking powder, cinnamon and salt. In another bowl, whisk the egg, milk, butter and vanilla. Stir into the dry ingredients just until moistened. Fold in apple and caramels.
2. Fill 12 paper-lined muffin cups about three-fourths full. Combine the topping ingredients; sprinkle over the batter.
3. Bake for 20-25 minutes or until a toothpick inserted in the cake portion comes out clean. Cool for 5 minutes before removing from pans to wire racks. Serve warm.

1 muffin: 245 cal., 8g fat (4g sat. fat), 33mg chol., 219mg sod., 41g carb. (26g sugars, 1g fiber), 4g pro.

CARAMEL APPLE MUFFINS

SWISS BEER BREAD

This recipe is a favorite because it isn't greasy like other cheese breads I have tried. It will not last long!
—Debi Wallace, Chestertown, NY

Prep: 15 min. • **Bake:** 50 min. + cooling
Makes: 1 loaf (12 slices)

- **4 oz. Jarlsberg or Swiss cheese**
- **3 cups all-purpose flour**
- **3 Tbsp. sugar**
- **3 tsp. baking powder**
- **1½ tsp. salt**
- **½ tsp. pepper**
- **1 bottle (12 oz.) beer or nonalcoholic beer**
- **2 Tbsp. butter, melted**

1. Preheat oven to 375°. Divide cheese in half. Cut half into ¼-in. cubes; shred the remaining cheese. In a large bowl, combine next five ingredients. Stir beer into dry ingredients just until moistened. Fold in cubed and shredded cheese.
2. Transfer to a greased 8x4-in. loaf pan. Drizzle with butter. Bake until a toothpick inserted in the center comes out clean, 50-60 minutes. Cool for 10 minutes before removing from pan to a wire rack.

1 slice: 182 cal., 5g fat (3g sat. fat), 11mg chol., 453mg sod., 28g carb. (4g sugars, 1g fiber), 6g pro.

ENGLISH BATTER BUNS

ENGLISH BATTER BUNS

Since receiving this easy-to-prepare recipe from a dear friend, I've made these rolls often for the holidays.
—Geraldine West, Ogden, UT

Prep: 15 min. + rising • **Bake:** 10 min.
Makes: 1 dozen

- **2 pkg. (¼ oz. each) active dry yeast**
- **1 cup warm whole milk (110° to 115°)**
- **½ cup shortening**
- **2 Tbsp. sugar**
- **1 tsp. salt**
- **2 large eggs, room temperature**
- **3½ cups all-purpose flour**
- **Melted butter**

1. In a large bowl, dissolve yeast in warm milk. Add the shortening, sugar, salt, eggs and 2 cups flour; beat on medium speed 3 minutes. Stir in remaining flour until smooth. Cover and let rise in a warm place until doubled, about 30 minutes.
2. Stir batter vigorously for 25 strokes (dough will be slightly sticky). Spoon into 12 greased muffin cups. Tap pans to settle the batter. Cover and let rise until batter reaches tops of cups, about 20 minutes. Meanwhile, preheat oven to 400°.
3. Bake 10-15 minutes or until golden brown. Brush with butter.

1 bun: 241 cal., 10g fat (3g sat. fat), 38mg chol., 218mg sod., 31g carb. (4g sugars, 1g fiber), 6g pro.

FAST FIX

CHEESY DROP BISCUITS

I wanted to capture the flavor of cheese biscuits from a popular restaurant. So I took my favorite buttermilk biscuit recipe and added to it.
—Milly Heaton, Richmond, IN

Takes: 20 min. • **Makes:** 10 biscuits

- **2 cups all-purpose flour**
- **2 tsp. baking powder**
- **1 tsp. salt**
- **¼ tsp. baking soda**
- **¼ tsp. garlic powder**
- **1 cup shredded cheddar cheese**
- **¼ cup grated Parmesan cheese**
- **⅔ cup buttermilk**
- **⅓ cup canola oil**
- **Additional Parmesan cheese, optional**

1. Preheat oven to 450°. In a large bowl, combine the first five ingredients. Add the cheeses.
2. In a small bowl, combine buttermilk and oil. Stir into dry ingredients just until moistened. Drop by ¼ cupfuls 2 in. apart onto a greased baking sheet. Sprinkle with additional Parmesan cheese if desired.
3. Bake 10-12 minutes or until golden brown. Serve warm.

1 biscuit: 176 cal., 10g fat (3g sat. fat), 12mg chol., 392mg sod., 17g carb. (1g sugars, 1g fiber), 5g pro.

COUNTRY CINNAMON SWIRL BREAD

With three active sons, I'm always busy — so this rich quick bread is a time-saving favorite. At the holidays, I give loaves a festive wrap and then give as gifts.
—Sharon Walker, Huntington Station, NY

Prep: 15 min. • **Bake:** 45 min. + cooling
Makes: 1 loaf (12 slices)

- **¼ cup butter, softened**
- **1⅓ cups sugar, divided**
- **1 large egg, room temperature**
- **2 cups all-purpose flour**
- **1 tsp. baking powder**
- **½ tsp. baking soda**
- **½ tsp. salt**
- **1 cup buttermilk**
- **1 Tbsp. ground cinnamon**

1. Preheat oven to 250°. Beat the butter, 1 cup sugar and the egg until blended. Combine flour, baking powder, baking soda and salt; add to the egg mixture alternately with buttermilk. Combine the cinnamon and the remaining sugar.

2. Pour a third of batter into a greased 8x4-in. loaf pan; sprinkle with a third of the cinnamon sugar. Repeat layers twice. Bake 45-50 minutes or until a toothpick inserted in the center comes out clean. Cool 10 minutes before removing from pan to a wire rack to cool completely.

1 slice: 212 cal., 5g fat (3g sat. fat), 26mg chol., 267mg sod., 40g carb. (23g sugars, 1g fiber), 3g pro.

KATE SMITH COFFEE CAKE

PICTURED ON P. 189

When I lived in an orphanage more than 50 years ago, I helped out in the kitchen, often making this wonderful coffee cake and following the recipe they used. Years later, seeing Kate Smith on television, I realized that I had been making a recipe from her cookbook!
—Ruth Nast, Waterford, CT

Prep: 15 min. • **Bake:** 20 min.
Makes: 6 servings

- **1 large egg, room temperature**
- **¼ cup butter, melted**
- **⅓ cup whole milk**
- **1 cup all-purpose flour**
- **¼ cup sugar**
- **2 tsp. baking powder**
- **¼ tsp. salt**
- **1 cup bran flakes, crushed**

TOPPING

- **2 tsp. butter, softened**
- **2 Tbsp. brown sugar**
- **⅓ cup bran flakes, crushed**

Preheat oven to 375°. In a bowl, combine the egg, butter and milk. Combine flour, sugar, baking powder and salt; stir into batter. Add bran flakes. Spread into a greased 8-in. round baking pan or 8-in. ovenproof skillet. Combine the topping ingredients; sprinkle over the batter. Bake 18-22 minutes or until a toothpick inserted in the center comes out clean. Serve warm.

1 slice: 253 cal., 11g fat (6g sat. fat), 61mg chol., 406mg sod., 37g carb. (15g sugars, 2g fiber), 5g pro.

COUNTRY CINNAMON SWIRL BREAD

CRANBERRY MUFFINS

There's an abundance of cranberries in our area during the fall, and this recipe is one of my favorite ways to use them. I often give these fresh-baked muffins as a small gift to friends.
—Ronni Dufour, Lebanon, CT

Prep: 15 min. • **Bake:** 20 min.
Makes: 1½ dozen

- **2 cups all-purpose flour**
- **1 cup sugar**
- **1½ tsp. baking powder**
- **1 tsp. ground nutmeg**
- **1 tsp. ground cinnamon**
- **½ tsp. baking soda**
- **½ tsp. ground ginger**
- **½ tsp. salt**
- **2 tsp. grated orange zest**
- **½ cup shortening**
- **¾ cup orange juice**
- **2 large eggs, room temperature, lightly beaten**
- **1 Tbsp. vanilla extract**
- **1½ cups coarsely chopped cranberries**
- **1½ cups chopped pecans**

1. Preheat oven to 375°. In a large bowl, combine the flour, sugar, baking powder, nutmeg, cinnamon, baking soda, ginger, salt and orange zest. Cut in shortening until crumbly. In a small bowl, combine the orange juice, eggs and vanilla. Stir into dry ingredients just until moistened. Fold in cranberries and nuts.
2. Fill 18 greased or paper-lined muffin cups two-thirds full. Bake until a toothpick inserted in the middle comes out clean, 18-20 minutes. Cool 10 minutes before removing to wire rack. Serve warm.

1 muffin: 231 cal., 13g fat (2g sat. fat), 24mg chol., 141mg sod., 26g carb. (13g sugars, 2g fiber), 3g pro.

CRANBERRY MUFFINS

ORANGE PECAN BREAD

PICTURED ON P. 189

My husband loves this scrumptious bread. Whenever I ask him to suggest a nice tea bread, he says, "What about that orange-pecan stuff?"
—Sondra Feldstein, Bondurant, IA

Prep: 25 min. • **Bake:** 30 min. + cooling
Makes: 1 loaf (6 slices)

- **¼ cup butter, softened**
- **¼ cup sugar**
- **1 large egg, room temperature, separated**
- **2 tsp. grated orange zest**
- **¾ cup all-purpose flour**
- **¾ tsp. baking powder**
- **⅛ tsp. baking soda**
- **Dash salt**
- **¼ cup orange juice**
- **⅓ cup chopped pecans**

GLAZE

- **1 Tbsp. sugar**
- **1 Tbsp. orange juice**

1. Preheat oven to 350°. In a small bowl, cream butter and sugar until light and fluffy. Add the egg yolk and orange zest; beat until blended. Combine the flour, baking powder, baking soda and salt; add to the creamed mixture alternately with orange juice.
2. In another small bowl, beat egg white until soft peaks form. Fold egg white and pecans into the batter.
3. Pour batter into a 5¾x3x2-in. loaf pan coated with cooking spray. Bake for 30-35 minutes or until a toothpick inserted in the center comes out clean.
4. Combine the glaze ingredients in a small microwave-safe bowl. Microwave, uncovered, at 50% power for 1 minute. Stir until sugar is dissolved. Pour over warm bread. Cool for 10 minutes before removing from the pan to a wire rack to cool completely.

1 slice: 229 cal., 13g fat (5g sat. fat), 56mg chol., 189mg sod., 25g carb. (12g sugars, 1g fiber), 3g pro. **Diabetic exchanges:** 2½ fat, 1 starch, ½ fruit.

CHIPPY CINNAMON SCONES

I love baking and I'm crazy about cinnamon rolls, but they take a lot of time to put together. I made this recipe to satisfy the craving!
—Camilla Saulsbury, Nacogdoches, TX

Prep: 20 min. • **Bake:** 20 min.
Makes: 6 scones

- **1⅔ cups all-purpose flour**
- **¼ cup packed brown sugar**
- **2 tsp. baking powder**
- **1 tsp. ground cinnamon**
- **⅛ tsp. salt**
- **1 cup heavy whipping cream**
- **½ cup miniature semisweet chocolate chips**
- **¼ cup chopped pecans, toasted**
- **¼ cup milk chocolate English toffee bits**
- **1 Tbsp. butter, melted**

GLAZE

- **¼ cup confectioners' sugar**
- **4½ tsp. spreadable cream cheese**
- **2¼ tsp. 2% milk**
- **¼ tsp. vanilla extract**

1. Preheat oven to 375°. In a large bowl, combine the flour, brown sugar, baking powder, cinnamon and salt. Stir in cream just until moistened. Stir in the chocolate chips, pecans and toffee bits.
2. Turn onto a floured surface; knead 10 times. Pat into an 8-in. circle; cut into six wedges. Separate wedges and transfer to a lightly greased baking sheet. Brush with butter.
3. Bake for 16-20 minutes or until golden brown. Combine the glaze ingredients; drizzle over scones. Serve warm.

1 scone: 499 cal., 29g fat (16g sat. fat), 70mg chol., 270mg sod., 57g carb. (22g sugars, 2g fiber), 6g pro.

CHIPPY CINNAMON SCONES

RHUBARB BREAD

Our family really enjoys this delicious, tangy bread. It's quick and easy to make; dicing the rhubarb is the hardest part!
—Grace Capen, Sacramento, CA

Prep: 15 min. • **Bake:** 45 min.
Makes: 2 loaves

- **1⅓ cups packed brown sugar**
- **⅔ cup vegetable oil**
- **1 large egg, room temperature, beaten**
- **1 tsp. vanilla extract**
- **1 cup buttermilk**
- **2½ cups all-purpose flour**
- **¾ tsp. salt**
- **½ tsp. ground cinnamon**
- **1 tsp. baking soda**
- **1½ to 2 cups finely diced rhubarb, ¼-in. cuts**
- **½ cup chopped nuts**

In a bowl, combine sugar and oil; blend in egg, vanilla and milk. Combine flour, salt, cinnamon and baking soda; add to moist ingredients. Stir in rhubarb and nuts. Transfer to two well-greased 8x4-in. loaf pans. Bake at 350° until a toothpick inserted in the center comes out clean, about 45 minutes. Cool for 10 minutes before removing from pans to wire racks.

1 slice: 129 cal., 6g fat (1g sat. fat), 7mg chol., 109mg sod., 17g carb. (10g sugars, 0 fiber), 2g pro.

CHOCOLATE CHIP PUMPKIN BREAD

I love making this bread in the fall. The aroma is mouthwatering.
—Vicki Raboine, Kansasville, WI

Prep: 15 min. • **Bake:** 45 min.
Makes: 4 mini loaves (6 slices each)

- **1 cup packed brown sugar**
- **1 cup sugar**
- **⅔ cup butter, softened**
- **3 large eggs, room temperature**
- **2⅓ cups all-purpose flour**
- **1½ cups canned pumpkin**
- **½ cup water**
- **2 tsp. baking soda**
- **1 tsp. ground cinnamon**
- **1 tsp. salt**
- **½ tsp. ground cloves**
- **2 cups (12 oz.) semisweet chocolate chips**

1. Preheat oven to 350°. In a bowl, cream sugars, butter and eggs. Add flour, pumpkin, water, baking soda, cinnamon, salt and cloves. Mix thoroughly. Fold in chocolate chips.
2. Pour into four greased and floured 5¾x3x2-in. loaf pans. Bake for 45 minutes or until breads test done.

1 slice: 239 cal., 10g fat (6g sat. fat), 37mg chol., 258mg sod., 37g carb. (26g sugars, 2g fiber), 3g pro.

Slow-Cooked Sensations

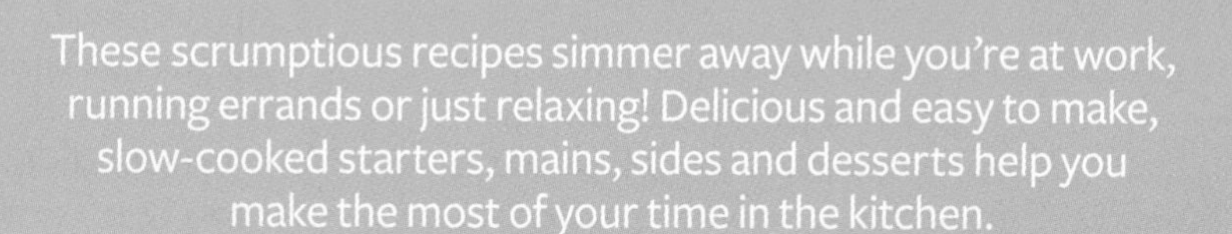

These scrumptious recipes simmer away while you're at work, running errands or just relaxing! Delicious and easy to make, slow-cooked starters, mains, sides and desserts help you make the most of your time in the kitchen.

Orange Chipotle Chicken (p. 208) **Spaghetti Squash with Tomatoes & Olives** (p. 222)
Pineapple Upside-Down Dump Cake (p. 204) **Slow-Cooked Golden Mashed Potatoes** (p. 205)
All-Day Red Beans & Rice (p. 225)

SPICY SAUSAGE MEATBALL SAUCE

SLOW COOKER | FREEZE IT

SPICY SAUSAGE MEATBALL SAUCE

I threw together three favorite veggies and spicy sausage for this incredible sauce that makes our mouths water the whole time it's cooking. Besides serving this with pasta (refrigerated tortellini is best), we've had it with brown basmati rice, as sloppy subs on toasted Italian rolls and as a stew with garlic bread.

—Ann Sheehy, Lawrence, MA

Prep: 40 min. • **Cook:** 5 hours
Makes: 12 servings (3¾ qt.)

- **2 cans (28 oz. each) crushed tomatoes**
- **2 cans (14½ oz. each) diced tomatoes, undrained**
- **¾ lb. sliced fresh mushrooms**
- **5 garlic cloves, minced**
- **4 tsp. Italian seasoning**
- **1 tsp. pepper**
- **¼ tsp. salt**
- **¼ tsp. crushed red pepper flakes**
- **1 large sweet onion**
- **1 large green pepper**
- **1 medium sweet red pepper**
- **1 medium sweet orange pepper**
- **1 medium sweet yellow pepper**
- **10 hot Italian sausage links (4 oz. each), casings removed**
- **¼ cup all-purpose flour**
- **2 Tbsp. canola oil**
- **Hot cooked pasta**

1. Place the first eight ingredients in a 6-qt. slow cooker. Chop the onion and peppers; stir into the tomato mixture.
2. Shape sausage into 1¾-in. balls; roll in flour to coat lightly. In a large skillet, heat oil over medium-high heat; cook the meatballs in batches until lightly browned, 5-8 minutes, turning occasionally. Drain on paper towels. Add to slow cooker, stirring gently into the sauce.
3. Cook, covered, on low until meatballs are cooked through and the vegetables are tender, 5-6 hours. Serve with pasta.

Freeze option: Freeze cooled meatball mixture in freezer containers. To use, partially thaw in refrigerator overnight. Place meatball mixture in a large skillet; heat through, stirring occasionally and adding a little water if necessary.

1¼ cups meatball sauce: 343 cal., 23g fat (7g sat. fat), 51mg chol., 984mg sod., 22g carb. (11g sugars, 5g fiber), 15g pro.

SLOW COOKER

PINEAPPLE UPSIDE-DOWN DUMP CAKE

PICTURED ON P. 203

No matter what the season, this dump cake recipe is wonderful! It works well with gluten-free and sugar-free cake mixes, too.

—Karin Gatewood, Dallas, TX

Prep: 10 min. • **Cook:** 2 hours + standing
Makes: 10 servings

- **¾ cup butter, divided**
- **⅔ cup packed brown sugar**
- **1 jar (6 oz.) maraschino cherries, drained**
- **½ cup chopped pecans, toasted**
- **1 can (20 oz.) unsweetened pineapple tidbits or crushed pineapple, undrained**
- **1 pkg. yellow cake mix (regular size)**
- **Vanilla ice cream, optional**

1. In a microwave, melt ½ cup butter; stir in brown sugar. Spread evenly onto bottom of a greased 5-qt. slow cooker. Sprinkle with cherries and pecans; top with pineapple. Sprinkle evenly with dry cake mix. Melt the remaining butter; drizzle over top.
2. Cook, covered, on high until the fruit mixture is bubbly, about 2 hours. (To avoid scorching, rotate slow cooker insert one-half turn midway through cooking, lifting carefully with oven mitts.)
3. Turn off the slow cooker; let stand, uncovered, for 30 minutes before serving. If desired, serve with ice cream.

Note: To toast nuts, bake in a shallow pan in a 350° oven for 5-10 minutes or cook in a skillet over low heat until lightly browned, stirring occasionally.

½ cup: 455 cal., 22g fat (10g sat. fat), 37mg chol., 418mg sod., 66g carb. (47g sugars, 1g fiber), 3g pro.

TEST KITCHEN TIP

Let the cake stand, uncovered, after cooking to allow the steam to escape. As it cools, the cake and saucy pineapple mixture will set up a bit.

Sprinkle the cake mix evenly over the pineapple. If it's piled high in the center, the middle may not cook completely. A large slow cooker keeps the ingredient layers thin and promotes even cooking.

SLOW COOKER

CHICKEN VEGETABLE CURRY

This comforting dish gets fabulous flavor when I add chicken, sweet red peppers, coconut milk and the all-important seasoning—curry powder.

—Roxana Lambeth, Moreno Valley, CA

Prep: 20 min. • **Cook:** 4 hours
Makes: 6 servings

- **1½ lbs. boneless skinless chicken thighs, cut into 1½-in. pieces**
- **2 medium red potatoes, chopped (about 1½ cups)**
- **1 small sweet red pepper, coarsely chopped**
- **1 medium onion, coarsely chopped**
- **1 medium carrot, chopped**
- **3 garlic cloves, minced**
- **1 can (13.66 oz.) coconut milk**
- **½ cup chicken broth**
- **3 tsp. curry powder**
- **1½ tsp. salt**
- **1 tsp. ground cumin**
- **1 Tbsp. minced fresh cilantro**
- **Hot cooked couscous**

1. Place the first six ingredients in a 3- or 4-qt. slow cooker. In a small bowl, whisk together coconut milk, broth and dry seasonings; stir into the chicken mixture.
2. Cook, covered, on low until the chicken and vegetables are tender, 4-5 hours. Stir in cilantro. Serve with couscous.

1 cup: 339 cal., 22g fat (14g sat. fat), 76mg chol., 755mg sod., 12g carb. (2g sugars, 2g fiber), 24g pro.

CHICKEN VEGETABLE CURRY

SLOW COOKER | EAT SMART

STEWED ZUCCHINI & TOMATOES

A fresh take on traditional vegetable sides, this dish stars zucchini, tomatoes and green peppers, with a bubbly cheddar cheese topping adding a down-home feel.

—Barbara Smith, Salem, OR

Prep: 20 min. • **Cook:** 3½ hours
Makes: 6 servings

- **3 medium zucchini, cut into ¼-in. slices**
- **1 tsp. salt, divided**
- **½ tsp. pepper, divided**
- **1 medium onion, thinly sliced**
- **1 medium green pepper, thinly sliced**
- **3 medium tomatoes, sliced**
- **⅔ cup condensed tomato soup, undiluted**
- **1 tsp. dried basil**
- **1 cup shredded cheddar cheese**
- **Minced fresh basil, optional**

1. Place zucchini in a greased 3-qt. slow cooker. Sprinkle with ½ tsp. salt and ¼ tsp. pepper. Layer with onion, green pepper and tomatoes. In a small bowl, combine the soup, basil and remaining salt and pepper; spread over tomatoes.
2. Cover and cook on low for 3-4 hours or until the vegetables are tender. Sprinkle with cheese. Cover and cook 30 minutes longer or until cheese is melted. If desired, top with fresh basil.

¾ cup: 126 cal., 6g fat (4g sat. fat), 20mg chol., 678mg sod., 14g carb. (8g sugars, 3g fiber), 7g pro. **Diabetic exchanges:** 1 vegetable, 1 fat, ½ starch.

SLOW COOKER | 5 INGREDIENTS

SLOW-COOKED GOLDEN MASHED POTATOES

PICTURED ON P. 203

Making a grand meal on Thanksgiving can be a little daunting, even for an experienced cook. Using a slow cooker for these spuds makes it one step easier.

—Samantha Six, Fredricksburg, IN

Prep: 20 min. • **Cook:** 4 hours
Makes: 14 servings

- **5 lbs. Yukon Gold potatoes (about 10 medium), chopped**
- **1 cup butter, cubed**
- **1 cup water**
- **3 tsp. salt**
- **¾ tsp. pepper**
- **½ cup mayonnaise**
- **¼ cup grated Parmesan cheese**
- **1 to 1½ cups 2% milk**

1. In a 6-qt. slow cooker, combine the first five ingredients. Cook, covered, on high 4-5 hours or until potatoes are tender (do not drain liquid).
2. Mash potatoes, gradually adding mayonnaise, cheese and enough milk to achieve desired consistency.

¾ cup: 327 cal., 20g fat (10g sat. fat), 38mg chol., 703mg sod., 33g carb. (3g sugars, 3g fiber), 5g pro.

SLOW COOKER
SPOON BREAD

Enjoy a super take on this southern specialty by using the slow cooker. It goes especially well with barbecue.
—*Taste of Home* Test Kitchen

Prep: 20 min. • **Cook:** 4 hours
Makes: 8 servings

- **1 pkg. (8 oz.) cream cheese, softened**
- **2 Tbsp. sugar**
- **2 large eggs, beaten**
- **1 cup 2% milk**
- **2 Tbsp. butter, melted**
- **½ tsp. salt**
- **¼ tsp. cayenne pepper**
- **⅛ tsp. pepper**
- **2 cups frozen corn**
- **1 can (14¾ oz.) cream-style corn**
- **1 cup yellow cornmeal**
- **1 cup shredded Monterey Jack cheese**
- **3 green onions, thinly sliced**
- **Coarsely ground pepper and thinly sliced green onions, optional**

1. In a large bowl, beat cream cheese and sugar until smooth. Gradually beat in eggs. Beat in the milk, butter, salt, cayenne and pepper until blended. Stir in the remaining ingredients.
2. Pour into a greased 3-qt. slow cooker. Cover and cook on low for 4-5 hours or until a toothpick inserted in the center comes out clean. If desired, top with additional pepper and green onions.

1 serving: 350 calories, 18g fat (11g saturated fat), 54mg cholesterol, 525mg sodium, 38g carbohydrate (8g sugars, 3g fiber), 12g protein.

PORK EDAMAME SOUP

SLOW COOKER
PORK EDAMAME SOUP

My husband grew up in a traditional Asian household and gives this soup high marks for authentic taste. I think the Asian hot chili sauce makes the dish, but any type of hot sauce would give it a kick!
—Kari Sue, Bend, OR

Prep: 25 min. • **Cook:** 4 hours 10 min.
Makes: 6 servings

- **4 tsp. canola oil**
- **2 lbs. boneless country-style pork ribs, trimmed, cut into 1-in. cubes**
- **2 medium carrots, cut into 1-in. pieces**
- **1 medium sweet red pepper, cut into 1-in. pieces**
- **1 can (8 oz.) sliced water chestnuts, drained**
- **6 garlic cloves, minced**
- **2 Tbsp. soy sauce**
- **1 Tbsp. hoisin sauce**
- **1 Tbsp. minced fresh gingerroot**
- **2 tsp. Sriracha Asian hot chili sauce**
- **2 cans (14½ oz. each) chicken broth**
- **1 pkg. (10 oz.) frozen shelled edamame, thawed**
- **1 pkg. (3 oz.) ramen noodles**
- **Thinly sliced green onions, optional**

1. In a large skillet, heat oil over medium-high heat. Brown pork in batches. Remove to a 5-qt. slow cooker. Stir in all remaining ingredients except edamame, noodles and green onions.
2. Cook, covered, on low until meat and vegetables are tender, 4-5 hours. Stir in edamame. Break up noodles; stir into soup. Discard or save seasoning packet for another use. Cook, covered, on low until noodles are al dente, 10-15 minutes.
3. Serve immediately. If desired, top with green onions.

1½ cups: 455 cal., 23g fat (7g sat. fat), 90mg chol., 1134mg sod., 25g carb. (6g sugars, 4g fiber), 36g pro.

TEST KITCHEN TIP

Adding the edamame toward the end of cooking keeps the color brighter. Cook the pork in batches to prevent overcrowding, which creates steam and keeps the meat from browning.

SLOW COOKER

SLOW-COOKER BANANAS FOSTER

The flavors of caramel, rum and walnut naturally complement fresh bananas in this version of a dessert classic. It's my go-to choice for any family get-together.
—Crystal Jo Bruns, Iliff, CO

Prep: 10 min. • **Cook:** 2 hours
Makes: 5 servings

- **5 medium firm bananas**
- **1 cup packed brown sugar**
- **¼ cup butter, melted**
- **¼ cup rum**
- **1 tsp. vanilla extract**
- **½ tsp. ground cinnamon**
- **⅓ cup chopped walnuts**
- **⅓ cup sweetened shredded coconut**
- **Vanilla ice cream or sliced pound cake**

1. Cut bananas in half lengthwise, then widthwise; layer in the bottom of a 1½-qt. slow cooker. Combine the brown sugar, butter, rum, vanilla and cinnamon; pour over the bananas. Cover and cook on low for 1½ hours or until heated through.
2. Sprinkle with walnuts and coconut; cook 30 minutes longer. Serve with ice cream or pound cake.

1 serving: 462 cal., 17g fat (8g sat. fat), 24mg chol., 99mg sod., 74g carb. (59g sugars, 4g fiber), 3g pro.

SLOW COOKER | 5 INGREDIENTS | EAT SMART

SLOW-COOKER BAKED POTATOES

This baked potato recipe is so easy—just add your favorite toppings. Save any extra potatoes to make baked potato soup the next day.
—Teresa Emrick, Tipp City, OH

Prep: 10 min. • **Cook:** 8 hours
Makes: 6 potatoes

- **6 medium russet potatoes**
- **3 Tbsp. butter, softened**
- **3 garlic cloves, minced**
- **1 cup water**
- **Salt and pepper to taste**
- **Optional toppings: sour cream, butter, crumbled bacon, guacamole, shredded cheddar cheese, minced fresh chives and cilantro**

1. Scrub potatoes; pierce several times with a fork. In a small bowl, mix butter and garlic. Rub potatoes with butter mixture. Wrap each tightly with a piece of foil.
2. Pour water into a 6-qt. slow cooker; add potatoes. Cook, covered, on low for 8-10 hours or until tender. Season and top as desired.

1 potato: 217 cal., 6g fat (4g sat. fat), 15mg chol., 59mg sod., 38g carb. (2g sugars, 5g fiber), 5g pro.

* HEALTH TIP * Skip high-calorie sour cream and try a dollop of fat-free Greek yogurt instead. Don't forget the chives!

*

TEST KITCHEN TIP

This is an ideal way to make potatoes for a baked potato bar at the office. Serve the potatoes right in the foil packets to enjoy the garlic butter.

SLOW-COOKER BAKED POTATOES

SLOW COOKER

CHILI MACARONI & CHEESE

What could taste better on a cold winter day than chili or mac and cheese? Put them together and you have a terrific dish that warms you up...and fills you up as well!
—Nancy Foust, Stoneboro, PA

Prep: 25 min. • **Cook:** 5 hours
Makes: 12 servings (4½ qt.)

- **2½ lbs. lean ground beef (90% lean)**
- **1 medium onion, chopped**
- **1 medium green pepper, chopped**
- **1 banana pepper, finely chopped**
- **2 cans (28 oz. each) diced tomatoes, undrained**
- **2 cans (16 oz. each) kidney beans, rinsed and drained**
- **2½ tsp. chili powder**
- **2 tsp. ground cumin**
- **2 cups uncooked elbow macaroni**
- **4 cups (16 oz.) shredded cheddar cheese**
- **Sour cream and additional shredded cheddar cheese, optional**

1. In a Dutch oven, cook beef, onion and peppers over medium-high heat until the beef is no longer pink and vegetables are tender, breaking up beef into crumbles, 8-10 minutes; drain. Transfer to a 7-qt. slow cooker. Stir in tomatoes, beans, chili powder and cumin. Cook, covered, on low until the flavors are blended, 5-6 hours.
2. Meanwhile, cook macaroni according to package directions; drain. Add to the slow cooker. Stir in cheese until melted. If desired, serve with sour cream and additional cheese.

1½ cups: 447 cal., 21g fat (10g sat. fat), 96mg chol., 646mg sod., 30g carb. (7g sugars, 7g fiber), 35g pro.

ORANGE CHIPOTLE CHICKEN

SLOW COOKER | EAT SMART

ORANGE CHIPOTLE CHICKEN

PICTURED ON P. 203

Even though this chicken dish cooks for hours, the citrus keeps things fresh. We're big on spice in our house, so sometimes I use two chipotle peppers.
—Deborah Biggs, Omaha, NE

Prep: 10 min. • **Cook:** 4 hours
Makes: 6 servings

- **½ cup thawed orange juice concentrate**
- **¼ cup barbecue sauce**
- **1 chipotle pepper in adobo sauce**
- **¼ tsp. salt**
- **¼ tsp. garlic powder**
- **6 boneless skinless chicken breast halves (6 oz. each)**
- **¼ cup chopped red onion**
- **4 tsp. cornstarch**
- **3 Tbsp. cold water**
- **Grated orange zest**

1. Place first five ingredients in a blender; cover and process until blended.
2. Place chicken and onion in a 3-qt. slow cooker; top with the juice mixture. Cook, covered, on low until a thermometer inserted in chicken reads at least 165°, 4-5 hours.
3. Remove chicken from slow cooker; keep warm. Transfer the cooking juices to a saucepan; bring to a boil. In a small bowl, mix cornstarch and water until smooth; gradually stir into juices. Return to a boil, stirring constantly; cook and stir until thickened, 1-2 minutes. Spoon over chicken; top with orange zest.

1 chicken breast with ¼ cup sauce: 246 cal., 4g fat (1g sat. fat), 94mg chol., 315mg sod., 15g carb. (11g sugars, 1g fiber), 35g pro.
Diabetic exchanges: 5 lean meat, 1 starch.

TEST KITCHEN TIP

Chipotle peppers are spicy, so you don't need much to add smoky heat. Freeze individual leftover peppers in ice cube trays, then store in an airtight container for the next time you want to add some spice!

FRENCH ONION SOUP

SLOW COOKER
FRENCH ONION SOUP

My husband and I love French onion soup, so I wondered if I could turn it into a less labor-intensive dish by adapting my recipe to the slow cooker. The rich, cheesy result was an instant winner at home.
—Ronda Eagle, Goose Creek, SC

Prep: 30 min. • **Cook:** 7 hours
Makes: 8 servings (2 qt.)

- **2 Tbsp. butter, cubed**
- **2 large sweet onions, halved and thinly sliced**
- **1 large red onion, halved and thinly sliced**
- **½ tsp. coarsely ground pepper**
- **2 cans (10½ oz. each) condensed beef broth, undiluted**
- **3 cups water**
- **¾ cup white wine or regular-strength beef broth**
- **2 fresh thyme sprigs**
- **1 fresh parsley sprig, optional**
- **1 bay leaf**
- **2 tsp. Worcestershire sauce**
- **16 slices French bread (¼ in. thick)**
- **¾ cup shredded Gruyere or Swiss cheese**

1. Place butter in a 5-qt. slow cooker. Top with sweet and red onions; sprinkle with pepper. Cook, covered, on low until the onions are tender, 5-6 hours.
2. Stir in broth, water, wine, herbs and Worcestershire sauce. Cook, covered, on low until flavors are blended, 2-3 hours. Remove herb sprigs and bay leaf.
3. To serve, preheat broiler. Place bread on a baking sheet; broil 4 in. from heat until lightly toasted, 1-2 minutes per side. Top bread with cheese; broil until cheese is melted, 1-2 minutes. Divide soup among eight bowls; top with the cheese toasts and serve immediately.

1 serving: 157 cal., 7g fat (4g sat. fat), 19mg chol., 706mg sod., 15g carb. (6g sugars, 1g fiber), 7g pro.

TEST KITCHEN TIP

Gruyere cheese is delicious in this recipe—its sweet, nutty flavor goes well with the oniony broth, and it melts wonderfully. Toasting the bread with cheese separately, instead of broiling on top of the soup in crocks, prevents the underside of the bread from becoming soggy.

SLOW COOKER
SLOW-COOKED PIZZAIOLA MEAT LOAF

I also like to add Italian Castelvetrano olives to the meat loaf mixture. Bright green, mild and fruity, they are available in the deli section of the grocery store.
—Ann Sheehy, Lawrence, MA

Prep: 35 min. • **Cook:** 4 hours
Makes: 8 servings

- **2 Tbsp. canola oil**
- **1 large onion, chopped**
- **1½ cups sliced fresh mushrooms**
- **1 cup chopped sweet red, yellow or green peppers**
- **2 garlic cloves, minced**
- **2 large eggs, lightly beaten**
- **1 cup seasoned bread crumbs**
- **1 cup (4 oz.) shredded Italian cheese blend**
- **1 tsp. Italian seasoning**
- **½ tsp. salt**
- **1¼ lbs. ground turkey**
- **1 lb. meat loaf mix (equal parts ground beef, pork and veal)**
- **Pizza sauce and shredded Parmesan cheese, optional**

1. Cut three 25x3-in. strips of heavy-duty foil; lay them crisscross so they resemble spokes of a wheel. Place strips on bottom and up the sides of a 5- or 6-qt. slow cooker. Coat strips with cooking spray.
2. In a large skillet, heat canola oil over medium-high heat. Add onions, peppers and mushrooms; cook and stir until the vegetables are tender, 4-6 minutes. Add garlic; cook 1 minute longer. Remove from heat and cool slightly.
3. In a large bowl, combine eggs, bread crumbs, cheese, Italian seasoning, salt and the cooked vegetables. Add the turkey and meat loaf mix; mix lightly but thoroughly. Shape into a loaf; transfer to slow cooker. Cook, covered, on low until a thermometer reads at least 160°, 4 to 5 hours. Using the foil strips as handles, remove meat loaf to a platter. If desired, serve with pizza sauce and Parmesan cheese.

1 slice: 356 cal., 19g fat (6g sat. fat), 139mg chol., 551mg sod., 14g carb. (3g sugars, 1g fiber), 31g pro.

SPICY CHICKEN EGG ROLLS

SLOW COOKER

SPICY CHICKEN EGG ROLLS

This crunchy delight gets its start in the slow cooker. Tuck the chicken mixture in egg roll wrappers and bake, or use smaller wonton wrappers for a bite-sized version.
—Tara Odegaard, Omaha, NE

Prep: 35 min. • **Cook:** 3 hours
Makes: 16 servings

- **1½ lbs. boneless skinless chicken breasts**
- **2 Tbsp. ranch salad dressing mix**
- **½ cup Buffalo wing sauce**
- **2 Tbsp. butter**
- **16 egg roll wrappers**
- **⅓ cup crumbled feta cheese**
- **⅓ cup shredded part-skim mozzarella cheese**
- **Ranch salad dressing, optional**

1. In a 3-qt. slow cooker, combine chicken, dressing mix and wing sauce. Cook, covered, on low until the chicken is tender, 3-4 hours.
2. Preheat oven to 425°. Shred chicken with two forks; stir in butter.
3. With one corner of an egg roll wrapper facing you, place 3 Tbsp. of the chicken mixture just below the center of the wrapper; top with 1 tsp. each feta and mozzarella cheeses. (Cover the remaining wrappers with a damp paper towel until ready to use.) Fold bottom corner of the wrapper over the filling; moisten the remaining edges of the wrapper with water. Fold side corners toward center over filling; roll up tightly, pressing at the tip to seal. Place on parchment-lined baking sheets, seam side down. Repeat.
4. Bake until wrapper is golden brown, 15-20 minutes. Let stand for 5 minutes before serving.

1 egg roll: 174 cal., 4g fat (2g sat. fat), 33mg chol., 716mg sod., 21g carb. (0 sugars, 1g fiber), 13g pro.

* **HEALTH TIP** * Lighten up this recipe by serving the chicken mixture in Bibb lettuce cups instead of egg roll wrappers.

*

TEST KITCHEN TIP

We tried brushing some of the egg rolls with oil before baking and they turned out about the same as the plain version—lightly browned and crisp. While they aren't quite as crunchy as deep-fried egg rolls, they are close!

CHICKEN & KALE TORTELLINI SOUP

SLOW COOKER

CHICKEN & KALE TORTELLINI SOUP

With tender tortellini, chicken, spinach and lots of herbs, this comforting soup is so flavorful. The fact that it's almost effortless is just a chilly-night bonus.
—Emily Hobbs, Springfield, MO

Prep: 15 min. • **Cook:** 2½ hours
Makes: 8 servings (3 qt.)

- **1 lb. boneless skinless chicken breasts, cut into 1¼-in. cubes**
- **2 garlic cloves, minced**
- **1½ tsp. Italian seasoning**
- **¼ tsp. pepper**
- **6 cups chicken broth**
- **1 pkg. (20 oz.) refrigerated cheese tortellini**
- **1 can (15 oz.) cannellini beans, rinsed and drained**
- **1 jar (7½ oz.) marinated quartered artichoke hearts, drained and coarsely chopped**
- **4 cups coarsely chopped fresh kale (about 2 oz.)**
- **Shaved Parmesan cheese, optional**

1. Place the first five ingredients in a 5- or 6-qt. slow cooker. Cook, covered, on low until chicken is no longer pink, 2-3 hours.
2. Stir in the tortellini, beans, artichoke hearts and kale. Cook, covered, on low until the tortellini and kale are tender, about 30 minutes, stirring halfway. Serve immediately. If desired, top with cheese.

1½ cups: 386 cal., 12g fat (4g sat. fat), 66mg chol., 1185mg sod., 43g carb. (4g sugars, 4g fiber), 24g pro.

* **HEALTH TIP** * Switch from regular broth to reduced-sodium broth to save about 300 milligrams sodium per serving.

*

TEST KITCHEN TIP

You can use chopped fresh spinach instead of kale for this soup. Stir it in during the last few minutes of cooking.

SLOW COOKER
PHILLY CHEESE SANDWICHES

I'm a big fan of Philly cheesesteaks, and this throw-it-together variation is right up my alley. Plus, my slow cooker does all the work. Win-win!
—Christina Addison, Blanchester, OH

Prep: 20 min. • **Cook:** 8 hours
Makes: 8 servings

- **1 boneless beef chuck roast (2½ to 3 lbs.), trimmed and cut into 1-in. cubes**
- **2 medium onions, halved and sliced**
- **¼ cup Worcestershire sauce**
- **2 garlic cloves, minced**
- **1 tsp. dried oregano**
- **½ tsp. dried basil**
- **1 medium sweet red pepper, sliced**
- **1 medium green pepper, sliced**
- **8 slices process American cheese or pepper jack cheese**
- **8 hoagie buns, split and toasted**

In a 3- or 4-qt. slow cooker, combine the first six ingredients. Cook, covered, on low 7 hours. Stir in peppers; cook, covered, until the meat and peppers are tender, 1-3 hours. Stir to break up meat. Serve beef mixture and cheese on buns.
1 sandwich: 546 cal., 23g fat (9g sat. fat), 97mg chol., 754mg sod., 42g carb. (9g sugars, 2g fiber), 40g pro.

PHILLY CHEESE SANDWICHES

SLOW COOKER | EAT SMART
APPLE PIE STEEL-CUT OATMEAL

I absolutely love this slow-cooked oatmeal. The steel cut oats have so much flavor and texture! My family loves to sprinkle toasted pecans on top.
—Angela Lively, Conroe, TX

Prep: 10 min. • **Cook:** 6 hours
Makes: 8 servings

- **6 cups water**
- **1½ cups steel-cut oats**
- **1½ cups unsweetened applesauce**
- **¼ cup maple syrup**
- **1½ tsp. ground cinnamon**
- **½ tsp. ground nutmeg**
- **⅛ tsp. salt**
- **1 large apple, chopped**
- **Sliced apples, toasted pecans and additional maple syrup, optional**

In a 4-qt. slow cooker, combine the first seven ingredients. Cover and cook on low for 6-8 hours or until liquid is absorbed. Stir in apples. If desired, top individual servings with apples, pecans and syrup.
1¼ cups: 171 cal., 2g fat (0 sat. fat), 0 chol., 39mg sod., 36g carb. (13g sugars, 4g fiber), 4g pro.

SLOW COOKER | FREEZE IT | EAT SMART
BAJA TACOS

This is my version of the most excellent Mexican food we ever had. The original recipe used beef, but this pork version comes mighty close to the same taste.
—Ariella Winn, Mesquite, TX

Prep: 10 min. • **Cook:** 8 hours
Makes: 12 servings

- **1 boneless pork sirloin roast (3 lbs.)**
- **5 cans (4 oz. each) chopped green chiles**
- **2 Tbsp. reduced-sodium taco seasoning**
- **3 tsp. ground cumin**
- **24 corn tortillas (6 in.), warmed**
- **3 cups shredded lettuce**
- **1½ cups shredded part-skim mozzarella cheese**

1. Cut roast in half; place in a 3- or 4-qt. slow cooker. Mix chiles, taco seasoning and cumin; spoon over pork. Cook, covered, on low until meat is tender, 8-10 hours.
2. Remove pork; cool slightly. Skim fat from the cooking juices. Shred meat with two forks. Return to the slow cooker; heat through. Serve in tortillas with lettuce and cheese.

Freeze option: Place the cooled pork mixture in freezer containers; freeze up to 3 months. To use, partially thaw in refrigerator overnight. Heat through in a covered saucepan, stirring gently and adding a little broth if necessary.
2 tacos: 320 cal., 11g fat (4g sat. fat), 77mg chol., 434mg sod., 26g carb. (1g sugars, 4g fiber), 30g pro. **Diabetic exchanges:** 3 medium-fat meat, 2 starch.
*** HEALTH TIP *** Using reduced-sodium taco seasoning saves about 80 milligrams sodium per serving.

LOW COOKER

MOLTEN MOCHA CAKE

When I first made my decadent slow-cooker chocolate cake, my family's expressions said it all. My daughter says it's one of er "most favorites." Once, I took one of hese to our next-door neighbors. Turns ut their teenage son, who answered the oor, ate the whole thing without telling nyone else about it!

–Aimee Fortney, Fairview, TN

rep: 10 min. • **Cook:** 2½ hours
Makes: 6 servings

- **4 large eggs**
- **1½ cups sugar**
- **½ cup butter, melted**
- **1 Tbsp. vanilla extract**
- **1 cup all-purpose flour**
- **½ cup baking cocoa**
- **1 Tbsp. instant coffee granules**
- **¼ tsp. salt**
- **Vanilla ice cream and fresh raspberries, optional**

1. Whisk together first four ingredients. In another bowl, whisk together flour, cocoa, coffee granules and salt; gradually beat into the egg mixture. Transfer to a greased 1½-qt. slow cooker.

2. Cook, covered, on low until a toothpick inserted in center comes out with moist crumbs, 2½ to 3 hours. Serve warm. If desired, serve with vanilla ice cream and fresh raspberries.

1 serving: 482 cal., 19g fat (11g sat. fat), 165mg chol., 269mg sod., 71g carb. (51g sugars, 2g fiber), 8g pro.

TEST KITCHEN TIP

Top with caramel and chopped nuts for a turtle flavor variation.

MOLTEN MOCHA CAKE

SLOW COOKER

ROSEMARY CAULIFLOWER PUREE

I love this delicious fake-take on mashed potatoes...even more because it doesn't heat up my kitchen! Treat leftovers as you would leftover mashed potatoes to make mock potato pancakes.

—Sharon Gibson, Hendersonville, NC

Prep: 15 min. • **Cook:** 4 hours
Makes: 6 servings

- **2 Tbsp. butter, melted**
- **1 medium onion, chopped**
- **1 large head cauliflower, cut into florets**
- **1 pkg. (6½ oz.) spreadable garlic and herb cheese**
- **½ cup grated Parmesan cheese**
- **½ tsp. Montreal steak seasoning**
- **¼ tsp. pepper**
- **1 tsp. minced fresh rosemary or ½ tsp. dried rosemary, crushed**
- **¼ cup heavy cream, warmed**
- **Additional minced fresh rosemary and pepper, optional**

1. Place melted butter and onion in a 4- or 5-qt. slow cooker. Add cauliflower; cook, covered, on high until cauliflower is tender, 3-4 hours.

2. Process in batches in a food processor to desired consistency. Add remaining ingredients and process just until blended. If desired, serve with additional rosemary and pepper.

⅔ cup: 245 cal., 20g fat (12g sat. fat), 54mg chol., 386mg sod., 11g carb. (5g sugars, 3g fiber), 6g pro.

*** HEALTH TIP *** At only 11 grams per serving, this is a flavorful lower-carb alternative to mashed potatoes. Replace heavy cream with half-and-half or 2% milk for a lighter version of this recipe.

TEST KITCHEN TIP

The garlic flavor comes from the cheese spread. For less garlic flavor, use only part of the spread in the recipe.

SLOW COOKER | EAT SMART

MEXI-STRONI SOUP

If you're a fan of classic minestrone but love bold Mexican flavors, this soup's perfect for you! It's pumped up with spices, veggies and pasta.

—Darlene Island, Lakewood, WA

Prep: 25 min. • **Cook:** 7½ hours
Makes: 10 servings (3¾ qt.)

- **1½ lbs. beef stew meat (1-in. pieces)**
- **1½ cups shredded carrots**
- **½ cup chopped onion**
- **1 jalapeno pepper, seeded and minced, optional**
- **1 tsp. ground cumin**
- **1 tsp. chili powder**
- **¾ tsp. seasoned salt**
- **½ tsp. Italian seasoning**
- **2 cans (10 oz. each) diced tomatoes and green chiles, undrained**
- **2 cups spicy hot V8 juice**
- **1 carton (32 oz.) reduced-sodium beef broth**
- **1 medium zucchini, halved and thinly sliced**
- **2 cups finely shredded cabbage**
- **2 celery ribs, thinly sliced**
- **1 can (16 oz.) kidney beans, rinsed and drained**
- **1 can (15 oz.) black beans, rinsed and drained**
- **1 cup small pasta shells**
- **¼ cup chopped fresh cilantro**

1. Place the first 11 ingredients in a 6- or 7-qt. slow cooker. Cook, covered, on low until the meat is tender, 7-9 hours.
2. Stir in remaining ingredients. Cook, covered, on high until the vegetables are tender, 30-45 minutes, stirring soup occasionally.

1½ cups: 249 cal., 5g fat (2g sat. fat), 44mg chol., 816mg sod., 29g carb. (5g sugars, 6g fiber), 21g pro. **Diabetic exchanges:** 2 starch, 2 lean meat.

TEST KITCHEN TIP

The V8 and diced tomatoes with green chiles add nice heat. If you like it even spicier, add the optional jalapeno. You can also use elbow macaroni instead of small pasta shells.

MEXI-STRONI SOUP

SLOW COOKER | FREEZE IT

EMERALD ISLE PEA SOUP WITH TARRAGON CREAM

This elegant and easy soup evokes memories of our honeymoon in Ireland and has become a true family favorite. The tarragon makes it taste so bright and springy.

—Sharon Marks, Waukesha, WI

Prep: 20 min. • **Cook:** 4 hours
Makes: 6 servings

- **1 cup dried green split peas**
- **1 large onion, chopped**
- **3 celery ribs, thinly sliced**
- **2 garlic cloves, minced**
- **3 to 4 tarragon sprigs**
- **1 tsp. salt**
- **¼ tsp. pepper**
- **4 cups chicken or vegetable stock**

TOPPING

- **¼ cup heavy whipping cream**
- **¼ cup sour cream**
- **1 tsp. minced fresh tarragon**

1. Place the first eight ingredients in a 4-qt. slow cooker. Cook, covered, on low until the peas are tender, 4-5 hours.
2. Remove tarragon sprigs. Puree soup using an immersion blender. Or, cool slightly and puree in batches in a blender; return to slow cooker and heat through.
3. Whisk whipping cream until slightly thickened. Whisk in sour cream and tarragon. Serve with soup.

Freeze option: Freeze cooled soup in freezer containers. To use, partially thaw in refrigerator overnight. Heat through in a saucepan.

1 cup soup with 4 tsp. tarragon cream: 198 cal., 6g fat (4g sat. fat), 14mg chol., 762mg sod., 26g carb. (5g sugars, 9g fiber), 12g pro.

TEST KITCHEN TIP

This is thinner than most pea soups, with a lighter consistency that pairs perfectly with the rich tarragon cream topping. Tarragon's delicately sweet licoricelike flavor goes well with cream and mustard, often in seafood, chicken and egg dishes.

CHERRY UPSIDE-DOWN BREAD PUDDING

SLOW COOKER

SLOW-COOKER CRAN-APPLE CHUTNEY

This sweet-tart chutney is perfect for Thanksgiving—it tastes amazing with turkey—but you may not want to wait that long!

—Raquel Haggard, Edmond, OK

Prep: 10 min. • **Cook:** 3 hours + chilling
Makes: 3 cups

- **1 pkg. (12 oz.) fresh or frozen cranberries, thawed**
- **1 medium Gala apple, peeled and finely chopped**
- **⅔ cup sugar or sugar substitute equivalent to ⅔ cup sugar**
- **⅓ cup honey**
- **2 Tbsp. brown sugar**
- **2 Tbsp. frozen orange juice concentrate, thawed**
- **1 tsp. ground cinnamon**
- **1 tsp. cider vinegar**
- **Dash ground ginger**

In a 1½-qt. slow cooker, combine all ingredients. Cook, covered, on low for 3-4 hours or until the cranberries pop and the mixture is slightly thickened. Transfer to a small bowl; cool slightly. Refrigerate until cold.

¼ cup: 103 cal., 0 fat (0 sat. fat), 0 chol., 2mg sod., 27g carb. (24g sugars, 1g fiber), 0 pro.

SLOW COOKER

CHERRY UPSIDE-DOWN BREAD PUDDING

I've always loved bread pudding, and I enjoy fixing this for my family on chilly days. For a completely different dessert, use another flavor of pie filling and omit the chocolate chips.

—Ronna Farley, Rockville, MD

Prep: 20 min. + cooling • **Cook:** 2¾ hours
Makes: 12 servings

- **1 loaf (16 oz.) sliced white bread**
- **1 can (21 oz.) cherry pie filling**
- **½ cup butter, softened**
- **1 cup sugar**
- **5 large eggs, room temperature**
- **2 cups 2% milk**
- **1 tsp. ground cinnamon**
- **1 tsp. vanilla extract**
- **¾ cup semisweet chocolate chips**
- **Sweetened whipped cream, optional**

1. Place bread on ungreased baking sheets. Broil each pan 3-4 in. from heat 1-2 minutes on each side or until golden brown; let cool. Cut into 1-in. pieces; set aside.
2. Spoon the pie filling into a greased 5- or 6-qt. slow cooker. In a large bowl, cream butter and sugar until crumbly. Add eggs, one at a time, beating well after each addition. Beat in milk, cinnamon and vanilla (the mixture may appear curdled). Gently stir in chocolate chips and bread cubes; let stand until the bread is softened, about 10 minutes. Transfer to slow cooker.
3. Cook, covered, on low 2¾-3¼ hours or until set and a knife inserted in the center comes out clean. Serve warm with whipped cream, if desired.

¾ cup: 393 cal., 15g fat (8g sat. fat), 101mg chol., 305mg sod., 58g carb. (27g sugars, 2g fiber), 8g pro.

SLOW-COOKER CHEESEBURGER DIP

SLOW COOKER

SLOW-COOKER CHEESEBURGER DIP

This fun dip recipe uses basic ingredients I always have in the fridge, ready to throw together on short notice.

—Cindi DeClue, Anchorage, AK

Prep: 25 min. • **Cook:** 1¾ hours
Makes: 16 servings

- **1 lb. lean ground beef (90% lean)**
- **1 medium onion, chopped**
- **1 pkg. (8 oz.) cream cheese, cubed**
- **2 cups shredded cheddar cheese, divided**
- **1 Tbsp. Worcestershire sauce**
- **2 tsp. prepared mustard**
- **¼ tsp. salt**
- **⅛ tsp. pepper**
- **1 medium tomato, chopped**
- **¼ cup chopped dill pickles**
- **Tortilla chips or crackers**

1. In a large skillet, cook beef and onion over medium-high heat until the beef is no longer pink and onion is tender, breaking up beef into crumbles, 6-8 minutes; drain. Transfer to a greased 1½- or 3-qt. slow cooker. Stir in the cream cheese, 1½ cups cheddar cheese, Worcestershire, mustard, salt and pepper. Sprinkle with remaining cheddar cheese.
2. Cook, covered, on low until the dip is heated through and the cheese is melted, 1¾-2¼ hours. Top with chopped tomatoes and pickles. Serve with tortilla chips.

¼ cup: 157 cal., 12g fat (6g sat. fat), 46mg chol., 225mg sod., 2g carb. (1g sugars, 0 fiber), 10g pro.

SLOW COOKER

CREAMY POLENTA WITH BALSAMIC GLAZE

This delicious and easy side dish goes incredibly well with braised meat. It makes any meal feel a little more special.

—Sarah Vasques, Milford, NH

Prep: 15 min. • **Cook:** 2 hours
Makes: 2 cups

- **4 Tbsp. butter, divided**
- **1½ cups half-and-half cream, divided**
- **1 cup 2% milk**
- **¼ tsp. salt**
- **⅓ cup cornmeal**
- **½ cup grated Parmesan cheese**
- **1 cup balsamic vinegar**
- **1 Tbsp. sugar**

1. In a medium saucepan, melt 2 Tbsp. butter over medium heat. Add 1 cup cream, the milk and salt. Bring to a low simmer. Gradually whisk in cornmeal. Cook and stir for 3 minutes.
2. Pour the polenta into a 3-qt. slow cooker coated with cooking spray. Cook, covered, on low for 2 hours, stirring every 30 minutes. Meanwhile, in a small saucepan, bring vinegar and sugar to a boil. Reduce heat; simmer, uncovered, until reduced to ⅓ cup. Just before serving, stir cheese and the remaining cream and butter into the polenta. To serve, drizzle with balsamic glaze.

½ cup polenta with 1 Tbsp. glaze: 415 cal., 25g fat (16g sat. fat), 89mg chol., 494mg sod., 37g carb. (25g sugars, 1g fiber), 9g pro.

TEST KITCHEN TIP

Don't try to speed this recipe along by cooking on high, or the outer edge is likely to get browned.

This recipe makes a generous amount of balsamic glaze. Try a drizzle on pork chops or roasted chicken.

SLOW COOKER

BREAD PUDDING WITH BOURBON SAUCE

There's nothing better on a cold, wintry day than this comforting bread pudding. The bourbon sauce tastes extravagant, but it's really simple to prepare. The slow cooker does the most of the work for you!
—Hope Johnson, Youngwood, PA

Prep: 15 min.
Cook: 3 hours.
Makes: 6 servings

- **3 large eggs**
- **1¼ cups 2% milk**
- **½ cup sugar**
- **3 tsp. vanilla extract**
- **½ tsp. ground cinnamon**
- **¼ tsp. ground nutmeg**
- **⅛ tsp. salt**
- **4½ cups day-old cubed brioche or egg bread**
- **1¼ cups raisins**

BOURBON SAUCE

- **¼ cup butter, cubed**
- **½ cup sugar**
- **¼ cup light corn syrup**
- **3 Tbsp. bourbon**

1. In a large bowl, whisk together first seven ingredients; stir in bread and raisins. Transfer to a greased 4-qt. slow cooker. Cook, covered, on low 3 hours. (To avoid scorching, rotate slow cooker insert one-half turn midway through cooking, lifting carefully with oven mitts.)
2. Place butter, sugar and corn syrup in a small saucepan; bring to a boil, stirring occasionally. Cook and stir until sugar is dissolved. Remove from heat; stir in the bourbon. Serve warm with bread pudding.

1 cup with 2 Tbsp. sauce: 477 cal., 12g fat (6g sat. fat), 130mg chol., 354mg sod., 84g carb. (59g sugars, 2g fiber), 8g pro.

* HEALTH TIP * This dessert is rich even without the sauce. Skip it and save nearly 200 calories and 8 grams fat per serving.

BREAD PUDDING WITH BOURBON SAUCE

SLOW COOKER | EAT SMART

BUTTERNUT SQUASH & CARROT SOUP

I got the recipe for this golden soup from a friend. Sometimes I add a few slices of red pepper to change up the flavor a bit.
—Pat Roberts, Thornton, ON

Prep: 25 min. • **Cook:** 7 hours
Makes: 8 servings (2 qt.)

- **1 Tbsp. canola oil**
- **1 medium onion, chopped**
- **2 garlic cloves, sliced**
- **¼ tsp. minced fresh gingerroot**
- **1 small butternut squash (about 2 lbs.), peeled and cut into 1-in. cubes (about 5 cups)**
- **1 lb. fresh baby carrots**
- **⅛ tsp. ground nutmeg**
- **½ tsp. salt**
- **1 carton (32 oz.) chicken broth**
- **½ cup half-and-half cream**
- **Sliced green onions, optional**

1. In a large skillet, heat canola oil over medium-high heat; saute onion, garlic and ginger until tender, 4-5 minutes. Transfer to a 5-qt. slow cooker.
2. Add all remaining ingredients except cream and green onions. Cook, covered, on low until vegetables are soft, 7-9 hours.
3. Puree soup using an immersion blender, or cool slightly and, in batches, puree in a blender and return to slow cooker. Stir in cream; heat through. If desired, top with green onions.

Freeze option: Freeze cooled soup in freezer containers. To use, partially thaw in refrigerator overnight. Heat through in a saucepan, stirring occasionally and adding a little broth or milk if necessary.

1 cup: 121 cal., 4g fat (1g sat. fat), 10mg chol., 695mg sod., 20g carb. (7g sugars, 5g fiber), 3g pro. **Diabetic exchanges:** 1 starch, 1 fat.

TEST KITCHEN TIP

Fresh ginger adds bright flavor, but you can use just a dash of ground ginger instead.

Stir in the cream at the end to prevent curdling from too much heat.

SLOW-COOKER BEEF TIPS BURGUNDY

Microwave, covered, on high in microwave-safe dishes until heated through, stirring gently and adding a little water if necessary. Sprinkle with parsley.

1 cup: 275 cal., 13g fat (5g sat. fat), 88mg chol., 536mg sod., 9g carb. (2g sugars, 1g fiber), 29g pro. **Diabetic exchanges:** 4 lean meat, ½ starch.

SLOW COOKER | EAT SMART

CHICKEN ENCHILADA STUFFED PEPPERS

Make leftover chicken seem brand new with super simple and tasty stuffed peppers! This is an ideal weekend meal; you can put it together quickly and run errands—or just relax!—while it cooks.

—Katie Jasiewicz, Belle Isle, FL

Prep: 20 min. • **Cook:** 3 hrs.
Makes: 6 servings

- **2 cups shredded cooked chicken**
- **1 pkg. (8.8 oz.) ready-to-serve long grain rice**
- **1 cup enchilada sauce**
- **¾ cup shredded cheddar cheese, divided**
- **3 Tbsp. minced red onion**
- **½ tsp. ground cumin**
- **⅓ cup water**
- **6 medium bell peppers**
- **Minced fresh cilantro, green onions and sour cream**

1. In a bowl, combine the chicken, rice, enchilada sauce, ½ cup cheese, red onion and cumin.
2. Pour water into a 6-qt. slow cooker. Cut and discard the tops from peppers; remove seeds. Fill peppers with the chicken mixture; place in slow cooker. Cover the slow cooker with a double layer of white paper towels; place lid securely over towels. Cook on low until peppers are tender, 3-4 hours. During the last 20 minutes, remove and discard paper towels and add the remaining cheese. Replace the cover and cook until cheese is melted. Serve with sour cream, cilantro and green onions.

1 stuffed pepper: 267 cal., 10g fat (4g sat. fat), 56mg chol., 364mg sod., 23g carb. (6g sugars, 3g fiber), 20g pro. **Diabetic exchanges:** 3 lean meat, 1 starch, 1 vegetable, ½ fat.

SLOW COOKER | EAT SMART

SLOW-COOKER BEEF TIPS BURGUNDY

Here's a heartwarming classic made simple in the slow cooker. Mushrooms, red wine and tender beef combine to create an enticing supper that is always welcome at our table!

—Deanna Zewen, Union Grove, WI

Prep: 15 min. • **Cook:** 6¾ hours
Makes: 10 servings

- **1 boneless beef chuck roast (3 lbs.), trimmed and cut into 1-in. pieces**
- **2 medium onions, halved and sliced**
- **½ lb. sliced fresh mushrooms**
- **4 garlic cloves, minced**
- **3 cups beef stock**
- **½ cup dry red wine or additional beef stock**
- **2 Tbsp. Worcestershire sauce**
- **2 Tbsp. red wine vinegar**
- **1¼ tsp. salt**
- **1 tsp. crushed red pepper flakes**
- **½ tsp. pepper**
- **⅓ cup cornstarch**
- **⅓ cup cold water**
- **Hot cooked egg noodles**
- **Minced fresh parsley**

1. In a 5-qt. slow cooker, combine beef, onions, mushrooms and garlic. In a small bowl, mix the next seven ingredients; pour over beef mixture. Cook, covered, on low until the meat is tender, 6-8 hours.
2. Skim fat from juices. In a small bowl, mix cornstarch and water until smooth; gradually stir into the slow cooker. Cook, covered, on high until thickened, about 45 minutes. Serve with noodles; sprinkle with parsley.

Freeze option: Omitting parsley, freeze the cooled meat mixture, sauce and egg noodles in freezer containers. To use, partially thaw in refrigerator overnight.

CHICKEN ENCHILADA
STUFFED PEPPERS

SLOW COOKER

SLOW-COOKED CORN ON THE COB

I like to eat corn all year long so I came up with this recipe. It's my favorite side with sloppy joes. You can use a butter substitute for a skinny version of this corn.
—Teresa Flowers, Sacramento, CA

Prep: 10 min. • **Cook:** 2 hours
Makes: 4 servings

- **4 medium ears sweet corn, cut into 2-in. pieces**
- **1 can (15 oz.) coconut milk**
- **1 medium onion, chopped**
- **¼ cup butter, cubed**
- **6 fresh thyme sprigs**
- **2 garlic cloves, minced**
- **1 bay leaf**
- **¾ tsp. salt**
- **¼ tsp. pepper**
- **¼ cup fresh cilantro leaves, chopped**
- **2 green onions, sliced**

In a 5- or 6-qt. slow cooker, combine the first nine ingredients. Cook, covered, on high for 2-3 hours or until tender. Serve with cilantro and green onions.
4 pieces: 161 cal., 9g fat (6g sat. fat), 8mg chol., 118mg sod., 21g carb. (7g sugars, 2g fiber), 4g pro.

SLOW COOKER

SLOW-COOKER BLUEBERRY COBBLER

I love blueberries and turn to this cake-mix cobbler to shows them off in style. Serve cobbler warm with a scoop of French vanilla ice cream or a dollop of whipped cream.
—Teri Rasey, Cadillac, MI

Prep: 15 min. • **Cook:** 3 hours
Makes: 12 servings

- **4 cups fresh or frozen blueberries**
- **1 cup sugar**
- **1 Tbsp. cornstarch**
- **2 tsp. vanilla extract**
- **1 pkg. French vanilla cake mix (regular size)**
- **½ cup butter, melted**
- **⅓ cup chopped pecans**
- **Vanilla ice cream, optional**

In a greased 5-qt. slow cooker, combine blueberries, sugar and cornstarch; stir in vanilla. In bowl, combine cake mix and melted butter. Crumble over blueberries. Top with pecans. Cover slow cooker with a double layer of white paper towels; place lid securely over towels. Cook, covered, on low 3-4 hours or until topping is set. If desired, serve with ice cream.
½ cup: 331 cal., 11g fat (6g sat. fat), 20mg chol., 343mg sod., 58g carb. (39g sugars, 2g fiber), 2g pro.

SLOW-COOKER BLUEBERRY COBBLER

SLOW COOKER | EAT SMART

SHREDDED GREEN CHILI BEEF

This Tex-Mex pulled beef roast is tender, juicy and slightly spicy. Serve over mashed potatoes or rice —or to make the best soft tacos you've ever had!

—Colleen Delawder, Herndon, VA

Prep: 25 min. • **Cook:** 7 hours
Makes: 12 servings

- **2 large sweet onions, halved and thinly sliced**
- **¼ cup packed brown sugar, divided**
- **1 Tbsp. paprika**
- **1½ tsp. salt**
- **1 tsp. cayenne pepper**
- **1 tsp. chili powder**
- **1 tsp. garlic powder**
- **½ tsp. pepper**
- **1 boneless beef chuck roast (about 3 lbs.)**
- **2 Tbsp. canola oil**
- **1 can (28 oz.) green enchilada sauce**
- **Mashed potatoes, optional**

1. Place onions and 3 Tbsp. brown sugar in a 5- or 6-qt. slow cooker. Combine remaining 1 Tbsp. brown sugar and next six ingredients; coat beef with mixture.
2. In a large skillet, heat the canola oil over medium-high heat; brown beef for 1-2 minutes on each side. Transfer to slow cooker; pour enchilada sauce over beef. Cook, covered, on low until the beef is tender, 7-9 hours.
3. Remove beef; shred meat with two forks. Return to slow cooker; heat through. If desired, serve over potatoes.

1 cup beef mixture: 278 cal., 15g fat (4g sat. fat), 74mg chol., 658mg sod., 14g carb. (8g sugars, 1g fiber), 23g pro. **Diabetic exchanges:** 3 lean meat, 1 starch, ½ fat.

TEST KITCHEN TIP

Save any leftover pulled beef in the liquid to prevent it from drying out.

TURKEY GINGER NOODLE SOUP

SLOW COOKER | EAT SMART

TURKEY GINGER NOODLE SOUP

I was looking for a craveworthy soup that's also healthy and tasty. Ginger is my favorite spice, making this recipe a shoo-in.

—Adina Monson, Nanaimo, BC

Prep: 20 min. • **Cook:** 4¼ hours
Makes: 8 servings (about 3 qt.)

- **2 medium carrots, sliced**
- **2 cans (8 oz. each) sliced water chestnuts, drained**
- **3 to 4 Tbsp. minced fresh gingerroot**
- **2 Tbsp. minced fresh parsley**
- **2 tsp. chili powder**
- **1 carton (32 oz.) chicken stock**
- **1 can (11.8 oz.) coconut water**
- **3 Tbsp. lemon juice**
- **2 lbs. uncooked skinless turkey breast, cut into 1-in. cubes**
- **2 tsp. pepper**
- **½ tsp. salt**
- **2 Tbsp. canola oil**
- **1 cup frozen corn (about 5 oz.), thawed**
- **1 cup frozen peas (about 4 oz.), thawed**
- **8 oz. rice noodles or thin spaghetti**

1. Place the first eight ingredients in a 4- or 5-qt. slow cooker.
2. Toss turkey with pepper and salt. In a large skillet, heat oil over medium-high heat; brown the turkey in batches. Add to slow cooker.
3. Cook, covered, on low until the carrots and turkey are tender, 4-5 hours. Stir in corn and peas; heat through.
4. Cook the noodles according to the package directions; drain. Add to the soup just before serving.

1½ cups: 351 cal., 6g fat (1g sat. fat), 65mg chol., 672mg sod., 41g carb. (5g sugars, 4g fiber), 33g pro. **Diabetic exchanges:** 3 starch, 3 lean meat.

BOURBON BARBECUE CHICKEN TACOS

SSLOW COOKER

BOURBON BARBECUE CHICKEN TACOS

I wanted to try a different take on taco night and decided on barbecue for the theme. Even my father enjoyed this taco, and he doesn't care for tacos!
—LaDale Hymer, Cleveland, OK

Prep: 30 min. • **Cook:** 3 hours
Makes: 8 servings

- **1 cup ketchup**
- **1 small red onion, finely chopped**
- **¼ cup packed brown sugar**
- **2 Tbsp. Worcestershire sauce**
- **2 Tbsp. maple syrup**
- **2 Tbsp. cider vinegar**
- **1 Tbsp. chopped fresh parsley**
- **2 garlic cloves, minced**
- **¼ tsp. pepper**
- **3 Tbsp. bourbon, divided**
- **1½ lbs. boneless skinless chicken breasts**

SALSA

- **2 cups fresh or thawed frozen corn**
- **1 cup chopped sweet red pepper**
- **½ cup finely chopped red onion**
- **2 medium limes, zested and juiced**
- **⅛ tsp. hot pepper sauce**
- **½ tsp. salt**
- **¼ tsp. pepper**
- **8 flour tortillas (8 in.)**
- **Minced cilantro**

1. In a 3-qt. slow cooker, combine first nine ingredients and 2 Tbsp. bourbon. Add chicken; turn to coat. Cook, covered, on low until a thermometer reads 165°, 3-4 hours. Remove chicken; shred with two forks. Return to slow cooker; stir in remaining bourbon. Heat through.
2. For salsa, combine corn, red pepper, onion, lime juice, lime zest, hot sauce, salt, and pepper in a bowl. Serve chicken in tortillas with salsa. Top with cilantro.

1 taco: 387 cal., 6g fat (2g sat. fat), 47mg chol., 855mg sod., 58g carb. (22g sugars, 4g fiber), 23g pro.

SLOW COOKER | **EAT SMART**

SPAGHETTI SQUASH WITH TOMATOES & OLIVES

PICTURED ON P. 203

Enjoy this squash as a side dish, or top it with canned tuna to serve as an entree. I use my own canned tomatoes for the best flavor.
—Carol Chase, Sioux City, IA

Prep: 15 min. • **Cook:** 5¼ hours
Makes: 10 servings

- **1 medium spaghetti squash, halved, seeds removed**
- **1 can (14 oz.) diced tomatoes**
- **¼ cup sliced green olives with pimientos, drained**
- **1 tsp. dried oregano**
- **½ tsp. salt**
- **½ tsp. pepper**
- **½ cup shredded cheddar cheese**
- **¼ cup minced fresh basil**

1. Place the squash in 6- or 7-qt. slow cooker, overlapping as needed to fit. Cook, covered, on low until tender, 5-7 hours.
2. Remove the squash from slow cooker; drain any cooking liquid from the slow cooker. Using a fork, separate squash into strands; discard the skin.
3. Return squash to slow cooker. Stir in the tomatoes, olives, oregano, salt and pepper; cook on low until heated through, about 15 minutes. Top with cheese and basil to serve.

¾ cup: 92 cal., 3g fat (1g sat. fat), 6mg chol., 296mg sod., 15g carb. (1g sugars, 4g fiber), 3g pro. **Diabetic exchanges:** 1 starch, ½ fat.

TEST KITCHEN TIP

Adding the tomato mixture after cooking the squash allows you to discard any condensed liquid before combining all the ingredients.

If you like cheesy goodness, top the squash mixture with cheese during the last 15 minutes of cooking, giving it time to get melty.

SLOW COOKER | EAT SMART

CREAMY CAULIFLOWER SOUP

I love indulgent cream soups but not the fat that goes along with them, so I came up with a healthier version. The velvety texture of this soup makes it feel so rich, and the spicy kick warms you up in a flash.
—Teri Rasey, Cadillac, MI

Prep: 20 min. • **Cook:** 6 hours
Makes: 14 servings (3½ qt.)

- **1¾ lbs. Yukon Gold potatoes (about 4 medium), peeled and cut into 1-in. cubes**
- **1 medium head cauliflower (about 1½ lbs.), cut into 1-in. pieces**
- **1 small onion, chopped**
- **3 garlic cloves, minced**
- **1 large bay leaf**
- **3 tsp. dried celery flakes**
- **1½ tsp. salt**
- **1½ tsp. adobo seasoning**
- **¾ tsp. ground mustard**
- **¼ tsp. cayenne pepper**
- **6 cups water**
- **¾ cup nonfat dry milk powder**
- **Optional toppings: shredded cheddar cheese, sliced green onions and croutons**

1. Place the first 10 ingredients in a 6-qt. slow cooker. Add water; sprinkle milk powder over top.
2. Cook, covered, on low until cauliflower is very tender, 6-8 hours. Remove bay leaf. Puree soup using an immersion blender, or cool slightly and puree in batches in a blender; return to slow cooker and heat through. Serve with toppings as desired.

1 cup: 80 cal., 0 fat (0 sat. fat), 1mg chol., 434mg sod., 17g carb. (4g sugars, 2g fiber), 3g pro. **Diabetic exchanges:** 1 vegetable, ½ starch.

TEST KITCHEN TIP

For added flavor, a 32-oz. carton of vegetable or chicken stock may be substituted for 4 cups of water.

Be sure to cook the vegetables until the cauliflower is very tender, so it can be processed to a smooth texture. If using a blender, cool the mixture slightly and don't fill the blender jar too much. Hold down the lid, protecting your hand with a thick towel or oven mitt, and begin blending at the lowest speed.

For a touch of indulgence, serve this soup with a small dollop of sour cream.

CREAMY CAULIFLOWER SOUP

SLOW COOKER

EFFORTLESS BLACK BEAN CHILI

My mom found the inspiration for this chili in a slow-cooker cookbook. After a few of her personal updates, all of us love it. It's even better served over rice!
—Amelia Gormley, Ephrata, PA

Prep: 25 min. • **Cook:** 6 hours
Makes: 6 servings (1½ qt.)

- **1 lb. ground turkey**
- **1 small onion, chopped**
- **3 tsp. chili powder**
- **2 tsp. minced fresh oregano or ¾ tsp. dried oregano**
- **1 tsp. chicken bouillon granules**
- **1 jar (16 oz.) mild salsa**
- **1 can (15¼ oz.) whole kernel corn, drained**
- **1 can (15 oz.) black beans, rinsed and drained**
- **1 can (14½ oz.) diced tomatoes, undrained**
- **½ cup water**
- **Optional toppings: sour cream, chopped cilantro, finely chopped red onion and corn chips**

1. In a large skillet, cook and crumble turkey with onion over medium-high heat until no longer pink, 5-7 minutes. Transfer to a 4-qt. slow cooker.
2. Stir in all remaining ingredients except the toppings. Cook, covered, on low until flavors are blended, 6-8 hours. Top chili as desired.

1 cup: 242 cal., 6g fat (1g sat. fat), 50mg chol., 868mg sod., 26g carb. (9g sugars, 6g fiber), 20g pro.

SLOW COOKER

SAVORY WINTER SOUP

Even my father, who doesn't particularly like soup, enjoys my full-flavored rendition of vegetable soup. He asked me to share the recipe with Mom, and I gladly obliged!
—Dana Simmons, Lancaster, OH

Prep: 20 min. • **Cook:** 6 hours
Makes: 14 servings (3½ qt.)

- **2 lbs. ground beef**
- **3 medium onions, chopped**
- **1 garlic clove, minced**
- **3 cans (10½ oz. each) condensed beef broth, undiluted**
- **1 can (28 oz.) diced tomatoes, undrained**
- **3 cups water**
- **1 cup each diced carrots and celery**
- **1 cup fresh or frozen cut green beans**
- **1 cup cubed peeled potatoes**
- **2 Tbsp. minced fresh parsley or 2 tsp. dried parsley flakes**
- **1 tsp. dried basil**
- **½ tsp. dried thyme**
- **Salt and pepper to taste**

1. In a large skillet, cook beef and onions over medium heat until the meat is no longer pink. Add garlic; cook 1 minute longer. Drain.
2. Transfer to a 5-qt. slow cooker. Stir in the remaining ingredients. Cover and cook on low until the vegetables are tender, 6-8 hours.

Note: Save chopping time by using frozen sliced carrots and cubed hash brown potatoes.

1 cup: 163 cal., 8g fat (3g sat. fat), 40mg chol., 583mg sod., 9g carb. (4g sugars, 2g fiber), 14g pro.

SLOW COOKER | EAT SMART

BEEF BURRITOS WITH GREEN CHILES

I created this recipe years ago, and it has become such a favorite that the wonderful aroma of it cooking makes my family instantly happy. It is hearty and flavorful and uses the long slow cook that truly defines comfort food. The beefy filling also works in tacos or quesadillas.
—Sally Pahler, Palisade, CO

Prep: 20 min. • **Cook:** 8 hours
Makes: 14 servings

- **2 garlic cloves, minced**
- **1 tsp. salt**
- **2 tsp. ground cumin**
- **1 tsp. cayenne pepper**
- **1 boneless beef chuck roast (4 lbs.)**
- **1 can (28 oz.) diced tomatoes**
- **4 cans (7 oz. each) whole green chiles, drained and coarsely chopped**
- **1 large onion, diced**
- **14 whole wheat tortillas (8 in.), warmed**
- **Optional toppings: shredded cheddar cheese, sour cream, salsa and sliced ripe olives**

1. Combine garlic, salt, cumin and cayenne; rub over roast. Place in a 5- or 6-qt. slow cooker. Add tomatoes, chiles and onion. Cook, covered, on low for 7-8 hours or until the meat is tender.
2. Remove roast from slow cooker; shred with two forks. Remove vegetables with a slotted spoon; discard the cooking juices. Return beef and vegetables to slow cooker and heat through. Serve in tortillas, with toppings if desired.

1 burrito: 355 cal., 13g fat (5g sat. fat), 84mg chol., 499mg sod., 28g carb. (4g sugars, 4g fiber), 30g pro. **Diabetic exchanges:** 4 lean meat, 2 starch.

TEST KITCHEN TIP

We liked the coarse texture of chiles chopped by hand, but if you're trying to save time, use diced green chiles.

BEEF BURRITOS WITH GREEN CHILES

SLOW COOKER | FREEZE IT | EAT SMART

ALL-DAY RED BEANS & RICE

PICTURED ON P. 203

My family loves New Orleans-style cooking, so I make this dish often. I appreciate how simple it is, and the smoky ham flavor is scrumptious.
—Celinda Dahlgren, Napa, CA

Prep: 20 min. + soaking
Cook: 8½ hours • **Makes:** 6 servings

- **1 cup dried red beans**
- **7 cups water, divided**
- **2 smoked ham hocks**
- **1 medium onion, chopped**
- **1½ tsp. minced garlic**
- **1 tsp. ground cumin**
- **1 medium tomato, chopped**
- **1 medium green pepper, chopped**
- **1 tsp. salt**
- **4 cups hot cooked rice**

1. Sort beans and rinse in cold water. Place in a 3-qt. slow cooker. Add 4 cups water; cover and let stand overnight.
2. Drain and rinse beans, discarding liquid. Return beans to slow cooker; add the ham hocks, onion, garlic, cumin and remaining water. Cover and cook on low 8-10 hours or until the beans are tender.
3. Remove the ham hocks; cool slightly. Remove meat from bones. Finely chop meat and return to slow cooker; discard bones. Stir in tomato, pepper and salt; cover and cook on high for 30 minutes or until the pepper is tender. Serve with rice.

Freeze option: Freeze cooled bean mixture in freezer containers. To use, partially thaw in refrigerator overnight. Microwave, covered, on high in a microwave-safe dish until heated through, gently stirring and adding a little water if necessary.

⅔ bean mixture with ⅔ cup rice: 297 cal., 7g fat (3g sat. fat), 33mg chol., 441mg sod., 50g carb. (3g sugars, 12g fiber), 17g pro.

Stovetop All-Day Red Beans & Rice: Prepare beans as directed using a Dutch oven. Add the ham hocks, onion, garlic, cumin and remaining water. Bring to a boil. Reduce heat; cover and simmer for 1 hour. Prepare ham as directed. Stir in tomato, pepper and salt. Bring to a boil. Reduce heat; cover and simmer for 45 minutes. Uncover and simmer 10-15 minutes longer or until the beans reach desired consistency.

TEXAS CHILI FRIES

SLOW COOKER

TEXAS CHILI FRIES

The delicious chili goes together in minutes and then cooks while you do other things. Then I make it even better by pouring it over crisp french fries and sprinkling it with shredded cheese!
—Joan Hallford, North Richland Hills, TX

Prep: 20 min. • **Cook:** 6 hours
Makes: 16 servings

- **1 medium onion, chopped**
- **1 medium carrot, finely chopped**
- **2 lbs. beef stew meat (cut into ½-in. pieces)**
- **3 Tbsp. all-purpose flour, divided**
- **2 Tbsp. canola oil**
- **1 can (14½ oz.) Mexican diced tomatoes**
- **1 envelope (1.25 oz.) chili seasoning mix**
- **1 can (15 oz.) pinto beans, rinsed and drained**
- **1 medium green pepper, chopped**
- **1 jalapeno pepper, seeded and finely chopped**
- **2 pkg. (32 oz. each) frozen french-fried potatoes**
- **2 cups shredded sharp cheddar cheese**
- **Sour cream and sliced jalapeno peppers, optional**

1. Place onion and carrot in a 5-qt. slow cooker. Toss beef with 2 Tbsp. flour. In a Dutch oven, heat oil over medium heat; brown beef in batches. Transfer meat to the slow cooker.
2. Drain tomatoes; reserving the liquid. In a small bowl, whisk the drained liquid with chili seasoning and the remaining flour until blended; pour over the beef. Stir in the tomatoes, beans and peppers. Cook, covered, on low for 6 hours or until the meat is tender.
3. Prepare fries according to package directions. Serve chili over fries; sprinkle with cheese. If desired, top with sour cream and jalapeno slices.

1 serving: 374 cal., 16g fat (6g sat. fat), 49mg chol., 824mg sod., 32g carb. (4g sugars, 5g fiber), 19g pro.

Hot off the Grill

Grilling isn't just for cooking burgers and steaks (although it's pretty incredible for those). Fire up the grill and turn out fabulous appetizers, mains, veggies and sides—even pizzas and desserts!

EAT SMART | FAST FIX

CAJUN GRILLED SHRIMP

The kicked-up marinade makes this a flavor-packed dish. Serve over rice, and make sure to squeeze the charred lemons over top—that makes the shrimp taste extra bright and delicious.
—Sharon Delaney-Chronis, South Milwaukee, WI

Takes: 30 min. • **Makes:** 6 servings

3 green onions, finely chopped
2 Tbsp. lemon juice
1 Tbsp. olive oil
3 garlic cloves, minced
2 tsp. paprika
1 tsp. salt
¼ tsp. pepper
¼ tsp. cayenne pepper
2 lbs. uncooked medium shrimp, peeled and deveined with tails on
4 medium lemons, each cut into 8 wedges

1. In a shallow dish or bowl, combine the first eight ingredients. Add shrimp and turn to coat. Refrigerate for 15 minutes.
2. Drain shrimp, discarding marinade. On 12 metal or soaked wooden skewers, thread the shrimp and lemon wedges.
3. Grill, covered, over medium heat or broil 4 in. from the heat until the shrimp turn pink, 6-8 minutes, turning once.
2 skewers: 168 cal., 5g fat (1g sat. fat), 184mg chol., 575mg sod., 7g carb. (1g sugars, 2g fiber), 25g pro. **Diabetic exchanges:** 3 lean meat, ½ fruit, ½ fat.

GARDEN-FRESH GRILLED VEGGIE PIZZA

GARDEN-FRESH GRILLED VEGGIE PIZZA

With my four gardens, I grow a good spread of veggies! I created this fun summer appetizer to use some of my best garden goodies. Carrot may seem a strange addition, but it adds a pleasant sweetness.
—Dianna Wara, Washington, IL

Prep: 30 min. • **Grill:** 15 min.
Makes: 6 servings

3 Tbsp. olive oil
3 garlic cloves, minced
3 medium tomatoes, cut into ½-in. slices
1 large sweet red pepper, halved, stemmed and seeded
1 small zucchini, cut lengthwise into ¼-in. slices
1 small onion, cut crosswise into ½-in. slices
1 tsp. coarsely ground pepper
1 prebaked 12-in. pizza crust
⅓ cup spreadable garden vegetable cream cheese
8 slices smoked provolone cheese, divided
½ cup minced fresh basil, divided
¼ cup shredded carrots
1 Tbsp. minced fresh oregano
1 tsp. minced fresh thyme

1. Mix oil and garlic; brush onto both sides of vegetables. Sprinkle with pepper. Grill, covered, over medium heat until tender, 4-5 minutes per side for pepper and onion, 3-4 minutes per side for zucchini, 2-3 minutes per side for tomatoes.
2. Coarsely chop the pepper, onion and zucchini. Spread pizza crust with cream cheese; layer with four slices provolone and the tomato slices. Sprinkle with ¼ cup basil, carrots, oregano and thyme. Top with grilled vegetables, then the remaining cheese.
3. Grill pizza, covered, over medium heat until the bottom is golden brown and the cheese is melted, 5-7 minutes. Top with the remaining basil.
1 slice: 395 cal., 22g fat (8g sat. fat), 23mg chol., 618mg sod., 36g carb. (6g sugars, 3g fiber), 16g pro.

APPLE THYME CHICKEN

Apples and chicken may seem like an unusual combination, but they make a wonderful meal when grilled to perfection.
—Peter Halferty, Corpus Christi, TX

Prep: 20 min. + marinating • **Grill:** 15 min.
Makes: 4 servings

- **½ cup apple juice**
- **½ cup lemon juice**
- **2 Tbsp. cider vinegar**
- **2 Tbsp. canola oil**
- **4 tsp. minced fresh thyme or 1½ tsp. dried thyme**
- **4 boneless skinless chicken breast halves (6 oz. each)**
- **2 medium tart apples, peeled and quartered**
- **1 Tbsp. honey**
- **½ tsp. salt**

SAUCE
- **2 tsp. cornstarch**
- **¾ tsp. minced fresh thyme or ¼ tsp. dried thyme**
- **¾ cup apple juice**

1. For marinade, in a bowl, mix the first five ingredients. In another bowl, combine chicken and ¾ cup marinade; refrigerate, covered, at least 2 hours. Reserve the remaining marinade; cover and refrigerate.
2. When ready to grill, toss the apples in reserved marinade; remove apples with a slotted spoon. Stir honey into the apple marinade. Place apples on an oiled grill rack over medium heat; grill, uncovered, until tender, 4-6 minutes, turning and brushing frequently with honey mixture.
3. Drain chicken, discarding the chicken marinade. Sprinkle the chicken with salt. Grill, covered, over medium heat until a thermometer reads 165°, 5-7 minutes per side; brush frequently with the remaining honey mixture during the last 4 minutes.
4. In a saucepan, mix sauce ingredients until smooth; bring to a boil. Cook and stir until thickened, about 2 minutes; stir in apples. Serve with chicken.
1 serving: 310 cal., 9g fat (1g sat. fat), 94mg chol., 380mg sod., 23g carb. (17g sugars, 2g fiber), 35g pro. **Diabetic exchanges:** 5 lean meat, 1½ fruit.

FAST FIX
SALMON CAESAR SALAD

This main course was invented out of a need to serve my family a balanced meal when time was tight. Even my young son just loves it!
—Ann Bagdonas, Antioch, CA

Takes: 30 min. • **Makes:** 4 servings

- **4 salmon fillets (4 oz. each)**
- **2 garlic cloves, minced**
- **½ cup teriyaki sauce**
- **1 pkg. (10 oz.) hearts of romaine salad mix**
- **¾ cup fat-free creamy Caesar salad dressing**
- **2 Tbsp. grated Parmesan cheese**
- **¼ cup slivered almonds, toasted**

1. Rub salmon with garlic; place in a shallow bowl. Add teriyaki sauce; turn salmon to coat. Let stand 10 minutes.
2. Preheat grill or broiler. Place salmon on an oiled grill rack over high heat or in a greased 15x10x1-in. pan. Grill, covered, or broil 3-4 in. from heat until the fish just begins to flake easily with a fork, 4-6 minutes per side.
3. Toss salad mix with salad dressing; place on four plates. Top with salmon. Sprinkle with cheese and almonds.
1 serving: 311 cal., 15g fat (3g sat. fat), 60mg chol., 928mg sod., 22g carb. (5g sugars, 3g fiber), 24g pro.
* **HEALTH TIP** * Sneak in an extra serving of fruit and veggies by adding sliced fresh strawberries, orange segments, blanched asparagus or chopped kale.

SALMON CAESAR SALAD

Hot & Sweet Corn

In the summer months, cook your corn right alongside your chicken or burgers for the perfect summer side.

EASY GRILLED CORN WITH CHIPOTLE-LIME BUTTER

Grilling corn in the husks is so easy. There's no need to remove the silk and tie the husk closed before grilling. Just soak, grill and add your favorite flavored butter.
—Taste of Home Test Kitchen

Prep: 5 min. + soaking • **Grill:** 25 min.
Makes: 8 servings

- **8 large ears sweet corn in husks**
- **½ cup butter, softened**
- **1½ tsp. grated lime zest**
- **1 tsp. minced fresh cilantro**
- **½ tsp. salt**
- **½ tsp. ground chipotle pepper**
- **Coarse sea salt, optional**

1 ear of corn with 2 Tbsp. butter: 225 cal., 13g fat (8g sat. fat), 31mg chol., 265mg sod., 27g carb. (9g sugars, 3g fiber), 5g pro.

HOW-TO

Cook Corn on the Cob on the Grill

1.

2.

3.

4.

1. Soak
Cover the corn with cold water and let the ears soak for 30 minutes. This prevents the husks from burning while cooking on the grill.

2. Grill
Over medium heat, grill the corn, covered, for 25-30 minutes or until the corn is tender. The husks will brown while the corn stays juicy.

3. Turn
While grilling, occasionally turn the ears so they cook evenly. Always re-cover the grill after turning. Meanwhile, comine the butter, zest, cilantro and seasonings.

4. Husk
Wearing oven mitts, carefully peel back the corn husks and remove the silk. Spread corn with the butter mixture.

EAT SMART | FAST FIX

GRILLED FISH SANDWICHES

season fish fillets with lime juice and emon pepper before grilling them. A simple honey mustard-mayo sauce puts these sandwiches ahead of the rest.
—Violet Beard, Marshall, IL

Takes: 20 min. • **Makes:** 4 servings

- **4 cod fillets (4 oz. each)**
- **1 Tbsp. lime juice**
- **½ tsp. lemon-pepper seasoning**
- **¼ cup fat-free mayonnaise**
- **2 tsp. Dijon mustard**
- **1 tsp. honey**
- **4 hamburger buns, split**
- **Lettuce leaves**
- **Tomato slices**

1. Brush cod with lime juice; sprinkle with lemon pepper. Place on an oiled grill rack over medium heat or in a greased 15x10x1-in. pan. Grill, covered, or broil 4 in. from heat until fish just begins to flake easily with a fork, 4-5 minutes per side.
2. Meanwhile, mix mayonnaise, mustard and honey; spread onto bun bottoms. Top with fish, lettuce, tomato and bun tops.
1 sandwich: 224 cal., 2g fat (1g sat. fat), 43mg chol., 499mg sod., 26g carb. (6g sugars, 1g fiber), 22g pro.

GRILLED FISH SANDWICHES

MOLASSES STEAK SANDWICHES

The classic steak and Swiss combo gets an added down-home sweetness thanks to a distinctive molasses-based marinade.
—*Taste of Home* Test Kitchen

Prep: 15 min. + marinating • **Grill:** 15 min.
Makes: 4 servings

- **¼ cup molasses**
- **2 Tbsp. brown sugar**
- **2 Tbsp. olive oil, divided**
- **1 Tbsp. Dijon mustard**
- **4 beef tenderloin steaks (1 in. thick and 4 oz. each)**
- **2 large portobello mushrooms, stems removed**
- **4 kaiser rolls, split**
- **4 slices Swiss cheese**

1. In a shallow dish, mix the molasses, brown sugar, 1 Tbsp. oil and mustard. Add steaks and turn to coat. Refrigerate up to 2 hours.
2. Drain beef, discarding the marinade. Brush mushrooms with remaining oil. Grill steaks, covered, over medium heat 5-7 minutes on each side or until meat reaches desired doneness (for medium-rare, a thermometer should read 135°; medium, 140°). Grill mushrooms, covered, until tender, turning occasionaly, 8-10 minutes. Remove steaks and mushrooms from grill; let stand 5 minutes.
3. Grill rolls, cut side down, until lightly toasted, 2-3 minutes. Cut steaks and mushrooms into slices. Serve in rolls with cheese.
1 sandwich: 452 cal., 17g fat (5g sat. fat), 59mg chol., 367mg sod., 40g carb. (9g sugars, 2g fiber), 34g pro.

GRILLED CHERRY-GLAZED CHICKEN WINGS

PICTURED ON P. 227

Cherry glaze makes grilled chicken wings into something special. When I take them to a party, there's never any left!
—Ashley Gable, Atlanta, GA

Prep: 20 min. • **Grill:** 15 min.
Makes: 1 dozen

- **12 chicken wings (about 3 lbs.)**
- **3 Tbsp. canola oil, divided**
- **1 garlic clove, minced**
- **1 cup ketchup**
- **½ cup cider vinegar**
- **½ cup cherry preserves**
- **2 Tbsp. Louisiana-style hot sauce**
- **1 Tbsp. Worcestershire sauce**
- **3 tsp. coarse salt, divided**
- **1 tsp. coarsely ground pepper, divided**

1. Using a sharp knife, cut through the two wing joints; discard wing tips.
2. In a small saucepan, heat 1 Tbsp. oil over medium heat. Add garlic; cook and stir 1 minute. Stir in ketchup, vinegar, preserves, hot sauce, Worcestershire sauce, 1 tsp. salt and ½ tsp. pepper. Cook and stir until heated through.
3. Brush wings with the remaining oil; sprinkle with remaining salt and pepper. Grill, covered, over medium heat for 15-18 minutes or until juices run clear, turning occasionally; brushing with glaze during the last 5 minutes of grilling. Serve with the remaining glaze.
1 chicken wing: 214 cal., 12g fat (3g sat. fat), 36mg chol., 867mg sod., 15g carb. (14g sugars, 0g fiber), 12g pro.

FAST FIX

VEGETABLE STEAK & EGGS

Low-carb doesn't have to be skimpy with this lighter take on steak and eggs. I love cooking with squash, but feel free to toss in any vegetable combination you like.
—Robert Deskin, Plantation, FL

Takes: 30 min. • **Makes:** 4 servings

- **1 beef skirt steak or flank steak (1 lb.)**
- **1 tsp. Montreal steak seasoning**
- **2 Tbsp. butter or coconut oil, divided**
- **1 medium zucchini, halved lengthwise and cut into ¼-in. slices**
- **1 medium yellow summer squash, halved lengthwise and cut into ¼-in. slices**
- **1 medium sweet red pepper, chopped**
- **5 oz. fresh baby spinach (about 6 cups)**
- **½ tsp. salt**
- **¼ tsp. pepper**
- **4 large eggs**
- **¼ cup shredded Parmesan cheese**

1. Rub steak with seasoning. Grill steak, covered, over medium-high heat or broil 3-4 in. from heat, 3-5 minutes on each side or until meat reaches desired doneness (for medium-rare, a thermometer should read 135°; medium, 140°; medium-well, 145°). Let stand 5 minutes.
2. Meanwhile, in a large nonstick skillet heat 1 Tbsp. butter over medium-high heat. Saute zucchini, squash and red pepper until crisp-tender, 5-7 minutes. Add spinach, salt and pepper; cook and stir until wilted, 2 minutes. Divide among four plates; keep warm.
3. In the same skillet, heat the remaining butter. Break eggs, one at a time, into pan; reduce heat to low. Cook to desired doneness. Thinly slice steak across the grain; serve over vegetables. Top with egg and cheese.

1 serving: 344 cal., 21g fat (10g sat. fat), 259mg chol., 770mg sod., 7g carb. (4g sugars, 2g fiber), 33g pro.

*** HEALTH TIP *** Swap canola oil for butter in this recipe and save a few grams of saturated fat per serving.

VEGETABLE STEAK & EGGS

FREEZE IT | EAT SMART | FAST FIX

SOUTHWEST TURKEY PATTIES WITH BEANS

PICTURED ON P. 227

These turkey patties are delicious and low in calories. Skip the rice if you're looking to cut carbs.
—Dot Carpenter, Washington, PA

Takes: 30 min. • **Makes:** 4 servings

- **⅓ cup shredded carrots**
- **⅓ cup finely chopped onion**
- **⅓ cup finely chopped green pepper**
- **¼ tsp. salt**
- **¼ tsp. pepper**
- **¾ lb. lean ground turkey**
- **1 can (15 oz.) black beans, rinsed and drained**
- **1 can (10 oz.) diced tomatoes and green chiles, undrained**
- **2 Tbsp. chopped fresh cilantro**
- **2 cups hot cooked brown rice**

1. In a large bowl, combine first five ingredients. Add turkey; mix lightly but thoroughly. Shape into four ½-in.-thick oval patties.
2. In a small saucepan, heat beans and tomatoes over medium heat, 8-10 minutes, stirring occasionally. Remove from heat; stir in cilantro. Keep warm.
3. Grill patties, covered, over medium heat or broil 4-5 in. from heat until a thermometer reads 165°, 4-5 minutes per side. Serve with rice and bean mixture.

Freeze option: Place patties on a waxed paper-lined baking sheet; wrap and freeze until firm. Remove from pan and transfer to an airtight container; return to freezer. To use, grill or broil frozen patties as directed, increasing time as necessary for a thermometer to read 165°.

1 serving: 356 cal., 8g fat (2g sat. fat), 59mg chol., 693mg sod., 46g carb. (2g sugars, 7g fiber), 25g pro. **Diabetic exchanges:** 3 starch, 3 lean meat.

5 INGREDIENTS | EAT SMART | FAST FIX

EASY GRILLED SQUASH

Butternut squash pairs beautifully with grilled steak or chicken—and is full of healthy vitamin A. This is one of my favorite ways to prepare it.
—Esther Horst, Monterey, TN

Takes: 20 min. • **Makes:** 4 servings

- **3 Tbsp. olive oil**
- **2 garlic cloves, minced**
- **¼ tsp. salt**
- **¼ tsp. pepper**
- **1 small butternut squash, peeled and cut lengthwise into ½-in. slices**

1. In a small bowl, combine the oil, garlic, salt and pepper. Brush over squash slices.
2. Grill squash, covered, over medium heat or broil 4 in. from the heat for 4-5 minutes on each side or until tender.
2 slices: 178 cal., 10g fat (1g sat. fat), 0 chol., 156mg sod., 23g carb. (5g sugars, 7g fiber), 2g pro. **Diabetic exchanges:** 1½ starch, 1½ fat.

FAST FIX

QUICK BARBECUED BEANS

PICTURED ON P. 227

This classic recipe gains subtle flavor from its time on the grill. It features a nice blend of beans and preparation time is minimal.
—Millie Vickery, Lena, IL

Takes: 25 min. • **Makes:** 5 servings

- **1 can (16 oz.) kidney beans, rinsed and drained**
- **1 can (15½ oz.) great northern beans, rinsed and drained**
- **1 can (15 oz.) pork and beans**
- **½ cup barbecue sauce**
- **2 Tbsp. brown sugar**
- **2 tsp. prepared mustard**

In an ungreased 8-in. square disposable foil pan, combine all the ingredients. Grill, covered, over medium heat 15-20 minutes or until heated through; stir occasionally.
¾ cup: 264 cal., 2g fat (0 sat. fat), 0 chol., 877mg sod., 51g carb. (15g sugars, 13g fiber), 14g pro.

EASY GRILLED SQUASH

ITALIAN MEATBALL KABOBS

When the temperature ramps up, these deliciously different kabobs are so fun to throw on the grill! Add a salad and rustic bread to make a complete summer meal.
—Marie Rizzio, Interlochen, MI

Prep: 30 min. • **Grill:** 10 min.
Makes: 12 kabobs

- **2 large eggs, lightly beaten**
- **⅔ cup seasoned bread crumbs**
- **½ cup grated Parmesan cheese**
- **¼ cup minced fresh parsley**
- **4 tsp. Italian seasoning**
- **½ tsp. salt**
- **½ tsp. garlic powder**
- **2½ lbs. ground beef**
- **1 medium onion, cut into 1-in. pieces**
- **1 medium sweet red pepper, cut into 1-in. pieces**
- **1 medium zucchini, cut into 1-in. pieces**
- **½ small eggplant, cut into 1-in. pieces**
- **½ cup balsamic vinegar**
- **½ cup olive oil**

1. In a large bowl, combine the first seven ingredients. Crumble beef over mixture and mix well. Shape into 1½-in. balls.
2. On 12 metal or soaked wooden skewers, alternately thread meatballs and vegetables. In a small bowl, combine vinegar and oil.
3. Grill kabobs, covered, over medium heat for 8-10 minutes or until meatballs are no longer pink and the vegetables are tender. Baste frequently with vinegar mixture and turn occasionally.
1 kabob: 325 cal., 22g fat (6g sat. fat), 97mg chol., 315mg sod., 10g carb. (4g sugars, 2g fiber), 21g pro.

BACON-CORN STUFFED PEPPERS

EAT SMART

BACON-CORN STUFFED PEPPERS

Filled with corn, salsa, green onions, mozzarella cheese and bacon, these grilled pepper halves are sure to liven up your next cookout. They give a fun twist to the usual corn on the cob.
—Mitzi Sentiff, Annapolis, MD

Prep: 20 min. • **Grill:** 25 min.
Makes: 4 servings

2 cups frozen corn, thawed
⅓ cup salsa
6 green onions, chopped
1 medium green pepper, halved and seeded
1 medium sweet red pepper, halved and seeded
¼ cup shredded part-skim mozzarella cheese
2 bacon strips, cooked and crumbled
Additional salsa, optional

1. In a large bowl, combine the corn, salsa and onions. Spoon into pepper halves. Place each stuffed pepper half on a piece of heavy-duty foil (about 18x12 in.). Fold foil around peppers and seal tightly.

2. Grill, covered, over medium heat for 25-30 minutes or until peppers are crisp-tender. Carefully open packets to allow steam to escape. Sprinkle with cheese and bacon. Return to the grill until cheese is melted, 3-5 minutes. Serve with additional salsa if desired.

1 stuffed pepper half: 130 cal., 4g fat (1g sat. fat), 9mg chol., 207mg sod., 21g carb. (5g sugars, 3g fiber), 6g pro. **Diabetic exchanges:** 1 starch, 1 vegetable, ½ fat.

EAT SMART | FAST FIX

SUMMER TURKEY KABOBS

PICTURED ON P. 227

These kabobs let you enjoy Thanksgiving flavors any time of year! We enjoy grilling them in the back yard in the summer.
—Angela Mathews, Fayetteville, NY

Takes: 30 min. • **Makes:** 6 kabobs

2 small yellow summer squash
2 small zucchini
1 can (about 15 oz.) whole potatoes, drained
2 Tbsp. olive oil
1 pkg. (20 oz.) turkey breast tenderloins
½ tsp. pepper
¼ tsp. salt
1 pkg. (5 oz.) torn mixed salad greens
1 cup salad croutons
½ cup red wine vinaigrette

1. Trim the ends of the yellow squash and zucchini; cut crosswise into 1-in. slices. Place the slices in a large bowl; add potatoes. Pour oil over the mixture, tossing to coat.
2. Cut turkey tenderloins into 24 cubes; add to the vegetables. Stir in pepper and salt; toss again.
3. On six metal or soaked wooden skewers, alternately thread turkey cubes, squash, zucchini and potatoes. Grill, covered, over medium heat, turning occasionally, until the turkey is no longer pink and the vegetables are crisp-tender, 12-15 minutes. Serve on greens with croutons. Drizzle with vinaigrette.

1 kabob: 274 cal., 13g fat (1g sat. fat), 38mg chol., 720mg sod., 15g carb. (3g sugars, 2g fiber), 26g pro. **Diabetic exchanges:** 2 lean meat, 1 vegetable, 1 fat, ½ starch.

AST FIX

FRUIT-GLAZED PORK CHOPS

PICTURED ON P. 227

These delectably grilled chops are done in less than half an hour. You can easily substitue other fruit preserves. They also broil nicely in the oven.
—Edie DeSpain, Logan, UT

Takes: 20 min. • **Makes:** 6 servings

- **⅓ cup hickory smoke-flavored barbecue sauce**
- **½ cup apricot or peach preserves**
- **1 Tbsp. corn syrup**
- **1 tsp. prepared mustard**
- **¼ tsp. ground cloves**
- **6 bone-in pork loin chops (¾ in. thick and 8 oz. each)**
- **½ tsp. salt**
- **½ tsp. pepper**

1. In a small bowl, combine the barbecue sauce, preserves, corn syrup, mustard and cloves; set aside.
2. Sprinkle pork chops with salt and pepper. On a lightly oiled grill, grill chops, covered, over medium heat or broil 4-5 in. from the heat for 4-5 minutes on each side or until a thermometer reads 145°; baste frequently with sauce mixture. Let meat stand for 5 minutes before serving.
1 pork chop: 336 cal., 10g fat (4g sat. fat), 98mg chol., 446mg sod., 26g carb. (19g sugars, 0 fiber), 35g pro.

FAST FIX

CHUTNEY TURKEY BURGERS

The secret to these burgers is the tangy mango chutney, but the arugula adds a special "Wow!" to the plate. I get lots of compliments when these appear at summer or fall cookouts.
—Jeanne Lueders, Weatherby Lake, MO

Takes: 25 min. • **Makes:** 4 servings

- **½ cup mango chutney, divided**
- **1 Tbsp. Dijon mustard**
- **2 tsp. lime juice**
- **¼ cup minced fresh parsley**
- **2 green onions, chopped**
- **½ tsp. salt**
- **¼ tsp. pepper**
- **1 lb. lean ground turkey**
- **4 hamburger buns, split**
- **Fresh arugula or baby spinach leaves**
- **Thinly sliced red onion**

1. For the sauce, mix ¼ cup of chutney, the mustard and lime juice. In a large bowl, combine parsley, green onions, salt, pepper and the remaining chutney. Add turkey; mix lightly but thoroughly. Shape into four ½-in.-thick patties.
2. Place burgers on a lightly oiled grill rack over medium heat or in a greased 15x10x1-in. pan. Grill, covered, or broil 3-4 in. from heat until a thermometer reads 165°, 5-7 minutes per side. Serve on buns with arugula, onion and sauce.
1 burger: 419 cal., 10g fat (3g sat. fat), 78mg chol., 1012mg sod., 51g carb. (21g sugars, 1g fiber), 27g pro.

EAT SMART | FAST FIX

GRILLED STEAK PINWHEELS

Living in Arizona, we try to keep the house cool, so we grill out often. I get most of the herbs in this recipe from my son's garden. I've been serving this to family and friends for 20 years and there are seldom any leftovers!
—Rhonda Knight, Scottsdale, AZ

Takes: 30 min. • **Makes:** 8 servings

- **2 beef flank steaks (1 lb. each), trimmed**
- **½ lb. bacon strips, cooked and crumbled**
- **1 cup finely chopped fresh mushrooms**
- **1 cup finely chopped green onions**
- **¼ cup finely chopped fresh basil or 4 tsp. dried basil**
- **2 Tbsp. minced chives**

1. Flatten steaks to ¼-in. In a large bowl, combine bacon, mushrooms, onions, basil and chives; spread evenly over the steaks.
2. Roll the meat up and secure with skewers or toothpicks. Cut each roll into ½- to ¾-in. slices and secure each with a toothpick.
3. Grill over medium-hot heat for 4-6 minutes on each side until meat reaches desired doneness (for medium-rare, a thermometer should read 135°; medium, 140°; medium-well, 145°). Remove toothpicks before serving.
2 pinwheels: 224 cal., 12g fat (5g sat. fat), 64mg chol., 250mg sod., 1g carb. (0 sugars, 0 fiber), 26g pro. **Diabetic exchanges:** 3 medium-fat meat.

GRILLED STEAK PINWHEELS

HERBED PORK CHOPS

5 INGREDIENTS | EAT SMART | FAST FIX

HERBED PORK CHOPS

Herbs are a fast and flavorful way to dress up pork. Plus, they make the chops look so pretty on a platter! I prepare these year-round as a way to capture the taste of summer.

—Dianne Esposite, New Middletown, OH

Takes: 20 min. • **Makes:** 4 servings

- **4 boneless pork loin chops (4 oz. each)**
- **2 tsp. lemon juice**
- **2 Tbsp. chopped fresh parsley**
- **½ tsp. dried rosemary, crushed**
- **½ tsp. dried thyme, crushed**
- **¼ tsp. pepper**

1. Sprinkle pork chops with lemon juice. In a small bowl, combine the parsley, rosemary, thyme and pepper; rub over the chops.

2. Grill, covered, over medium heat for 4-5 minutes on each side or until a thermometer reads 145°. Let the meat stand for 5 minutes before serving.

1 pork chop: 154 cal., 6g fat (2g sat. fat), 55mg chol., 33mg sod., 1g carb. (0 sugars, 0 fiber), 22g pro. **Diabetic exchanges:** 3 lean meat.

5 INGREDIENTS | FAST FIX

GRILLED CAJUN GREEN BEANS

I created this recipe when the weather was hot and I didn't want to cook in the house. I threw the green beans on the grill and forgot about them, and they turned out fabulous! These are such a hit with my family that I'm often asked to bring them to our get-togethers.

—Shannon Lewis, Andover, MN

Takes: 30 min. • **Makes:** 4 servings

- **1 lb. fresh green beans, trimmed**
- **½ tsp. Cajun seasoning**
- **1 Tbsp. butter**

1. Place the green beans on a double thickness of heavy-duty foil (about 18 in. square). Sprinkle with Cajun seasoning and dot with butter. Fold foil around beans, sealing tightly.

2. Grill, covered, over medium heat 9-11 minutes on each side or until the beans are tender. Open foil carefully to allow steam to escape.

¾ cup: 56 cal., 3g fat (2g sat. fat), 8mg chol., 109mg sod., 7g carb. (3g sugars, 3g fiber), 2g pro. **Diabetic exchanges:** 1 vegetable, ½ fat.

EAT SMART

TACOS ON A STICK

Kids like assembling these creative kabobs almost as much as they like devouring them. The sensational southwestern flavor is a taco-night twist on traditional beef shish kabobs.

—Dixie Terry, Goreville, IL

Prep: 15 min. + marinating • **Grill:** 15 min.
Makes: 6 servings

- **1 envelope taco seasoning**
- **1 cup tomato juice**
- **2 Tbsp. canola oil**
- **2 lbs. beef top sirloin steak, cut into 1-in. cubes**
- **1 medium green pepper, cut into chunks**
- **1 medium sweet red pepper, cut into chunks**
- **1 large onion, cut into wedges**
- **16 cherry tomatoes**
- **Salsa con queso or sour cream, optional**

1. In a large bowl or dish, combine the taco seasoning, tomato juice and oil; mix well. Remove ½ cup for basting; refrigerate. Add beef to the bowl and turn to coat. Refrigerate for at least 5 hours.

2. Drain and discard the marinade from the beef. On metal or soaked wooden skewers, alternately thread beef, peppers, onion and tomatoes. Grill, uncovered, over medium heat for 3 minutes on each side. Baste with the reserved marinade. Continue turning and basting until meat reaches desired doneness, 8-10 minutes. If desired, serve with salsa con queso or sour cream.

1 kabob: 277 cal., 10g fat (3g sat. fat), 61mg chol., 665mg sod., 12g carb. (4g sugars, 2g fiber), 34g pro. **Diabetic exchanges:** 4 lean meat, 2 vegetable, 1 fat.

TACOS ON A STICK

BLUEBERRY CHOPS WITH CINNAMON SWEET POTATOES

The sweet and spicy combo is the perfect accent for the meaty chops. Serve the pork on a bed of cinnamon-spiked mashed sweet potatoes to really set off the flavor of the blueberries! With a fresh green veggie, it's a hearty meal but lighter than traditional meat and potatoes.
—Laura Davis, Chincoteague, VA

Prep: 40 min. • **Grill:** 10 min.
Makes: 4 servings

- **1 cup fresh or frozen blueberries**
- **¼ cup water**
- **3 Tbsp. brown sugar**
- **1 Tbsp. red wine vinegar**
- **1 Tbsp. chopped chipotle peppers in adobo sauce**

SWEET POTATOES

- **1½ lbs. sweet potatoes (about 2 medium), peeled and cut into 1-in. cubes**
- **2 Tbsp. butter**
- **1 Tbsp. packed brown sugar**
- **1 Tbsp. half-and-half cream**
- **¼ tsp. kosher salt**
- **¼ tsp. ground cinnamon**

PORK

- **4 pork rib chops (1 in. thick and 8 oz. each)**
- **2 tsp. kosher salt**
- **1 tsp. coarsely ground pepper**

1. For the sauce, combine the first five ingredients in a small saucepan; bring to a boil over medium-high heat. Reduce heat; simmer, uncovered, until liquid is reduced by half, 8-10 minutes. Remove from heat; keep warm.

2. Place sweet potatoes with water to cover in a large saucepan; bring to a boil. Reduce heat; cook, uncovered, until tender, 10-15 minutes. Drain; return to pan. Mash potatoes until smooth, adding butter, brown sugar, cream, salt and cinnamon. Cover; keep warm.

3. Meanwhile, preheat grill or broiler. Sprinkle pork chops with salt and pepper. Grill, covered, over medium heat or broil 4 in. from heat on a broiler pan until a thermometer reads 145°, 4-6 minutes per side. Remove from heat; let stand, covered, 5 minutes. Serve over sweet potatoes; top with sauce.

1 serving: 520 cal., 16g fat (8g sat. fat), 90mg chol., 1216mg sod., 61g carb. (34g sugars, 6g fiber), 32g pro.

TEST KITCHEN TIP

If you're making this dish for company, you can prepare the potatoes and sauce ahead of time and keep them warm. Cook the chops just before serving.

FAST FIX

GRILLED ANGEL FOOD CAKE WITH FRUIT SALSA

When I need dessert fast, I go with this cake. Mix the fruit salsa ahead of time, and pop the cake on the grill.
—Glorimar Jimenez, Indianapolis, IN

Takes: 15 min. • **Makes:** 6 servings

- **½ cup each fresh raspberries, blueberries and chopped strawberries**
- **1 medium kiwifruit, peeled and chopped**
- **2 Tbsp. sugar**
- **1 Tbsp. lime juice**
- **1 loaf-shaped angel food cake (10½ oz.), split horizontally**
- **Whipped topping, optional**

In a small bowl, combine berries, kiwi, sugar and lime juice. Grill cake, cut side down, over medium heat or broil 4 in. from heat 1-3 minutes or until lightly browned. Cut into slices. Serve with fruit salsa and, if desired, whipped topping.

1 slice with ¼ cup salsa: 169 cal., 1g fat (0 sat. fat), 0 chol., 372mg sod., 39g carb. (30g sugars, 2g fiber), 3g pro.

GRILLED ANGEL FOOD CAKE WITH FRUIT SALSA

ROMANO BASIL TURKEY BREAST

Guests will appreciate slices of this golden, grilled turkey breast, dressed up with a flavorful layer of basil and cheese under the skin.
—Darlene Markham, Rochester, NY

Prep: 15 min. • **Grill:** 1½ hours + standing
Makes: 8 servings

- **1 cup Romano cheese, shredded**
- **½ cup fresh basil leaves, chopped**
- **4 lemon slices**
- **4 garlic cloves, minced**
- **1 bone-in turkey breast (4 to 5 lbs.)**
- **2 Tbsp. olive oil**
- **½ tsp. salt**
- **¼ tsp. pepper**

1. Combine the cheese, basil, lemon slices and garlic. With fingers, carefully loosen skin from the turkey breast; place mixture under the skin. Secure skin to underside of breast with toothpicks. Rub skin with oil and sprinkle with salt and pepper.
2. Prepare grill for indirect heat, using a drip pan. Place turkey over drip pan. Grill, covered, over indirect medium heat until a thermometer reads 170°, 1½-2 hours. Remove toothpicks. Cover and let stand for 10 minutes before slicing.
6 oz. cooked turkey: 402 cal., 20g fat (7g sat. fat), 136mg chol., 493mg sod., 1g carb. (0 sugars, 0 fiber), 53g pro.

ROMANO BASIL TURKEY BREAST

CAMPFIRE POTATOES

Butter, onion and cheddar cheese combine to make a delectable potato side dish for any grilled meat. Cooking in the foil packet makes cleanup a breeze.
—JoAnn Dettbarn, Brainerd, MN

Prep: 5 min. • **Grill:** 35 min.
Makes: 4-6 servings

- **5 medium potatoes, peeled and thinly sliced**
- **1 medium onion, sliced**
- **6 Tbsp. butter**
- **⅓ cup shredded cheddar cheese**
- **2 Tbsp. minced fresh parsley**
- **1 Tbsp. Worcestershire sauce**
- **Salt and pepper to taste**
- **⅓ cup chicken broth**

1. Place the potatoes and onion on a large piece of heavy-duty foil (about 20x20 in.); dot with butter. Combine the cheese, parsley, Worcestershire sauce, salt and pepper; sprinkle over potatoes.
2. Fold foil up around potatoes and add broth. Seal the edges of the foil well. Grill, covered, over medium heat for 35-40 minutes or until the potatoes are tender.
1 cup: 276 cal., 13g fat (8g sat. fat), 37mg chol., 245mg sod., 35g carb. (4g sugars, 3g fiber), 6g pro.

5 INGREDIENTS | **EAT SMART**

DIJON GRILLED PORK CHOPS

The recipe for these savory chops with a sweet and tangy apple-mustard marinade came from my mom. With a vegetable and some rice or pasta, you have a feast!
—Babette Watterson, Atglen, PA

Prep: 10 min. + marinating • **Grill:** 10 min.
Makes: 4 servings

- **6 Tbsp. brown sugar**
- **6 Tbsp. Dijon mustard**
- **3 Tbsp. unsweetened apple juice**
- **3 Tbsp. Worcestershire sauce**
- **4 bone-in pork loin chops (8 oz. each)**

1. For the marinade, in a small bowl, mix the first four ingredients. Place the pork chops and ⅔ cup of marinade in a large bowl or dish; turn to coat. Reserve the remaining marinade; cover and refrigerate with pork 8 hours or overnight.
2. Place the chops on a lightly oiled grill rack over medium heat; discard the marinade remaining in the bowl. Grill the chops, covered, until a thermometer reads 145°, 4-6 minutes per side, basting with the reserved marinade during the last 3 minutes. Let stand for 5 minutes before serving.
1 pork chop: 295 cal., 10g fat (4g sat. fat), 98mg chol., 408mg sod., 13g carb. (12g sugars, 0 fiber), 34g pro. **Diabetic exchanges:** 1 starch, 4 lean meat.

FAST FIX
SAUSAGE SQUASH KABOBS

Expect a crowd to gather around the grill when these flavorful kabobs are cooking. The zesty honey-mustard glaze gives a lovely sheen to the sausage and veggies.
—Lisa Malynn-Kent,
North Richland Hills, TX

Takes: 20 min. • **Makes:** 4 servings

- **1 lb. small red potatoes**
- **1 Tbsp. water**
- **½ cup honey**
- **¼ cup Dijon mustard**
- **½ tsp. grated orange zest**
- **1 lb. smoked turkey kielbasa, sliced ½ in. thick**
- **2 small yellow summer squash, sliced ½ in. thick**
- **2 small zucchini, sliced ½ in. thick**

1. In a large microwave-safe bowl, combine the potatoes and water. Cover and microwave on high 6-8 minutes or until tender; drain and set aside. For the glaze, combine the honey, mustard and orange zest in a small bowl.
2. On eight metal or soaked wooden skewers, alternately thread the sausage, potatoes, yellow squash and zucchini; brush with half of the glaze.
3. On a lightly oiled grill rack, grill kabobs, uncovered, over medium heat or broil 4 in. from the heat for 10-16 minutes or until the vegetables are tender and the sausage is heated through, turning and basting frequently with glaze.

2 kabobs: 385 cal., 7g fat (2g sat. fat), 71mg chol., 1491mg sod., 58g carb. (40g sugars, 3g fiber), 22g pro.

SPINACH & MUSHROOM SMOTHERED CHICKEN

EAT SMART | FAST FIX
SPINACH & MUSHROOM SMOTHERED CHICKEN

Chicken breasts stay nice and moist tucked under their blanket of melted cheese. This dish is extra special to serve but not at all tricky to make.
—Katrina Wagner, Grain Valley, MO

Takes: 30 min. • **Makes:** 4 servings

- **1½ tsp. olive oil**
- **1¾ cups sliced fresh mushrooms**
- **3 green onions, sliced**
- **3 cups fresh baby spinach**
- **2 Tbsp. chopped pecans**
- **4 boneless skinless chicken breast halves (4 oz. each)**
- **½ tsp. rotisserie chicken seasoning**
- **2 slices reduced-fat provolone cheese, halved**

1. Preheat grill or broiler. In a large skillet, heat oil over medium-high heat; saute mushrooms and green onions until tender. Stir in spinach and pecans until the spinach is wilted. Remove from heat; keep warm.
2. Sprinkle the chicken with seasoning. Grill, covered, on an oiled grill rack over medium heat or broil 4 in. from heat on a greased broiler pan until a thermometer reads 165°, 4-5 minutes per side. Top with provolone cheese; grill or broil until cheese is melted. To serve, top with the mushroom mixture.

1 serving: 203 cal., 9g fat (2g sat. fat), 68mg chol., 210mg sod., 3g carb. (1g sugars, 2g fiber), 27g pro. **Diabetic exchanges:** 3 lean meat, 1 vegetable, 1 fat.

*** HEALTH TIP *** This low-carb main dish is also gluten-free.

5 INGREDIENTS

GRILLED SWEET POTATOES WITH GORGONZOLA SPREAD

My husband first tried this recipe with plain potatoes. Then we tried sweet potatoes—they were even better! With the Gorgonzola, they're irresistible.
—Kristen Minello, Macomb, MI

Prep: 25 min. • **Grill:** 10 min.
Makes: 8 servings

- **4 large sweet potatoes**
- **1 cup (4 oz.) crumbled Gorgonzola cheese**
- **½ cup mayonnaise**
- **1 to 2 Tbsp. lemon juice**
- **3 Tbsp. olive oil**
- **½ tsp. salt**
- **¼ tsp. pepper**
- **Minced chives, optional**

1. Scrub and pierce sweet potatoes with a fork; place on a microwave-safe plate. Microwave, uncovered, on high just until tender, turning once, 6-8 minutes.

2. Meanwhile, in a small bowl, combine cheese, mayonnaise and lemon juice. Refrigerate until serving.

3. Slice potatoes into ½-in.-thick rounds; brush both sides with oil. Sprinkle with salt and pepper. Grill, covered, over medium heat or broil 4 in. from heat on each side until browned, 4-5 minutes. Serve with spread. If desired, sprinkle with chives.

1 serving with 3 Tbsp. spread: 362 cal., 19g fat (5g sat. fat), 14mg chol., 425mg sod., 42g carb. (17g sugars, 6g fiber), 6g pro.

FAST FIX

GRILLED PORK BURGERS

We live on a working hog farm and love this savory burger made with fresh pork. Everyone will love these burgers—even if your pork comes from the grocery store!
—Dawnita Phillips, Drexel, MO

Takes: 25 min. • **Makes:** 6 servings

- **1 large egg, lightly beaten**
- **¾ cup soft bread crumbs**
- **¾ cup grated Parmesan cheese**
- **1 Tbsp. dried parsley flakes**
- **2 tsp. dried basil**
- **½ tsp. salt**
- **½ tsp. garlic powder**
- **¼ tsp. pepper**
- **2 lbs. ground pork**
- **6 hamburger buns, split**
- **Lettuce leaves, sliced tomato and sweet onion, optional**

1. In a large bowl, combine the first eight ingredients. Crumble pork over the mixture and mix well. Shape into six patties.

2. Grill burgers, covered, over medium heat for 4-5 minutes on each side or until a thermometer reads 160°. Serve the burgers on buns; top with lettuce, tomato and onion if desired.

1 burger: 522 cal., 28g fat (11g sat. fat), 145mg chol., 690mg sod., 28g carb. (4g sugars, 2g fiber), 38g pro.

GRILLED SWEET POTATOES WITH GORGONZOLA SPREAD

Potlucks & Parties

Open house, game day, church supper or office party—the delicious recipes in this chapter all feed a crowd. Whether you're dressing up or down, you'll find something to keep your guests happy.

Fudgy Macaroon Bars (p. 249) **Pepper Jack Hash Brown Casserole** (p. 245) **One-Pot Bacon Cheeseburger Pasta** (p. 246) **Zippy Party Roll-Ups** (p. 253) **Chili Queso Dip** (p. 252)

SLOW-COOKER PIZZA DIP

FREEZE IT

FIESTA PINWHEELS

Whenever I serve these appetizers, they disappear fast. A friend from the office shared them with me, and after one bite I knew I'd be bringing her recipe home.
—Diane Martin, Brown Deer, WI

Prep: 15 min. + chilling
Makes: about 5 dozen

- **1 pkg. (8 oz.) cream cheese, softened**
- **½ cup sour cream**
- **¼ cup picante sauce**
- **2 Tbsp. taco seasoning**
- **Dash garlic powder**
- **1 can (4½ oz.) chopped ripe olives, drained**
- **1 can (4 oz.) chopped green chilies**
- **1 cup finely shredded cheddar cheese**
- **½ cup thinly sliced green onions**
- **8 flour tortillas (10 in.)**
- **Salsa**

1. In a small bowl, beat cream cheese, sour cream, picante sauce, taco seasoning and garlic powder until smooth. Stir in olives, chilies, cheese and onions. Spread about ½ cup on each tortilla.

2. Roll up jelly-roll style; wrap in plastic. Refrigerate for 2 hours or overnight. Slice into 1-in. pieces. Serve with salsa.

Freeze option: Pinwheels may be prepared ahead and frozen. Thaw in refrigerator.

3 pinwheels: 170 cal., 9g fat (5g sat. fat), 22mg chol., 402mg sod., 15g carb. (1g sugars, 3g fiber), 5g pro.

SLOW COOKER | FREEZE IT

SLOW-COOKER PIZZA DIP

I created this dip for my daughter's pizza-themed birthday party. It was such a hit I've continued to bring it to other gatherings. Everyone loves it!
—Stephanie Gates, Waterloo, IA

Prep: 15 min. • **Cook:** 2 hours
Makes: 20 servings

- **½ lb. ground beef**
- **½ lb. bulk pork sausage**
- **1 can (28 oz.) crushed tomatoes**
- **½ cup diced green pepper**
- **¼ cup grated Parmesan cheese**
- **2 Tbsp. tomato paste**
- **2 tsp. Italian seasoning**
- **1 garlic clove, minced**
- **¾ tsp. crushed red pepper flakes**
- **¼ tsp. salt**
- **¼ tsp. pepper**
- **Hot garlic bread**

In a large skillet, cook and crumble beef and sausage over medium heat until no longer pink, 5-7 minutes. Using a slotted spoon, transfer meat to a 3-qt. slow cooker. Stir in all remaining ingredients except garlic bread. Cook, covered, on low until heated through, 2-3 hours. Serve with garlic bread.

Freeze option: Freeze cooled dip in freezer containers. To use, partially thaw in refrigerator overnight. Heat through in a saucepan, stirring occasionally.

¼ cup dip: 68 cal., 4g fat (1g sat. fat), 14mg chol., 198mg sod., 4g carb. (2g sugars, 1g fiber), 4g pro.

TEST KITCHEN TIP

You can use 1 pound of Italian sausage instead of the ½ pound ground beef and ½ pound pork sausage.

Top this dip with sliced ripe olives, pepperoni or grated Parm and dried oregano for even more pizza flavor.

SPINACH ARTICHOKE-STUFFED MUSHROOMS

I used this recipe when I was in a culinary arts program and had to prepare an entire buffet by myself. It's an impressive party appetizer yet goes together so easily.
—Amy Gaisford, Salt Lake City, UT

Prep: 20 min. • **Bake:** 20 min.
Makes: about 2½ dozen

- **3 oz. cream cheese, softened**
- **½ cup mayonnaise**
- **½ cup sour cream**
- **¾ tsp. garlic salt**
- **1 can (14 oz.) water-packed artichoke hearts, rinsed, drained and chopped**
- **1 pkg. (10 oz.) frozen chopped spinach, thawed and squeezed dry**
- **⅓ cup shredded part-skim mozzarella cheese**
- **3 Tbsp. shredded Parmesan cheese**
- **30 to 35 large fresh mushrooms, stems removed**
- **Additional shredded Parmesan cheese, optional**

1. Preheat oven to 400°. Mix first four ingredients. Stir in artichoke hearts, spinach, mozzarella cheese and 3 Tbsp. Parmesan cheese.
2. Place mushrooms on foil-lined baking sheets, stem side up. Spoon about 1 Tbsp. filling into each. If desired, top with additional Parmesan cheese. Bake until mushrooms are tender, 16-20 minutes.

1 stuffed mushroom: 51 cal., 4g fat (1g sat. fat), 4mg chol., 116mg sod., 2g carb. (0 sugars, 0 fiber), 2g pro.

So-Easy Stuffed Mushrooms: Omit first eight ingredients. Mix 1 package (6½ oz.) garlic-herb spreadable cheese and 2 Tbsp. Parmesan cheese. Fill mushroom caps; sprinkle with 1 Tbsp. Parmesan cheese. Reduce baking time to 10-12 minutes.

Sausage-Stuffed Mushrooms: Omit first eight ingredients. Finely chop mushroom stems. Cook ½ pound bulk sausage and chopped mushrooms over medium heat until meat is no longer pink; drain. Remove from heat; stir in ½ cup shredded mozzarella cheese and ¼ cup seasoned bread crumbs. Fill and bake as recipe directs.

Canadian Bacon-Stuffed Mushrooms: Omit first eight ingredients. Finely chop mushroom stems. Cook mushrooms, ¼ pound diced Canadian bacon, ⅓ cup sweet red pepper, ¼ cup chopped red onion, ½ tsp. salt and ½ tsp. pepper in 2 Tbsp. canola oil until vegetables are crisp-tender. Add 1 minced garlic clove; cook 1 minute. Remove from heat; stir in ½ cup crumbled goat or feta cheese and ½ cup shredded cheddar cheese. Fill and bake as recipe directs.

SPINACH ARTICHOKE-STUFFED MUSHROOMS

PEPPER JACK HASH BROWN CASSEROLE

PICTURED ON P. 243

I found myself in need of an impromptu potato dish, but I had no potatoes. Frozen hash browns and the plethora of cheeses I keep in the freezer offered me a perfect solution to my side-dish dilemma.
—Cyndy Gerken, Naples, FL

Prep: 25 min. • **Bake:** 30 min.
Makes: 12 servings

- **1 pkg. (30 oz.) frozen shredded hash brown potatoes, thawed**
- **1 can (10½ oz.) condensed cream of chicken soup, undiluted**
- **2 cups shredded pepper jack cheese**
- **1½ cups heavy whipping cream**
- **½ cup butter, melted**
- **½ cup sour cream**
- **¼ cup shredded Parmesan cheese**
- **½ tsp. salt**
- **½ tsp. onion powder**
- **¼ tsp. garlic powder**
- **¼ tsp. pepper**

TOPPING

- **1 cup crushed potato chips**
- **5 bacon strips, cooked and crumbled**
- **¾ cup shredded Parmesan cheese**
- **1 tsp. paprika**

1. Preheat oven to 350°. In a large bowl, combine the first 11 ingredients. Transfer to a greased 13x9-in. baking dish.
2. For topping, combine crushed potato chips, bacon and Parmesan; sprinkle over casserole. Top with paprika.
3. Bake, uncovered, until the edges are bubbly and the topping is golden brown, 25-30 minutes.

⅔ cup: 416 cal., 33g fat (19g sat. fat), 87mg chol., 682mg sod., 20g carb. (2g sugars, 2g fiber), 12g pro.

POTATO & CHORIZO CASSEROLE

I love the smoky flavor chorizo gives this dish, but I've also made it with Italian sausage and swapped out the Mexican cheese for an Italian blend. Or you can use cream of mushroom soup and fresh mushrooms for a vegetarian option.
—Ana Beteta, Aberdeen, MD

Prep: 25 min. • **Bake:** 40 min.
Makes: 12 servings

- **8 oz. fresh chorizo or bulk spicy pork sausage**
- **1 pkg. (32 oz.) frozen cubed hash brown potatoes, thawed**
- **1 can (10½ oz.) condensed cream of chicken soup, undiluted**
- **2 cups shredded Mexican cheese blend**
- **1 pkg. (8 oz.) cream cheese, cubed**
- **1 medium onion, chopped**
- **1 small sweet red pepper, chopped**
- **1 small green pepper, chopped**
- **½ tsp. crushed red pepper flakes**
- **¾ cup panko (Japanese) bread crumbs**
- **Chopped fresh parsley and cilantro**

1. Preheat oven to 375°. In a small skillet, cook chorizo over medium heat until cooked through, breaking into crumbles, 5-7 minutes; drain. Transfer to a large bowl. Stir in the hash browns, soup, cheeses, onion, peppers and pepper flakes. Transfer to a greased 13x9-in. baking dish. Sprinkle with panko.
2. Bake, uncovered, until golden brown and bubbly, 40-45 minutes. Sprinkle with parsley and cilantro before serving.

¾ cup: 316 cal., 20g fat (9g sat. fat), 54mg chol., 611mg sod., 22g carb. (3g sugars, 2g fiber), 12g pro.

POTATO & CHORIZO CASSEROLE

ONE-POT BACON CHEESEBURGER PASTA

PICTURED ON P. 243

When it's too chilly to grill burgers, I whip up a pot of this cheesy pasta. Believe it or not, it tastes like a bacon cheeseburger, and it's much easier for my young children to enjoy. For a more grown-up taste, use Dijon mustard!
—Carly Terrell, Granbury, TX

Prep: 15 min. • **Cook:** 35 min.
Makes: 12 servings

- **8 bacon strips, chopped**
- **2 lbs. ground beef**
- **½ large red onion, chopped**
- **12 oz. uncooked spiral pasta**
- **4 cups chicken broth**
- **2 cans (15 oz. each) crushed tomatoes**
- **1 can (8 oz.) tomato sauce**
- **1 cup water**
- **¼ cup ketchup**
- **3 Tbsp. prepared mustard**
- **2 Tbsp. Worcestershire sauce**
- **¼ tsp. salt**
- **¼ tsp. pepper**
- **2 cups shredded cheddar cheese, divided**
- **⅓ cup chopped dill pickle**
- **Chopped tomatoes and thinly sliced green onions, optional**

1. In a 6-qt. stockpot, cook bacon over medium heat, stirring occasionally, until crisp, 6-8 minutes. Remove with a slotted spoon; drain on paper towels. Discard drippings.
2. In the same pot, cook ground beef and onion over medium heat until meat is no longer pink, breaking into crumbles, 6-8 minutes; drain. Add next ten ingredients; bring to a boil. Reduce the heat; simmer, covered, until pasta is al dente, stirring occasionally, about 10 minutes.
3. Stir in 1 cup cheese, pickle and bacon; cook and stir until cheese is melted. Serve with remaining cheese and, if desired, tomatoes and green onions.

1⅓ cups: 390 cal., 18g fat (8g sat. fat), 73mg chol., 1023mg sod., 31g carb. (7g sugars, 3g fiber), 25g pro.

TEST KITCHEN TIP

Take the time to shred cheese from a block for this recipe; it stirs in with a smoother texture than pre-shredded cheese.

SLOW COOKER | FREEZE IT

PULED PORK DOUGHNUT HOLE SLIDERS

Our family created this slider recipe by accident when we had a surplus of root beer left over from a party. Now we can't have barbecue any other way! The root beer adds flavor to the shredded meat, but doesn't make it too sweet.
—Eden Dranger, Los Angeles, CA

Prep: 55 min. • **Cook:** 8 hours.
Makes: 5 dozen

- **1 bottle (2 liters) root beer**
- **1½ cups barbecue sauce**
- **1½ tsp. salt**
- **1 tsp. minced fresh gingerroot**
- **1 bone-in pork shoulder roast (about 3 lbs.)**

SLAW

- **½ cup mayonnaise or Miracle Whip**
- **2 Tbsp. white vinegar**
- **1 Tbsp. maple syrup**
- **1 pkg. (14 oz.) coleslaw mix**

ASSEMBLY

- **60 plain doughnut holes**
- **60 appetizer skewers**
- **Additional barbecue sauce, optional**

1. In a large saucepan, bring root beer to a boil. Reduce heat to medium-high; cook, uncovered, until liquid is reduced by half, 30-45 minutes. Transfer to a 5- or 6-qt. slow cooker. Stir in barbecue sauce, salt and ginger. Add roast, turning to coat.
2. Cook, covered, on low until pork is tender, 8-10 hours. For slaw, in a large bowl, mix mayonnaise, vinegar and syrup. Stir in coleslaw mix. Refrigerate, covered, until flavors are blended, at least 1 hour.
3. Remove pork from slow cooker; skim fat from cooking juices. Remove meat from bones; shred with two forks. Return juices and pork to slow cooker; heat through.
4. To serve, cut doughnut holes in half; cut a thin slice off bottoms to level. Serve pork and slaw in doughnut holes; secure with skewers. If desired, serve sliders with additional barbecue sauce.

Freeze option: Freeze cooled pork mixture in freezer containers. To use, partially thaw in refrigerator overnight. Heat through in a covered saucepan, stirring gently.

1 slider: 138 cal., 7g fat (2g sat. fat), 13mg chol., 218mg sod., 14g carb. (10g sugars, 0 fiber), 5g pro.

FAST FIX

SHRIMP TARTLETS

Mini tart shells are filled with a cream cheese mixture, then topped with seafood sauce and shrimp for this picture-perfect, tasty appetizer. You could also serve several as a fast, light meal.
—Gina Hutchison, Smithville, MO

Takes: 20 min. • **Makes:** 2½ dozen

- **1 pkg. (8 oz.) cream cheese, softened**
- **1½ tsp. Worcestershire sauce**
- **1 to 2 tsp. grated onion**
- **1 tsp. garlic salt**
- **⅛ tsp. lemon juice**
- **2 pkg. (1.9 oz. each) frozen miniature phyllo tart shells**
- **½ cup seafood cocktail sauce**
- **30 peeled and deveined cooked shrimp (31-40 per lb.), tails removed**
- **Minced fresh parsley and lemon wedges, optional**

Beat the first five ingredients until blended. Place tart shells on a serving plate. Fill with cream cheese mixture; top with cocktail sauce and shrimp. Refrigerate until serving. If desired, sprinkle with parsley and serve with lemon wedges.

1 tartlet: 61 cal., 4g fat (2g sat. fat), 23mg chol., 143mg sod., 4g carb. (1g sugars, 0 fiber), 3g pro.

TACO TATER SKINS

I wanted to make a version of these with ingredients most people have on hand. We make a meal out of these skins, but they're also great for parties as appetizers.
—Phyllis Douglas, Fairview, MI

Prep: 20 min. + cooling • **Bake:** 65 min.
Makes: 2 dozen

- **6 large baking potatoes (about 13 oz. each)**
- **½ cup butter, melted**
- **2 Tbsp. taco seasoning**
- **1 cup shredded cheddar cheese**
- **15 bacon strips, cooked and crumbled**
- **3 green onions, chopped**
- **Salsa and sour cream, optional**

1. Preheat oven to 375°. Scrub potatoes; pierce several times with a fork. Place on a baking sheet; bake until tender, 60-70 minutes. Cool slightly. Reduce oven setting to 350°.
2. Cut potatoes lengthwise into quarters; remove pulp, leaving a ¼-in. shell (save pulp for another use). Mix melted butter and seasoning; brush over both sides of potato skins. Place on greased baking sheets, skin side down. Sprinkle with cheese, bacon and green onions.
3. Bake until the cheese is melted, 5-10 minutes. If desired, serve with salsa and sour cream.

1 piece: 153 cal., 7g fat (4g sat. fat), 20mg chol., 227mg sod., 17g carb. (1g sugars, 2g fiber), 5g pro.

CINNAMON CHIP CHAI-SPICED SNICKERDOODLES

CINNAMON CHIP CHAI-SPICED SNICKERDOODLES

I love cinnamon chips and am always looking for a way to use them. Make sure to stock up on them during the holiday season so you have plenty to last during the year.
—Marietta Slater, Justin, TX

Prep: 30 min. + chilling
Bake: 15 min./batch + cooling
Makes: about 6 dozen

- **½ cup sugar**
- **2 tsp. ground cardamom**
- **2 tsp. ground cinnamon**
- **½ tsp. ground ginger**
- **½ tsp. ground cloves**
- **¼ tsp. ground nutmeg**

DOUGH

- **½ cup butter, softened**
- **½ cup shortening**
- **1 cup sugar**
- **2 large eggs**
- **1 tsp. vanilla extract**
- **2¾ cups all-purpose flour**
- **2 tsp. cream of tartar**
- **1 tsp. baking soda**
- **Dash salt**
- **1 pkg. (10 oz.) cinnamon baking chips**

1. Preheat oven to 350°. For the spiced sugar, mix first six ingredients.
2. In a large bowl, cream softened butter, shortening, sugar and 2 Tbsp. spiced sugar until light and fluffy. Beat in the eggs and vanilla. In another bowl, whisk together flour, cream of tartar, baking soda and salt; gradually beat into creamed mixture. Stir in baking chips. Refrigerate, covered, until firm enough to shape, about 1 hour.
3. Shape dough into 1-in. balls; roll in the remaining spiced sugar. Place 2 in. apart on greased baking sheets.
4. Bake until set, 11-13 minutes. Remove from pans to wire racks to cool.

1 cookie: 81 cal., 4g fat (2g sat. fat), 9mg chol., 59mg sod., 10g carb. (7g sugars, 0 fiber), 1g pro.

FUDGY MACAROON BARS

PICTURED ON P. 243

Everyone with a sweet tooth makes a beeline for my dessert tray when these rich squares show up. They're attractive on the platter and absolutely delectable.
—Beverly Zdurne, East Lansing, MI

Prep: 25 min. • **Bake:** 35 min.
Makes: 3 dozen

- 4 oz. unsweetened chocolate
- 1 cup butter
- 2 cups sugar
- 1 cup all-purpose flour
- ¼ tsp. salt
- 1 tsp. vanilla extract
- 3 large eggs, lightly beaten

FILLING
- 3 cups sweetened shredded coconut
- 1 can (14 oz.) sweetened condensed milk
- 1 tsp. vanilla extract
- ½ tsp. almond extract

TOPPING
- 1 cup (6 oz.) semisweet chocolate chips
- ½ cup chopped walnuts

1. Preheat oven to 350°. In a microwave, melt the chocolate and butter; stir until smooth. Cool slightly. Stir in the sugar, flour, salt, vanilla and eggs. Spread half the batter into a greased 13x9-in. baking pan.
2. In a large bowl, combine the filling ingredients. Spoon over the chocolate layer. Carefully spread the remaining chocolate mixture evenly over filling.
3. Bake for 35-40 minutes or until the sides pull away from the pan. Immediately sprinkle with chocolate chips. Allow the chips to soften for a few minutes, then spread evenly. Sprinkle with walnuts. Cool completely before cutting.

1 bar: 219 cal., 12g fat (7g sat. fat), 35mg chol., 108mg sod., 27g carb. (22g sugars, 1g fiber), 3g pro.

SLOW COOKER | FREEZE IT | EAT SMART

CHINESE MEATBALLS

These were a huge hit at our last cookout! They're a great alternative to the expected meatballs. You can use two tablespoons of chopped crystallized ginger in place of the fresh ginger if you like.
—Pat Barnes, Panama City, FL

Prep: 35 min. • **Cook:** 3 hours
Makes: about 6 dozen

- 2 large eggs, lightly beaten
- 2 Tbsp. soy sauce
- 1 tsp. salt
- 6 green onions, sliced
- 2 lbs. lean ground pork
- 2 cans (8 oz. each) sliced water chestnuts, drained and chopped
- 1 cup dry bread crumbs

SAUCE
- ¼ cup cornstarch
- 1 cup pineapple juice
- ⅓ cup sugar
- 4 tsp. minced fresh gingerroot
- 1 can (10½ oz.) condensed beef consomme, undiluted
- ½ cup white vinegar

1. Preheat oven to 400°. In a large bowl, combine the first four ingredients. Add pork, water chestnuts and bread crumbs; mix lightly but thoroughly. Shape mixture into 1-in. balls. Place in a greased 15x10x1-in. pan. Bake 15 minutes.
2. In a 5- or 6-qt. slow cooker, mix cornstarch and juice until smooth. Stir in remaining ingredients. Add meatballs; stir gently to coat. Cook, covered, on low until meatballs are cooked through and sauce is thickened, 3-4 hours.

Freeze option: Freeze cooled meatball mixture in freezer containers. To use, partially thaw in refrigerator overnight. Heat through in a covered saucepan, stirring gently. Add a little broth if necessary.

1 meatball: 41 cal., 2g fat (1g sat. fat), 12mg chol., 109mg sod., 4g carb. (2g sugars, 0 fiber), 3g pro.

TEST KITCHEN TIP

Add 1 tsp. crushed red pepper flakes to the sauce mixture for a Szechuan profile. These meatballs and their gingery sauce are also delicious served over rice for a main dish. Meatballs made with ground pork are lighter and more delicate than beef meatballs.

CHINESE MEATBALLS

RHUBARB-FILLED COOKIES

RHUBARB-FILLED COOKIES

I won a blue ribbon at our local fair for these tender cookies. They're so pretty with the ruby red filling peeking through the dough. If you have leftover filling, it's great as a spread on toast or a topping for ice cream.

—Pauline Bondy, Grand Forks, ND

Prep: 25 min. • **Bake:** 10 min.
Makes: about 4½ dozen

- **1 cup butter, softened**
- **1 cup sugar**
- **1 cup packed brown sugar**
- **4 large eggs**
- **4½ cups all-purpose flour**
- **1 tsp. baking soda**
- **1 tsp. salt**

FILLING

- **3½ cups chopped fresh or frozen rhubarb, thawed**
- **1½ cups sugar**
- **6 Tbsp. water, divided**
- **¼ cup cornstarch**
- **1 tsp. vanilla extract**

1. In a large bowl, cream the butter and sugars until light and fluffy. Add eggs, one at a time, beating well after each addition. Combine the flour, baking soda and salt; gradually add to the creamed mixture and mix well. (Dough will be sticky.)
2. For filling, combine rhubarb, sugar and 2 Tbsp. water in a large saucepan; bring to a boil. Reduce heat; simmer, uncovered, until thickened, stirring frequently, about 10 minutes. Combine cornstarch and the remaining water until smooth; stir into rhubarb mixture. Bring to a boil; cook and stir until thickened, about 2 minutes. Remove from heat; stir in vanilla.
3. Drop dough by tablespoonfuls 2 in. apart onto ungreased baking sheets. Using the end of a wooden spoon handle, make an indentation in center of each cookie; fill with a rounded teaspoon of filling. Top with ½ tsp. of dough, allowing some of the filling to show. Bake at 375° until lightly browned, 8-10 minutes.

Note: If using frozen rhubarb, measure rhubarb while still frozen, then thaw completely. Drain in a colander, but do not press liquid out.

1 cookie: 129 cal., 4g fat (2g sat. fat), 23mg chol., 101mg sod., 22g carb. (13g sugars, 0 fiber), 2g pro.

ZUCCHINI PANZANELLA SALAD

EAT SMART

ZUCCHINI PANZANELLA SALAD

I learned how to make panzanella from a dear friend's grandmother. This is a version I crave during the summer. What a tasty way to use day-old bread and your garden's bounty of zucchini!

—Felicity Wolf, Kansas City, MO

Prep: 20 min. + cooling • **Bake:** 40 min.
Makes: 14 cups

- **3 medium zucchini, cut into ¼-in. slices**
- **¼ cup olive oil, divided**
- **1 French bread baguette (10½ oz.), cubed**
- **1½ cups heirloom mini or cherry tomatoes, halved**
- **1 medium green pepper, coarsely chopped**
- **½ medium red onion, thinly sliced**
- **¼ cup balsamic vinegar**
- **1 tsp. jarred roasted minced garlic**
- **1 tsp. Italian seasoning**
- **½ tsp. crushed red pepper flakes**
- **1 tsp. kosher salt**
- **½ tsp. coarsely ground pepper**
- **1½ cups fresh mozzarella cheese pearls**

1. Preheat oven to 400°. Place zucchini in a 15x10x1-in. baking pan. Toss with 1 Tbsp. olive oil. Bake, uncovered, for 25-30 minutes or until tender and lightly browned, stirring halfway. Remove from the oven and cool.
2. Meanwhile, in a large bowl, toss bread cubes with 1 Tbsp. olive oil. Transfer to a baking sheet. Bake for 12-14 minutes or until lightly browned, stirring occasionally.
3. Place the cooled zucchini, toasted bread, tomatoes, green pepper, and red onion in a large bowl. In a small bowl, whisk together vinegar, garlic, seasonings and remaining oil. Drizzle over salad; toss gently to combine. Add the mozzarella and stir to combine. Serve immediately.

1 cup: 152 cal., 8g fat (3g sat. fat), 13mg chol., 301mg sod., 16g carb. (4g sugars, 1g fiber), 5g pro. **Diabetic exchanges:** 1½ fat, 1 starch.

TEST KITCHEN TIP

If the raw onion is too pungent for you, roast it with the zucchini.

CRANBERRY SAUERKRAUT MEATBALLS

SLOW COOKER
CRANBERRY SAUERKRAUT MEATBALLS

I tried these meatballs at a friend's birthday party, and now I make them all the time. They are super easy to prepare and perfect for a potluck or a Sunday afternoon football game.
—Lisa Castelli, Pleasant Prairie, WI

Prep: 15 min. • **Cook:** 4 hours
Makes: about 5 dozen

- **1 can (14 oz.) whole-berry cranberry sauce**
- **1 can (14 oz.) sauerkraut, rinsed and well drained**
- **1 bottle (12 oz.) chili sauce**
- **¾ cup packed brown sugar**
- **1 pkg. (32 oz.) frozen fully cooked homestyle meatballs, thawed**
- **Minced chives, optional**

In a 4-qt. slow cooker, combine the cranberry sauce, sauerkraut, chili sauce and brown sugar. Stir in the meatballs. Cover and cook on low until heated through, 4-5 hours. If desired, top with chives to serve.

1 meatball with about 1 Tbsp. sauce: 76 cal., 4g fat (2g sat. fat), 6mg chol., 250mg sod., 8g carb. (6g sugars, 0 fiber), 2g pro.

ANTIPASTO KABOBS

My husband and I met at a cooking class and have loved entertaining and creating menus ever since. These make-ahead appetizers are a favorite to serve.
—Denise Hazen, Cincinnati, OH

Prep: 35 min. + marinating
Makes: 40 appetizers

- **1 pkg. (9 oz.) refrigerated cheese tortellini**
- **40 pimiento-stuffed olives**
- **40 large pitted ripe olives**
- **¾ cup Italian salad dressing**
- **40 thin slices pepperoni**
- **20 thin slices hard salami, halved**
- **Fresh parsley sprigs, optional**

1. Cook tortellini according to package directions; drain and rinse in cold water. In a large bowl, combine the tortellini, olives and salad dressing. Toss to coat; cover and refrigerate 4 hours or overnight.
2. Drain and discard marinade. For each appetizer, thread a stuffed olive, folded pepperoni slice, tortellini, folded salami piece, ripe olive and, if desired, parsley sprig on a toothpick or short skewer.

1 kabob: 66 cal., 5g fat (1g sat. fat), 9mg chol., 315mg sod., 4g carb. (0 sugars, 0 fiber), 2g pro.

SLOW COOKER
CHILI QUESO DIP

PICTURED ON P. 243

I've had this recipe for more than 42 years, but have updated it from time to time. This is an easy party favorite, and everyone loves the taquito dippers.
—Joan Hallford, North Richland Hills, TX

Prep: 20 min. • **Cook:** 2 hours
Makes: 40 servings

- **1 lb. ground beef**
- **1 lb. bulk pork sausage**
- **1 small onion, chopped**
- **2 jalapeno peppers, seeded and finely chopped**
- **1 garlic clove, minced**
- **1 can (15 oz.) chili con carne (without beans)**
- **1 can (10¾ oz.) reduced-fat reduced-sodium condensed cream of mushroom soup, undiluted**
- **1 can (10 oz.) diced tomatoes and green chilies, drained**
- **1 jar (4 oz.) diced pimientos, drained**
- **1 pkg. (2 lbs.) process cheese (Velveeta), cubed**
- **Prepared taquitos, tortilla chips or corn chips**

1. In a large skillet, cook and crumble beef and sausage with onion, jalapenos and garlic over medium-high heat until no longer pink, 5-7 minutes. Using a slotted spoon, transfer to a 5-qt. slow cooker. Stir in chili, soup, tomatoes, pimientos and cheese.
2. Cook, covered, on low until heated through, 2-3 hours, stirring halfway through cooking. Serve warm with taquitos or chips.

¼ cup dip: 147 cal., 11g fat (5g sat. fat), 39mg chol., 473mg sod., 4g carb. (2g sugars, 0 fiber), 8g pro.

TEST KITCHEN TIP

This recipe uses reduced-fat, reduced-sodium soup for taste reasons, not for health reasons. The dip tasted a bit too salty when made with regular soup.

COCONUT TRES LECHES CUPCAKES

Three types of milk wonderfully moisten these cupcakes. Toasted coconut on top adds an elegant touch.
—*Taste of Home* Test Kitchen

Prep: 35 min. + chilling
Bake: 20 min. + cooling
Makes: about 1½ dozen

- **½ cup butter, softened**
- **1½ cups sugar**
- **1½ tsp. vanilla extract**
- **4 large egg whites**
- **2 cups all-purpose flour**
- **1 tsp. baking powder**
- **½ tsp. baking soda**
- **¼ tsp. salt**
- **1⅓ cups buttermilk**
- **1 can (14 oz.) sweetened condensed milk**
- **⅔ cup evaporated milk**
- **½ cup coconut milk**
- **1½ cups heavy whipping cream**
- **⅓ cup confectioners' sugar**
- **Toasted sweetened shredded coconut**

1. Preheat oven to 350°. Line 18 muffin cups with paper liners.
2. Cream butter and sugar until light and fluffy. Beat in vanilla and egg whites, one at a time, beating well after each addition. In another bowl, whisk together flour, baking powder, baking soda and salt; add to creamed mixture alternately with buttermilk, beating after each addition.
3. Fill prepared cups about two-thirds full. Bake until a toothpick inserted in center comes out clean, 17-20 minutes. Cool 10 minutes. Remove cupcakes to a 15x10x1-in. pan.
4. In a bowl, mix sweetened condensed, evaporated and coconut milks. Poke holes in cupcakes with a skewer, about ½ in. apart. Slowly spoon the milk mixture over top, allowing it to absorb into the cake. Refrigerate, covered, at least 2 hours.
5. To serve, beat cream until it begins to thicken. Add confectioners' sugar; beat until soft peaks form. Spread or pipe over cupcakes. Top with coconut. Store in the refrigerator.

1 cupcake: 342 cal., 16g fat (11g sat. fat), 47mg chol., 226mg sod., 44g carb. (33g sugars, 0 fiber), 6g pro.

COCONUT TRES LECHES CUPCAKES

ZIPPY PARTY ROLL-UPS

PICTURED ON P. 243

A guaranteed crowd-pleaser, these zesty appetizers are a great way to pep up a party! The recipe won a blue ribbon at the county fair, and even when I double the recipe—which I always do—I never seem to make enough.
—Dana Gonzalez del Valle, Battle Ground, WA

Prep: 20 min. + chilling • **Makes:** 6 dozen

- **1 pkg. (8 oz.) cream cheese, softened**
- **6 flour tortillas (8 in.)**
- **36 spinach leaves**
- **1 pkg. (6 oz.) thinly sliced deli ham**
- **1 can (4¼ oz.) chopped ripe olives**
- **1 can (4 oz.) chopped green chilies, drained**

Spread about 3 Tbsp. cream cheese over each tortilla; layer each with six spinach leaves and three slices of ham. Sprinkle with olives and chilies. Roll up tightly and wrap in plastic. Refrigerate until firm. Unwrap and cut each roll into 12 slices.

1 roll-up: 32 cal., 2g fat (1g sat. fat), 4mg chol., 85mg sod., 3g carb. (0 sugars, 0 fiber), 1g pro.

EAT SMART | FAST FIX

WATERMELON TOMATO SALAD

Watermelon and tomatoes may seem an unlikely pair, but they team up to make a winning combination in this bright, eye-catching salad.
—Matthew Denton, Seattle, WA

Takes: 25 min. • **Makes:** 18 servings

- **10 cups cubed seedless watermelon**
- **2 pints yellow grape or pear tomatoes, halved**
- **1 medium red onion, chopped**
- **½ cup minced fresh parsley**
- **½ cup minced fresh basil**
- **¼ cup lime juice**

In a large bowl, combine the watermelon, tomatoes and onion. In a small bowl, combine the parsley, basil and lime juice. Pour over watermelon mixture and toss to coat. Refrigerate until serving.

¾ cup: 33 cal., 0 fat (0 sat. fat), 0 chol., 7mg sod., 10g carb. (8g sugars, 1g fiber), 1g pro.
Diabetic exchanges: ½ fruit.

IRISH CREME CHOCOLATE TRIFLE

This trifle calls for Irish creme coffee creamer, but I first created it when I was given a bottle of Irish cream liqueur—so if you're serving adults, you can use that instead. Both ways are rich and delicious!
—Margaret Wilson, San Bernardino, CA

Prep: 20 min. + chilling
Bake: 30 min. + cooling
Makes: 16 servings

- **1 pkg. devil's food cake mix (regular size)**
- **1 cup refrigerated Irish creme nondairy creamer**
- **3½ cups 2% milk**
- **2 pkg. (3.9 oz. each) instant chocolate pudding mix**
- **3 cups whipped topping**
- **12 mint Andes candies, chopped**

1. Prepare and bake cake mix according to package directions, using a 13x9-in. pan. Cool in pan on a wire rack for 1 hour.
2. With a meat fork or wooden skewer, poke holes in cake about 2 in. apart. Slowly pour the creamer over cake; refrigerate, covered, for 1 hour.
3. In a large bowl, whisk milk and pudding mixes 2 minutes; let stand until soft-set, about 2 minutes.
4. Cut cake into 1½-in. cubes. In a 3-qt. trifle or glass bowl, layer a third of each of the following: cake cubes, pudding, whipped topping and candies. Repeat layers twice. Refrigerate until serving.

1 serving: 343 cal., 14g fat (5g sat. fat), 39mg chol., 363mg sod., 49g carb. (32g sugars, 1g fiber), 5g pro.

SLOW COOKER

JALAPENO MAC & CHEESE

Many years ago, after I had knee surgery, a friend brought me a big casserole of mac and cheese along with the recipe. Over the years, I fiddled with the recipe. Most recently, I added jalapenos at the request of my son. What an awesome spicy twist!
—Teresa Gustafson, Elkton, MD

Prep: 25 min. • **Cook:** 3 hours
Makes: 15 servings

- **1 pkg. (16 oz.) uncooked elbow macaroni**
- **6 Tbsp. butter, divided**
- **4 jalapeno peppers, seeded and finely chopped**
- **3 cups shredded cheddar cheese**
- **2 cups shredded Colby-Monterey Jack cheese**
- **2 cups whole milk**
- **1 can (10¾ oz.) condensed cream of onion soup, undiluted**
- **1 can (10¾ oz.) condensed cheddar cheese soup, undiluted**
- **½ cup mayonnaise**
- **¼ tsp. pepper**
- **1 cup crushed Ritz crackers (about 25 crackers)**

1. Cook macaroni according to package directions for al dente; drain. Transfer to a greased 5-qt. slow cooker.
2. Melt 2 Tbsp. butter in a large skillet over medium-high heat. Add jalapenos; cook and stir until crisp-tender, about 5 minutes. Add to slow cooker. Stir in the cheeses, milk, soups, mayonnaise and pepper.
3. Cook, covered, on low until cheese is melted and the mixture is heated through, 3 hours. Melt the remaining butter; stir in crackers. Sprinkle over macaroni mixture.

¾ cup: 428 cal., 27g fat (13g sat. fat), 53mg chol., 654mg sod., 33g carb. (5g sugars, 2g fiber), 14g pro.

TEST KITCHEN TIP

Be sure to cook the pasta just short of tender. It will continue to cook in the slow cooker.

JALAPENO MAC & CHEESE

CRANBERRY NUT COOKIES

CRANBERRY NUT COOKIES

Tangy cranberries are a nice addition to a buttery cookie. In fall, I stock up on fresh cranberries and freeze them so I can make these cookies throughout the year.
—Machelle Wall, Rosamond, CA

Prep: 15 min. • **Bake:** 20 min./batch
Makes: 5 dozen

- ⅔ **cup butter, softened**
- 1 **cup sugar**
- 1 **cup packed brown sugar**
- 1 **large egg**
- ¼ **cup 2% milk**
- 2 **Tbsp. lemon juice**
- 3 **cups all-purpose flour**
- ¼ **cup ground walnuts**
- 1 **tsp. baking powder**
- ½ **tsp. salt**
- ¼ **tsp. baking soda**
- 2½ **cups halved fresh or frozen cranberries**
- 1 **cup chopped walnuts**

1. Cream butter and sugars until light and fluffy. Beat in egg, milk and lemon juice. Combine flour, ground walnuts, baking powder, salt and baking soda; gradually add to the creamed mixture and mix well. Stir in cranberries and chopped walnuts.
2. Drop by heaping tablespoonfuls 2 in. apart onto lightly greased baking sheets. Bake at 350° for 16-18 minutes or until golden brown. Remove to wire racks.

1 cookie: 87 cal., 4g fat (1g sat. fat), 9mg chol., 52mg sod., 13g carb. (7g sugars, 0 fiber), 1g pro.

SLOW COOKER

HOT CRAB DIP

I have a large family, work full time and coach soccer and football, so I value easy-to-assemble recipes. This rich, creamy dip is a fun appetizer to whip up for any gathering.
—Teri Rasey, Cadillac, MI

Prep: 5 min. • **Cook:** 3 hours
Makes: about 5 cups

- ½ **cup whole milk**
- ⅓ **cup salsa**
- 3 **pkg. (8 oz. each) cream cheese, cubed**
- 2 **pkg. (8 oz. each) imitation crabmeat, flaked**
- 1 **cup thinly sliced green onions**
- 1 **can (4 oz.) chopped green chilies**
- **Assorted crackers or fresh vegetables**

In a small bowl, combine milk and salsa. Transfer to a greased 3-qt. slow cooker. Stir in cream cheese, crab, onions and chilies. Cover and cook on low for 3-4 hours, stirring every 30 minutes. Serve with crackers.

¼ cup: 148 cal., 12g fat (7g sat. fat), 38mg chol., 274mg sod., 6g carb. (2g sugars, 0 fiber), 5g pro.

SLOW-COOKER CHICKPEA TAGINE

SLOW COOKER | EAT SMART

SLOW-COOKER CHICKPEA TAGINE

While traveling in Morocco, my wife and I fell in love with the complex flavors of the many tagines we tried. Resist the urge to stir this; that breaks down the veggies. For a one-pot meal, add shredded cooked chicken in the last 10 minutes.
—Raymond Wyatt, West St. Paul, MN

Prep: 20 min. • **Cook:** 4 hours
Makes: 12 servings

- **1 small butternut squash (about 2 lbs.), peeled and cut into ½-in. cubes**
- **2 medium zucchini, cut into ½-in. pieces**
- **1 medium sweet red pepper, coarsely chopped**
- **1 medium onion, coarsely chopped**
- **1 can (15 oz.) chickpeas or garbanzo beans, rinsed and drained**
- **12 dried apricots, halved**
- **2 Tbsp. olive oil**
- **2 garlic cloves, minced**
- **2 tsp. paprika**
- **1 tsp. ground ginger**
- **1 tsp. ground cumin**
- **½ tsp. salt**
- **¼ tsp. pepper**
- **¼ tsp. ground cinnamon**
- **1 can (14.5 oz.) crushed tomatoes**
- **2 to 3 tsp. harissa chili paste**
- **2 tsp. honey**
- **¼ cup chopped fresh mint leaves**
- **Plain Greek yogurt, optional**
- **Additional olive oil, honey and fresh mint, optional**

1. Place the first six ingredients in a 5- or 6-qt. slow cooker.
2. In a skillet, heat oil over medium heat. Add garlic, paprika, ginger, cumin, salt, pepper and cinnamon; cook and stir until fragrant, about 1 minute. Add tomatoes, harissa and honey; bring to a boil. Pour tomato mixture over vegetables; stir to combine. Cook, covered, on low until vegetables are tender and sauce has thickened, 4-5 hours. Stir in mint.
3. If desired, top with yogurt, and additional mint, olive oil and honey to serve.

¾ cup: 127 cal., 3g fat (0 sat. fat), 0 chol., 224mg sod., 23g carb. (9g sugars, 6g fiber), 4g pro. **Diabetic exchanges:** 1½ starch, ½ fat.

TEST KITCHEN TIP

For a meatless main dish, serve this over couscous. If you don't have harissa paste but still want some heat, add a little hot pepper sauce or crushed red pepper flakes.

FREEZE IT

ITALIAN PASTA SAUCE

When my daughter got married, her new husband made something special for their wedding buffet—a big batch of this thick flavorful pasta sauce. His grandmother brought the recipe from Italy 80 years ago.
—Judy Braun, Juneau, WI

Prep: 15 min. • **Cook:** 2½ hours
Makes: 20 servings

- **4 lbs. ground beef**
- **1 lb. bulk Italian sausage**
- **1 large onion, finely chopped**
- **3 celery ribs, finely chopped**
- **4 garlic cloves, minced**
- **2 Tbsp. olive oil**
- **3 cans (28 oz. each) crushed tomatoes in puree**
- **3 cans (6 oz. each) tomato paste**
- **3 cups chicken or beef broth**
- **1 lb. fresh mushrooms, sliced**
- **¾ cup minced fresh parsley**
- **1 Tbsp. sugar**
- **2 to 3 tsp. salt**
- **½ tsp. pepper**
- **½ tsp. ground allspice, optional**
- **Hot cooked pasta**

1. In a Dutch oven or soup kettle, cook beef in two batches over medium heat until no longer pink; drain and set aside. Cook sausage over medium heat until no longer pink; drain and set aside. In the same pot, saute onion, celery and garlic in oil until vegetables are tender.
2. Return the beef and sausage to the pot. Add the next nine ingredients, including allspice if desired, and bring to a boil. Reduce heat; cover and simmer until the sauce reaches desired thickness, stirring occasionally, 2-3 hours. Serve over pasta.

Freeze option: Freeze cooled sauce in freezer containers. To use, partially thaw in refrigerator overnight. Heat through in a saucepan, stirring occasionally. Add a little broth or water if necessary.

1 cup: 284 cal., 15g fat (5g sat. fat), 57mg chol., 821mg sod., 16g carb. (9g sugars, 3g fiber), 23g pro.

STRAWBERRY OATMEAL BARS

A fruity filling and fluffy coconut topping truly make these bars one of a kind. They really dress up a cookie tray!
—Flo Burtnett, Gage, OK

Prep: 15 min. • **Bake:** 25 min.
Makes: 2 dozen

- **1¼ cups all-purpose flour**
- **1¼ cups quick-cooking oats**
- **½ cup sugar**
- **½ tsp. baking powder**
- **¼ tsp. salt**
- **¾ cup butter, melted**
- **2 tsp. vanilla extract**
- **1 cup strawberry preserves**
- **½ cup sweetened shredded coconut**

Preheat oven to 350°. Combine first five ingredients. Add butter and vanilla; stir until crumbly. Set aside 1 cup. Press remaining crumb mixture evenly into an ungreased 13x9-in. baking pan. Spread preserves over crust. Combine coconut and the reserved crumb mixture; sprinkle over preserves. Bake 25-30 minutes or until coconut is lightly browned. Cool.

1 bar: 150 cal., 7g fat (4g sat. fat), 15mg chol., 86mg sod., 22g carb. (13g sugars, 1g fiber), 1g pro.

BLUE CHEESE ONION DIP

I decided to tweak the onion soup dip you see at every gathering, and everyone seems to be glad I did. Serve with crisp veggies or potato chips, and you're set.
—Vicki Desy, Tucson, AZ

Prep: 10 min. + chilling
Makes: 12 servings

- **2 cups sour cream**
- **⅔ cup mayonnaise**
- **2 Tbsp. onion soup mix**
- **1 garlic clove, minced**
- **1 cup crumbled blue cheese**
- **⅓ cup chopped walnuts, toasted**
- **Assorted fresh vegetables**

Mix the first four ingredients until blended; stir in cheese. Refrigerate, covered, until the flavors are blended, at least 2 hours. To serve, top with walnuts. Serve with vegetables.

Note: To toast nuts, bake in a shallow pan in a 350° oven for 5-10 minutes or cook in a skillet over low heat until lightly browned, stirring occasionally.

¼ cup dip: 224 cal., 22g fat (8g sat. fat), 19mg chol., 306mg sod., 3g carb. (2g sugars, 0 fiber), 4g pro.

STRAWBERRY OATMEAL BARS

PUMPKIN TORTE

A local newspaper featured this potluck-friendly recipe years ago. A creamy alternative to pumpkin pie, it quickly became one of my favorite desserts.
—Peggy Shea, Lowell, IN

Prep: 30 min. • **Bake:** 25 min. + chilling
Makes: 15 servings

- **1⅔ cups graham cracker crumbs**
- **⅓ cup sugar**
- **½ cup butter, melted**

CREAM CHEESE FILLING

- **2 pkg. (8 oz. each) cream cheese, softened**
- **¾ cup sugar**
- **2 large eggs**

PUMPKIN FILLING

- **2 envelopes unflavored gelatin**
- **½ cup cold water**
- **1 can (30 oz.) pumpkin pie filling**
- **1 can (5½ oz.) evaporated milk**
- **2 large eggs, lightly beaten**

TOPPING

- **1 carton (12 oz.) frozen whipped topping, thawed**

1. Preheat oven to 350°. Combine the crumbs, sugar and butter. Press onto the bottom of an ungreased 13x9-in. baking dish; set aside. In a large bowl, beat cream cheese and sugar until smooth. Add eggs; beat on low speed just until combined. Pour over crust. Bake until center is almost set, 25-30 minutes.
2. Meanwhile, in a small bowl, sprinkle gelatin over cold water; let stand for 1 minute. In a large saucepan, combine pie filling and evaporated milk. Bring to a boil. Add gelatin; stir until dissolved. Whisk a small amount of the hot mixture into the eggs. Return all to the pan, whisking constantly.
3. Cook and stir over low heat until the mixture is thickened and coats the back of a spoon. Cool for 10 minutes. Spread over the cream cheese layer. Spread whipped topping over top. Cover and refrigerate overnight.

1 piece: 413 cal., 24g fat (15g sat. fat), 109mg chol., 296mg sod., 42g carb. (32g sugars, 2g fiber), 7g pro.

Holiday & Seasonal Pleasers

Easter, Fourth of July, Halloween, Thanksgiving, Christmas... whatever the occasion, the delightful recipes in this chapter will help you navigate seasonal parties in style and give your guests a holiday to remember.

Buttermilk Smashed Potatoes (p. 269) **Banana Cream Chocolate Truffles** (p. 281) **Horseradish-Glazed Ham** (p. 261) **Festive Holiday Sliders** (p. 274) **Swift Strawberry Salad** (p. 263)

Just Right for Easter

Celebrate with delicious main course options, a side perfect for a springtime feast and a dessert that's sure to please the Easter Bunny! And we know just the way to make your Easter basket special.

GRANDMA'S CARROT CAKE

GRANDMA'S CARROT CAKE

My Grandma was very special to me. She had a big country kitchen that was full of wonderful aromas any time we visited. This was one of her prized cake recipes, which continues to be a favorite from generation to generation.
—Denise Strasz, Detroit, MI

Prep: 30 min. • **Bake:** 50 min. + cooling
Makes: 16 servings

- 2 cups sugar
- 1½ cups canola oil
- 4 large eggs, room temperature
- 2 tsp. vanilla extract
- 2½ cups all-purpose flour
- 1½ tsp. baking soda
- ½ tsp. salt
- 1 tsp. ground cinnamon
- 3 cups shredded carrots (about 6 medium)
- 1 cup chopped walnuts

FROSTING
- 1 pkg. (8 oz.) cream cheese, softened
- ¼ cup butter, softened
- 3 cups confectioners' sugar

1. Preheat oven to 350°. Grease and flour a 10-in. fluted tube pan.
2. Beat the first four ingredients until well blended. Whisk together the flour, baking soda, salt and cinnamon; gradually beat into the sugar mixture. Stir in carrots and walnuts.
3. Transfer batter to prepared pan. Bake until a toothpick inserted in center comes out clean, 50-60 minutes. Cool in pan 10 minutes before removing to a wire rack; cool completely.
4. For frosting, beat cream cheese and butter until smooth. Gradually beat in confectioners' sugar. Spread over cake.

Note: To remove cakes easily, use solid shortening to grease plain and fluted tube pans.

1 slice: 593 cal., 35g fat (7g sat. fat), 68mg chol., 292mg sod., 67g carb. (49g sugars, 2g fiber), 6g pro.

* HEALTH TIP * Skip the heavy frosting and dust this cake with confectioners' sugar to save almost 150 calories and 10 grams fat per serving.

5 INGREDIENTS

LEEKS AU GRATIN

Leeks are too delicious to serve only as an enhancement. Here, they're the star of a side dish, with a bit of French flair.
—Chuck Mallory, Chicago, IL

Prep: 35 min. • **Bake:** 15 min. + standing
Makes: 8 servings

- 6 medium leeks (white and pale green portion only)
- 1½ cups heavy whipping cream
- 1 tsp. kosher salt
- ½ tsp. pepper
- ½ cup grated Pecorino Romano cheese

1. Preheat oven to 375°. Cut leeks lengthwise in half; cut halves crosswise into 3-in. pieces. Place cream, salt, pepper and leeks in an ovenproof large skillet; bring to a boil over medium-high heat. Reduce heat; simmer, covered, 5 minutes. Uncover; simmer 15 minutes. Remove from heat; sprinkle with cheese.
2. Bake, uncovered, until golden and leeks are tender, 15-20 minutes. Let stand for 5-10 minutes before serving.

½ cup: 224 cal., 19g fat (12g sat. fat), 52mg chol., 378mg sod., 11g carb. (4g sugars, 1g fiber), 5g pro.

TEST KITCHEN TIP

Leeks are part of the onion family, although their flavor is more subtle.

Leeks tend trap dirt between their layers of leaves. To prepare, cut off the roots and trim the tough leaf ends. Slit the leek from end to end and wash thoroughly under cold water.

Peeps House

Create a sweet house for your favorite Easter basket treat. Use pastel candies to decorate the roof and nest.

Use frosting to join and decorate six graham cracker squares—roof, three walls and floor. Set Peeps candy on green-tinted coconut.

FIG-GLAZED CHICKEN WITH WHITE BEANS

Sauteed shallots, fig jam, rosemary, lemon and sherry vinegar make a delightful sauce for both the chicken and beans. My husband couldn't believe how well the beans absorbed the flavor, making this a grand slam. If you like, add matchstick carrots to the bean mixture for extra color, flavor and crunch.
—Arlene Erlbach, Morton Grove, IL

Prep: 10 min. • **Cook:** 30 min.
Makes: 6 servings

- **¾ cup fig preserves**
- **⅓ cup water**
- **2 Tbsp. lemon juice**
- **2 Tbsp. sherry vinegar**
- **4 tsp. minced fresh rosemary or 1 tsp. dried rosemary, crushed**
- **1 Tbsp. Worcestershire sauce**
- **¼ tsp. salt**
- **¼ tsp. pepper**
- **6 bone-in chicken thighs (about 2¼ lbs.)**
- **4 shallots, coarsely chopped**
- **1 can (15 oz.) cannellini beans, rinsed and drained**

1. Combine the first eight ingredients. In a large skillet over medium-high heat, brown the chicken in batches, starting skin side down. Remove from pan; reserve the drippings.
2. Saute shallots in the reserved drippings until golden brown, 2-3 minutes. Stir in the preserves mixture; bring to a boil, stirring to loosen browned bits from pan. Add the chicken. Reduce heat; simmer, covered, for 5 minutes.
3. Add the beans; return to a boil. Cook, uncovered, until a thermometer inserted in the chicken reads 170°-175°, about 12-15 minutes.

1 serving: 405 cal., 15g fat (4g sat. fat), 81mg chol., 287mg sod., 42g carb. (25g sugars, 3g fiber), 26g pro.

TEST KITCHEN TIP

Shallots add a mild yet distinctive flavor to sauces. Choose shallots that are firm and heavy, with dry, papery skins. Avoid any that have shoots or feel soft. Store them as you would onions, in a cool, dry place with good air circulation.

The flavorful sauce of this dish coats the chicken but will pool slightly, so serve it in a shallow bowl.

5 INGREDIENTS

HORSERADISH-GLAZED HAM

PICTURED ON P. 259

This glaze is my favorite way to really spark a baked ham. The leftovers make excellent sandwiches—with more horseradish, of course!
—Cathy & Monte Seus, Tulelake, CA

Prep: 15 min. • **Bake:** 1 hour 40 min.
Makes: 12 servings

- **1 fully cooked bone-in ham (5 to 6 lbs.)**
- **Whole cloves**
- **1 cup packed brown sugar**
- **⅓ cup prepared horseradish**
- **¼ cup lemon juice**

Using a sharp knife, score surface of ham with ¼-in.-deep cuts in a diamond pattern; insert a clove in each diamond. Bake the ham according to package directions Meanwhile, mix remaining ingredients. Brush over ham during the last 30 minutes of cooking.

4 oz. cooked ham: 232 cal., 5g fat (2g sat. fat), 83mg chol., 1026mg sod., 20g carb. (19g sugars, 0 fiber), 28g pro.

Star-Spangled Summer Party

Pull out the stops this Fourth of July with a picnic table full of scrumptious summer dishes. Mains and sides, salads and sweets, they're all here!

BOSTON BAKED BEANS

SLOW COOKER

BOSTON BAKED BEANS

Simmered in molasses, these beans are perfect to take to your next potluck. The sauce is sweet, dark and rich and they complement anything you serve with them.

—Darlene Duncan, Langhorne, PA

Prep: 20 min. + soaking • **Cook:** 10 hours
Makes: 10 servings

- **1 lb. dried navy beans**
- **6 cups water, divided**
- **¼ lb. diced salt pork or 6 bacon strips, cooked and crumbled**
- **1 large onion, chopped**
- **½ cup packed brown sugar**
- **½ cup molasses**
- **¼ cup sugar**
- **1 tsp. ground mustard**
- **1 tsp. salt**
- **½ tsp. ground cloves**
- **½ tsp. pepper**

1. Sort beans and rinse in cold water. Place the beans in a 3- or 4-qt. slow cooker; add 4 cups water. Cover and let stand overnight.
2. Drain and rinse the beans, discarding the liquid. Return beans to slow cooker; add salt pork.
3. In a small bowl, combine the onion, brown sugar, molasses, sugar, mustard, salt, cloves, pepper and remaining water. Pour mixture over beans; stir to combine.
4. Cover and cook on low for 10-12 hours or until the beans are tender.

⅔ cup: 331 cal., 6g fat (2g sat. fat), 12mg chol., 511mg sod., 58g carb. (27g sugars, 7g fiber), 13g pro.

*** HEALTH TIP *** Making baked beans from scratch allows you to control the amount of sodium, which is typically high in prepared baked beans. Decrease the salt in this recipe, if you are following a lower-sodium diet.

EAT SMART | FAST FIX

TOMATOES WITH BUTTERMILK VINAIGRETTE

I like to make the most of tomatoes when they are in season and plentiful—and I love an old-fashioned homemade dressing with summery taste.

—Judith Foreman, Alexandria, VA

Takes: 20 min.
Makes: 12 servings

- **¾ cup buttermilk**
- **¼ cup minced fresh tarragon**
- **¼ cup white wine vinegar**
- **3 Tbsp. canola oil**
- **1½ tsp. sugar**
- **½ tsp. ground mustard**
- **¼ tsp. celery salt**
- **¼ tsp. pepper**
- **4 lbs. cherry tomatoes, halved**
- **⅓ cup minced fresh chives**

1. In a small bowl, whisk the first eight ingredients until blended. Refrigerate, covered, until serving.
2. Just before serving, arrange tomatoes on a platter; drizzle with vinaigrette. Sprinkle with chives.

¾ cup: 79 cal., 4g fat (0 sat. fat), 1mg chol., 63mg sod., 10g carb. (6g sugars, 2g fiber), 2g pro. **Diabetic exchanges:** 1 vegetable, ½ starch, ½ fat.

EAT SMART

CREAMY LAYERED BLUEBERRY ICE POPS

Try these delicious pops with either raspberries or blackberries. The rosemary sprig and lemon rind bring another layer of taste. Kids love this make-ahead dessert, but do save some for the grown-ups, too.
—Gloria Bradley, Naperville, IL

Prep: 25 min. + freezing
Cook: 10 min. + cooling
Makes: 10 servings

- **⅓ cup agave nectar**
- **¼ cup water**
- **1 fresh rosemary sprig**
- **1 lemon zest strip (2 in.)**
- **1 Tbsp. lemon juice**
- **2 cups fresh or frozen blueberries**
- **2 Tbsp. sugar**
- **2¼ cups frozen whipped topping, thawed**
- **10 freezer pop molds or 10 paper cups (3 oz. each) and wooden pop sticks**

1. For the lemon syrup, place the first four ingredients in a small saucepan; bring to a boil, stirring occasionally. Remove from heat; let stand, covered, 10 minutes. Remove rosemary and lemon zest. Stir in lemon juice; cool completely.
2. Place blueberries and sugar in another saucepan; cook and stir over medium heat until the berries pop, 5-7 minutes. Cool completely.
3. Add whipped topping to the lemon syrup, whisking to blend. Transfer half of the mixture to food-safe plastic bag; cut a small hole in a corner of bag. Pipe into molds. Layer with blueberries. Pipe the remaining whipped topping mixture over top. Close molds with holders. For paper cups, top with foil and insert sticks through foil.
4. Freeze until firm, about 4 hours. To serve, dip molds briefly in warm water before removing.

1 frozen pop: 104 cal., 3g fat (3g sat. fat), 0 chol., 0 sod., 19g carb. (18g sugars, 1g fiber), 0 pro. **Diabetic exchanges:** 1 starch, ½ fat.

TEST KITCHEN TIP

Agave nectar, made from the plant used to make tequila, is a sweetener that can be used like sugar or honey. The flavor of lime works well in this recipe, too. Substitute equal parts lime zest and juice for the lemon.

5 INGREDIENTS | FAST FIX

SWIFT STRAWBERRY SALAD

PICTURED ON P. 259

A simple blend of syrup, orange juice and caramel topping forms the light dressing for fresh berries and crunchy cashews found in this sensational salad.
—*Taste of Home* Test Kitchen

Takes: 10 min. • **Makes:** 6 servings

- **4 cups sliced fresh strawberries**
- **2 Tbsp. caramel ice cream topping**
- **2 Tbsp. maple syrup**
- **1 Tbsp. orange juice**
- **⅓ cup salted cashew halves**

Place strawberries in a large bowl. Mix the caramel topping, syrup and orange juice; drizzle over the strawberries. Top with cashews.

⅔ cup: 116 cal., 4g fat (1g sat. fat), 0 chol., 59mg sod., 20g carb. (14g sugars, 3g fiber), 2g pro.

Firecracker Nachos

Dig into a patriotic platter of red, white and blue nachos–it couldn't be easier.

EAT SMART

RUBY RASPBERRY SLAW

Give ordinary coleslaw a berry twist. With its bright colors and tangy flavor, this is sure to get raves at your next picnic or potluck.
—Deborah Biggs, Omaha, NE

Prep: 15 min. + chilling
Makes: 6 servings

- **2 cups shredded red cabbage**
- **2 cups shredded cabbage**
- **1 cup shredded carrots**
- **¼ cup prepared raspberry vinaigrette**
- **3 Tbsp. mayonnaise**
- **¼ tsp. pepper**
- **½ cup fresh raspberries**

In a large bowl, combine cabbages and carrots. In a small bowl, whisk vinaigrette, mayonnaise and pepper until blended. Add to the cabbage mixture; toss to coat. Refrigerate, covered, for10 minutes. Top with raspberries.

¾ cup: 122 cal., 11g fat (1g sat. fat), 3mg chol., 144mg sod., 6g carb. (2g sugars, 2g fiber), 1g pro. **Diabetic exchanges:** 2 fat, 1 vegetable.

5 INGREDIENTS

ROASTED RED POTATO SALAD

For me, cooking is a family affair. I learned to cook from the two best cooks I know: my mom and my Grandma Etta. I got this much-loved (and often requested) recipe from my sister-in-law.
—Ginger Cusano, Sandusky, OH

Prep: 40 min. + chilling
Makes: 6-8 servings

- **2 lbs. red potatoes, cut into 1-in. cubes**
- **1 medium onion, chopped**
- **4 large hard-boiled large eggs, sliced**
- **6 bacon strips, cooked and crumbled**
- **1 cup mayonnaise**
- **½ tsp. salt**
- **¼ tsp. pepper**
- **Paprika, optional**

1. Preheat oven to 400°. Place the potatoes in a greased 15x10x1-in. baking pan. Bake, uncovered, for 25-30 minutes or until tender and golden brown, stirring occasionally. Cool for 15 minutes.
2. Transfer potatoes to a large bowl; add onion, eggs, bacon, mayonnaise, salt and pepper. Toss to coat. Cover and refrigerate for several hours or overnight. Sprinkle with paprika if desired.

1 serving: 355 cal., 27g fat (5g sat. fat), 120mg chol., 412mg sod., 20g carb. (3g sugars, 2g fiber), 7g pro.

STRAWBERRY GELATO

You'll love this smooth and creamy gelato with bright strawberry flavor and just a hint of sea salt and honey.
—Shelly Bevington, Hermiston, OR

Prep: 10 min. + chilling
Process: 25 min. • **Makes:** 1½ qt.

- **2 cups whole milk**
- **2 Tbsp. light corn syrup**
- **1 Tbsp. honey**
- **¾ cup sugar**
- **½ tsp. sea salt**
- **2½ cups fresh strawberries (about 12 oz.), halved**
- **½ cup heavy whipping cream**
- **1 tsp. lemon juice**

1. Place the first six ingredients in a blender; cover and process until blended. While processing, gradually add cream, processing just until combined. Remove to a bowl; stir in lemon juice. Refrigerate, covered, until cold, about 4 hours.
2. Fill cylinder of ice cream maker no more than two-thirds full; freeze according to manufacturer's directions. (Refrigerate any remaining mixture until ready to freeze.)
3. Transfer ice cream to airtight freezer containers, allowing headspace for expansion. Freeze until firm, 3-4 hours.

½ cup: 160 cal., 6g fat (4g sat. fat), 18mg chol., 124mg sod., 26g carb. (25g sugars, 1g fiber), 2g pro.

*

TEST KITCHEN TIP

This recipe makes 4¾ cups of strawberry mixture before freezing and yields about 6 cups after freezing. If you have a 1-qt. ice cream maker, you will probably need to make the gelato in two batches. Be sure to follow your manufacturer's instruction manual.

Corn syrup and honey contribute to the smoothness of this frozen treat by preventing the formation of ice crystals. If your berries are tart, you may want to add a touch more sugar or honey.

STRAWBERRY GELATO

SLOW COOKER

COUNTRY-STYLE BARBECUE RIBS

These get a good sear under the broiler, then go into the slow cooker until they're fall-apart tender. Enjoy them with sides, or shred and serve on a bun. Either way, they're the most amazing ribs ever.
—Shannon Copley, Upper Arlington, OH

Prep: 15 min. • **Cook:** 3 hours
Makes: 10 servings

- **2 Tbsp. paprika**
- **2 Tbsp. brown sugar**
- **2 tsp. salt**
- **2 tsp. garlic powder**
- **2 tsp. chili powder**
- **1 tsp. onion powder**
- **1 tsp. ground chipotle pepper**
- **1 tsp. pepper**
- **¾ tsp. dried thyme**
- **4 lbs. boneless country-style pork ribs**
- **1 bottle (18 oz.) barbecue sauce**
- **¾ cup amber beer or reduced-sodium chicken broth**

1. Preheat broiler. Mix the first nine ingredients. Place pork ribs in a foil-lined 15x10x1-in. pan; rub generously with the seasoning mixture. Broil 4-5 in. from heat until browned, 2-3 minutes per side.
2. Transfer to a 5-qt. slow cooker. Whisk together barbecue sauce and beer; pour over the ribs. Cook, covered, on low until tender, 3-4 hours.
3. Remove ribs. Reserve 2 cups of the cooking juices; discard the remaining juices. Skim fat from the reserved juices. Serve with ribs.

1 serving: 393 cal., 17g fat (6g sat. fat), 105mg chol., 1098mg sod., 26g carb. (20g sugars, 1g fiber), 33g pro.

No Trick, All Treats!

Satisfy your sweet tooth this Halloween with a cool collection of mouthwatering treats, perfect for a spooky holiday party!

GHOSTLY CUSTARDS

EAT SMART

GHOSTLY CUSTARDS

You'll hear shrieks of delight when these not-too-spooky custards appear for dessert. These ghosts will be gobbled up in no time!
—Suzanne Strocsher, Bothell, WA

Prep: 10 min. • **Bake:** 40 min. + cooling
Makes: 8 servings

- **1 can (15 oz.) solid-pack pumpkin**
- **1 can (12 oz.) evaporated milk**
- **⅓ cup sugar**
- **2 Tbsp. honey**
- **1 tsp. ground cinnamon**
- **¾ tsp. ground allspice**
- **2 large eggs**
- **2 cups whipped topping**
- **Miniature semisweet chocolate chips**

In a bowl, combine the first seven ingredients; beat on low until smooth. Place eight ungreased 4-oz. custard cups in two 8-in. square baking pans. Fill each cup with ½ cup pumpkin mixture. Pour hot water around cups into the pans to a depth of 1 in. Bake at 325° for 40-50 minutes or until a knife inserted in the center comes out clean. Remove from pans to cool on wire racks. Before serving, top each with dollops of whipped topping in the shape of a ghost; add chocolate chips for eyes.

1 serving: 189 cal., 7g fat (5g sat. fat), 60mg chol., 61mg sod., 25g carb. (23g sugars, 2g fiber), 5g pro. **Diabetic exchanges:** 1½ starch, 1½ fat.

FROSTY GINGER PUMPKIN SQUARES

My family loves getting together to sample good food. While pumpkin is perfect for the fall holidays, this ice cream dessert is requested year-round.
—Kathryn Reeger, Shelocta, PA

Prep: 30 min. + freezing
Makes: 15 servings

- **¼ cup butter, melted**
- **1 cup crushed graham cracker (about 16 squares)**
- **1 cup crushed gingersnaps (about 18 cookies)**
- **2 cups canned pumpkin**
- **1 cup sugar**
- **½ to 1 tsp. ground cinnamon**
- **½ tsp. salt**
- **½ tsp. ground ginger**
- **¼ tsp. ground nutmeg**
- **1 cup chopped walnuts**
- **½ gallon vanilla ice cream, slightly softened**

1. In a large bowl, combine the butter, graham crackers and gingersnaps. Press two-thirds of the crumb mixture into an ungreased 13x9-in. dish.
2. In a large bowl, combine the pumpkin, sugar, cinnamon, salt, ginger and nutmeg. Stir in walnuts. Fold in ice cream. Spoon into crust. Sprinkle the remaining crumb mixture over top. Freeze until firm, about 3 hours.

1 piece: 351 cal., 18g fat (8g sat. fat), 39mg chol., 234mg sod., 46g carb. (33g sugars, 2g fiber), 5g pro.

Candy Corn Pudding Pops

Turn a Halloween favorite into a sweet freeze.

Whisk instant cheesecake pudding mix (3.4 oz.) with 2 cups 2% milk and ½ cup heavy cream. Color one-third orange and one-third yellow. Add in layers to freezer pop molds.

BROWNED BUTTER CEREAL BARS

Crispy rice treats were one of the first recipes I ever made as a kid. This version is similar but more special. Friends and family think using Cap'n Crunch and browned butter is genius, but I just call them delicious.
—Kelly Krauss, Lebanon, NJ

Prep: 15 min. + freezing
Cook: 20 min. + cooling • **Makes:** 5 dozen

- **4 cups white fudge-covered miniature pretzels**
- **1 pkg. (10½ oz.) miniature marshmallows**
- **1 pkg. (10 to 12 oz.) white baking chips**
- **2 cups butter, cubed**
- **3 pkg. (10 oz. each) large marshmallows**
- **2 tsp. vanilla extract**
- **1 tsp. salt**
- **8 cups Cap'n Crunch**

1. Place pretzels, miniature marshmallows and baking chips in the freezer for 1 hour. Line a 15x10x1-in. pan with parchment, letting ends extend over sides; set aside.
2. In a large bowl, combine frozen pretzels, marshmallows and baking chips. In a Dutch oven, melt butter over medium heat. Heat 10-13 minutes or until golden brown, stirring constantly. Add the large marshmallows; cook and stir until blended. Remove from heat; stir in vanilla and salt.
3. Stir in cereal until coated. Stir in the pretzel mixture; transfer to the prepared pan, pressing evenly with a buttered spatula. Cool completely.
4. Lifting with parchment, remove the cereal mixture from pan. Cut into bars. Store in airtight containers.

1 bar: 186 cal., 9g fat (6g sat. fat), 17mg chol., 172mg sod., 27g carb. (18g sugars, 0 fiber), 1g pro.

FAST FIX

APPLE BRICKLE DIP

I first tasted this delectable dip at a friend's Christmas party. I just kept going back for more—and knew it was a must-have recipe.
—Karen Wydrinski, Woodstock, GA

Takes: 10 min. • **Makes:** 2 cups

- **1 pkg. (8 oz.) cream cheese, softened**
- **½ cup packed brown sugar**
- **¼ cup sugar**
- **1 tsp. vanilla extract**
- **1 pkg. almond brickle chips (7½ oz.) or English toffee bits (10 oz.)**
- **3 medium tart apples, cut into chunks**

In a bowl, beat cream cheese, sugars and vanilla. Fold in brickle chips. Serve with apples. Refrigerate any leftovers.

2 Tbsp.: 174 cal., 9g fat (5g sat. fat), 20mg chol., 120mg sod., 22g carb. (21g sugars, 1g fiber), 1g pro.

Thanksgiving Feast

A spiced cider to start things off, the perfect roast turkey, cranberry sauce, sides and a beautiful change-of-pace pumpkin dessert...everything you need for a memorable Thanksgiving dinner is here, making it easy to get a full feast on the table!

RICE DRESSING

RICE DRESSING

This yummy rice mixture is a delightful change from our traditional cornbread dressing. To make it a meal in itself, I'll add finely chopped cooked chicken and a little more broth before baking.
—Linda Emery, Bearden, AR

Prep: 35 min. • **Bake:** 30 min.
Makes: 10 servings

- **4 cups chicken broth, divided**
- **1½ cups uncooked long grain rice**
- **2 cups chopped onion**
- **2 cups chopped celery**
- **½ cup butter, cubed**
- **2 cans (4 oz. each) mushroom stems and pieces, drained**
- **3 Tbsp. minced fresh parsley**
- **1½ to 2 tsp. poultry seasoning**
- **¾ tsp. salt**
- **½ tsp. pepper**
- **Fresh sage and thyme, optional**

1. Preheat oven to 350°. In a saucepan, bring 3½ cups broth and the rice to a boil. Reduce heat; cover and simmer until tender, about 20 minutes.
2. Meanwhile, in a skillet, saute onion and celery in butter until tender. Stir in rice, mushrooms, parsley, poultry seasoning, salt, pepper and the remaining broth. Pour into a greased 13x9-in. baking dish. Bake, uncovered, for 30 minutes. Garnish with sage and thyme if desired.

¾ cup: 221 cal., 10g fat (6g sat. fat), 26mg chol., 727mg sod., 29g carb. (2g sugars, 1g fiber), 4g pro.

SPICED CIDER PUNCH

I've shared this punch with many friends, and it never wears out its welcome. Serve it warm to take the chill off in winter.
—Charles Piatt, Little Rock, AR

Prep: 5 min. + chilling • **Cook:** 5 min.
Makes: 12 servings (about 3¼ qt.)

- **1 cup sugar**
- **1 tsp. ground cinnamon**
- **1 tsp. ground allspice**
- **1 bottle (64 oz.) apple cider or apple juice, divided**
- **1 can (12 oz.) frozen orange juice concentrate**
- **1 liter ginger ale, chilled**
- **Orange slices, optional**

1. Place sugar, spices and 1 cup cider in a saucepan; cook and stir over medium heat until sugar is dissolved. Remove from heat; stir in juice concentrate until melted.
2. Transfer to a large pitcher. Stir in the remaining cider. Refrigerate, covered, until cold.
3. To serve, pour cider mixture into a punch bowl. Stir in ginger ale. If desired, garnish with orange slices.

1 cup: 217 cal., 0 fat (0 sat. fat), 0 chol., 25mg sod., 55g carb. (50g sugars, 0 fiber), 1g pro.

5 INGREDIENTS | FAST FIX

BUTTERMILK SMASHED POTATOES

PICTURED ON P. 259

This recipe of buttermilk, potatoes and butter tastes luscious and decadent, but it's made using reduced-fat ingredients. My family loves it. Serve with your favorite toppings and indulge!

—Marla Clark, Albuquerque, NM

Takes: 30 min. • **Makes:** 8 servings

- **4 lbs. Yukon Gold potatoes, peeled and cubed (about 8 cups)**
- **½ cup butter, softened**
- **1¼ tsp. salt**
- **¼ tsp. pepper**
- **¾ to 1 cup buttermilk**
- **Optional toppings: crumbled cooked bacon, sour cream and thinly sliced green onions**

1. Place potatoes in a 6-qt. stockpot; add water to cover. Bring to a boil. Reduce heat; cook, uncovered, 10-15 minutes or until tender.

2. Drain; return potatoes to pan. Mash potatoes, gradually adding butter, salt, pepper and enough buttermilk to reach the desired consistency. Serve with toppings as desired.

¾ cup: 313 cal., 12g fat (7g sat. fat), 31mg chol., 531mg sod., 46g carb. (4g sugars, 4g fiber), 6g pro.

SWEET POTATO CRANBERRY BAKE

In October, my husband helps harvest cranberries at a friend's bogs, so I have access to the very freshest ingredients. Their bold autumn flavor pairs perfectly with sweet potatoes to make a seasonal side dish that my family looks forward to every year.

—Jill Doyle, Kingston, MA

Prep: 50 min. • **Bake:** 40 min.
Makes: 8 servings

- **4 large sweet potatoes**
- **2 cups fresh or frozen cranberries**
- **½ cup packed brown sugar**
- **2 Tbsp. butter, melted**
- **½ cup orange juice**

TOPPING

- **½ cup chopped walnuts**
- **¼ cup packed brown sugar**
- **½ tsp. ground cinnamon**
- **3 Tbsp. cold butter**

1. Place sweet potatoes in a Dutch oven; cover with water. Bring to a boil. Reduce heat; cover and simmer until tender, 20-30 minutes. Drain. When cool enough to handle, peel potatoes and cut into ¼-in. slices.

2. Preheat oven to 350°. Place half of the sweet potatoes in a greased 2½-qt. baking dish. Top with half the cranberries, brown sugar and butter. Repeat layers. Pour orange juice over top. Cover and bake for 30 minutes.

3. In a small bowl, combine the walnuts, brown sugar and cinnamon; cut in butter. Sprinkle over the sweet potato mixture. Bake, uncovered, until topping is golden brown, about 10 minutes longer.

¾ cup: 386 cal., 12g fat (5g sat. fat), 19mg chol., 81mg sod., 68g carb. (40g sugars, 7g fiber), 4g pro.

* HEALTH TIP * One serving of this classic side provides all the vitamin A your body needs for the day.

Roll With It!

Serve a showstopping holiday dessert? Piece of cake! Bake this gorgeous rolled cake as a grand finale for your Thanksgiving feast.

PUMPKIN CAKE ROLL

This lovely cake is a slice of heaven—especially if you like cream cheese and pumpkin. With such excellent attributes, consider it as a fancy alternative to pumpkin pie for Thanksgiving dessert.
—Elizabeth Montgomery, Allston, MA

Prep: 25 min. • **Bake:** 15 min. + chilling
Makes: 10 servings

- 3 large eggs, room temperature
- 1 cup sugar
- ⅔ cup canned pumpkin
- 1 tsp. lemon juice
- ¾ cup all-purpose flour
- 2 tsp. ground cinnamon
- 1 tsp. baking powder
- ½ tsp. salt
- ¼ tsp. ground nutmeg
- 1 cup finely chopped walnuts

CREAM CHEESE FILLING

- 6 oz. cream cheese, softened
- 1 cup confectioners' sugar
- ¼ cup butter, softened
- ½ tsp. vanilla extract
- Additional confectioners' sugar

1 slice: 365 cal., 20g fat (8g sat. fat), 85mg chol., 279mg sod., 44g carb. (33g sugars, 2g fiber), 6g pro.

TEST KITCHEN TIP

Be patient when beating eggs. Aerating them (a fancy term for incorporating air) lends structure and light texture to this delicate cake. This tender cake can tear easily, so work slowly when spreading the filling.

Cool the rolled cake seam-side down to prevent it from unrolling.

HOW-TO

Make a Pumpkin Cake Roll

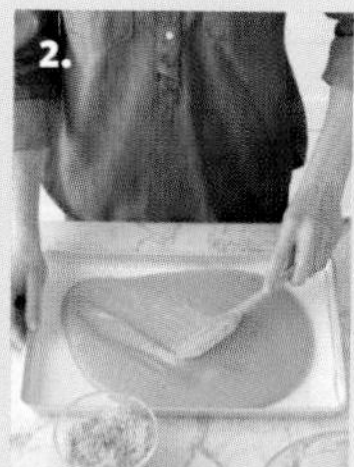

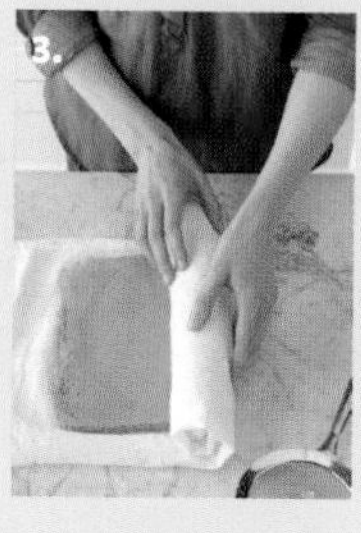

1. Mix
Beat eggs on high for 5 minutes. Gradually beat in sugar until thick and lemon-colored. Add pumpkin and lemon juice. Combine the next five ingredients; fold into the pumpkin mixture.

2. Bake
Grease a 15x10x1-in. baking pan and line with greased and floured parchment. Spread batter into pan; sprinkle with walnuts. Bake at 375° until the cake springs back, about 15 minutes.

3. Roll
Immediately turn out cake onto a clean dish towel dusted lightly with confectioners' sugar. Peel off parchment and roll cake up in the towel, starting with a short end. Cool.

4. Fill
Beat softened cream cheese, confectioners' sugar, butter and vanilla until fluffy. Carefully unroll the cake. Spread filling over cake to within 1 in. of edges. Roll up cake without the towel. Cover and chill until serving. Dust with confectioners' sugar.

HERB-GLAZED TURKEY

Honey and corn syrup blend with savoy herbs and seasonings to give this turkey a slightly sweet flavor. My tried-and-true recipe never fails to win compliments.
—Charlene Melenka, Vegreville, AB

Prep: 10 min. • **Bake:** 4 hours + standing
Makes: 18 servings

- **1 turkey (14 to 16 lbs.)**
- **¼ cup olive oil**
- **2 tsp. dried thyme**
- **1½ tsp. salt, divided**
- **1¼ tsp. pepper, divided**
- **1 cup honey**
- **1 cup corn syrup**
- **¼ cup butter, melted**
- **2 tsp. dried rosemary, crushed**
- **1 tsp. rubbed sage**
- **1 tsp. dried basil**

1. Preheat oven to 325°. Brush turkey with oil; tie the drumsticks together. Place the turkey breast-side up on a rack in a roasting pan. Combine the thyme, 1 tsp. of salt and 1 tsp. of pepper; sprinkle evenly over turkey. Bake, uncovered, for 2 hours.
2. In a small bowl, combine honey, corn syrup, butter, rosemary, sage, basil and remaining salt and pepper. Brush over the turkey. Bake until a thermometer inserted in the thickest part of a thigh reads 170°-175°, basting frequently with pan drippings, about 90 minutes longer. Cover turkey loosely with foil if it browns too quickly. Remove from oven. Cover and let stand for 15 minutes before carving.

7 oz. cooked turkey: 570 cal., 25g fat (8g sat. fat), 197mg chol., 380mg sod., 30g carb. (24g sugars, 0 fiber), 56g pro.

HERB-GLAZED TURKEY

5 INGREDIENTS

CRANBERRY SAUCE

I turn to this recipe frequently because I can prepare it a day ahead—it's so convenient when company's coming. And with only a trace of fat, the fruity condiment is nutritious and delicious.
—Nancy Zimmerman, Cape May Court House, NJ

Prep: 5 min. • **Cook:** 15 min. + chilling
Makes: about 2¾ cups

- **1 pkg. (12 oz.) fresh or frozen cranberries**
- **1 cup sugar**
- **1 cup cranberry-raspberry juice**
- **1 Tbsp. lemon juice**

Place cranberries, sugar and cranberry-raspberry juice in a large saucepan; bring to a boil, stirring to dissolve the sugar. Reduce heat; simmer, covered, until the cranberries pop, 10-15 minutes, stirring occasionally Remove from heat; stir in lemon juice. Transfer to a bowl; cool slightly. Refrigerate, covered, until cold.

¼ cup: 106 cal., 0 fat (0 sat. fat), 0 chol., 2mg sod., 27g carb. (24g sugars, 1g fiber), 0 pro.

Deck the Halls

Welcome friends to your home with an array of holiday appetizers, drinks and sweets to warm the heart and the belly—all perfect for a friendly Christmas get-together or holiday open house.

SPRUCED-UP CHEESE SPREAD

FAST FIX

SPRUCED-UP CHEESE SPREAD

A neighbor who is a wonderful cook gave me the recipe for this zippy cracker spread. I sometimes shape it into a Christmas tree for a festive occasion.
—Judy Grimes, Brandon, MS

Takes: 20 min.
Makes: 32 servings (2 Tbsp. each)

- **1 cup mayonnaise**
- **1 small onion, grated**
- **1 to 2 Tbsp. prepared mustard**
- **1 Tbsp. Worcestershire sauce**
- **1 tsp. celery seed**
- **½ tsp. paprika**
- **¼ tsp. garlic salt**
- **1 jar (4 oz.) diced pimientos, drained, divided**
- **3 cups finely shredded sharp cheddar cheese**
- **Minced fresh parsley**
- **2 Tbsp. finely chopped pecans**
- **Assorted crackers**

Mix the first seven ingredients and ⅓ cup pimientos. Stir in cheese. Transfer to a serving dish. Sprinkle with parsley, pecans and the remaining pimientos. Serve with crackers.

2 Tbsp. spread: 93 cal., 9g fat (3g sat. fat), 11mg chol., 131mg sod., 1g carb. (0 sugars, 0 fiber), 3g pro.

SLOW COOKER

HOT SPICED WINE

My friends, family and I enjoy this spiced wine during cold-winter gatherings. This warm drink will be especially pleasing to people who enjoy dry red wines.
—Noel Lickenfelt, Bolivar, PA

Prep: 10 min. • **Cook:** 4 hours
Makes: 8 servings

- **2 cinnamon sticks (3 in.)**
- **3 whole cloves**
- **3 medium tart apples, peeled and sliced**
- **½ cup sugar**
- **1 tsp. lemon juice**
- **2 bottles (750 ml each) dry red wine**

Place cinnamon sticks and cloves on a double thickness of cheesecloth. Gather corners of the cloth to enclose spices; tie securely with string. Place in a 3-qt. slow cooker. Add the remaining ingredients. Cook, covered, on low until flavors are blended, 4-5 hours. Discard spice bag. Serve warm.

¾ cup: 231 cal., 0 fat (0 sat. fat), 0 chol., 8mg sod., 24g carb. (19g sugars, 1g fiber), 0 pro.

COOKIES & CREAM STUFFED SANTA BELLIES

All hands will be reaching for these cute cookies, and you know kids love 'em! If your kitchen is warm from baking all day, chill your dough for a bit before rolling it out.
—Crystal Schlueter, Babbitt, MN

Prep: 55 min. + chilling
Bake: 10 min./batch + cooling
Makes: about 2 dozen

- **1 cup unsalted butter, softened**
- **1 cup sugar**
- **2 large eggs, room temperature**
- **1 Tbsp. vanilla extract**
- **3½ cups all-purpose flour**
- **1 Tbsp. baking powder**
- **½ tsp. salt**
- **6 to 7 Hershey's Cookies 'n' Creme candy bars (1.55 oz. each), broken into 3-section pieces**
- **2½ cups vanilla frosting**
- **Red, black and yellow paste food coloring**

1. Cream butter and sugar until light and fluffy. Beat in eggs and vanilla. In another bowl, whisk together flour, baking powder and salt; gradually beat into the creamed mixture. Divide dough in half; shape each into a disk. Wrap and refrigerate until firm enough to roll, at least 1 hour.
2. Preheat oven to 350°. On a lightly floured surface, roll each portion of dough to ⅛-in. thickness. Cut with a floured 3-in. round cutter.
3. Place half of the circles 1 in. apart on ungreased baking sheets; top with candy bar pieces. Top with the remaining circles, pinching the edges to seal.
4. Bake until the bottoms are light brown, 10-12 minutes. Remove from pans to wire racks to cool completely.
5. Tint 1⅔ cups of the frosting red; spread over cookies. Tint ⅔ cup of the frosting black; pipe belts and buttons over top. Tint the remaining frosting yellow; pipe buckles on belts.

1 filled cookie: 350 cal., 16g fat (8g sat. fat), 37mg chol., 202mg sod., 49g carb. (30g sugars, 0 fiber), 3g pro.

5 INGREDIENTS | FAST FIX

CREAMY HOT CHOCOLATE

You need just a few basic ingredients to stir up this spirit-warming sipper. The comforting beverage is smooth and not too sweet, making it just right for cozy chilly nights.
—Flo Snodderly, North Vernon, IN

Takes: 15 min. • **Makes:** 8 servings

- **1 can (14 oz.) sweetened condensed milk**
- **½ cup baking cocoa**
- **6½ cups water**
- **2 tsp. vanilla extract**
- **Sweetened whipped cream, optional**

Place milk and cocoa in a large saucepan; cook and stir over medium heat until blended. Gradually stir in water; heat through, stirring occasionally. Remove from heat; stir in vanilla. If desired, top with whipped cream.

1 cup: 177 cal., 5g fat (3g sat. fat), 17mg chol., 63mg sod., 30g carb. (27g sugars, 1g fiber), 5g pro.

Quick & Easy Chocolate Sauce

Looking for a just-right gift for neighbors, teachers or co-workers? Take care of the chocolate lovers on your list with DIY reindeer jars filled with luscious homemade fudge.

REINDEER SNACK MIX

Rudolph and his pals will be dashing, dancing and prancing to gobble up this savory snack mix. Humans also will enjoy the buttery, perfectly seasoned and wonderfully crunchy combination.
—*Taste of Home* Test Kitchen

Prep: 10 min. • **Bake:** 1 hour
Makes: 12 servings (about 2¼ qt.)

- **2 cups Bugles**
- **2 cups pretzel sticks**
- **2 cups cheese-flavored snack crackers**
- **1 cup bite-sized Shredded Wheat**
- **1 cup Corn Chex**
- **1 cup pecan halves**
- **½ cup butter, cubed**
- **1 Tbsp. maple syrup**
- **1½ tsp. Worcestershire sauce**
- **¾ tsp. Cajun seasoning**
- **¼ tsp. cayenne pepper**

1. Preheat oven to 250°. Place the first six ingredients in a large bowl. In a microwave, melt butter; stir in remaining ingredients. Drizzle over snack mixture; toss to combine. Transfer to an ungreased 15x10x1-in. pan.
2. Bake 1 hour, stirring every 15 minutes. Cool completely before storing in an airtight container.

¾ cup: 239 cal., 16g fat (6g sat. fat), 21mg chol., 331mg sod., 22g carb. (2g sugars, 2g fiber), 3g pro.

FAST FIX
FESTIVE HOLIDAY SLIDERS

PICTURED ON P. 259

My mini turkey sandwiches with cranberry sauce, horseradish and ginger keep well in the refrigerator. I like to have a batch on hand for holiday get-togethers.
—Pamela Miller, Big Rapids, MI

Takes: 30 min. • **Makes:** 2 dozen

- **1 pkg. (8 oz.) cream cheese, softened**
- **½ cup mayonnaise**
- **¼ cup Creole mustard**
- **2 Tbsp. minced fresh gingerroot**
- **1 Tbsp. grated orange zest**
- **1½ tsp. prepared horseradish**
- **1 cup whole-berry cranberry sauce**
- **4 green onions, sliced**
- **2 pkg. (12 oz. each) Hawaiian sweet rolls or 24 dinner rolls, split**
- **1½ lbs. thinly sliced cooked turkey**

1. Beat cream cheese and mayonnaise until smooth. Beat in the mustard, ginger, orange zest and horseradish. In another bowl, combine the cranberry sauce and green onions.
2. Spread the cream cheese mixture onto roll bottoms. Top with turkey, the cranberry mixture and roll tops.

1 slider: 231 cal., 10g fat (4g sat. fat), 54mg chol., 221mg sod., 22g carb. (10g sugars, 1g fiber), 13g pro

SLOW COOKER

CINNAMON ROLL CASSEROLE

Because we love cinnamon rolls, I created a slow cooker recipe suitable for a weekend breakfast or brunch. This delicious, simple, no-fuss recipe is perfect for both company and family.

—Joan Hallford, North Richland Hills, TX

Prep: 20 min. • **Cook:** 2½ hours
Makes: 10 servings

- **2 tubes (12.40 oz. each) refrigerated cinnamon rolls with icing, cut into quarters**
- **½ cup chopped toasted pecans, divided**
- **½ cup miniature semisweet chocolate chips, divided**
- **½ cup evaporated milk**
- **3 Tbsp. maple syrup**
- **2 tsp. vanilla extract**
- **1 tsp. ground cinnamon**
- **½ cup all-purpose flour**
- **½ cup packed brown sugar**
- **¼ tsp. pumpkin pie spice**
- **½ cup cold butter, cubed**

1. Place half of the cinnamon roll pieces in a greased 4- or 5-qt. slow cooker. Sprinkle with ¼ cup pecans and ¼ cup chocolate chips. In a small bowl, whisk milk, syrup, vanilla and cinnamon until blended; pour over the rolls. Top with the remaining cinnamon roll pieces and the remaining chocolate chips. Top with one packet of the icing.
2. For topping, mix flour, brown sugar and pie spice; cut in butter until crumbly. Stir in the remaining pecans. Sprinkle over icing. Cook, covered, on low for 2½ to 3 hours or until the rolls are set. Remove insert and top with the remaining icing. Serve warm.

1 serving: 492 cal., 25g fat (11g sat. fat), 28mg chol., 638mg sod., 65g carb. (36g sugars, 2g fiber), 5g pro.

CINNAMON ROLL CASSEROLE

FAST FIX

CHRISTMAS MEATBALLS

Cranberry sauce and brown sugar create a tangy glaze for meatballs that are good as an appetizer or as a main dish over rice. We love them so much, I prepare them year-round.

—Joyce Bentley, Redlands, CA

Takes: 30 min. • **Makes:** about 3 dozen

- **2 large eggs, lightly beaten**
- **1 envelope onion soup mix**
- **½ cup seasoned bread crumbs**
- **¼ cup chopped dried cranberries**
- **2 Tbsp. minced fresh parsley**
- **1½ lbs. lean ground beef (90% lean)**

SAUCE

- **1 can (14 oz.) whole-berry cranberry sauce**
- **¾ cup ketchup**
- **½ cup beef broth**
- **3 Tbsp. brown sugar**
- **3 Tbsp. finely chopped onion**
- **2 tsp. cider vinegar**

1. In a large bowl, combine the first five ingredients. Add ground beef; mix lightly but thoroughly. Shape into 1-in. balls.
2. Place a third of the meatballs on a microwave-safe plate. Cover with waxed paper; microwave on high until cooked through, 2-3 minutes. Drain on paper towels. Repeat twice with the remaining meatballs.
3. In a 2-qt. microwave-safe dish, mix sauce ingredients. Microwave, covered, on high until heated through, 3-4 minutes, stirring halfway. Gently stir in meatballs. Microwave, covered, on high until heated through, 1-2 minutes.

1 meatball: 71 cal., 2g fat (1g sat. fat), 22mg chol., 190mg sod., 9g carb. (6g sugars, 0 fiber), 4g pro

5 INGREDIENTS

HOMEMADE LIMONCELLO

Homemade limoncello is as good, if not better, than store bought. The after-dinner liqueur is considered the national drink of Italy. Just one sip and you'll understand why.
—Jenni Sharp, Milwaukee, WI

Prep: 40 min. + standing • **Makes:** 1½ qt.

10 medium lemons
1 bottle (750 ml) vodka
3 cups water
1½ cups sugar

1. Using a vegetable peeler, peel rind from lemons (save lemons for another use). With a sharp knife, scrape pith from the peels and discard. Place lemon peels and vodka in a large glass or plastic container. Cover and let stand at room temperature for at least 2 weeks, stirring once a week.
2. In a large saucepan, bring water and sugar to a boil. Reduce heat; simmer, uncovered, for 10 minutes. Let cool completely.
3. Strain the vodka mixture; discard the lemon peels. Return the mixture to the container; stir in the sugar mixture. Pour into glass bottles; seal tightly. Let stand for 2 weeks. Serve chilled.

1½ oz.: 87 cal., 0 fat (0 sat. fat), 0 chol., 0 sod., 9g carb. (9g sugars, 0 fiber), 0 pro.

GINGERBREAD TORTE

GINGERBREAD TORTE

This old-fashioned gingerbread cake is excellent! Lemon zest in the cream cheese frosting adds a bright note and keeps the frosting from being too sweet.
—Ginger Hendricksen, Wisconsin Rapids, WI

Prep: 30 min. • **Bake:** 20 min. + cooling
Makes: 12 servings

¾ cup butter, softened
¾ cup sugar
2 large eggs, room temperature
1 cup molasses
3 cups all-purpose flour
2 tsp. baking soda
3 tsp. ground ginger
1½ tsp. ground cinnamon
¾ tsp. salt
1 cup 2% milk

FROSTING

1 pkg. (8 oz.) cream cheese, softened
¼ cup butter, softened
2 tsp. grated lemon zest
3¾ cups confectioners' sugar
Chopped crystallized ginger, optional

1. Preheat oven to 350°. Line the bottoms of three greased 9-in. round baking pans with parchment; grease the parchment.
2. Cream butter and sugar until light and fluffy. Beat in eggs, one at a time. Gradually beat in molasses. In another bowl, whisk together flour, baking soda, spices and salt; add to creamed mixture alternately with milk. Transfer to the prepared pans.
3. Bake until a toothpick inserted in the center comes out clean, 20-25 minutes. Cool in pans 10 minutes before removing to wire racks; remove the parchment. Cool completely.
4. Beat cream cheese, butter and lemon zest until blended; gradually beat in confectioners' sugar. Spread or pipe ⅔ cup frosting between each layer. Top with the remaining frosting. If desired, sprinkle with crystallized ginger. Store in refrigerator.

1 slice: 612 cal., 23g fat (14g sat. fat), 92mg chol., 571mg sod., 97g carb. (71g sugars, 1g fiber), 6g pro.

CHERRY WALDORF SALAD

Classic Waldorf salad gets a fun holiday spin when tart cherries and dried cranberries are added to the crunchy-creamy mix.
—Marie Hattrup, Sonoma, CA

Prep: 15 min. + chilling
Makes: 8 servings

- **¼ cup mayonnaise**
- **¼ cup sour cream**
- **2 Tbsp. honey**
- **⅛ tsp. salt**
- **2 large apples (about 1 lb.), cubed**
- **1 Tbsp. lemon juice**
- **2 celery ribs, chopped**
- **½ cup dried cranberries**
- **½ cup slivered almonds, toasted**
- **1 cup fresh or frozen pitted tart cherries, thawed**

For dressing, whisk together first four ingredients. In a large bowl, toss apples with lemon juice. Add celery, cranberries and almonds; toss with dressing. Gently stir in cherries. Refrigerate, covered, for 1 hour before serving.

Note: To toast nuts, bake in a shallow pan in a 350° oven for 5-10 minutes or cook in a skillet over low heat until lightly browned, stirring occasionally.

¾ cup: 181 cal., 10g fat (2g sat. fat), 2mg chol., 84mg sod., 23g carb. (19g sugars, 3g fiber), 2g pro.

VERY CHERRY CRESCENT RING

My mother used to prepare this pretty coffee cake on Christmas Eve for our family to enjoy the next morning after opening gifts. It's an easy way to add an elegant touch to a holiday breakfast or brunch.
—Karen Sevensky, Hackettstown, NJ

Prep: 25 min. • **Bake:** 20 min.
Makes: 16 servings

- **1 jar (10 oz.) maraschino cherries, drained well and chopped**
- **1 pkg. (8 oz.) cream cheese, softened**
- **½ cup sugar**
- **½ tsp. almond extract**
- **¾ cup chopped pecans**
- **2 tubes (8 oz. each) refrigerated crescent rolls**

GLAZE

- **1 cup confectioners' sugar**
- **1 to 2 Tbsp. 2% milk**
- **¼ tsp. almond extract**
- **Additional pecans**

1. Preheat oven to 375°. Reserve 3 Tbsp. cherries for topping. For filling, beat the cream cheese, sugar and extract until smooth. Stir in ¾ cup pecans and the remaining cherries.
2. On a lightly floured surface, unroll crescent dough into one long rectangle; press perforations to seal. Fold the dough lengthwise in half; roll into an 18x12-in. rectangle. Spread filling over top to within 1 in. of edges. Roll up tightly jelly-roll style, starting with a long side; pinch the seam to seal.
3. Transfer roll to a greased baking sheet, seam-side down; shape into a ring, pinching ends to seal. Using kitchen scissors, start at the outside edge and cut two-thirds of the way through the ring at 1-in. intervals. Separate sections slightly and twist to show the filling.
4. Bake until golden brown, 20-30 minutes. (Cover loosely with foil if it browns too quickly.)
5. Using two large spatulas, remove from pan to a wire rack. Mix confectioners' sugar, milk and extract; spoon over the warm coffeecake. Top with reserved cherries and, if desired, additional pecans.

1 slice: 273 cal., 15g fat (5g sat. fat), 14mg chol., 268mg sod., 33g carb. (23g sugars, 0 fiber), 3g pro.

VERY CHERRY CRESCENT RING

EGGNOG BISCOTTI

You may substitute additional eggnog for the rum if rum isn't your thing. As a variation, try using one of the flavored eggnogs available around the holidays.
—Shannon Dobos, Calgary, AB

Prep: 25 min. • **Bake:** 40 min. + cooling
Makes: about 3 dozen

- **½ cup butter, softened**
- **1 cup sugar**
- **2 large eggs, room temperature**
- **¼ cup eggnog**
- **½ tsp. vanilla extract**
- **2⅓ cups all-purpose flour**
- **2 tsp. baking powder**
- **½ tsp. ground nutmeg**
- **Dash salt**

GLAZE

- **¾ cup confectioners' sugar**
- **3 to 5 tsp. eggnog**
- **1 tsp. dark rum, optional**

1. Preheat oven to 375°. Beat butter and sugar until blended. Beat in eggs, one at a time. Beat in eggnog and vanilla. In another bowl, whisk together flour, baking powder, nutmeg and salt; gradually beat into the butter mixture (the dough will be sticky).
2. Divide dough in half. On a greased baking sheet, shape each portion into a 12x3-in. rectangle. Bake until a toothpick inserted in the center comes out clean, 16-19 minutes. Reduce oven setting to 300°. Remove biscotti from pans to wire racks; cool 10 minutes.
3. Place rectangles on a cutting board. Using a serrated knife, trim the ends of the rectangles and cut diagonally into ½-in. slices. Return to baking sheets, cut-side down. Bake until firm, about 10 minutes per side. Remove from pans to wire racks; cool completely.
4. Mix the glaze ingredients. Drizzle over biscotti with a spoon.

Note: This recipe was tested with commercially prepared eggnog.

1 cookie: 90 cal., 3g fat (2g sat. fat), 18mg chol., 56mg sod., 15g carb. (8g sugars, 0 fiber), 1g pro.

EGGNOG BISCOTTI

SANTA CUPCAKES

My children decorate these cupcakes every year for Christmas. We use chocolate chips for Santa's eyes and a Red Hot for his nose, but you can use any kind of candy you like.
—Sharon Skildum, Maple Grove, MN

Prep: 30 min. • **Bake:** 20 min. + cooling
Makes: about 1½ dozen

- **1 pkg. white cake mix (regular size)**
- **1 can (16 oz.) vanilla frosting (about 1⅔ cups)**
- **Red gel or paste food coloring**
- **Miniature marshmallows**
- **Brown M&M's minis**
- **Red Hots**
- **Red jimmies**
- **Sweetened shredded coconut**

1. Prepare and bake cake mix according to the package directions for cupcakes; fill paper-lined muffin cups two-thirds full. Cool in pans for 10 minutes before removing to wire racks to cool completely.
2. Tint ⅔ cup of the frosting red with food coloring. Place 3 Tbsp. of white frosting in a food-safe plastic bag; cut a ¼-in. hole in one corner and reserve for piping.
3. Use the remaining white frosting to cover two-thirds of each cupcake. For the hats, cover the remaining third of each cupcake with red frosting. Pipe fur trim with white frosting; add marshmallows for pompoms. Decorate with M&M's, Red Hots and jimmies for faces; add shredded coconut for beards.

1 cupcake: 276 cal., 12g fat (2g sat. fat), 31mg chol., 249mg sod., 40g carb. (28g sugars, 0 fiber), 2g pro.

SANTA CUPCAKES

Candy for Christmas

Set out on trays for family members to savor, or box with a ribbon as gifts to dear friends. These delightful homemade holiday candies bring the magic of the season wherever they go.

5 INGREDIENTS

CREAM CHEESE CANDIES

This four-ingredient recipe was recommended by friends and shared throughout our neighborhood. The rich, simple mints make a perfect last-minute addition to holiday candy trays.
—Katie Koziolek, Hartland, MN

Prep: 15 min. + standing
Makes: about 6 dozen

- **3 oz. cream cheese, softened**
- **¼ tsp. peppermint or almond extract**
- **3 cups confectioners' sugar, divided**
- **Sugar or colored sugar, optional**

1. Mix cream cheese and extract until blended. Beat in 1½ cups confectioners' sugar. Knead in remaining 1½ cups sugar.
2. Shape into ½-in. balls. If desired, roll in sugar or colored sugar. Place on waxed paper. Flatten with a fork. Let stand until firm, 1-2 hours. Store between layers of waxed paper in an airtight container in the refrigerator.

1 piece: 24 cal., 0 fat (0 sat. fat), 1mg chol., 4mg sod., 5g carb. (5g sugars, 0 fiber), 0 pro.

FAST FIX

CRUNCHY CHOCOLATE CLUSTERS

Sweet, salty and crunchy, this no-bake candy brings a bit of south-of-the-border flavor with cinnamon, chocolate and coffee.
—Roxanne Chan, Albany, CA

Takes: 25 min. • **Makes:** ¾ lb. (12 pieces)

- **¾ cup coarsely crushed pretzels**
- **¼ cup raisins**
- **2 Tbsp. pine nuts, toasted**
- **1⅓ cups (8 oz.) semisweet chocolate chips**
- **½ tsp. instant coffee granules**
- **¼ tsp. ground cinnamon**
- **¼ cup sour cream**
- **Coarse sea salt**

1. Place the pretzels, raisins and pine nuts in a bowl. In a microwave, melt chocolate chips; stir until smooth. Stir in the coffee granules, cinnamon and sour cream. To rewarm, microwave in additional 5- to 10-second intervals. Add to the pretzel mixture; toss until combined.
2. Drop mixture by tablespoonfuls onto a waxed paper-lined baking sheet. Sprinkle with salt.
3. Refrigerate until set, about 10 minutes. Store in an airtight container in the refrigerator.

1 piece: 139 cal., 8g fat (4g sat. fat), 1mg chol., 86mg sod., 19g carb. (12g sugars, 1g fiber), 2g pro.

CASHEW BRITTLE

3. Immediately pour onto prepared pan, spreading with a metal spatula; cool slightly. Refrigerate until set, 15-20 minutes.
4. Break the brittle into pieces. Store between layers of waxed paper in an airtight container.
1 oz.: 184 cal., 6g fat (2g sat. fat), 2mg chol., 170mg sod., 32g carb. (29g sugars, 0 fiber), 2g pro.

BANANA CREAM CHOCOLATE TRUFFLES

PICTURED ON P. 259

This recipe began with ripe bananas and a little imagination, and the outcome blew my family and friends away! I could eat these truffles all day long.
—Michele Lassuy, Orlando, FL

Prep: 35 min. + freezing
Makes: about 4 dozen

1 pkg. (14.3 oz.) Golden Oreo cookies
1 pkg. (8 oz.) cream cheese, softened
2 tsp. banana extract
⅓ cup mashed ripe banana
1 lb. milk chocolate candy coating, melted
Dried banana chips, coarsely crushed

1. Pulse cookies in a food processor until fine crumbs form. In a bowl, beat cream cheese and extract until blended. Beat in mashed banana. Stir in cookie crumbs. Freeze, covered, until firm enough to shape, about 2 hours.
2. Shape mixture into 1-in. balls. Dip cookie balls in candy coating; place on waxed paper-lined baking sheets. Top immediately with banana chips.
3. Refrigerate until set, about 30 minutes. Store in a covered container in the refrigerator.
1 truffle: 110 cal., 6g fat (4g sat. fat), 5mg chol., 45mg sod., 13g carb. (9g sugars, 0 fiber), 1g pro.

TEST KITCHEN TIP

To coat the truffles, use two forks to dip and turn them in the chocolate coating.

5 INGREDIENTS

PECAN CARAMEL CANDIES

The perfect combination of salty and sweet, these candies make an ideal treat at the holidays! Get kids involved by having them help you unwrap the candies and place the pretzels on baking sheets. You'll soon have several ready to give as gifts—and have fun making them.
—Julie Wemhoff, Angola, IN

Prep: 30 min. • **Bake:** 5 min. + standing
Makes: 4½ dozen

54 pretzels
54 Rolo candies (about 11 oz.)
54 pecan halves

1. Preheat oven to 250°. Place pretzels 1 in. apart on foil-lined baking sheets. Top each with a candy.
2. Bake 3-4 minutes or until the candies are softened. (Rolos will still retain their shape.) Immediately top with pecans, pressing to spread the candy into the pretzel. Let stand until set.
1 piece: 44 cal., 2g fat (1g sat. fat), 1mg chol., 24mg sod., 6g carb. (4g sugars, 0 fiber), 1g pro.

CASHEW BRITTLE

No candy thermometer needed for this enticing brittle. Pack it in clear jars for a gift that people will instantly open.
—Rhonda Glenn, Prince Frederick, MD

Prep: 10 min. • **Cook:** 10 min. + chilling
Makes: ¾ lb.

2 tsp. butter, divided
1 cup sugar
½ cup light corn syrup
1 to 1½ cups salted cashew halves
1 tsp. baking soda
1 tsp. vanilla extract

1. Grease a baking sheet with 1 tsp. butter.
2. In a microwave-safe bowl, mix sugar and corn syrup; microwave, uncovered, on high for 3 minutes. Stir to dissolve sugar; microwave 2 minutes longer. Stir in cashews and remaining butter; microwave on high for 40 seconds. Stir; continue microwaving in 20-second intervals until the mixture turns a light amber color, about 1-2 minutes. (Mixture will be very hot.) Quickly stir in baking soda and vanilla until light and foamy.

PISTACHIO CRANBERRY BARK

5 INGREDIENTS

CHOCOLATE-COVERED POMEGRANATE SEEDS

I dunk pomegranate seeds in chocolate to get these easy-to-make little treats friends and family love.

—Jim Javorsky, Havre de Grace, MD

Prep: 5 min. + chilling • **Cook:** 5 min.
Makes: 2 dozen (about 1 lb.)

- **1 pkg. (12 oz.) dark chocolate chips**
- **1 cup pomegranate seeds, patted dry**

1. In a microwave-safe bowl, melt the chocolate chips; stir until smooth. Stir in pomegranate seeds.
2. Drop by tablespoonfuls onto waxed paper-lined baking sheets. Refrigerate until firm, about 1 hour. Store between layers of waxed paper in an airtight container in the refrigerator.

1 piece: 70 cal., 4g fat (3g sat. fat), 0 chol., 5mg sod., 10g carb. (9g sugars, 1g fiber), 1g pro.

5 INGREDIENTS

PISTACHIO CRANBERRY BARK

This bark makes a lovely holiday gift. Fill a plate or cup with candy, then gather clear cellophane around it and tie with red and green ribbons.

—Susan Wacek, Pleasanton, CA

Prep: 20 min. + chilling
Makes: about 1 lb.

- **2 cups (12 oz.) semisweet chocolate chips**
- **1 cup chopped pistachios, toasted, divided**
- **¾ cup dried cranberries, divided**
- **5 oz. white candy coating, melted**

1. In a microwave-safe bowl, microwave the chocolate chips until melted; stir until smooth. Stir in ¾ cup of the pistachios and half the cranberries; spread onto a waxed paper-lined baking sheet. Drizzle with melted candy coating. Cut through the layers with a knife to swirl. Sprinkle with the remaining pistachios and cranberries. Refrigerate until firm.
2. Cut or break into pieces. Store in an airtight container in refrigerator.

1 oz.: 215 cal., 12g fat (6g sat. fat), 0 chol., 36mg sod., 28g carb. (24g sugars, 2g fiber), 3g pro.

Almond Cranberry Bark: Substitute slivered almonds for the pistachios

Cherry Pretzel Bark: Substitute ½ cup each slivered almonds and crushed pretzels for the pistachios; substitute chopped dried cherries for the cranberries.

Chocolate Peppermint Bark: Omit pistachios and cranberries. Stir ½ cup crushed peppermint candies into the melted chocolate. Sprinkle swirled chocolate with another ½ cup crushed peppermint candies.

5 INGREDIENTS

EASY HOLIDAY TRUFFLES

You may be tempted to save this recipe for a special occasion since these smooth, creamy chocolates are divine. With just a few ingredients, the smarter plan is remembering how easy they are to make.
—*Taste of Home* Test Kitchen

Prep: 25 min. + chilling • **Cook:** 5 min.
Makes: about 6 dozen

- **3 cups semisweet chocolate chips**
- **1 can (14 oz.) sweetened condensed milk**
- **1 Tbsp. vanilla extract**
- **Toasted finely chopped nuts or assorted jimmies**

1. Place chocolate chips and milk in a microwave-safe bowl; microwave on high for 3 minutes, stirring halfway through. Stir in vanilla. Refrigerate, covered, until firm enough to shape, about 3 hours.
2. Shape into 1-in. balls; roll in nuts or jimmies. Place in a 15x10x1-in. pan; refrigerate until firm, about 1 hour.

1 truffle: 52 cal., 3g fat (2g sat. fat), 2mg chol., 8mg sod., 7g carb. (7g sugars, 0 fiber), 1g pro.

EASY HOLIDAY TRUFFLES

WHITE CHOCOLATE FUDGE

When December arrives, friends and family eagerly await my creamy white fudge. It's something a little different from the traditional chocolate.
—Gioviana Buser, Riverside, CA

Prep: 10 min. • **Cook:** 15 min. + chilling
Makes: about 3 lbs. (117 pieces)

- **1½ tsp. plus ¾ cup butter, softened, divided**
- **3 cups sugar**
- **1 can (5 oz.) evaporated milk (about ⅔ cup)**
- **1 pkg. (12 oz.) white baking chips**
- **1 jar (7 oz.) marshmallow creme**
- **1 tsp. vanilla extract**

1. Line a 13x9-in. pan with foil; grease foil with 1½ tsp. butter.
2. In a heavy saucepan, combine sugar, milk and remaining butter; bring to a rapid boil over medium heat, stirring constantly. Boil for 4 minutes, stirring constantly. Remove from heat; stir in baking chips and marshmallow creme until melted. Stir in vanilla. Immediately spread into prepared pan. Refrigerate until firm, 1-2 hours.
3. Using foil, lift fudge out of pan. Remove the foil; cut fudge into 1-in. squares. Store between layers of waxed paper in an airtight container.

1 piece: 54 cal., 2g fat (1g sat. fat), 4mg chol., 15mg sod., 8g carb. (8g sugars, 0 fiber), 0 pro.

Delectable Desserts

Finish off any meal with an irresistible dessert! Choose from cakes, crisps, pies, cookies, bars...everything your sweet tooth could crave. Each one is easy to make, so you'll be serving up the perfect treat in practically no time!

Frosted Butter Rum Brickle Bites (p. 291) **Golden Peach Pie** (p. 301)
Blackberry White Chocolate Cheesecake Cups (p. 290)
Spiced Upside-Down Apple Pie (p. 303) **Streuseled Zucchini Bundt Cake** (p. 289)

CRANBERRY-CHERRY NUT PIE

CRANBERRY-CHERRY NUT PIE

This delightful, stress-free pie combines cranberries with convenient cherry pie filling for a fresh, fun flavor.
—*Taste of Home* Test Kitchen

Prep: 20 min. • **Bake:** 40 min. + cooling
Makes: 8 servings

- **1 can (21 oz.) cherry pie filling**
- **2 cups fresh or frozen cranberries, thawed**
- **¾ cup sugar**
- **½ cup chopped walnuts**
- **2 Tbsp. cornstarch**
- **1 tsp. vanilla extract**
- **½ tsp. ground cinnamon**
- **⅛ tsp. ground allspice**
- **1 pkg. (14.1 oz.) refrigerated pie pastry**
- **2 Tbsp. butter**
- **1 tsp. 2% milk**
- **1 Tbsp. coarse sugar**

1. Preheat oven to 375°. For filling, mix first eight ingredients. Unroll one crust into a 9-in. pie plate. Add filling; dot top with butter.
2. Unroll the remaining crust onto a work surface; make cutout vents using small cookie cutters. Place top crust over filling; seal and flute edge. Decorate top with cutouts. Brush with milk; sprinkle with coarse sugar.
3. Bake on a lower oven rack until the crust is golden brown and filling is bubbly, 40-45 minutes. Cover edge with foil during the last 30 minutes if needed to prevent overbrowning. Cool on a wire rack.

1 piece: 482 cal., 21g fat (8g sat. fat), 17mg chol., 223mg sod., 71g carb. (24g sugars, 2g fiber), 3g pro.

DREAM CUPCAKES

My grandchildren love these cream-filled cupcakes. Fill some dreamy cupcakes for your people, too.
—Dorothy Bahlmann, Clarksville, IA

Prep: 20 min. • **Bake:** 25 min.
Makes: about 2½ dozen

- **1 pkg. chocolate cake mix (regular size)**
- **3 oz. cream cheese, softened**
- **⅓ cup sugar**
- **1 large egg, room temperature**
- **⅛ tsp. salt**
- **1 cup (6 oz.) semisweet chocolate chips**
- **¼ cup sweetened shredded coconut, optional**

1. Preheat oven to 350°. Prepare the cake mix according to package directions for cupcakes. Fill paper-lined muffin cups half full with batter.
2. In a large bowl, beat cream cheese and sugar until fluffy. Beat in egg and salt until smooth. Stir in chocolate chips and, if desired, coconut.
3. Drop about 2 teaspoonfuls of cream cheese mixture into the center of each cupcake. Bake for 25-30 minutes or until cake springs back when lightly touched. Cool for 5 minutes before removing from pans to wire racks to cool completely. Store in the refrigerator.

1 cupcake: 155 cal., 8g fat (3g sat. fat), 34mg chol., 153mg sod., 20g carb. (14g sugars, 1g fiber), 2g pro. **Diabetic exchanges:** 1½ fat, 1 starch.

DOUBLE-LAYER CHEESECAKE BARS

Can't choose between chocolate or vanilla cheesecake? You don't have to when you make this two-layer bar.
—Andrea Price, Grafton, WI

Prep: 35 min. • **Bake:** 30 min. + chilling
Makes: 2 dozen

- **1 pkg. yellow cake mix (regular size)**
- **¼ cup canola oil**
- **3 large eggs, room temperature, divided use**
- **1¼ cups milk chocolate chips, divided**
- **3 pkg. (8 oz. each) cream cheese, softened**
- **½ cup sugar**
- **½ cup sour cream**
- **½ cup heavy whipping cream**
- **1 tsp. vanilla extract**

1. Preheat oven to 350°. Reserve 1 cup dry cake mix for filling. In a large bowl, combine oil, 1 egg and the remaining cake mix; stir until blended. Stir in ½ cup of the chocolate chips. Press onto the bottom of a greased 13x9-in. baking pan. Bake until set, 10-12 minutes.
2. Meanwhile, in a large bowl, beat cream cheese and sugar until smooth. Beat in sour cream, heavy cream, vanilla and the reserved cake mix. Add the remaining eggs; beat on low speed just until blended. Remove 2 cups for chocolate topping; pour the remaining batter over crust.
3. For topping, melt remaining chocolate chips. Stir into reserved cream cheese mixture; spoon over the filling. Bake until center is almost set, 30-35 minutes. Cool 1 hour on a wire rack. Refrigerate 4 hours before serving. Refrigerate leftovers.

1 bar: 292 cal., 19g fat (10g sat. fat), 61mg chol., 248mg sod., 28g carb. (19g sugars, 1g fiber), 4g pro.

EAT SMART

MOCHA MERINGUE SANDWICH COOKIES

These crisp, chewy cookies can be made any size you choose. They're also tasty with a variety of fillings—try them with fruit preserves.
—Marie Valdes, Brandon, FL

Prep: 30 min. + standing
Bake: 15 min./batch + cooling
Makes: about 2 dozen

MOCHA MERINGUE SANDWICH COOKIES

- **3 large egg whites**
- **1 tsp. instant coffee granules**
- **½ cup confectioners' sugar**
- **¼ cup baking cocoa**
- **¼ tsp. cream of tartar**
- **¾ cup sugar**
- **¾ cup chocolate frosting**
- **Additional confectioners' sugar**

1. Place egg whites in a bowl; let stand at room temperature 30 minutes. Preheat oven to 350°. Sift coffee granules through a fine sieve to break them up, pressing with a spoon as needed. Sift together ½ cup confectioners' sugar, cocoa and the coffee.
2. Add cream of tartar to egg whites; beat on medium speed until foamy. Gradually beat in sugar, 1 Tbsp. at a time, beating on high after each addition until the sugar is dissolved. Continue beating until stiff glossy peaks form. Fold in coffee mixture.
3. Cut a small hole in the tip of a pastry bag or in a corner of a food-safe plastic bag; insert a #11 round pastry tip. Add the meringue; pipe 1¾-in. spirals 1 in. apart onto parchment-lined baking sheets.
4. Bake the meringues until set and dry, 12-15 minutes. Cool completely before removing from paper.
5. To assemble, spread about 1½ tsp. frosting onto the bottom of half of the meringues; cover with the remaining meringues. Dust with additional confectioners' sugar.

1 sandwich cookie: 76 cal., 2g fat (1g sat. fat), 0 chol., 25mg sod., 15g carb. (14g sugars, 0 fiber), 1g pro. **Diabetic exchanges:** 1 starch, ½ fat.

TEST KITCHEN TIP

When foaming egg whites, do not allow any yolk or grease into the mixture. The fat will prevent the egg whites from beating up.

For more coffee flavor, use espresso powder instead of instant coffee granules. Since the texture is finer than instant coffee, skip the first sift.

Cream of tartar is an acid that makes meringue more stable. If you don't have cream of tartar, use ½ tsp. lemon juice or white vinegar.

CRANBERRY BOG BARS

These homespun bars combine the flavors of oats, cranberries, brown sugar and pecans. I like to sprinkle them with confectioners' sugar before serving.
—Sally Wakefield, Gans, PA

Prep: 25 min. • **Bake:** 25 min. + cooling
Makes: 2 dozen

- **1¼ cups butter, softened, divided**
- **1½ cups packed brown sugar, divided**
- **3½ cups old-fashioned oats, divided**
- **1 cup all-purpose flour**
- **1 can (14 oz.) whole-berry cranberry sauce**
- **½ cup finely chopped pecans**

1. Preheat oven to 375°. In a large bowl, cream 1 cup butter and 1 cup brown sugar until light and fluffy. Combine 2½ cups oats and flour. Gradually add to the creamed mixture until crumbly. Press into a greased 13x9-in. baking pan. Spread with cranberry sauce.
2. In a microwave-safe bowl, melt the remaining butter; stir in pecans and the remaining brown sugar and oats. Sprinkle over cranberry sauce. Bake until lightly browned, 25-30 minutes. Cool on a wire rack. Cut into bars.

1 bar: 239 cal., 12g fat (6g sat. fat), 25mg chol., 88mg sod., 32g carb. (18g sugars, 2g fiber), 2g pro.

COCONUT KEY LIME THUMBPRINTS

I created this cookie recipe for the 2013 Las Vegas World Food Championships. It's similar to a shortbread thumbprint cookie, but with lots more personality. To save time, you can also make these with prepared lime curd.
—Amy Freeze, Avon Park, FL

Prep: 40 min. + cooling
Bake: 15 min./batch + cooling
Makes: about 2½ dozen

- **2 Tbsp. cornstarch**
- **⅔ cup Key lime juice**
- **¾ cup sugar**
- **2 large egg yolks**

COOKIES

- **1 cup butter, softened**
- **½ cup confectioners' sugar**
- **⅛ tsp. salt**
- **1 tsp. vanilla extract**
- **½ tsp. coconut extract**
- **2 cups all-purpose flour**
- **2 large egg whites**
- **2 tsp. water**
- **2½ cups sweetened shredded coconut**

DRIZZLE

- **4 oz. white baking chocolate, chopped**
- **1 Tbsp. shortening**

1. For lime curd, in a small saucepan, whisk cornstarch and lime juice until smooth. Whisk in sugar and egg yolks; cook and stir over medium heat until boiling. Transfer to a bowl; cool slightly. Press plastic wrap onto the surface of the curd; refrigerate until cold.
2. Preheat oven to 400°. Cream butter, confectioners' sugar and salt until light and fluffy. Beat in extracts. Gradually beat in flour.
3. In a small bowl, whisk together egg whites and water. Place coconut in a separate bowl. Shape dough into 1¼-in. balls. Dip each ball in egg whites, then roll in coconut, coating well. Place 2 in. apart on parchment-lined baking sheets. Press a deep indentation in center of each with the handle of a wooden spoon.
4. Bake until the edges are golden brown, 12-14 minutes. Reshape indentations as needed. Cool on pans 5 minutes. Remove to wire racks to cool completely.
5. To serve, fill each cookie with about 1½ tsp. curd. In a microwave, melt white chocolate and shortening; stir until smooth. Drizzle over cookies. Refrigerate leftover filled cookies.

1 cookie: 182 cal., 11g fat (7g sat. fat), 29mg chol., 76mg sod., 21g carb. (13g sugars, 1g fiber), 2g pro.

COCONUT KEY LIME THUMBPRINTS

EAT SMART

STREUSELED ZUCCHINI BUNDT CAKE

PICTURED ON P. 285

Inspired by an abundance of zucchini, I came up with this spiced and lightly sweet cake. It even won a blue ribbon at our county fair!

—Regina Stock, Topeka, KS

Prep: 25 min. • **Bake:** 55 min. + cooling
Makes: 14 servings

- **2 cups shredded zucchini, patted dry**
- **1⅓ cups fat-free plain yogurt**
- **¾ cup sugar**
- **2 large egg whites, room temperature**
- **⅓ cup canola oil**
- **1 large egg, room temperature**
- **4 tsp. vanilla extract, divided**
- **3 cups all-purpose flour**
- **1½ tsp. baking powder**
- **1 tsp. baking soda**
- **½ tsp. salt**
- **1 Tbsp. dry bread crumbs**
- **⅓ cup packed brown sugar**
- **⅓ cup chopped walnuts**
- **⅓ cup raisins**
- **1 Tbsp. ground cinnamon**
- **½ tsp. ground allspice**
- **¾ cup confectioners' sugar**
- **2 to 3 tsp. fat-free milk**

1. Preheat oven to 350°. In a large bowl, beat zucchini, yogurt, sugar, egg whites, oil, egg and 3 tsp. vanilla until well blended. In a small bowl, combine flour, baking powder, baking soda and salt; gradually beat into zucchini mixture until blended.
2. Coat a 10-in. fluted tube pan with cooking spray; sprinkle with bread crumbs. Pour a third of the batter into pan. Combine brown sugar, walnuts, raisins, cinnamon and allspice; sprinkle half over the batter. Top with another third of the batter. Sprinkle with the remaining brown sugar mixture; top with the remaining batter.
3. Bake 55-65 minutes or until a toothpick inserted in the center comes out clean. Cool for 10 minutes before removing from pan to a wire rack to cool completely.
4. In a small bowl, combine confectioners' sugar, the remaining vanilla and enough milk to achieve desired consistency; drizzle over cake.

MANGO ALMOND ICEBOX CAKE

1 slice: 287 cal., 8g fat (1g sat. fat), 14mg chol., 259mg sod., 49g carb. (26g sugars, 2g fiber), 6g pro.

*** HEALTH TIP *** Fat-free plain yogurt replaces some of the oil and helps make this cake tender and moist.

MANGO ALMOND ICEBOX CAKE

A dear friend asked me to make a mango cake—and I came up with this. It's easy to prepare, with a light, refreshing taste. You can also make it with strawberries, if you prefer.

—Rachel simoneau, Danbury, CT

Prep: 35 min. + chilling
Makes: 12 servings

- **1 cup water**
- **½ cup sugar**
- **¼ tsp. almond extract**
- **1 pkg. (16 oz.) frozen mango chunks, thawed**
- **4 oz. cream cheese, softened**
- **½ cup confectioners' sugar**
- **½ tsp. vanilla extract**
- **2 cups heavy whipping cream**
- **22 crisp ladyfinger cookies**
- **1 pkg. (5 oz.) miniature meringue cookies, coarsely crushed**
- **1 cup sliced almonds**

1. For syrup, place water in a microwave-safe bowl; microwave on high 30 seconds. Stir in sugar and extract until the sugar is dissolved; cool completely.
2. Finely chop ¼ cup mango chunks; place in a large bowl. Add cream cheese, confectioners' sugar and vanilla; beat until blended. In another bowl, beat cream until stiff peaks form; fold into mango mixture.
3. To assemble, line the bottom of a 9-in. springform pan with 11 ladyfingers; slowly drizzle with half the syrup. Layer with half of each of the following: cream mixture, meringue cookies, remaining mango and almonds. Repeat layers. Refrigerate, covered, 8 hours or overnight. To serve, loosen sides from pan with a knife; remove rim. Refrigerate leftovers.

1 slice: 389 cal., 22g fat (11g sat. fat), 71mg chol., 72mg sod., 45g carb. (38g sugars, 2g fiber), 5g pro.

TEST KITCHEN TIP

To get the smoothest whipped cream, beat on medium speed, not high.

For a nuttier flavor and added crunch and color, toast almonds before using.

BLACKBERRY WHITE CHOCOLATE CHEESECAKE CUPS

PICTURED ON P. 285

I read that white chocolate intensifies the flavor of blackberries. It's true! With white chocolate chips, blackberry puree and a sweet and salty pretzel crust, this is a sensational mini dessert.
—Arlene Erlbach, Morton Grove, IL

Prep: 25 min. + chilling
Makes: 6 servings

- **1½ cups miniature pretzels**
- **2 Tbsp. plus ⅓ cup sugar, divided**
- **3 Tbsp. butter, melted**
- **1 cup heavy whipping cream**
- **1 pkg. (8 oz.) cream cheese, softened**
- **½ cup confectioners' sugar**
- **1 tsp. vanilla extract**
- **½ cup white baking chips**
- **1½ cups fresh blackberries**
- **Additional blackberries**

1. Pulse pretzels in a food processor until fine crumbs form. Add 2 Tbsp. granulated sugar and melted butter; pulse just until combined. Divide mixture between six half-pint canning jars or dessert dishes.
2. For the cheesecake layer, beat cream until stiff peaks form. In another bowl, beat cream cheese, confectioners' sugar and vanilla until smooth. Fold in 1½ cups whipped cream, then baking chips. Spoon over pretzel mixture. Refrigerate, covered, until cold, about 3 hours.
3. In a clean food processor, puree the blackberries with the remaining sugar; remove to a bowl. Cover and refrigerate berry mixture and remaining whipped cream until serving.
4. To serve, top with blackberry mixture, reserved whipped cream and additional blackberries.

1 serving: 553 cal., 38g fat (23g sat. fat), 102mg chol., 359mg sod., 49g carb. (38g sugars, 2g fiber), 6g pro.

TEST KITCHEN TIP

When blackberries aren't in season, you can use thawed frozen blackberries in place of the 1½ cups fresh berries in the puree.

DATE-FILLED RUGELACH

DATE-FILLED RUGELACH

I like to take old recipes and make them my own and that's how these cookies came about. They're so special to my family. Sometimes I roll the dough in cinnamon sugar instead of flour.
—Barb Estabrook, Appleton, WI

Prep: 40 min. + chilling
Bake: 25 min./batch
Makes: 32 cookies

- **1¼ cups coarsely chopped dates (about 6 oz.)**
- **1 Tbsp. minced crystallized ginger**
- **1 tsp. grated orange zest**
- **¼ cup orange juice**
- **2 cups all-purpose flour**
- **2 Tbsp. plus ⅔ cup sugar, divided**
- **½ tsp. salt**
- **1 cup cold unsalted butter, cubed**
- **6 oz. cold cream cheese, cubed**
- **1 tsp. ground cinnamon**
- **6 Tbsp. coarsely chopped walnuts, toasted**

1. Place the first four ingredients in a small heavy saucepan; bring to a boil, stirring frequently. Reduce heat; simmer, uncovered, until thickened, 5 minutes. Cool completely.
2. Place flour, 2 Tbsp. sugar and salt in a food processor; pulse to combine. Add butter; pulse until the butter is the size of peas. Add cream cheese; pulse just until a dough forms. Divide dough in half; shape each into a disk. Wrap disks and refrigerate 1 hour.
3. Preheat oven to 350°. Mix cinnamon and remaining sugar. On a lightly floured surface, roll each portion of dough into a 12-in. circle. Spread each with half of the date mixture and sprinkle with ⅓ cup sugar mixture and 3 Tbsp. walnuts. Cut each into 16 wedges. Roll up wedges from the wide ends; place 2 in. apart on parchment-lined baking sheets.
4. Bake until light golden brown, for 25-28 minutes. Cool on pans 10 minutes. Remove to wire racks to cool.

1 cookie: 144 cal., 9g fat (5g sat. fat), 21mg chol., 55mg sod., 16g carb. (9g sugars, 1g fiber), 2g pro.

CASHEW GINGER COOKIE TWISTS

This is a fun cookie for a party or cookie exchange. As a variation, dip just one side in melted dark chocolate and sprinkle with orange zest or finely chopped cashews.

—Carole Holt, Mendota Heights, MN

Prep: 55 min. + chilling
Bake: 10 min./batch + cooling
Makes: 40 cookies

- ¾ cup butter, softened
- ⅓ cup confectioners' sugar
- 1½ tsp. grated orange zest
- ¼ tsp. ground ginger
- 1 large egg, room temperature
- ¾ tsp. vanilla extract
- 2 cups all-purpose flour, divided
- ½ cup honey-roasted cashews
- 1½ cups white baking chips
- 1 Tbsp. shortening
- ⅓ cup finely chopped crystallized ginger

1. Beat the first four ingredients until blended; beat in the egg and vanilla. Place ¼ cup flour and cashews in a food processor; pulse until the cashews are ground. Add the remaining flour; pulse to blend. Gradually beat the flour mixture into the butter mixture.
2. Divide dough in half; shape each into a 10-in.-long log. Wrap and refrigerate until firm, about 1 hour.
3. Preheat oven to 375°. Unwrap each log and cut into twenty ½-in. slices. Roll each slice into an 8-in. rope and shape into a pretzel. Place twists 2 in. apart on ungreased baking sheets.
4. Bake until the edges are light brown, 8-10 minutes. Cool on pans 2 minutes. Remove to wire racks to cool completely.
5. In a microwave, melt baking chips and shortening; stir until smooth. Dip tops of cookies in baking chips; sprinkle with crystallized ginger. Let stand until set.

1 cookie: 113 cal., 7g fat (4g sat. fat), 15mg chol., 42mg sod., 12g carb. (6g sugars, 0 fiber), 1g pro.

CASHEW GINGER COOKIE TWISTS

FROSTED BUTTER RUM BRICKLE BITES

PICTURED ON P. 285

Rum, real butter and toffee bits turned these cookies into my husband's new favorite. If you'd like them less sweet, skip the frosting and sprinkle with a little confectioners' sugar while the cookies are still warm.

—Cindy Nerat, Menominee, MI

Prep: 35 min.
Bake: 10 min./batch + cooling
Makes: about 4 dozen

- 1 cup butter, softened
- ¾ cup confectioners' sugar
- 2 tsp. rum extract
- ½ tsp. salt
- 2 cups all-purpose flour
- 1 pkg. (8 oz.) brickle toffee bits

ICING

- ⅓ cup butter, cubed
- 2 cups confectioners' sugar
- ½ tsp. rum extract
- 2 to 3 Tbsp. 2% milk

1. Preheat oven to 375°. Beat first four ingredients until blended. Beat in flour. Stir in toffee bits. Shape dough into 1-in. balls; place 2 in. apart on parchment-lined baking sheets.
2. Bake until edges are light brown and toffee bits begin to melt, 8-10 minutes. Cool on pans 5 minutes. Remove to wire racks to cool completely.
3. In a small heavy saucepan, melt the butter over medium heat. Heat until golden brown, about 5 minutes, stirring constantly. Remove from heat; stir in the confectioners' sugar, rum extract and enough milk to reach desired consistency. Spread over the cookies.

1 cookie: 112 cal., 6g fat (4g sat. fat), 15mg chol., 89mg sod., 13g carb. (9g sugars, 0 fiber), 1g pro.

TEST KITCHEN TIP

This icing is thick and buttery with a hint of toasted flavor. It would also enhance pecan shortbreads or pumpkin cookies.

HO HO HO CAKE

5 INGREDIENTS

HO HO HO CAKE

With just a few alterations, this became an amazingly elegant dessert. It has a light texture and chocolaty flavor, and the cute presentation can't be beat!
—Lynne Bargar, Saegertown, PA

Prep: 25 min. + chilling
Makes: 12 servings

1½ pkg. (13 oz. each) Swiss cake rolls
2¾ cups 2% milk
2 pkg. (3.9 oz. each) instant chocolate fudge pudding mix
2 cups whipped topping

1. Cut each cake roll into six slices; reserve any broken chocolate coating for the topping. Line the bottom and sides of a 9-in. springform pan with cake slices, covering the pan completely.
2. Whisk milk and pudding mixes for 2 minutes (mixture will be thick); spread onto the bottom layer of cake rolls. Cover with whipped topping. Sprinkle with the reserved chocolate pieces. Refrigerate, covered, at least 2 hours before serving.

1 slice: 331 cal., 12g fat (5g sat. fat), 16mg chol., 382mg sod., 46g carb. (35g sugars, 1g fiber), 4g pro.

PINEAPPLE PRETZEL FLUFF

I often bring this special salad to potlucks, and everyone goes crazy for the sweet and crunchy combination. Be sure to add the pretzel mixture right before serving to keep it crispy.
—Beth Olby, Ashland, WI

Prep: 15 min. + chilling
Bake: 10 min. + cooling
Makes: 12 servings

1 cup coarsely crushed pretzels
½ cup butter, melted
1 cup sugar, divided
1 pkg. (8 oz.) cream cheese, softened
1 can (20 oz.) unsweetened crushed pineapple, drained
1 carton (12 oz.) frozen whipped topping, thawed

1. Preheat oven to 400°. Mix pretzels, melted butter and ½ cup sugar. Press into a 13x9-in. pan. Bake 7 minutes. Cool completely on a wire rack.
2. Meanwhile, in a large bowl, beat cream cheese and the remaining sugar until creamy. Fold in pineapple and whipped topping; refrigerate, covered, until serving.
3. To serve, break pretzel mixture into small pieces. Stir into pineapple mixture.

½ cup: 334 cal., 19g fat (13g sat. fat), 39mg chol., 230mg sod., 37g carb. (31g sugars, 1g fiber), 2g pro.

FROZEN PEANUT BUTTER & CHOCOLATE TERRINE

FREEZE IT

FROZEN PEANUT BUTTER & CHOCOLATE TERRINE

This frozen dessert is a great option for making ahead of time, so it's ready when needed. When served, it cuts easily and the lovely layers of banana, peanut butter, and chocolate give it a real "Wow!" factor.
—Jennifer Jackson, Keller, TX

Prep: 30 min. + freezing
Makes: 12 servings

15 Nutter Butter cookies, crushed (about 2 cups)
1 carton (16 oz.) mascarpone cheese
1 cup sugar
2 tsp. vanilla extract
1 carton (8 oz.) frozen whipped topping, thawed
1 medium banana, sliced
1 cup semisweet chocolate chips, melted and cooled slightly
1 Tbsp. baking cocoa
1 cup chunky peanut butter

1. Line a 9x5-in. loaf pan with plastic wrap, letting edges extend up all sides. Sprinkle with a third of the crushed cookies.
2. In a large bowl, mix mascarpone, sugar and vanilla; fold in whipped topping. Divide mixture evenly between three bowls.
3. To one portion, fold in sliced banana; spread evenly in loaf pan. Repeat cookie layer. To a second portion, stir in melted chocolate and cocoa; add to pan. Sprinkle with remaining cookies. Stir peanut butter into the third portion. Spread over top.
4. Freeze, covered, until firm, at least 5 hours. To serve, invert onto a platter; remove plastic wrap. Cut into slices.

1 slice: 568 cal., 39g fat (18g sat. fat), 47mg chol., 190mg sod., 49g carb. (38g sugars, 3g fiber), 10g pro.

TEST KITCHEN TIP

The melted chocolate should be fluid enough to stir smoothly into the mascarpone mixture, but not warm enough to melt it.

Instead of whipped topping, you can use homemade whipped cream. Beat 1¾ cups heavy whipping cream with 2-3 Tbsp. confectioners' sugar until soft peaks form.

CURRY-KISSED COCONUT FUDGE

If you love Thai flavors and you love fudge, then you'll adore this creamy coconut fudge sprinkled with a hint of sweet curry powder.
—Sarah Meuser, New Milford, CT

Prep: 25 min. + chilling
Makes: about 4½ lbs.

2 tsp. plus ¼ cup butter, divided
4 pkg. (10 to 12 oz. each) white baking chips
2 cans (14 oz. each) sweetened condensed milk
1½ tsp. coconut extract
½ tsp. sea salt
¼ tsp. curry powder

1. Line a 13x9-in. pan with foil or parchment; grease foil with 2 tsp. butter.
2. In a large heavy saucepan, cook and stir the baking chips, milk and remaining ¼ cup butter over low heat until smooth. Remove from heat; stir in extract and salt. Spread into prepared pan; sprinkle with curry powder. Refrigerate, covered, until firm, about 2 hours.
3. Using foil, lift fudge out of pan. Remove foil; cut fudge into 1-in. squares. Store in an airtight container in the refrigerator.

1 piece: 78 cal., 4g fat (3g sat. fat), 6mg chol., 29mg sod., 9g carb. (9g sugars, 0 fiber), 1g pro.

TRIPLE CHOCOLATE MOUSSE TORTE

TRIPLE CHOCOLATE MOUSSE TORTE

When it's too hot to bake something sweet, but you're craving chocolate, my triple chocolate mousse tart is all you need. Stack up the layers anyway you like.
—Samantha Hernandez, Vacaville, CA

Prep: 35 min. + chilling
Cook: 20 min. + cooling
Makes: 16 servings

18 Oreo cookies
⅓ cup butter, melted
6 tsp. unflavored gelatin, divided
3 Tbsp. cold water, divided
5 oz. bittersweet chocolate, chopped
4½ cups heavy whipping cream, divided
5 oz. milk chocolate, chopped
5 oz. white baking chocolate, chopped
2 tsp. vanilla extract
Additional Oreo cookies, chocolate shavings or cocoa powder, optional

1. Pulse cookies in a food processor until fine crumbs form. Add the melted butter; pulse until combined. Press onto the bottom of a greased 9-in. springform pan. Refrigerate while preparing filling.
2. In a small saucepan, sprinkle 2 tsp. gelatin over 1 Tbsp. cold water; let stand for 1 minute. Heat and stir over low heat until gelatin is completely dissolved; remove from heat.
3. Place bittersweet chocolate and ½ cup of the cream in a metal bowl over a small saucepan of hot water; heat and stir until the mixture is smooth. Stir in the gelatin mixture. Transfer to a medium bowl; cool completely. Repeat twice with milk and white chocolates.
4. In a large bowl, beat vanilla and the remaining 3 cups cream until stiff peaks form. Fold 2 cups whipped cream (⅓ of total) into cooled bittersweet chocolate; spread over crust. Refrigerate until set, 25-30 minutes. Repeat twice with milk and white chocolates, keeping the remaining whipped cream chilled until needed.
5. Refrigerate the torte, covered, until set, about 4 hours. To serve, loosen sides from pan with a knife. Carefully remove rim from pan. Garnish with additional crumbled cookies, shavings of chocolate or a dusting of cocoa powder, if desired.

1 slice: 467 cal., 39g fat (24g sat. fat), 90mg chol., 112mg sod., 24g carb. (19g sugars, 1g fiber), 5g pro.

TEST KITCHEN TIP

An envelope of unflavored gelatin contains 1 Tbsp., so you'll need two packages for this recipe.

We found it best to cut this torte using a clean, wet knife. Wipe the knife clean after each cut.

GINGERED CHERRY PEAR COBBLER

This cobbler is warm, sweet and filling—comfort food at its best! Think of it for those crisp and cool autumn days and remember to serve it warm.
—Taste of Home Test Kitchen

Prep: 25 min. • **Bake:** 55 min.
Makes: 8 servings

- **4 cups chopped peeled fresh pears**
- **½ cup dried cherries**
- **¼ cup packed brown sugar**
- **2 Tbsp. finely chopped crystallized ginger**
- **1 Tbsp. all-purpose flour**
- **3 Tbsp. butter**

TOPPING

- **¼ cup sugar**
- **2 Tbsp. finely chopped crystallized ginger**
- **1 cup all-purpose flour**
- **1½ tsp. baking powder**
- **⅛ tsp. baking soda**
- **¼ tsp. salt**
- **5 Tbsp. cold butter, cubed**
- **½ cup buttermilk**

1. Preheat oven to 350°. In a large bowl, combine the first five ingredients; transfer to a greased 12-in. cast-iron skillet or 2-qt. baking dish. Heat butter in a small saucepan over medium heat for 7 minutes or until golden brown; pour over the pear mixture. Cover and bake for 20-25 minutes or until bubbly.
2. In a food processor, combine sugar and ginger; cover and process until finely chopped. Add the flour, baking powder, baking soda and salt; cover and process for 3 seconds or until blended. Add butter; process until mixture resembles coarse crumbs. Add buttermilk and pulse just until a soft dough forms. Drop by tablespoonfuls over warm pear mixture.
3. Bake, uncovered, for 35-40 minutes or until the topping is golden brown. Serve warm.

½ cup: 332 cal., 12g fat (7g sat. fat), 31mg chol., 274mg sod., 56g carb. (33g sugars, 4g fiber), 3g pro.

Gingered Cranberry-Pear Cobbler: Substitute dried cranberries for the cherries in this recipe.

Gingered Raisin-Pear Cobbler: Substitute golden raisins for the cherries.

PEANUT BUTTER CHOCOLATE CHIP ZUCCHINI CAKE

Years ago, I added some zucchini to a peanut butter bar I had created, with delicious results. This time, I wanted to try it with a cake. The zucchini makes it super moist, but doesn't get in the way of the chocolate and peanut butter goodness.
—Marilyn Blankschien, Clintonville, WI

Prep: 20 min. • **Bake:** 20 min.
Makes: 10 servings

- **⅓ cup creamy peanut butter**
- **¼ cup butter, softened**
- **1 cup packed brown sugar**
- **1½ cups all-purpose flour, divided**
- **½ tsp. salt**
- **½ tsp. baking soda**
- **1 large egg, room temperature**
- **1 tsp. vanilla extract**
- **¼ cup buttermilk**
- **1 cup shredded zucchini**
- **¼ tsp. ground cinnamon**
- **½ cup semisweet chocolate chips**

1. Preheat oven to 350°. In a large bowl, cream peanut butter, butter and brown sugar until blended. In another bowl, whisk 1¼ cups flour, salt and baking soda; add to the creamed mixture. Beat just until the mixture is sandy. Remove ½ cup of the crumb mixture for topping.
2. To the remaining mixture, beat in the remaining flour, egg, vanilla, and buttermilk. Stir in zucchini. Spread into a greased 9-in. round baking pan. Stir cinnamon into reserved topping. Sprinkle over batter; top with chocolate chips.
3. Bake until a toothpick inserted in center comes out with moist crumbs, 20-25 minutes. Cool in pan on a wire rack.

1 piece: 297 cal., 12g fat (6g sat. fat), 31mg chol., 281mg sod., 44g carb. (28g sugars, 2g fiber), 5g pro.

TEST KITCHEN TIP

If you like a chunky streusel topping, squeeze it into clumps as you sprinkle it over the batter.

PEANUT BUTTER CHOCOLATE CHIP ZUCCHINI CAKE

FRUITCAKE COOKIES WITH RUM GLAZE

Like fruitcake—only better! You can either make these cookies with rum or opt for a kid-friendly version. If you make these without alcohol, you may wish to increase the rum extract for flavor.
—Sheila Joan Suhan, Scottdale, PA

Prep: 45 min. + cooling
Bake: 15 min./batch + cooling
Makes: about 4 dozen

- **1 cup golden raisins**
- **¾ cup dried cherries**
- **½ cup diced dried apricots**
- **¾ cup water**
- **¼ cup rum or additional water**
- **¾ cup chopped pecans**
- **⅓ cup diced crystallized ginger**
- **⅓ cup diced candied orange zest**
- **1 cup butter, softened**
- **2 cups sugar, divided**
- **2 large eggs, room temperature**
- **1½ tsp. rum extract**
- **3½ cups all-purpose flour**
- **1 tsp. baking soda**
- **½ tsp. salt**

GLAZE

- **3 cups confectioners' sugar**
- **3 to 5 Tbsp. 2% milk**
- **3 Tbsp. rum or additional milk**

1. Place the first five ingredients in a small saucepan; bring to a boil. Reduce heat; simmer, uncovered, until liquid is almost absorbed, 12-15 minutes. Cool completely. Stir in pecans, ginger and orange zest.
2. Preheat oven to 350°. Cream butter and 1½ cups sugar until light and fluffy. Beat in the eggs and extract. In another bowl, whisk together the flour, baking soda and salt; gradually beat into the creamed mixture. Stir in fruit mixture. Place remaining ½ cup sugar in a shallow bowl. Shape 2 Tbsp. of dough into balls; toss balls in sugar to coat lightly. Place 2 in. apart on parchment-lined baking sheets.
3. Bake until golden brown and just set, 11-13 minutes. Remove from pans to wire racks; cool completely.
4. Mix glaze. Drizzle over cookies.

1 cookie: 176 cal., 5g fat (3g sat. fat), 18mg chol., 92mg sod., 31g carb. (21g sugars, 1g fiber), 2g pro.

TEST KITCHEN TIP

These cookies can be baked on greased baking sheets if you don't have parchment. Use a metal spatula when removing because they'll stick just a bit.

FRUITCAKE COOKIES WITH RUM GLAZE

CARAMEL DUMPLINGS

My family just loves these tender dumplings in a sweet, rich sauce. I love them because they turn out wonderful every time I make them...which is a lot!
—Faye Johnson, Connersville, IN

Prep: 10 min. • **Cook:** 30 min.
Makes: 6-8 servings

- **2 Tbsp. butter**
- **1½ cups packed brown sugar**
- **1½ cups water**

DUMPLINGS

- **1¼ cups all-purpose flour**
- **½ cup sugar**
- **2 tsp. baking powder**
- **½ tsp. salt**
- **½ cup whole milk**
- **2 Tbsp. butter, softened**
- **2 tsp. vanilla extract**
- **½ cup coarsely chopped peeled apple, optional**

1. In a large skillet, heat butter, brown sugar and water to boiling. Reduce heat to simmer.
2. Meanwhile, combine the dumpling ingredients. Drop by tablespoonfuls into the simmering sauce. Cover tightly and simmer for 20 minutes. Do not lift lid. If desired, serve warm with cream or ice cream.

½ cup: 336 cal., 6g fat (4g sat. fat), 17mg chol., 329mg sod., 68g carb. (53g sugars, 1g fiber), 3g pro.

STREUSEL-TOPPED LEMON TART

A sweet streusel topping pairs well with citrusy slices of this tart. It's a spectacular spin on basic lemon bars.
—Lisa Varner, El Paso, TX

Prep: 20 min. • **Bake:** 40 min. + cooling
Makes: 12 servings

- **1¼ cups all-purpose flour**
- **⅓ cup confectioners' sugar**
- **½ tsp. grated lemon zest**
- **½ cup plus 2 Tbsp. cold butter**

FILLING

- **4 large eggs, room temperature**
- **1½ cups sugar**
- **¼ cup lemon juice**
- **¼ cup all-purpose flour**
- **1 tsp. baking powder**
- **1 tsp. grated lemon zest**

TOPPING

- **⅓ cup all-purpose flour**
- **⅓ cup packed brown sugar**
- **3 Tbsp. cold butter**
- **2 Tbsp. chopped pecans**
- **Confectioners' sugar**

1. Preheat oven to 350°, In a small bowl, combine flour, confectioners' sugar and lemon zest; cut in butter until crumbly. Press onto the bottom and ½ in. up the sides of a greased 9-in. springform pan. Bake 10-15 minutes or until crust is lightly browned. Cool on a wire rack.
2. In a small bowl, beat eggs, sugar and lemon juice until thick and lemon-colored. Beat in flour, baking powder and lemon zest until blended. Pour into crust. Bake 20-25 minutes or until set.
3. For topping, in a small bowl, combine flour and brown sugar; cut in butter until crumbly. Stir in pecans. Sprinkle over the filling. Bake until a toothpick inserted in center comes out clean, 20-25 minutes. Cool completely on a wire rack. Remove sides of pan. Dust with confectioners' sugar. Refrigerate leftovers.

1 slice: 350 cal., 15g fat (8g sat. fat), 103mg chol., 147mg sod., 51g carb. (36g sugars, 1g fiber), 4g pro.

Streusel-Topped Lime Tart: Substitute lime zest for the lemon zest and lime juice for the lemon juice.

CHOCOLATE CARAMEL HAZELNUT PIE

CHOCOLATE CARAMEL HAZELNUT PIE

I love chocolate, caramel and hazelnuts so I came up with a recipe that has all three. Take this one to your next potluck or party and watch the pie lovers line up.
—Debbie Anderson, Mount Angel, OR

Prep: 25 min. + chilling
Makes: 8 servings

- **1½ cups salted caramel pretzel pieces**
- **12 Lorna Doone shortbread cookies**
- **¼ cup sugar**
- **6 Tbsp. butter, melted**
- **5 Tbsp. caramel topping, divided**

FILLING

- **1 pkg. (8 oz.) cream cheese, softened**
- **½ cup Nutella**
- **1 jar (7 oz.) marshmallow creme**
- **1 carton (8 oz.) frozen whipped topping, thawed**
- **1 cup miniature marshmallows**
- **1 Snickers candy bar (1.86 oz.), chopped**

1. Place pretzel pieces and cookies in a food processor; pulse until fine crumbs form. Add sugar and melted butter; pulse just until blended. Press onto bottom and sides of a 9-in. pie plate. Drizzle with 3 Tbsp. caramel topping. Freeze while preparing filling.
2. For filling, beat cream cheese and Nutella until smooth. Gradually beat in marshmallow creme. Gently fold in whipped topping and marshmallows. Spoon into crust.
3. Refrigerate until set, 3-4 hours. Top with chopped candy and the remaining caramel topping before serving.

1 piece: 663 cal., 35g fat (19g sat. fat), 60mg chol., 327mg sod., 74g carb. (57g sugars, 1g fiber), 6g pro.

TEST KITCHEN TIP

Short on time? You can quick-chill this pie in the freezer in about one hour.

SHORTCUT COCONUT-PECAN CHOCOLATE TASSIES

5 INGREDIENTS

SHORTCUT COCONUT-PECAN CHOCOLATE TASSIES

Anyone who loves German chocolate cake will adore these bite-sized versions. Garnish them with chocolate chips or pecan halves before baking, or drizzle them with melted chocolate after taking them out of the oven.
—Deb Villenauve, Krakow, WI

Prep: 25 min.
Bake: 10 min./batch + cooling
Makes: about 3 dozen

- **1 pkg. chocolate cake mix (regular size)**
- **½ cup quick-cooking oats**
- **1 large egg, room temperature, lightly beaten**
- **6 Tbsp. butter, melted and cooled slightly**
- **¾ cup coconut-pecan frosting**
- **Pecan halves, melted semisweet chocolate, or chocolate chips, optional**

1. Preheat oven to 350°. Mix cake mix and oats; stir in egg and melted butter. Shape mixture into 1-in. balls. Press onto bottom and up sides of greased mini-muffin cups.
2. Bake just until set, 8-10 minutes. Cool slightly before removing to wire racks; cool completely.
3. Top each with about 1 tsp. frosting. If desired, top with pecans or drizzle with melted chocolate.

1 tassie: 94 cal., 4g fat (2g sat. fat), 10mg chol., 105mg sod., 13g carb. (8g sugars, 1g fiber), 1g pro.

CHERRY-FILLED CUTOUTS

Mom has been making these cookies since 1953. They will freeze for over two months, though they may not last that long in the freezer, either.
—Beth Neels, Ontario, NY

Prep: 40 min. + chilling
Bake: 15 min./batch
Makes: about 2 dozen

- **1 cup butter, softened**
- **1 cup sugar**
- **½ cup packed brown sugar**
- **2 large eggs, room temperature**
- **1 tsp. vanilla extract**
- **4 cups all-purpose flour**
- **1 tsp. baking soda**
- **½ tsp. salt**
- **1 cup cherry preserves**
- **¼ cup chopped slivered almonds**

1. Cream butter and sugars until light and fluffy. Beat in eggs and vanilla. In another bowl, whisk together flour, baking soda and salt; gradually beat into creamed mixture. Divide dough in half. Shape each into a disk; wrap and refrigerate 4 hours or until firm enough to roll.
2. Preheat oven to 375°. On a lightly floured surface, roll each portion of dough to ⅛-in. thickness. Using floured 2¾-in. and 3-in. cookie cutters, cut an equal number of circles in each size. Using a floured 1-in. cookie cutter, cut out the centers from larger circles.
3. For filling, mix preserves and almonds. Place the solid circles 1½ in. apart on parchment-lined baking sheets. Spoon 2 tsp. filling on center of each. Top with the cutout circles.
4. Bake until golden brown, for 12-15 minutes. Cool on pans 5 minutes. Remove to wire racks to cool completely.

1 sandwich cookie: 240 cal., 9g fat (5g sat. fat), 36mg chol., 170mg sod., 38g carb. (21g sugars, 1g fiber), 3g pro.

5 INGREDIENTS

MIMOSA BUTTER COOKIES

You can add many different flavors to butter cookies to make them your own. Try an alternate type of citrus zest, or add an alternate liquid to change things up.
—Sara Lark, Raton, NM

Prep: 25 min. • **Bake:** 10 min./batch
Makes: about 3 dozen

- **1 cup butter, softened**
- **1¼ cups confectioners' sugar**
- **2 tsp. grated orange zest**
- **1 tsp. salt**
- **¼ cup orange juice**
- **¼ cup champagne**
- **2½ cups all-purpose flour**

1. Preheat oven to 350°. In a large bowl, cream first four ingredients until light and fluffy. Mix juice and champagne. Add flour to creamed mixture alternately with juice mixture, beating well after each addition.
2. Cut a small hole in the tip of a pastry bag or in a corner of a food-safe plastic bag; insert a #1M star tip. Transfer dough to bag; pipe 2-in. circles 2 in. apart onto parchment-lined baking sheets.
3. Bake until edges are set, 10-12 minutes. Cool on pan 5 minutes. Remove to wire racks to cool.

1 cookie: 95 cal., 5g fat (3g sat. fat), 14mg chol., 106mg sod., 11g carb. (4g sugars, 0 fiber), 1g pro.

MIMOSA BUTTER COOKIES

SNICKERDOODLE BLONDIE BARS

When asked to bring a dessert to share for my boys' football team, I whipped up these blondies and was instantly named the greatest mom!
—Valonda Seward, Coarsegold, CA

Prep: 15 min. • **Bake:** 35 min. + cooling
Makes: 20 bars

- **1 cup butter, softened**
- **2 cups packed brown sugar**
- **3 tsp. vanilla extract**
- **2 large eggs, room temperature**
- **2⅔ cups all-purpose flour**
- **2 tsp. baking powder**
- **1 tsp. ground cinnamon**
- **¼ tsp. ground nutmeg**
- **½ tsp. salt**

TOPPING

- **1½ tsp. sugar**
- **½ tsp. ground cinnamon**

1. Preheat oven to 350°. Cream butter and brown sugar until light and fluffy. Beat in vanilla and eggs, one at a time. In another bowl, whisk together flour, baking powder, spices and salt; gradually beat into the creamed mixture. Spread into a greased 9-in. square baking pan.
2. Mix the topping ingredients; sprinkle over top. Bake until set and golden brown, 35-40 minutes. Cool in pan on a wire rack. Cut into bars when completely cool.

1 bar: 235 cal., 10g fat (6g sat. fat), 45mg chol., 180mg sod., 35g carb. (22g sugars, 1g fiber), 2g pro.

TEST KITCHEN TIP

For thinner bars, prepare recipe as directed, spreading batter in a 13x9-in. greased baking pan. Bake 25-30 minutes.

PECAN CAKE WITH COOKIE BUTTER FROSTING

My mom and I bought a jar of cookie butter to try it out and we fell in love with it. I knew the flavor would go well with maple syrup and pecans so I came up with this cake. Make a pretty design on top of the cake with pecan halves.
—Natalie Larsen, Columbia, MD

Prep: 20 min. • **Bake:** 25 min. + cooling
Makes: 20 servings

- **½ cup pecan halves**
- **½ cup sugar**
- **½ cup packed brown sugar**
- **1 cup butter, softened**
- **4 large eggs, room temperature**
- **¼ cup maple syrup**
- **2 Tbsp. 2% milk**
- **1⅔ cups all-purpose flour**
- **3 tsp. baking powder**
- **½ tsp. salt**

FROSTING

- **½ cup butter, softened**
- **2 cups confectioners' sugar**
- **1 cup Biscoff creamy cookie spread**
- **¼ cup 2% milk**

1. Preheat oven to 350°. Grease a 13x9-in. baking pan; set aside.
2. Place pecans and sugars in a food processor; process until ground. In a large bowl, cream butter and the pecan mixture until blended. Add eggs, one at a time, beating well after each addition. Beat in syrup and milk. In another bowl, whisk flour, baking powder and salt; gradually add to the creamed mixture, beating well.
3. Transfer batter to the prepared pan. Bake until a toothpick inserted in center comes out clean, 25-30 minutes. Cool completely in pan on a wire rack.
4. In a large bowl, combine all the frosting ingredients; beat until smooth. Spread over the cake. Refrigerate leftovers.

1 piece: 363 cal., 21g fat (10g sat. fat), 74mg chol., 259mg sod., 41g carb. (29g sugars, 1g fiber), 3g pro.

PECAN CAKE WITH COOKIE BUTTER FROSTING

GOLDEN PEACH PIE

PICTURED ON P. 285

Years ago, I entered this pie in the Park County Fair in Livingston. It won a first-place blue ribbon plus a purple ribbon for Best All Around! Family and friends agree with the judges—it's a perfectly peachy pie.
—Shirley Olson, Polson, MT

Prep: 20 min. • **Bake:** 50 min. + cooling
Makes: 8 servings

- **2 sheets refrigerated pie crust**
- **5 cups sliced peeled fresh peaches (about 5 medium)**
- **2 tsp. lemon juice**
- **½ tsp. grated orange zest**
- **⅛ tsp. almond extract**
- **1 cup sugar**
- **¼ cup cornstarch**
- **¼ tsp. ground nutmeg**
- **⅛ tsp. salt**
- **2 Tbsp. butter**

1. Preheat oven to 400°. Line a 9-in. pie plate with one crust; trim, leaving a 1-in. overhang around edge. Set aside. In a large bowl, combine the peaches, lemon juice, orange zest and extract. In another smaller bowl, combine the sugar, cornstarch, nutmeg and salt. Add to the peach mixture; toss gently to coat. Pour into crust; dot with butter.
2. Roll out the remaining crust to a ⅛-in.-thick circle; cut into strips of various widths. Arrange over the filling in a lattice pattern. Trim and seal the strips to the bottom crust; fold over the overhang. Lightly press or flute edge. Cover edges loosely with foil.
3. Bake for 40 minutes. Remove foil; bake 10-15 minutes longer or until the crust is golden brown and the filling is bubbly. Cool on a wire rack. Store in the refrigerator.

1 piece: 425 cal., 17g fat (8g sat. fat), 18mg chol., 267mg sod., 67g carb. (36g sugars, 2g fiber), 3g pro.

NO-BAKE CHOCOLATE CHIP CANNOLI CHEESECAKE

NO-BAKE CHOCOLATE CHIP CANNOLI CHEESECAKE

This flavorful and refreshing cheesecake is perfect as a summer dessert. Not needing to turn on the oven and heat up the house is an added bonus.
—Kristen Heigl, Staten Island, NY

Prep: 25 min. + chilling
Makes: 8 servings

- **1 pkg. (4 oz.) cannoli shells**
- **½ cup sugar**
- **½ cup graham cracker crumbs**
- **⅓ cup butter, melted**

FILLING

- **2 pkg. (8 oz. each) cream cheese, softened**
- **1 cup confectioners' sugar**
- **½ tsp. grated orange zest**
- **¼ tsp. ground cinnamon**
- **¾ cup part-skim ricotta cheese**
- **1 tsp. vanilla extract**
- **½ tsp. rum extract**
- **½ cup miniature semisweet chocolate chips**
- **Chopped pistachios, optional**

1. Pulse cannoli shells in a food processor until coarse crumbs form. Add sugar, cracker crumbs and melted butter; pulse just until combined. Press onto bottom and sides of a greased 9-in. pie plate. Refrigerate until firm, about 1 hour.
2. Beat first four filling ingredients until blended. Beat in ricotta cheese and extracts. Stir in chocolate chips. Spread into crust.
3. Refrigerate, covered, until set, about 4 hours. If desired, top with pistachios.

1 piece: 548 cal., 36g fat (20g sat. fat), 88mg chol., 292mg sod., 51g carb. (38g sugars, 1g fiber), 8g pro.

TEST KITCHEN TIP

Pistachios are classic in cannoli, but if you don't have them, you can add crunch by topping the pie with more crumbled cannoli shells.

PINA COLADA ICEBOX CAKE

PINA COLADA ICEBOX CAKE

This icebox cake has all of the flavors of a pina colada—it takes just one bite to escape to a tropical island!
—Rachel Lewis, Danville, VA

Prep: 25 min. + chilling
Makes: 12 servings

- **1 pkg. (8 oz.) cream cheese, softened**
- **½ cup confectioners' sugar**
- **½ tsp. rum extract**
- **1 can (13.66 oz.) coconut milk, divided**
- **1 pkg. (3.4 oz.) instant vanilla pudding mix**
- **1 container (8 oz.) frozen whipped topping, thawed**
- **15 whole graham crackers**
- **1 can (20 oz.) crushed pineapple, drained**
- **1 cup sweetened shredded coconut, toasted**

1. In a large bowl, beat cream cheese, confectioners' sugar and extract until smooth. Gradually beat in 1 cup coconut milk. Add pudding mix; beat on low speed until smooth. Fold in the whipped topping.
2. Pour the remaining coconut milk into a shallow dish. Quickly dip half the graham crackers into the milk; allow excess to drip off. Arrange in a single layer in the bottom of a 13x9 baking dish, breaking to fit as needed. Layer with half each of the cream cheese mixture, pineapple and coconut. Repeat layers. Refrigerate, covered, at least 4 hours before serving.

Note: To toast coconut, bake in a shallow pan at 350° for 5-10 minutes or cook in a skillet over low heat until golden brown, stirring occasionally.

1 piece: 377 cal., 20g fat (15g sat. fat), 19mg chol., 259mg sod., 47g carb. (33g sugars, 1g fiber), 3g pro.

TEST KITCHEN TIP

This can be made in a slightly smaller dish, but we liked that the dessert didn't fill the dish completely. That makes it easier to cover when chilling (and transporting to potlucks).

RHUBARB CHEESECAKE SQUARES

Rich and tangy, this cheese bar is bound to be a hit with the rhubarb lovers you know—and even those who haven't fallen for the ruby red goodness just yet.
—Sharon Schmidt, Mandan, ND

Prep: 25 min. • **Bake:** 40 min. + chilling
Makes: 16 servings

- **1¼ cups all-purpose flour**
- **½ cup old-fashioned oats**
- **½ cup packed brown sugar**
- **½ cup cold butter, cubed**
- **1 pkg. (8 oz.) cream cheese, softened**
- **¾ cup sugar**
- **½ tsp. salt**
- **¼ tsp. ground cinnamon**
- **⅛ tsp. ground nutmeg**
- **1 large egg, room temperature, lightly beaten**
- **½ tsp. vanilla extract**
- **1½ cups diced fresh or frozen rhubarb, thawed**

1. Preheat oven to 350°. In a small bowl, mix flour, oats and brown sugar; cut in butter until crumbly. Reserve 1 cup mixture for topping. Press the remaining mixture onto the bottom of a greased 9-in. square baking pan.
2. For the filling, beat cream cheese, sugar, salt and spices until smooth. Add egg and vanilla; beat on low speed just until combined. Fold in rhubarb. Spread over the crust. Sprinkle with topping.
3. Bake until golden brown and filling is set, about 40 minutes. Cool on a wire rack 1 hour. Refrigerate, covered, until cold, about 2 hours. Cut into squares.

Note: If using frozen rhubarb, measure it while still frozen, then thaw completely. Drain in a colander, but do not press liquid out.

1 square: 216 cal., 11g fat (7g sat. fat), 41mg chol., 171mg sod., 27g carb. (17g sugars, 1g fiber), 3g pro.

CHOCOLATE MARSHMALLOW PEANUT BUTTER SQUARES

I combined a couple of different recipes to create these crunchy, chocolaty bars bursting with peanut butter flavor, marshmallows and pretzel pieces. These bars could pass for fudge!
—Dawn E. Lowenstein, Huntingdon Valley, PA

Prep: 15 min. + chilling • **Cook:** 5 min.
Makes: 5 dozen

- 1 can (14 oz.) sweetened condensed milk
- 1 pkg. (11 oz.) peanut butter and milk chocolate chips
- ½ cup milk chocolate chips
- ½ cup creamy peanut butter
- 1 tsp. vanilla extract
- 1½ cups miniature marshmallows
- 1 cup broken miniature pretzels
- 1 cup Rice Krispies

1. Place the first five ingredients in a heavy saucepan; cook and stir over low heat until smooth and blended, about 5 minutes (the mixture will be very thick). Remove from heat; stir in the remaining ingredients. Spread mixture into a greased 13x9-in. pan.
2. Refrigerate, covered, until firm, about 4 hours. Cut into squares. Store in an airtight container in the refrigerator.

1 square: 85 cal., 4g fat (2g sat. fat), 3mg chol., 50mg sod., 12g carb. (8g sugars, 0 fiber), 1g pro.

TEST KITCHEN TIP

For easier cutting, line your pan with greased foil, letting the ends extend up the sides. This makes it simple to pull the candy out and cut even pieces.

For more of a rocky road visual, sprinkle the top with chopped peanuts.

CHOCOLATE MARSHMALLOW PEANUT BUTTER SQUARES

SPICED UPSIDE-DOWN APPLE PIE

PICTURED ON P. 285

My grandma taught me to make this pie when I was 4 years old. Over the years I've kept it about the same with just a few changes. Flip it out of the pan the second it stops bubbling. The glaze it makes looks like stained glass.
—Francine Bryson, Pickens, SC

Prep: 20 min. • **Bake:** 50 min. + cooling
Makes: 8 servings

- 2 cups pecan halves
- ½ cup butter, melted
- 1 cup packed brown sugar
- Pastry for double-crust pie (9 in.)
- ½ cup sugar
- 3 Tbsp. all-purpose flour
- 1 Tbsp. apple pie spice
- ½ tsp. ground nutmeg
- 6 cups thinly sliced peeled tart apples
- 2 Tbsp. lemon juice
- 1 tsp. vanilla extract

1. Preheat oven to 450°. Arrange the pecans, rounded-side down, on the bottom of a 9-in. deep-dish pie plate; drizzle with butter. Sprinkle with brown sugar; press lightly.
2. Roll out dough to fit the pie plate; place over brown sugar. Press the crust firmly against brown sugar and the sides of the pie plate. Trim edges.
3. In a large bowl, combine sugar, flour, pie spice and nutmeg. Add the apples, lemon juice and vanilla; toss to coat. Fill crust. Roll out the remaining dough to fit the top of the pie; place over filling. Trim, seal and flute edges. Cut slits in top crust.
4. Place the pie on the center oven rack; place a foil-lined baking sheet on a rack below to catch any spills. Bake pie at 450° for 10 minutes, then reduce heat to 350° and bake until golden brown and apples are tender, 40-45 minutes longer. Cool for 10 minutes before inverting onto a serving plate. Serve warm.

1 piece: 825 cal., 53g fat (23g sat. fat), 91mg chol., 409mg sod., 87g carb. (50g sugars, 5g fiber), 7g pro.

Easy Odds & Ends

Bowls, jars or a tall, chilled glass—this chapter is full of one-dish meals. Have a fresh and healthy meal in a bowl, pack your lunch in a jar filled with lovely layers, or blend up the perfect homemade smoothie. Once you learn the basic recipes, start experimenting to create your own!

Pulled Pork Parfait (p. 310) **Poached Egg Buddha Bowls** (p. 307) **Taco Salad in a Jar** (p. 311) **Thai Salmon Brown Rice Bowls** (p. 306) **Frosty Orange Smoothie** (p. 315)

Super Bowls

These mighty meals are brimming with good-for-you grains, fresh produce and serious flavor. Easy, nutritious and delicious—all in one bowl? Time to dig in!

GREEK BROWN & WILD RICE BOWL

FAST FIX

GREEK BROWN & WILD RICE BOWL

This fresh rice dish tastes like the Mediterranean in a bowl! It calls for only a few ingredients but packs in so much flavor. For a hand-held version, omit the rice and tuck the rest of the ingredients in a pita pocket.
—Darla Andrews, Schertz, TX

Takes: 15 min. • **Makes:** 2 servings

- **1 pkg. (8½ oz.) ready-to-serve whole grain brown and wild rice medley**
- **¼ cup Greek vinaigrette, divided**
- **½ medium ripe avocado, peeled and sliced**
- **¾ cup cherry tomatoes, halved**
- **¼ cup crumbled feta cheese**
- **¼ cup pitted Greek olives, sliced**
- **Minced fresh parsley, optional**

In a microwave-safe bowl, combine the rice mix and 2 Tbsp. vinaigrette. Cover and cook on high until heated through, about 2 minutes. Divide between two bowls. Top with avocado, tomatoes, cheese, olives, remaining dressing and, if desired, parsley.

1 serving: 433 cal., 25g fat (4g sat. fat), 8mg chol., 1355mg sod., 44g carb. (3g sugars, 6g fiber), 8g pro.

*** HEALTH TIP *** These otherwise healthy bowls are high in sodium because of the prepared rice, dressing, feta cheese and Greek olives. Save on sodium by cooking the rice from scratch and using a simple oil and vinegar dressing.

TEST KITCHEN TIP

For more protein, add some tuna or grilled chicken to these bowls.

One package of prepared rice mix equals about two cups.

EAT SMART | FAST FIX

THAI SALMON BROWN RICE BOWLS

Turn to this salmon recipe for a quick and nourishing meal. The store-bought ginger-sesame dressing saves time and adds extra flavor to this healthy dish.
—Naylet LaRochelle, Miami, FL

Takes: 15 min. • **Makes:** 4 servings

- **4 salmon fillets (4 oz. each)**
- **½ cup sesame ginger salad dressing, divided**
- **3 cups hot cooked brown rice**
- **½ cup chopped fresh cilantro**
- **¼ tsp. salt**
- **1 cup julienned carrot**
- **Thinly sliced red cabbage, optional**

1. Preheat oven to 400°. Place salmon in a foil-lined 15x10x1-in. pan; brush with ¼ cup dressing. Bake until fish just begins to flake easily with a fork, 8-10 minutes. Meanwhile, toss rice with cilantro and salt.

2. To serve, divide rice mixture among four bowls. Top with the salmon, carrots and, if desired, cabbage. Drizzle with the remaining dressing.

1 serving: 486 cal., 21g fat (4g sat. fat), 57mg chol., 532mg sod., 49g carb. (8g sugars, 3g fiber), 24g pro.

EAT SMART

POACHED EGG BUDDHA BOWLS

PICTURED ON P. 305

My husband and I celebrate the arrival of spring with this dish, enjoying it in the backyard. I often include fresh peas and other spring delights.
—Amy McDonough, Carlton, OR

Prep: 5 min. • **Cook:** 65 min.
Makes: 2 servings

- **¾ cup wheat berries**
- **3½ cups water, divided**
- **2 Tbsp. olive oil**
- **2 Tbsp. lemon juice**
- **1 Tbsp. thinly sliced fresh mint leaves**
- **¼ tsp. salt**
- **⅛ tsp. freshly ground pepper**
- **½ cup quartered cherry tomatoes**
- **½ cup reduced-fat ricotta cheese**
- **2 Tbsp. sliced Greek olives**
- **2 large eggs**
- **Additional olive oil and pepper, optional**

1. Place wheat berries and 2½ cups water in a large saucepan; bring to a boil. Reduce heat; simmer, covered, until tender, about 1 hour. Drain; transfer to a bowl. Cool wheat berries slightly.
2. Stir in oil, lemon juice, mint, salt and pepper; divide between two bowls. Top with tomatoes, ricotta cheese and olives.
3. To poach egg, place ½ cup water in a small microwave-safe bowl or glass measuring cup. Break an egg into water. Microwave, covered, on high 1 minute. Microwave in 10-second intervals until white is set and yolk begins to thicken; let stand 1 minute.
4. Using a slotted spoon, transfer warm egg to one of the bowls. Repeat. If desired, drizzle with additional oil and sprinkle with more pepper.
1 serving: 526 cal., 24g fat (5g sat. fat), 201mg chol., 563mg sod., 58g carb. (5g sugars, 10g fiber), 21g pro.

TEST KITCHEN TIP

Wheat berries are whole kernels of wheat. They cook up to a chewy texture with a hint of buttery flavor. Look for them near other whole grains, usually in the baking aisle in small packages.

EAT SMART | FAST FIX

EDAMAME & SOBA NOODLE BOWL

Toothsome soba noodles are made from buckwheat flour.
—Matthew Hass, Ellison Bay, WI

Takes: 30 min. • **Makes:** 6 servings

- **1 pkg. (12 oz.) uncooked Japanese soba noodles or whole wheat spaghetti**
- **2 Tbsp. sesame oil**
- **2 cups fresh small broccoli florets**
- **1 medium onion, halved and thinly sliced**
- **3 cups frozen shelled edamame, thawed**
- **2 large carrots, cut into ribbons with a vegetable peeler**
- **4 garlic cloves, minced**
- **1 cup reduced-fat Asian toasted sesame salad dressing**
- **¼ tsp. pepper**
- **Sesame seeds, toasted, optional**

1. In a 6 qt. stockpot, cook noodles according to package directions; drain and return to pan.
2. Meanwhile, in a large skillet, heat oil over medium heat. Add broccoli and onion; cook and stir until crisp-tender, 4-6 minutes. Add edamame and carrots; cook and stir until tender, 6-8 minutes. Add garlic; cook 1 minute longer. Add vegetable mixture, dressing and pepper to noodles; toss to combine. Sprinkle with sesame seeds, if desired.
1⅓ cups: 414 cal., 12g fat (1g sat. fat), 0 chol., 867mg sod., 64g carb. (12g sugars, 4g fiber), 18g pro.

EDAMAME & SOBA NOODLE BOWL

EAST COAST SHRIMP
& LENTIL BOWLS

EAT SMART

EAST COAST SHRIMP & LENTIL BOWLS

With frozen shrimp, a few seasonings, bagged spinach and lentils, this dish comes together effortlessly, creating a marvelous medley of flavor and texture.
—Mary Kay LaBrie, Clermont, FL

Prep: 10 min. • **Cook:** 25 min.
Makes: 4 servings

- **½ cup dried brown lentils, rinsed**
- **1 Tbsp. olive oil**
- **⅛ tsp. salt**
- **1¾ cups water**
- **2 Tbsp. garlic powder, divided**
- **1 lb. uncooked shrimp (26-30 per lb.), peeled and deveined**
- **2 tsp. seafood seasoning**
- **2 Tbsp. butter**
- **½ tsp. crushed red pepper flakes**
- **2 tsp. lemon juice**
- **3 cups fresh baby spinach**
- **¼ tsp. ground nutmeg**
- **¼ cup finely chopped sweet onion**
- **Lemon wedges**

1. Place first four ingredients and 1 Tbsp. garlic powder in a small saucepan; bring to a boil. Reduce heat; simmer, covered, until lentils are tender, 17-20 minutes.
2. Toss shrimp with seafood seasoning. In a large skillet, melt the butter over medium-high heat. Add pepper flakes and the remaining 1 Tbsp. garlic powder; cook and stir for 30 seconds. Add the shrimp; cook and stir until shrimp turns pink, 3-4 minutes. Stir in lemon juice; remove from pan and keep warm.
3. Add spinach and nutmeg to the pan; cook and stir over medium-high heat until the spinach is wilted. Remove from heat.
4. To serve, divide lentils among four bowls. Top with shrimp, spinach and onion. Serve with lemon wedges.
1 serving: 289 cal., 11g fat (5g sat. fat), 153mg chol., 645mg sod., 22g carb. (1g sugars, 4g fiber), 26g pro. **Diabetic exchanges:** 3 lean meat, 1½ starch, 1 fat.

TEST KITCHEN TIP

We tested our recipe with Old Bay seafood seasoning.

Shrimp that are 26-30 per pound are sometimes labeled as large shrimp.

CHICKEN QUINOA BOWLS WITH BALSAMIC DRESSING

EAT SMART

CHICKEN QUINOA BOWLS WITH BALSAMIC DRESSING

The simplicity of this recipe allows me to spend time with my family, while not sacrificing on health or flavor. The fresh spring flavors really shine through!
—Allyson Meyler, Greensboro, NC

Prep: 30 min. + cooling • **Broil:** 10 min.
Makes: 2 servings

- **¼ cup balsamic vinegar**
- **⅔ cup water**
- **⅓ cup quinoa, rinsed**
- **2 boneless skinless chicken breast halves (6 oz. each)**
- **3 tsp. olive or coconut oil, divided**
- **¼ tsp. garlic powder**
- **½ tsp. salt, divided**
- **¼ tsp. pepper, divided**
- **½ lb. fresh asparagus, trimmed**
- **¼ cup plain Greek yogurt**
- **½ tsp. spicy brown mustard**
- **½ medium ripe avocado, peeled and sliced**
- **6 cherry tomatoes, halved**

1. Place balsamic vinegar in a small saucepan; bring to a boil. Cook until slightly thickened, 2-3 minutes. Transfer to a bowl; let cool completely.
2. In a small saucepan, bring water to a boil. Add quinoa. Reduce heat; simmer, covered, until the liquid is absorbed, 10-12 minutes. Keep warm.
3. Preheat broiler. Toss the chicken with 2 tsp. oil, garlic powder, ¼ tsp. salt and ⅛ tsp. pepper. Place on one half of a 15x10x1-in. pan coated with cooking spray. Broil 4 in. from heat for 5 minutes. Meanwhile, toss the asparagus with the remaining oil, salt and pepper.
4. Remove pan from oven; turn chicken over. Add the asparagus. Broil until a thermometer inserted in chicken reads 165° and asparagus is tender, 3-5 minutes. Let chicken stand 5 minutes before slicing.
5. For dressing, stir yogurt and mustard into the balsamic reduction. To serve, spoon the quinoa into bowls; top with the chicken, asparagus, avocado slices and tomatoes. Serve with dressing.
1 serving: 491 cal., 21g fat (5g sat. fat), 101mg chol., 715mg sod., 35g carb. (12g sugars, 6g fiber), 42g pro.

Some Assembly Required

Grab your go-to jar and build a layered lunch that will be the envy of the office crowd. These simple make-and-take meals make workdays wonderful.

PULLED PORK PARFAIT

5 INGREDIENTS | FREEZE IT | FAST FIX

PULLED PORK PARFAIT

I tried a version of this meaty parfait at Miller Park, home of my favorite baseball team, the Brewers. I take it up a notch by layering in corn and creamy mac and cheese, so it truly is a full barbecue meal you can take on the go—and freeze until you're ready to hit the road!
—Rachel Seis, Milwaukee, WI

Takes: 15 min. • **Makes:** 4 servings

- **1 pkg. (16 oz.) refrigerated fully cooked barbecued shredded pork**
- **1 cup frozen corn**
- **2 cups refrigerated mashed potatoes**
- **2 cups prepared macaroni and cheese**

In each of four 1-pint wide-mouth canning jars, divide and layer ingredients in the following order: pulled pork, corn, mashed potatoes, and macaroni and cheese. Cover and refrigerate until serving time. When ready to serve, remove lid and microwave until heated through.

Freeze option: Freeze after assembly. To serve, partially thaw in refrigerator overnight before microwaving.

1 serving: 349 cal., 8g fat (4g sat. fat), 45mg chol., 1116mg sod., 41g carb. (20g sugars, 1g fiber), 17g pro.

FAST FIX

CHOPPED GREEK SALAD IN A JAR

Jenn Tidwell from Fair Oaks, California, sent us a fabulous recipe for a chopped Greek salad. Here it's lunchbox-friendly.
—*Taste of Home* Test Kitchen

Takes: 20 min. • **Makes:** 4 servings

- **¼ cup pepperoncini juice**
- **¼ cup extra virgin olive oil**
- **¼ cup minced fresh basil**
- **2 Tbsp. lemon juice**
- **½ tsp. pepper**
- **¼ tsp. salt**
- **¼ cup finely chopped pepperoncini**
- **1 can (15 oz.) garbanzo beans or chickpeas, rinsed and drained**
- **2 celery ribs, sliced**
- **½ cup Greek olives**
- **1 medium tomato, chopped**
- **½ cup crumbled feta cheese**
- **8 cups chopped romaine**

In a small bowl, whisk the first six ingredients. In each of four 1-qt. wide-mouth canning jars, divide and layer ingredients in the following order: olive oil mixture, pepperoncini, garbanzo beans, celery, Greek olives, tomato, feta and romaine. Cover and refrigerate until serving. Transfer salads into bowls; toss to combine.

1 serving: 332 cal., 23g fat (4g sat. fat), 8mg chol., 795mg sod., 25g carb. (5g sugars, 8g fiber), 9g pro.

* HEALTH TIP * The Greek olives and feta cheese add a lot of flavor, but also a fair amount of fat and sodium. Leave them out and save 7 grams fat and more than 400 milligrams sodium per serving.

AT SMART
CALIFORNIA ROLL IN A JAR
m a big sushi fan but don't always ave time to make those intricate rolls t home. This jar is layered with my avorite California roll ingredients, for ll the flavor without the fuss.
—James Schend, Pleasant Prairie, WI

Prep: 20 min. • **Cook:** 15 min. + standing
Makes: 4 servings

- **1 cup uncooked sushi rice**
- **1 cup water**
- **½ tsp. salt**
- **1 Tbsp. rice vinegar**
- **1 Tbsp. sugar**
- **2 medium ripe avocados, peeled and cubed**
- **1 cup lump crabmeat, drained**
- **1 cup chopped cucumber**
- **2 nori sheets, thinly sliced**
- **Pickled ginger slices, soy sauce and toasted sesame seeds, optional**

1. Wash rice in a colander until water runs clear. In a large saucepan, combine rice, 1 cup water and salt; bring to a boil. Reduce heat; cover. Simmer until water is absorbed and rice is tender, 15-20 minutes. Remove from heat. Let stand 10 minutes. Combine rice vinegar and sugar, stirring until sugar is dissolved. Stir into rice.

2. Place ⅓ cup rice into each of four 1-pint wide-mouth canning jars; layer with half of the avocados, crabmeat, cucumber and nori. Top with the remaining rice and repeat layers. Cover and refrigerate until serving. Transfer into bowls; toss to combine. If desired, serve with optional ingredients.

1 serving: 349 cal., 11g fat (2g sat. fat), 33mg chol., 562mg sod., 52g carb. (6g sugars, 7g fiber), 11g pro.

TEST KITCHEN TIP

Imitation crabmeat makes a very acceptable substitute for the more costly lump crabmeat. Tuna, smoked salmon and smoked trout are also good replacements for the crab. Add any other ingredients you like, such as matchstick carrots or cubed cream cheese.

To keep avocados green, toss in rice vinegar before layering.

CALIFORNIA ROLL IN A JAR

FAST FIX
TACO SALAD IN A JAR
PICTURED ON P. 305

Inspired by Elissa Dougherty's recipe for taco salad, we created a make-and-take version for lunch on the go.
—*Taste of Home* Test Kitchen

Takes: 30 min. • **Makes:** 4 servings

- **1 lb. lean ground beef (90% lean)**
- **⅔ cup water**
- **1 envelope reduced-sodium taco seasoning**
- **1 medium ripe avocado, peeled and cubed**
- **1 Tbsp. finely chopped red onion**
- **1 garlic clove, minced**
- **½ tsp. lemon juice**
- **¾ cup reduced-fat sour cream**
- **¾ cup salsa**
- **2 medium tomatoes, chopped**
- **1 can (2¼ oz.) sliced ripe olives, drained**
- **1 small cucumber, peeled and chopped**
- **5 green onions, chopped**
- **1 cup shredded cheddar cheese**
- **4 cups shredded lettuce**
- **Tortilla chips, optional**

1. In a small skillet, cook beef over medium heat until no longer pink; drain. Stir in water and taco seasoning. Bring to a boil; cook and stir for 2 minutes. Cool.

2. In a small bowl, mash avocado with onion, garlic and lemon juice. In each of four 1-qt. wide-mouth canning jars, divide and layer ingredients in the following order: sour cream, salsa, beef, tomatoes, olives, cucumber, green onions, avocado mixture, cheese and lettuce. Cover and refrigerate until serving. Transfer salads into bowls; toss to combine. If desired, serve with tortilla chips.

1 serving: 483 cal., 29g fat (12g sat. fat), 103mg chol., 1087mg sod., 24g carb. (11g sugars, 5g fiber), 34g pro.

FAST FIX

TURKEY & APPLE ARUGULA SALAD IN A JAR

Stack up the flavors—sweet, savory and spicy—in this adaptation of a turkey and apple salad recipe from Nancy Heishman of Las Vegas, Nevada.
—*Taste of Home* Test Kitchen

Takes: 20 min. • **Makes:** 4 servings

- **½ cup orange juice**
- **3 Tbsp. red wine vinegar**
- **1 to 3 Tbsp. sesame oil**
- **2 Tbsp. minced fresh chives**
- **¼ tsp. salt**
- **¼ tsp. coarsely ground pepper**

SALAD

- **4 cups cubed cooked turkey**
- **4 tsp. curry powder**
- **½ tsp. coarsely ground pepper**
- **¼ tsp. salt**
- **1 large apple, chopped**
- **1 Tbsp. lemon juice**
- **1 cup green grapes, halved**
- **1 can (11 oz.) mandarin oranges, drained**
- **½ cup pomegranate seeds or dried cranberries**
- **½ cup chopped walnuts**
- **4 cups fresh arugula or baby spinach**

1. In a small bowl, whisk the first six ingredients. Place turkey in a large bowl; sprinkle with seasonings and toss to combine. In a separate bowl, toss the chopped apple with lemon juice.
2. In each of four 1-qt. wide-mouth canning jars, divide and layer ingredients in the following order: orange juice mixture, seasoned turkey, apple, grapes, oranges, pomegranate seeds, walnuts and arugula. Cover and refrigerate until serving. To serve, transfer salads into bowls; toss to combine.

1 serving: 471 cal., 19g fat (3g sat. fat), 141mg chol., 453mg sod., 33g carb. (25g sugars, 5g fiber), 45g pro.

TURKEY & APPLE ARUGULA SALAD IN A JAR

FAST FIX

DIY RAMEN SOUP

This jarred version of ramen soup is a healthier alternative to most commercial varieties. You can customize the veggies to your taste.
—Michelle Clair, Seattle, WA

Takes: 25 min. • **Makes:** 2 servings

- **1 pkg. (3 oz.) ramen noodles**
- **1 Tbsp. reduced-sodium chicken base**
- **1 to 2 tsp. Sriracha Asian hot chili sauce**
- **1 tsp. minced fresh gingerroot**
- **½ cup shredded carrots**
- **½ cup shredded cabbage**
- **2 radishes, halved and sliced**
- **½ cup sliced fresh shiitake mushrooms**
- **1 cup shredded cooked chicken breast**
- **¼ cup fresh cilantro leaves**
- **1 hard-boiled large egg, halved**
- **2 lime wedges**
- **4 cups boiling water**

1. Cook ramen according to package directions; cool. In each of two 1-qt. wide-mouth canning jars, divide and layer the ingredients in the following order: ramen noodles, chicken base, Sriracha, ginger, carrots, cabbage, radishes, mushrooms, chicken and cilantro. Place egg and lime wedge in 4-oz. glass jars or other airtight containers. Place on top of cilantro in 1-qt. jars. Cover and refrigerate until serving.
2. To serve, remove egg and lime. Pour 2 cups boiling water into each 1-qt. glass jar; let stand until warmed through or until the chicken base has dissolved. Stir to combine seasonings. Squeeze lime juice over soup and place egg on top.

1 serving: 401 cal., 14g fat (6g sat. fat), 153mg chol., 1092mg sod., 35g carb. (4g sugars, 2g fiber), 31g pro.

Smooth & Satisfying

Crisp, sweet or tangy, a homemade smoothie can help start the day or replenish your energy in a healthy way. It's also a sweet (but not too sweet) indulgent treat!

CUCUMBER MELON SMOOTHIES

5 INGREDIENTS | EAT SMART | FAST FIX

CUCUMBER MELON SMOOTHIES

My cool honeydew and cucumber smoothie has only five ingredients. I sometimes add a small avocado when I want to make an extra-creamy version.
—Crystal Schlueter, Babbitt, MN

Takes: 15 min. • **Makes:** 6 servings

- **2 cups reduced-fat plain Greek yogurt**
- **⅓ cup honey**
- **3 cups chopped honeydew melon**
- **2 medium cucumbers, peeled, seeded and chopped**
- **1 to 2 Tbsp. fresh mint leaves, optional**
- **2 cups crushed ice cubes**

Place half of each of the following in a blender: yogurt, honey, melon, cucumber and, if desired, mint. Cover; process until blended. Add 1 cup ice; cover and process until smooth. Pour into three glasses; repeat with remaining ingredients.

1 cup: 155 cal., 2g fat (1g sat. fat), 4mg chol., 48mg sod., 28g carb. (26g sugars, 2g fiber), 9g pro.

5 INGREDIENTS | FAST FIX

HAZELNUT MOCHA SMOOTHIES

This smooth blend of coffee, cocoa and nutty flavors is better than any coffeehouse version we've tried.
—*Taste of Home* Test Kitchen

Takes: 10 min. • **Makes:** 3 servings

- **1 cup whole milk**
- **½ cup Nutella**
- **4 tsp. instant espresso powder**
- **6 ice cubes**
- **2 cups vanilla ice cream**
- **Chocolate curls, optional**

In a blender, combine the milk, Nutella and espresso powder; cover and process until blended. Add the ice cubes; cover and process until smooth. Add the ice cream; cover and process until smooth. Pour into chilled glasses; serve immediately. Garnish with chocolate curls if desired.

1 cup: 474 cal 27g fat (10g saturated fat), 47mg chol, 124mg sod, 55g carb. (46g sugars, 2g fiber), 9g pro

CHERRY FRUIT SMOOTHIES

5 INGREDIENTS | FAST FIX

CHERRY FRUIT SMOOTHIES

You need just four ingredients to blend these super fast smoothies for breakfast. Whip up a batch on a hot summer day for a cool treat.

—Macy Plummer, Avon, IN

Takes: 5 min. • **Makes:** 4 servings

- **1½ cups unsweetened apple juice**
- **1 cup frozen unsweetened raspberries**
- **1 cup frozen pitted dark sweet cherries**
- **1½ cups raspberry sherbet**

In a blender, combine the apple juice, raspberries and cherries. Add sherbet; cover and process until well blended. Pour smoothies into chilled glasses; serve immediately.

1 cup: 160 cal., 2g fat (1g sat. fat), 3mg chol., 29mg sod., 37g carb. (31g sugars, 2g fiber), 2g pro.

5 INGREDIENTS | FAST FIX

BERRY SMOOTHIES

Add a blush of color and a frosty burst of berry flavor to your meal with these scrumptious summery smoothies.

—Patricia Mahoney, Presque Isle, ME

Takes: 5 min. • **Makes:** 2 servings

- **⅔ cup 2% milk**
- **¾ cup frozen unsweetened strawberries**
- **⅓ cup frozen unsweetened raspberries**
- **2 Tbsp. sugar**
- **¾ cup ice cubes**

Place the milk, berries and sugar in a blender; cover and process until blended. Add ice cubes; cover and process until smooth. Pour into chilled glasses; serve immediately.

1 cup: 106 cal., 0 fat (0 sat. fat), 2mg chol., 44mg sod., 24g carb. (21g sugars, 2g fiber), 3g pro.

5 INGREDIENTS | FAST FIX

FROSTY ORANGE SMOOTHIE

PICTURED ON P. 305

This refreshing, fun sipper makes a tasty alternative to soft drinks.

—Rita Swanson, Three Hills, AB

Takes: 10 min. • **Makes:** 4 servings

- **1 can (6 oz.) frozen orange juice concentrate, thawed**
- **1 cup milk**
- **1 cup water**
- **¼ cup sugar**
- **1 tsp. vanilla extract**
- **10 to 12 ice cubes**

In a blender, combine the orange juice, milk, water, sugar and vanilla. Cover and blend until smooth. With blender running, add ice cubes, one at a time, through the opening in lid. Blend until smooth. Serve immediately.

1 cup: 156 cal., 2g fat (1g sat. fat), 8mg chol., 31mg sod., 32g carb. (31g sugars, 0 fiber), 3g pro.

General Recipe Index

This handy index lists every recipe by food category, major ingredient and cooking method, so you can easily locate the recipes that suit your needs.

NORTHWEST CHERRY SALSA, P. 11

SPICY THAI COCONUT CHICKEN SOUP, P. 55

TRIPLE CHOCOLATE MOUSSE TORTE, P.294

MUFFINS & QUICK BREADS

MUSHROOMS

MUSTARD

NUTS

OATS

OLIVES

ONIONS

ORANGES

PASTA & NOODLES

CRANBERRY MUFFINS, P. 200

JALAPENO MAC & CHEESE, P.254

SALADS
(continued)

SANDWICHES & WRAPS
(also see Burgers)

SAUSAGE, PEPPERONI & HOT DOGS

SEAFOOD
(also see Fish)

SIDE DISHES

SLOW-COOKER RECIPES

EFFORTLESS BLACK BEAN CHILI, P. 223

SOUPS, CHILI & STEWS

SOUPS, CHILI & STEWS *(continued)*

SPINACH

SQUASH

(also see Zucchini & Summer Squash)

STRAWBERRIES

SWEET POTATOES

TOMATOES

DILLY TURKEY MELT, P. 62

Alphabetical Recipe Index

This index lists every recipe in alphabetical order so you can easily find all of your favorites.

A

B

C

D

E

EGG-TOPPED AVOCADO TOAST, P. 61

GOLDEN PEACH PIE, P. 301

F

G

H

I

PAPRIKA CHICKEN STROGANOFF, P. 169

Q

R

S

QUICK CARBONARA, P. 96

SWEET POTATO-CRUSTED CHICKEN NUGGETS, P. 104

T

V

W

Y

Z

ZUCCHINI PANZANELLA SALAD, P. 251